W9-BMZ-090

LET'S READ!

Elizabeth Crosby Stull

**THE CENTER FOR APPLIED
RESEARCH IN EDUCATION**
West Nyack, New York 10994

Library of Congress Cataloging-in-Publication Data

Stull, Elizabeth Crosby.
    Let's read! : a complete month-by-month activities program for
beginning readers / Elizabeth Crosby Stull.
        p.   cm.
    Includes bibliographical references (p.   ).
    ISBN 0-87628-489-6
    1. Reading (Primary)—United States.   2. Education, Primary—
Activity programs—United States.   I. Title.
    LB1573.S896   2000
    372.4—dc21   99-38923
                                                                                   CIP

DEDICATED TO MARCHING BANDS EVERYWHERE

Just as a good band requires teamwork, so too does putting together a book. Special thanks go to:

- ♩ Deborah C. Wright, illustrator, the *Visual Arranger* of the whimsical ABC Marching Band and creator of the lovely drawings . . .

- ♩ Diane Turso, development editor, the *Drum Majorette* who diligently shaped and improved the manuscript . . .

- ♩ Susan Kolwicz, education editor, the *Band Conductor,* who with patience and good taste, skillfully juggled all the tunes, kept us in step, and saw to it that we finished when the last note was sounded!

© 2000 by The Center for Applied Research in Education

Acquisitions Editor: *Susan Kolwicz*
Production Editor: *Mariann Hutlak*
Interior Design/Composition: *Publications Development Company*

All rights reserved.

Permission is given for individual educators to reproduce pages for classroom use.
Reproduction of these materials for an entire school system is strictly forbidden.

Printed in the United States of America
10 9 8 7 6 5 4 3 2

ISBN 0-87628-489-6 (spiral wire)

ISBN 0-13-032019-6 (lay-flat pbk)

ATTENTION: CORPORATIONS AND SCHOOLS

Prentice Hall books are available at quantity discounts with bulk purchase for educational, business, or sales promotional use. For information, please write to: Prentice Hall Career & Personal Development Special Sales, 240 Frisch Court, Paramus, NJ 07652. Please supply: title of book, ISBN, quantity, how the book will be used, date needed.

**THE CENTER FOR APPLIED RESEARCH
IN EDUCATION**
West Nyack, NY 10994

www.phdirect.com

About the Author

Elizabeth Crosby Stull, Ph.D. (The Ohio State University) has over 30 years of experience in education as a primary teacher and teacher educator. She began her career as a teacher of grades 1, 2, and 4 in public schools of Greece Central, Camillus, and Pittsford in upstate New York, and is currently teaching part-time for Ohio State at Marion.

Dr. Stull has published many articles in professional journals such as *Instructor Teaching K–8* and is coauthor with Carol Lewis Price of *Kindergarten Teacher's Month-by-Month Activities Program* (The Center, 1987). In addition, she has written *First Grade Teacher's Month-by-Month Activities Program* (The Center, 1990), *Alphabet Animal Activities Kit* (The Center, 1991), *Second Grade Teacher's Month-by-Month Activities Program* (The Center, 1992), *Multicultural Discovery Activities for the Elementary Grades* (The Center, 1995), and *Kindergarten Teacher's Survival Guide* (The Center, 1997).

Dr. Stull is a member of the National Association for the Education of Young Children, The International Reading Association, as well as Phi Delta Kappa and Delta Kappa Gamma, two education societies.

About the Book

Teaching young children to read is one of the most rewarding experiences a teacher can have. It takes time, skill, and patience. There may seem to be a bit of magic about it when Springtime rolls around and children begin to make spurts of progress. Is it magic? No, it's consistent effort and hard work on the part of the teacher as well as the student.

This book is designed so that the reading activities can be used sequentially throughout the year. Sometimes we may have a list of reading activities and ideas, but are not certain when it is appropriate to use them, especially if there is no structured reading program in place. The approach here is one of skill building.

Work with the September section to help set up the classroom for reading in the content areas as well, since reading does not take place in isolation. On a daily basis, review previously taught skills and reinforce and introduce new skills.

PHONICS. There is a heavy emphasis on phonics in this book because without a strong letter–sound relationship, children will have difficulty with reading and may be unsuccessful. With this book, we begin with the ABC's, and learn the sound that each letter makes. Then, we build from that point.

Teaching and learning phonics can be fun. Somewhere along the line that message needs to be communicated. Learning to read is a skill that requires drill and practice. In this book, the strong phonics component comes through with the *ABC Marching Band.* Each letter is represented by a different animal with that letter sound, or sounds, and an instrument that makes the sound. Children meet the letters as animal characters and participate in stories, chants and activities that enable them to move to the rhythm of the letter sounds and to make the sounds as well. The teacher acts as the director of the marching band. The letters are not introduced sequentially, and this is deliberate. The alphabet is not static—letters move about in words, just as a marching band moves about on the playing field.

A mediocre band requires drill and practice. A good band requires drill and practice. A superior band requires . . . drill and practice. Reading also requires drill and practice. Learning to read can be likened to learning to play an instrument. It doesn't just happen. The more you work at it, the better you get. Children need to be given that important message. Learning is hard work so the teacher needs to give encouragement and support as the beginner struggles with a page of print. The process is not automatic. *The reward is in the learning of the skill, using it, perfecting it, and expanding it.* This requires formal, consistent instruction.

LINKS TO WRITING. During the 1990s much attention was given to the child as a creator of print, rather than as one who deciphers print. Thus, writing in journals, writing "like an author," and making books are activities in which many children were engaged. Since the speaking vocabulary of children is far ahead of their reading vocabulary, an effort has been made to get the words that the child speaks down on paper. This involves writing, and so writing has come to the forefront in the curriculum.

This is fine as long as the child gets a balanced program and enjoys it, learns from it, and still gets the basic reading skills instruction necessary to decipher a page of print. If all or a great deal of the child's time is spent creating print, it is akin to asking a beginning music student to become a composer while still struggling with the fundamentals.

Meanwhile, set up a Writing Center in the classroom and provide materials for students so they practice writing with care. Value and encourage their efforts. Many activities are suggested each month.

LINKS TO HOLIDAYS. Reading holiday books to children is essential because they are introduced to new vocabulary words and learn how to pronounce them. They catch the rhythm and the rhyme and even the magic of words with a good picture book. Many other language arts opportunities are suggested herein that enable the students to write and draw and learn about important holidays.

LINKS TO MATH. Math, too, is a language with its own set of symbols. So students need to learn the configuration (shape) of the numerals, and what the symbols stands for (as with phonics). In addition, children must learn the symbols for equality (=) and inequality (≠), for greater than/less than, (>/<), as well as the symbols for the four basic operations of addition, subtraction, multiplication and division. This requires direct instruction.

Children need to get a sense of numbers and this is best accomplished with the use of math manipulative materials. There are many suggestions in this material for math links.

Since math is an exact science and a form of communication, it is important that children learn to print the numerals with care. Also, knowledge of math is sequential and requires skill building. It doesn't just happen.

LINKS TO SOCIAL STUDIES AND SCIENCE AND HEALTH. There are many suggestions throughout the book for activities that deal with these very important content areas. Since this is a reading book, much of the focus is upon the skills of reading, writing, speaking and listening in conjunction with the content. However, in these critical areas it is well to keep in mind that the language arts act as the "glue" that holds together the content, and does not itself become the content.

LINKS TO AUTHOR STUDIES. At the end of each month there is an author-of-the-month study selection, with an annotated bibliography of suggested books. Also, there are many activities involving art and music that help to make the books come to life for the reader or listeners. It is with these activities that children catch the magic and enthusiasm for reading, storytelling, visual art and dramatic play. Here is where they can be encouraged to write their own stories, discuss the stories, make predictions, and so on.

These books help to enrich the classroom, and the teacher and children enjoy the stories together. Imagination takes flight. This is as important to the reading process as the drill and practice mentioned previously.

SUGGESTED BOOKS FOR THE MONTH. In each section, ten picture books are listed with annotations. There is usually an alphabet book among them, and many choice books by well–known and respected authors and illustrators. The books were selected because they have been well received by teachers and children. But, with over 4,000 books being printed yearly, it is impossible to list all of the quality books available.

At the end of the book, an extensive bibliography of picture books is listed. Again, it is important to read daily to young children. It motivates them to keep trying to learn to read by themselves. And, it creates a bond between teacher and student, and among the students.

ADDITIONAL HELP. The information at the beginning of the book can be used throughout the school year. It is designed to be informative and helpful, especially the sample letters and forms. Information about the interrelationship between visual art and print may be useful with parent conferencing.

As an adult, most people don't remember the daily routine that enabled them to become proficient readers. They don't recall many of the drill and practice activities carefully planned by the teacher. What is important, is that they learned how to read! As a teacher, you are responsible for being a strong leader in that process, especially during the early years. I hope you find some helpful ideas here.

Elizabeth Crosby Stull

Learning to Read with Ann

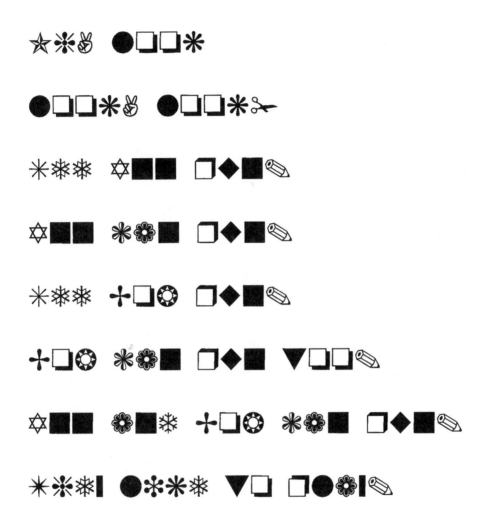

© 2000 by The Center for Applied Research in Education

Reading is a process, and one aspect of reading is decoding symbols. Can you decode these unfamiliar symbols so that you can read this short story? Now you know what it feels like to be a beginning reader. Work with this exercise to determine what you see, what you know, and what you'd like to know. Do you find the process challenging? It is! To teach this to a beginner, you need a wide variety of techniques. THE FOLLOWING IS THE STORY as seen by a beginner and as seen by a reader. Share this with parents.

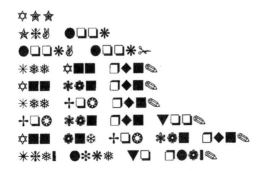

ANN
Oh, look
look, look!
See Ann run.
Ann can run.
See Bob run.
Bob can run too.
Ann and Bob can run.
They like to play.

Print Is Everywhere!

ENVIRONMENTAL PRINT. In our culture, students are bombarded by "environmental print" long before they come to school.

Environmental print is all around us—on billboards, gas station pumps, grocery store window signs, neon light messages that flash on and off, highway signs, street signs, traffic Rebus signs, a variety of logos for fast-food restaurants, and so on. A visit to the shopping mall bombards you with logos for food, clothing, and "specials" for sales. The mall's food court is another "print-rich environment."

Both children and adults are like walking advertisements with print messages and/or logos on shirts, jackets, shoes, pants, T-shirts, sweatshirts, and hats.

Children watch television with a variety of commercials that have catchy tunes and chants and words that go along with the pictures. Many foreign students who come to the United States have said that watching television commercials has helped them to learn English because they *hear* the word, *see* the word, and see a picture of what the word represents—not once but over and over again, until they have learned to memorize the information.

So, long before children come to school, they are exposed to letters and sounds and sound–symbol relationships. This gives many students a jump-start on reading.

PRINT-RICH ENVIRONMENT. In school, a "print-rich" environment means having a wide variety of written materials in the classroom. This includes labels on items (desk, sink, clock), name tags, bus schedule, special class schedule, classroom rules, the alphabet, a calendar, experience chart stories, a book nook or book center for reading, an area for writing that is well equipped with supplies, and a wide variety of children's work on display which sends out the message: "Learning Going on Here."

A print-rich environment is not to be confused with a cluttered environment. The 21st-century teacher needs a professional sense of color and design, and needs to take care with printing and writing that is teacher-generated, since it serves as a model for students. Keeping up this inviting environment is a lot of work, but worth the effort to provide a learning environment that not only looks appealing but is rich with learning opportunities.

Setting Up an Inviting Cozy Reading Area

You will need:

picture books	floor pillows
magazines	end table
newspapers	lamp
cozy chair with pillow	alarm clock
rug	stuffed animals

Procedure:

1. Set up this area in a corner of the room so that students can sign up to go there and read during a designated time of the day. Determine how many students can be accommodated successfully and stay with that number. For example, you may decide that one person can be in the chair and from two to five on the rug with a reading pillow, stuffed animal, and book.

2. Students can sign up for five minutes or ten minutes, and keep track of time with the alarm clock. An interest in telling time is a side benefit when there is a clock to assist with movement in and out of this area.

3. When students bring in a stuffed animal, encourage them to go to the school library to find a book (preferably one that they can read) that has that animal as one of the characters. Students return with the book and set it by the stuffed animal along with a sign-up sheet. If there is an animal and no book to accompany it, chances are the animal would like to listen to a story anyway.

4. Students enjoy going to this area to read quietly to a stuffed animal. Later, you can engage several students in a conversation about the book they read to a stuffed animal. For example, if students read *Goldilocks and the Three Bears* aloud to a stuffed bear, you can ask:

   - What part did the bear like best when you read it?
   - What part made the bear laugh when you read it?
   - Was the bear ever frightened by what you read?
   - What did your bear think of Goldilocks?
   - What new word did the bear learn to read?

   By doing this, the students are talking about characters, plot, setting, and purpose of the story. This is all done on an informal basis and in conversational tone.

5. *Enlist* the help of parents for materials for the cozy corner. Many parents can loan rugs, a couch, a rocking chair, pillows, and the stuffed animals for this type of cozy area. (See the sample letter to parents.) This is a hit with students and makes reading a pleasurable experience. *Let's read!*

"Cozy Corner"
Letter to Parents

Date _____

Dear Parents,

Greetings! It's the beginning of the school year and we're happy to be here. We have a wonderful group—maybe you've heard about us already from your youngster.

Have you heard this news? We want to set up a Cozy Corner for reading in our classroom. We need some materials for this project and would appreciate some help from you, if possible.

For our Cozy Corner, we need the following:

- a wicker chair or a rocking chair
- a gently used area rug
- an end table
- a lamp for atmosphere
- an alarm clock to help us with telling time
- cozy pillows
- stuffed animals that we can read to
- back issues of children's magazines

When we put the corner all together, we'll be sure to take a picture for you. When we have Open House later in the autumn, we hope you will come and see this corner for yourself.

ALSO, things that may be throw-away items for you may be gems for us! We would be happy with the following, any time you no longer need them:

- colored pencils
- wallpaper samples
- clothing for dress-up
- colored felt-tip pens
- computer paper scraps
- used baskets to hold "stuff"

Please send a note to me if you have something we can use. It will be greatly appreciated. You'll be hearing from us soon . . . we plan to send out a newsletter called "What's Going on Here?"

Sincerely,

_____
Teacher

Basic Skills Program, Whole Language Approach, and the Phonics Debate

Reading instruction is multifaceted. There is no one way that works best for all students, but all students should be exposed to a variety of techniques.

The **Basic Skills Program** (basal reader) focuses upon the following systematic skill development: letter–sound relationship (phonics); decoding and word recognition (word identification, word analysis); vocabulary (taught by definition, context, repetition, practice); comprehension (main idea, drawing conclusions, predicting outcomes, recognizing cause-and-effect relationships, understanding the author's purpose); reference and study skills (locating information, evaluating information, workbook practice); and language and literature skills (analysis of story, elements of story, writing devices, dramatic play and art activities, enrichment).

You can see from this list that phonics is *only one of the necessary skills* for teaching reading. It is a critical skill, however. To say that there is a "Whole Language vs. Phonics" debate is misleading. It would be more accurate to say there has been a debate that involves the "Whole Language vs. Basic Skills" approach, of which phonics is one component.

The **Whole Language Approach** grew rapidly. Essentially, it means that language is the focal point of the whole curriculum. Language arts is the "glue" that helps hold together the content of the math, science, social studies, and health curriculum with its reading, speaking, listening, writing, and visual and dramatic arts components. Critics are concerned that too much focus has been placed upon the glue to the detriment of the content.

With this movement, a great deal of emphasis has been placed upon what children know rather than what they don't know. Children's writing is valued, and they are encouraged to become authors, engage in daily journal writing, and produce stories and visuals. Partner reading and book browsing with a wide choice of reading materials is advocated. The skills are taught when the student is ready to learn them. To do all of this—and to do it effectively—takes a master teacher in order that the basic skills necessary for learning to read are not lost along the way. Notice that whole language has been referred to as an "approach," so guidelines are recommended but there is no set program. It is subject to the interpretation of the individual teacher.

In order to teach children effectively, you have to keep their welfare in the forefront. The question is how do children learn best. You have to rid yourselves

of the mistaken idea that all learning must be fun. Learning requires hard work and perseverance. The fun, or joy, comes from having learned how to do something and then being able to do it again independently.

The beginning teacher is well advised to follow a prescribed program. It is one way of assessing student needs, interests, and skills. You need patience and perseverance. Reading is a skill that increases with practice, and a teacher must develop a variety of techniques to capture and maintain student interest and motivation. Also, the socio-economic level of the student population figures into the program selection and helps determine how much structure is necessary for a reading program.

There are good features and ill-chosen features for any approach. But one single approach is not an answer—whether it is whole language or just one of the basic skills, namely phonics alone. You need to take what is most effective from each.

Once again, the reading pendulum is swinging . . .

A Visual–Verbal Relationship

When we look at children's art and the stories they tell about them, we find some interesting and complex relationships. For example:

- Children whose drawings are rich in detail often exhibit verbal language that is rich and embellished. (See Figure 1.)
- Children whose drawings are sparse in detail often exhibit language that is sparse in detail. (See Figure 2.)
- Children who experience success in reading also experience success with oral language.

Figure 1. Detailed drawing, with accompanying detailed story of 156 words, showing good imagination. The squirrel came down from the tree and took the girl's doll back to its nest. She persuaded him to give it back in return for a flower she would pick for him.

Figure 2. Sparse drawing, with accompanying sparse story of 8 words: "This is a house. This is a sun."

It is wise to let children draw and then tell you a story about it. Never ask, "What is it?" Instead, say something about the picture, such as "That's an interesting shape," or "Nice colors," or "Tell me something about your drawing."

The drawing in Figure 3 could look meaningless to the adult eye, but a 6-year-old boy laboriously drew these two lines of numerals along the bottom of a paper. Only when he told his story did the picture make visual sense.

The story was about a rocket that went to the moon with an astronaut. Perhaps the child was influenced by the countdown often seen along the bottom of a TV screen during a space shuttle blast off.

Give children plenty of time with their drawings. Do not hurry them!

Figure 3.

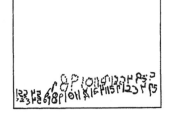

Some children, when asked to draw a picture of "anything you want to," may draw scattered objects. In Figure 4, a 6-year-old boy drew many items. When asked to tell a story about his picture, he named the objects: "This is a sun, this is a star, this is a house," and so on.

Figure 4.

Figure 5.

Five weeks later when the 6-year-old's naming story was read back to him, he attempted to portray a visually coherent unit. There is a baseline and the picture makes "visual sense."

The question is, did the structure of the language influence the orderliness of the second picture shown in Figure 5?

Visual art can be one predictor of success with reading. Art researcher Florence Goodenough devised a "Draw a Person" test whereby the more detail the child drew, the higher the child's score.

Figure 6 shows a child who is aware of a person, body parts, and extra features such as eyebrows, eyelashes, nose, lips, jewelry, and bracelets. Figure 7, on the other hand, does not have the same degree of awareness outside of the self.

What does this tell us? In order to be ready to learn to read, a child needs to be able to attend to figures and symbols and to focus attention outside of him- or herself, and to notice and retain details. The child who draws similar to Figure 6 will have success with reading activities, whereas the child who draws similar to Figure 7 is simply not yet ready for abstract symbols.

Figure 6.

Figure 7.

Source: "Drawing a Story and Listening to a Picture, A Visual–Verbal Relationship," *Arts and Activities,* January 1982. (See Bibliography.)

A Reading Portfolio

A reading portfolio can be as simple as a file folder of information about reading progress for each student in the classroom. The portfolio is maintained by you, although the student can have input. Keep the folders in a secure area. In this file folder, labeled with the student's name, there can be a representative sampling of the following items. The folder is designed to give a profile of the child as a reader and is helpful for conferencing with child, parents, or special needs counselor.

1. **ASSESSMENT:** A statement, made monthly, of the child's progress, the skill group to which student is assigned, and the child's interest in reading. This can be handwritten or in the form of a checklist. You can put a plus sign, or check mark, or minus sign after each item. These ideas can help get you started:
   - shows interest in reading books
   - listens attentively to stories
   - tries to figure out new words
   - is building a reading vocabulary
   - is making letter–sound relationship progress
   - excells in _____ ; needs work in _____

2. **READING TESTS:** Samples of work that are graded and evaluated using a districtwide measure.

3. **VOCABULARY CHECKLIST:** Use the First 100 Words, as an example, and periodically check the child's progress. Keep good records of dates.

4. **READING LIST:** What is the child's reading interest? What books has this student read? (This is one place where the child can have input into the portfolio and help keep this record.)

5. **ALPHABET AND PHONETIC PROGRESS:** Forms or teacher statements about ability, interest, progress.

6. **PRODUCER OF INFORMATION:** Keep representative samples. The following will help you get started:
   - likes to draw pictures to accompany text
   - interested in writing story sentences
   - interested in writing stories
   - likes to make books
   - engages in reading enrichment activities (drama, construction, puppets)
   - writes book summaries
   - writes journal entries

7. **GENERAL COMMENTS** (dated record)

8. **SPECIFIC COMMENTS** (dated record)

How Parents Can Help With Reading

There are many informal ways that parents can help children with the reading process. A child's social, emotional, and intellectual growth all figure into the reading process. Here are some ideas that may be helpful:

1. **LANGUAGE DEVELOPMENT**
   - Talk with your child. When you are engaged in a task, tell the child what you are doing.
   - Point out different things in the natural environment, such as flowers, trees, rocks, shells.
   - Take your child on outings to the zoo. Talk about the habitats and habits of the animals.
   - Go on an outdoor picnic, or go swimming and enjoy the experience. Then talk about what you did.
   - When driving a car, explain where you are going and what you are going to do next. "We turn right here." "We stop at the red light." "It's green which means we can go now." "We go one block past the school," etc.
   - On a familiar route, ask the child to tell you where to turn and what landmarks or signs to look for.

2. **READ TO YOUR CHILD**
   - Read picture books aloud and enjoy and discuss the story.
   - Visit the library weekly. Take out a card in the child's name. Have the child go to story hour, if appropriate.
   - Pay attention to what interests the child, and then find a book at the library that addresses the subject.
   - Set up a special time for everyone to read quietly at home.
   - Set up a library corner for your child—table, chair, books, paper for writing, pencils.
   - Limit television time.

3. **OTHER ACTIVITIES THAT ASSIST IN THE READING PROCESS**
   - Encourage your child to print and to write stories and notes to relatives.
   - Have your child classify items that you bring home from the grocery store: the liquids, meats, fruits, cereals, vegetables, and so on.
   - Have your child help sort laundry and fold it.

- Take your child to a play, concert, ballgame—a place where attention is required, and the child can have a different type of experience.

4. INDEPENDENCE AND FOLLOW-THROUGH

- Give your child responsibilities, such as cleaning up toys, straightening up the room, taking out the garbage.
- Leave notes for you child with directions.
- Have a place near the phone for pencil and paper. Teach your child how to answer the phone and how to take a message.
- Have the child help set the table and help clean up.
- Express confidence in the child—a "can do" attitude.
- Be patient, loving, and *consistent* so the child can grow naturally.
- Have a set bed time and stick to it.

Contents

September   1

October   63

December   185

January   241

February   293

March **335**

April 383

May and June   439

CHILDREN'S PICTURE BOOKS

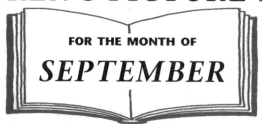

FOR THE MONTH OF
SEPTEMBER

Carle, Eric. *From Head to Toe* **(New York: HarperCollins Publishers, 1997)** Written in the question-and-answer format, this colorful book invites the child to imitate the movement of different animals. The familiar refrain "Can You Do It? I Can Do It" appear with each exercise. Aside from enjoying the book, the child gets a good workout. (Mr. Carle has dedicated this book to his teachers.)

Davis, Lee. *P. B. Bear's Treasure Hunt* **(New York: DK (Dorling Kindersley), 1995)** This book is a wonderful adventure, filled with large colorful photographs, maps, and picture writing (rebus style). The teddy bears have set out to look for a treasure at sea, while the reader is busy guessing what's in the box, and noting other picture clues.

Engel, Diane. *Josephina Hates Her Name* **(New York: Morrow Jr. Books, 1989)** Josephina thinks her name is ugly and wonders how she could have such a name. After a talk with Grandmother—who suggested the name—she has a better feeling. (A good story for children who are in the process of learning new names of classmates, and for some who would prefer a different name.)

Heller, Ruth. *Color, Color, Color, Color* **(New York: Putnam & Grosset, 1995)** An imaginative book about four basic colors (yellow, magenta, cyan blue, black) and how secondary colors are formed. Through the use of acetate pages, the colors are mixed before your eyes and then disappear at the end one by one. Children are fascinated by this color experience.

Ho, Minfong. *HUSH! A Thai Lullaby.* **Pictures by Holly Meade (New York: Orchard Books, 1996)** A mother goes in search of a variety of animals who are nearby making sounds that might keep her baby awake. The text is done in a question-and-answer format with rhythmical verse. Children will like joining in. (A Caldecott award winner.)

Johnson, Dolores. *What Will Mommy Do When I'm at School?* **(New York: Macmillan, 1990)** A tender story about a little girl who deals with her own feelings about school by fretting about her mother. Will her mother be scared without her? What will her mother do all day? After a reassuring talk with Mother, an amiable arrangement is worked out.

Keller, Holly. *What Alvin Wanted* **(New York: Greenwillow Books. 1990)** In this mouse family, Mother leaves Alvin in the care of his brother and sister, but he's fussy and cries and nothing they suggest will help. When Mother returns, she knows just what Alvin needs . . . the kiss she forgot to give him before she left.

Martin, Bill, Jr. and John Archambault. *Chicka Chicka Boom Boom!* **Illustrated by Lois Ehlert (New York: Simon & Schuster, Inc., 1989)** A rhythmic alphabet chant by letters that decide to meet on top of the coconut tree. But, can they all fit? Oops! A tangled mass of letters results, and the reader is invited to find them in their twisted and turned positions.

Tax, Meredith. *Families.* **Illustrated by Marylin Hafner (Boston: Little Brown, 1981)** This is an introduction to a wide variety of families—big, small, single parent, adopted children in the family, couples without children, and then on to dogs and other animal families. The main ingredient is the same—love. (A good start to a discussion of our own families.)

Woodruff, Elvira. *Show and Tell.* **Illustrated by Denise Brunkus (New York: Holiday House, 1991)** Andy never brought in anything exciting for Show and Tell. Once he brought a paper clip; another time, a shoelace. No one was interested until he found a blue bottle with a label that read: **CAUTION: BUBBLES MAY CAUSE TROUBLES.** (A good discussion book for appropriate items to share.)

SEPTEMBER

SEPTEMBER GREETINGS! Welcome to school! We're off on a challenging and rewarding adventure. Remember, children thrive on routine, so in the beginning keep the daily activities similar and predictable.

Learning to read takes practice. Just like the professional baseball player who has reached the height of proficiency and yet practices the same skills daily, or the renowned concert pianist who practices the same skills every day, beginning readers also need to practice the same skills daily. Instruction and practice are two sides of the same coin. The experience can be rich, varied and enjoyable too, as children note their improvement.

September's Focus on Reading. During this month you will be engaged in a variety of reading activities. Specific skills to focus on are: (1) Awareness of Alphabet Letters *(visual, auditory, kinesthetic);* (2) Letter–Sound Relationships *(phonics);* (3) The ABC Marching Band Letters of the Month—M, S, R, T, B, and L (special attention paid to six alphabet letters); and (4) More Skill-Building Activities for Letters M, S, R, T, B, L.

Awareness of Alphabet Letters

Alphabet on Parade *(Visual Awareness)*

Make sure you have a colorful copy of the manuscript alphabet on display across the front of the room. It's a good idea to have two copies—one above the chalkboard so that it can be seen from a distance and one below the chalkboard so that children can sit in front of it and use it to work with ABC activities.

There are many commercial alphabet sets available. Some teachers choose to create their own, using colorful sheets of 9″ × 12″ construction paper or card stock. Cut out the upper- and lower-case letter for each page, and place either a picture on the page or use an actual object.

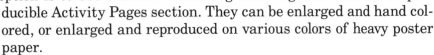

Another option is to use the ABC Marching Band figures from the Reproducible Activity Pages section. They can be enlarged and hand colored, or enlarged and reproduced on various colors of heavy poster paper.

Note: The large ABC book entitled *A Farmer's Alphabet* by Mary Azarian consists of striking woodblock prints in black, white, and red that Azarian was commissioned to do for the Vermont Board of Education. These big, bright, bold prints can be seen hanging in the primary classrooms throughout the state of Vermont.

In addition, there is a small paperback version of the same book that teachers have carefully cut up, laminated, and used for flashcard ABC matching games.

Also, Mary Azarian is the 1999 Caldecott Award winner for her woodcut illustrations in the book *Snowflake Bentley* by Mary Briggs Martin.

ABC Hint: Be on the lookout for used alphabet books at garage sales or used and slightly damaged books at community library book sales. Carefully cut them up and laminate them for artistic, yet sturdy, large, ABC flashcards. You can start a collection.

If you have several cut-up books, the cards can be mixed together and students can sort them by visual cues (i.e., bold print, color, style) and then, when they have done this, they can put the individual cards in alphabetical order.

The Alphabet Song Activities *(Auditory Awareness)*

To the tune of "Twinkle, Twinkle Little Star," sing the alphabet song daily. Many children will already know it and their voices will help carry the letters, words, and tune. Do this every day! This is the dominant rhythm pattern:

ABCD EFG
HIJK LMNOP
Q and R and S and T
UVW XYZ
Now I know my ABC's
Tell me what you think of me.

- Use a pointer and point to the letters as they are sung.
- Sing this at opening exercise time.
- Have two sets of ABC flashcards. Line one set up along the chalkboard and distribute the other. Sing the ABC song two or three times while children go to the chalkboard and place their letter in front of the corresponding letter on the ledge.
- "Change that Tune." Branch out from the traditional Alphabet Song by changing the rhythm, the pattern, and tempo. Sing the song, and have students echo the pattern. This strengthens good listening habits. Here is one sample to get you started. You can think up many more.

Teacher (Singing)	*Students (Echo Singing)*
ABC	ABC
DE . . . FG	DE . . . FG
HI	HI
JKLM . . . NOP	JKLM . . . NOP
QRS	QRS
TUV	TUV
W and XYZ	W and XYZ

Letters Are "Touchy" *(Kinesthetic Awareness)*

Students learn how a letter is shaped by tracing it with their finger. Make letter cutouts from rough paper (sandpaper) so students can get the feel of the letter.

Also, make balls of soft clay or plasticene and put them into plastic bags. Students can roll out snake coils with the clay on top of a slick counter or cookie sheet, and shape them into alphabet letters—thus feeling every inch of the letter.

The Sewing Shop *(Kinesthetic Awareness)*

You will need large alphabet letters made from sturdy cardboard or oaktag. Punch holes along the letter edge. Have students use a long shoelace to sew the letter—in and out, around and around. They gain a sense of the letter shape from this activity.

Letter–Sound Relationships

Calling All First Names! *(Phonics)*

Make a set of student name cards, one for each person in the class. Hold up a single name card and call attention to the beginning letter. For variety, this can be done in a number of ways. Using the letter "S" as an example, here are some ideas to get you started.

"This name begins with the letter S." *(direct instruction)*

"This is our *Science* letter." *(auditory clue—general)*

"We can hear this letter in *swing*" *(auditory discrimination)*

"Can this person identify his name?" *(personal response)*

"Raise your hand if you know this beginning letter." *(group response)*

"Who are you?" *(individual response)*

"This name has the sound of *s-s-s-s*, and the person is wearing a pink shirt with blue stripes." *(auditory/visual clues)*

Once the name is identified, the person can claim his or her card by saying the letter and name (S—Samuel or S—Stephanie). Do this until all cards are either lined up along the ledge, or distributed and then returned in alphabetical order.

Note: You are adding variety to this drill activity by changing the questions being asked. It helps to keep the children on task. Also, students are: (1) learning their own name, (2) learning the names of classmates, and (3) working with letter–sound relationships.

Listen for Beginning Letter–Sound Patterns *(Phonics)*

"Everyone should be very quiet. Let's put on our listening ears. Keep feet still and mouths closed, so 'ear windows' can open."

Slowly say three words, two of which will have the same beginning sound. Repeat. When students think they know the sound or letter of *two that are the same,* have them hold up their pointer finger to their ear as a signal. Tell them what pattern to listen for. Here are some starters:

(AAB pattern)	cake, candy, rose
	plate, party, boy
	acorn, able, mouse
(ABA pattern)	sister, flower, salt
	glass, horse, gold
	neighbor, ball, nest
(ABB pattern)	witch, ball, balloon
	key, popcorn, pepper
	laugh, tree, ticket

More Beginning Sounds *(Phonics)*

Another activity for those at the very beginning of formal reading instruction is to identify a letter sound by a clue that you give. Print the letter on the chalkboard. Say it aloud. Next, tell students that you will say a target word that begins with that sound. After that you will say three additional words; however, only two of the words will begin with the target word sound and one word will not. Say the words carefully and slowly (twice) and ask students to find the words that sound exactly the same at the start of the target word. Raise their pointer finger when they know them.

For example, print the letter *s* and say, "Listen for the *s-s-s* sound in the word *snake.* (Repeat target word *snake.*) Now, I'll say three words. Two will begin with the same sound as *s-s-s* in *snake,* and one will be different. See if you can listen carefully and remember the ones that are the same. If you know, raise your pointer finger." Say "snake" slowly, pause, and then say the other three words. Repeat. Call upon someone whose pointer finger is raised even if someone has called out the response; this serves as a reminder that you're looking for the hand signal.

Snake:	sun	flower	soldier
Snake:	Sally	Suzie	Andy
Snake:	lamp	sandwich	salami

Students can also listen for the one that is different, or *does not belong*. Do this exercise with all of the consonant sounds. Make up your own words in advance. When you find that you have from three to five minutes to spare—sometimes just before lining up at the door to go to a special activity class—you can use this exercise to help students review and learn.

Can You Name the Letter? *(Phonics)*

"Everyone quiet, ready to listen. I will say three letters. Two will be the same. I will say the letters twice, or two times. Raise your pinky finger if you think you know the letter that I've said twice." Do this listening exercise daily, using different letters. This will get you started:

(AAB pattern)	r, r, s	v, v, l
	d, d, x	c, c, g
(ABA pattern)	r, s, r	v, l, v
	d, x, d	c, g, c
(ABB, pattern)	s, r, r	l, v, v
	x, d, d	g, c, c

For variation, have students raise their hand and be able to tell the letter that is different. This strengthens listening skills.

Constructing Big Letters

Make straight and curved shapes from cardboard or styrofoam pieces. Store them in a large box. Have students sit in a circle. Spread out the shapes. Then, call upon students to work in pairs to construct the designated letters while others observe. Take turns.

Constructing Feather Letters

At the local craft store, get a big bag of colored feathers. Have students construct alphabet letters using feathers. The idea is to gain a kinesthetic awareness of the letter shape. Feathers are very quiet, too. Pompom balls are available in large bags at craft stores and also work well.

During circle time, each student can contribute to constructing a large letter on the floor.

We've Got Some Name Envelopes

Make two sets of first-name flashcards for each student and laminate them. Cut up one set into individual letters. Place the name card and the individual letter cards in an envelope with the student's name printed on the outside. These name envelopes can be kept in the Writing Center. Students can match the letters and print their name.

Let's Get Acquainted—Name Envelope Activities

Students can take out their name cards and letter cards. Match the letters by placing the individual letters on top of, or beneath, the corresponding letters on the name card.

- Students can use their name cards as a model and practice printing their name.
- Students can spell out their name using Scrabble® letters.
- Students can locate letters in magazines that are in their first name, cut them out, and glue them onto another name card. They will become aware of a variety of fonts, sizes, slants, and colors of letters.

Those Puzzling ABC's

Print puffy, large-sized letters on different colors of sturdy oaktag paper. Next, use a marking pen to create swirling and interlocking lines on the letter shape. Then, cut out the letter and puzzle shapes. These puzzles can be individually stored in small plastic bags with one letter puzzle per bag. Make sure the letter is printed on the outside of the container for students to see as a model.

Clay Is Cool—Making "Dog Tags"

Students can form the letter of their first name out of baking clay. Use a toothpick to make a hole at the top. Bake according to directions on the package. When done, allow clay to cool. String yarn through the letter and wear as a necklace or identification tag.

Snacking with Carrot-Stick Letters

For snack time, have a large container of carrot sticks and ask children to pretend that they are rabbits. Give each student a handful on a little plate, and practice making stick letters—those letters that do not have rounded edges.

For capital letters, try the following: A, E, F, H, I, K, L, M, N, T, V, W, X, Y, and Z. Then have students make just one or two that they would like to eat. Have them form and say the letter(s) they plan to devour, and then start nibbling like a rabbit.

For lower-case letters, try the following: i, k, l, t, v, w, x, y, and z. Which ones use straight lines just like the capitals? (Ii, Kk, Ll, Tt, Vv, Ww, Xx, Yy, and Zz) Point out to students that lower-case letters a, e, f, h, m, and n use both straight and curved lines, unlike their capital counterparts.

The ABC Marching Band Letters of the Month— M, S, R, T, B, and L

Introduction to the ABC Marching Band

Information for the teacher: The 26 alphabet letters can be presented or reinforced with the ABC Marching Band. There is a page for each letter in the Reproducible Activity Pages throughout the book on which is printed the capital and lower-case letters, the animal character, and the instrument that the character plays. (For example, April Alligator plays the accordion with two notes—the long *a* and the short *a;* Barry Bear plays a bugle with the sound of *b-b-b-b;* Cindy Cat plays both the clarinet [hard sound of *c*] and the cymbals [soft sound of *c*]; Dolby Dog plays the drums; and so on.) For a complete list of the ABC Marching Band and the month in which they appear, see Bibliography.)

The Marching Band members can provide much instruction for students in terms of the sounds they make, rhythms and rhyme, and kinesthetic formation of the letters. They provide an opportunity to develop listening skills. This section also makes students aware of how they produce sounds (tongue, teeth, etc.). The letters can be introduced in order or via the following Marching Band focus letters section, which does not introduce them in order. The reason for this is to mix them up in an effort to approach the letters in a unique way that is playful, instructive, and nonthreatening. *These band member letters move about just as letters move about to make words!*

Get into the spirit of the ABC Marching Band with rhythm and background music, body motions, and marching. There are also links to other areas of the curriculum as well.

Focusing Attention on September's Letters

Each month you can focus upon at least four to six alphabet letters. They do not have to be in order. For September, use the following letters: M, S, R, T, B, and L. How do you work through this material? Here is a suggested procedure.

Tap the baton (dowel rod, ruler, stick) for order. All eyes are on the bandleader (teacher). Then: (1) say the name of the letter; (2) demonstrate the shape of the letter (draw both upper case and lower case on the chalkboard); (3) introduce the ABC Marching Band member by name and the instrument he or she plays and simulate this movement (use the Reproducible Activity Pages to help); and (4) reinforce the letter sound that the ABC Marching Band member makes. (Focus upon mouth, teeth, tongue, and lips, and how to make the sound.)

Use the ABC Band Member Reproducible Activity Pages for the following: An ABC marching band for the classroom wall; an individual ABC book for each student; an ABC stick puppet collection for help with phonics; an ABC card collection for use with suggested activities; as "posters" to carry when the class is marching around in a circle while band music is playing in the background; and for other activities suggested in the ABC Marching Band sections of the book.

Students enjoy rhythm, rhyme, movement, and physical activity so let's capitalize upon these strengths and interests for part of the time, as they learn letters and sounds.

Meet Manny Mouse and His Marimba *(Letter M)*

Use the procedure in the order referred to above. Manny Mouse plays the marimba. The marimba is a real instrument that resonates when struck with a mallet. When Manny strikes the marimba, it makes the sound of "mmm."

Have students practice the letter sound along with Manny Mouse. First, model the sound of the letter *m* with lips together and the prolonged *mmmmm* sound. Then have children do this, noting that their lips are together and they are making a humming sound in their throat. They can make the sound high or low, or glide up and down.

Note: Have students take a deep breath and hold the sound of "mmm" until all air is expelled from their lungs. Then they usually take a gulp of air. This is effective in showing students that the lungs and air play a part in using their own instrument (voice) and in playing instruments.

(This will help with procedure. You, otherwise known as the bandleader, hold a baton or ruler level until all is quiet. Then, with a flourish, lift the baton up as a signal to make the sound, then swing the baton down as a signal that the sound is to stop.) All band members have to pay attention and learn when to stop and start, just as in a real band. To be effective, you have to take on an air of authority as the bandleader—a baton, a hat, a jacket, or a business attitude will help. Later, students can take over this role and model the behavior of the teacher.

Here is a short, rhythmic verse to help provide an opportunity for students to pretend to be in the marching band, making the sound of the letter *m*. First, model the verse; then have students repeat it, section by section, after you. When the practice is going along well, try the following "dress rehearsal."

Here's Manny Mouse. *(Bandleader: Baton swings up.)*
He's come to say
It's fun to play
His letter today!
MMM, MMM, MMM! *(Baton swings down.)*

He plays the marimba *(Baton swings up.)*
In a mariache band.
He's from down south
In Mexico land.
MMM, MMM, MMM! *(Baton swings down.)*

Three Things That Start with "M" *(Letter M)*

Have three items that begin with the sound of the letter M in a basket with a tag attached. The tag should have the large and small letters printed on it (M,m).

Take the items out one at a time and say the names. If they sound like they begin with the "mmm" sound, they can be returned to the basket. If not, then they will have to be set aside.

Encourage students to bring in items for the "M,m Basket."

The Letter Head Sweat Bands *(Letter M)*

Make the connection between the marching band and the head band. The word "band" serves as a word with double meaning. Cut long construction paper strips and have students practice writing the letter "M" on it. Then, encircle the band around the head of each student for a good fit, remove it, staple the band together, and have students wear the head band today. This can be done for several letters or for all of them.

Another approach is to ask students to bring in head sweat bands. Then, each time you are emphasizing the band letter, they can wear the head band with a cut-out of the letter tucked underneath the band or attached to it. Wear it as the letter of the day.

Meet Sally Squirrel and the Saxophone *(Letter S)*

Sally plays one note on her saxophone and it comes out sounding like "sss." The saxophone is a reed instrument and curves, similar to a snake; this is another association you can make with the letter—the hissing sound of a snake, or "sss, sss, sss."

Point out to students that when saying the sound of the letter *s,* the teeth are together (edge of top teeth resting on edge of bottom teeth). Inhale, or take a deep breath, and then slowly let the air out between the teeth. Note that it also sounds like air escaping from a tire.

Where is the tongue? The tip is resting behind the bottom row of teeth. Have students inhale, put teeth together, and blow air from their lungs while shifting their tongue around inside the mouth in different positions—on the roof or on the back of the floor to make the sound of the letter *s.* It just isn't the same, is it? Point out that the position of the tongue is important when making the sound of *s.*

Here is a verse to say and learn about Sally. Go slowly. Model the entire verse while students listen. Say only a part and have students repeat that part. Then try for an entire verse.

Tap for the quiet signal, just as a conductor would do. All eyes are on you. "Stand tall, feet together, arms at sides. Ready, go." *(Raise baton.)*

I called Sally on the telephone
But she was practicing the saxophone.
SSS, SSS, SSS!

I said, "Hey, Sally! Turn on the TV.
There are lots of cartoons for you to see."
SSS, SSS, SSS!

But Sally said on the telephone,
"I'd rather practice my saxophone."
SSS, SSS, SSS!

So here I am, and I'm all alone
Maybe *I'll* take up the saxophone!
SSS, SSS, SSS! *(Lower baton.)*

You and the students can make up motions to go with the verses, or use the following: For the first one, raise hand to ear for talking on the telephone; then, twist the wrist for turning on the TV; and then put both hands in front of the chest and pretend to push down buttons for playing the saxophone.

Silly Sentences with Sally *(Letter S)*

Have students repeat these simple sentences after you. Then have them determine which words begin with the sound that the letter *s* makes.

Sally saw a snake.
Sally saw a silver snake.
Sally saw a silver snake in the sink.

Sally saw a squirrel.
Sally saw a silver squirrel.
Sally saw a squirrel eating a sunflower seed.

Write the simple sentence on the chalkboard and, one by one, have students circle or underline the letter *S* in Sally, the letter *s* in saw, and so on.

Meet Rusty Rabbit and the Rhapsodia *(Letter R)*

Rusty plays one note on his rhapsodia, and it comes out sounding like "ur." What is the rhapsodia? It's a make-believe instrument that looks like a shoe box with rubber bands around it. However, *rhapsodia* has its roots in the Latin word *rhapsodia* and Greek word *rhapsoidos* which means "weaver of songs." Also, the word *rhapsody* means a sweeping melody.

Point out to the students that this sound is made in the back of the throat. Have them gently touch their throat and feel the purring sound. Have a mirror available so that students can see themselves when making this sound. Point out that the lips are parted to let the air out and the corners of the mouth are drawn together. The tongue is at rest.

The following is a song (make up the tune) to be said or sung with gusto! For each line *(r-r-r)*, the voice can go higher; then repeat and have the voice go lower. Introduce these musical terms.

I hear a melody, r-r-r.   *(Raise baton.)*
I hear a rhapsody, r-r-r.
I hear a symphony, r-r-r.
I am in ecstacy, R-R-R!   *(Lower baton.)*

Real Items That Have the Letter "R" Sound *(Letter R)*

Have a container with five items in it. Three or four items can begin with the sound of the letter *r;* one is different. Which letter got into the wrong basket? Students say the names of those that belong.

It's a Red-Letter Day *(Letter R)*

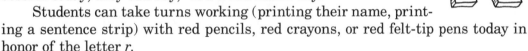

A red-letter day is a "saying" or an expression that means "It's a good day!" Students can trace and cut out red letters for their head bands or for a letter badge. Every time someone is successful today, they can say, "It's a red-letter day!"

Students can take turns working (printing their name, printing a sentence strip) with red pencils, red crayons, or red felt-tip pens today in honor of the letter *r.*

Meet Tootsie Turtle and the Trumpet *(Letter T)*

Tootsie plays the trumpet with a toot, toot, toot! Students may be familiar with the trumpet, as it is an actual instrument and a popular one. Have a picture available, or a real trumpet, and have students simulate holding a trumpet with two hands in front of their face, pressing down on a key, and making a "toot, toot" sound.

Point out to students that when making the sound for the letter *t,* the tongue plays a big part. The lips are slightly parted, the teeth are slightly parted, and the tip of the tongue is pressed against the ridge on the roof of the mouth just behind the top teeth, as air is expelled from the lungs. While the letter name sounds like "tee," the actual sound is more like "tuh."

Here is a rhyme students can learn as they march around the circle with their make-believe trumpet. They are getting kinesthetically involved with the letter sound and reinforcing directions (up, down, left, right). Make sure the feet are raised high off the floor during marching. You, as bandleader, demonstrate the sing-song rhythm of this verse. Children will quickly learn it.

Tootsie plays the trumpet *(Leader: Baton swings up.)*
With a toot, toot, toot! *(Baton swings back/forth.)*
She's never without
Her marching suit!

She's snappy and she's happy
And she loves to play,
So, won't you join
Ms. Tootsie today?

With a toot to the right *(Turn right from waist.)*
And a toot to the left *(Turn left from waist.)*
And a toot up high *(Turn toward ceiling.)*
And a toot down low. *(Turn toward floor.)*

Ready now?
Here's the way to blow.
TOOT. TOOT.   TOOT, TOOT, TOOT.
TOOT. TOOT.   TOOT, TOOT, TOOT! *(Leader: Baton swings down.)*

Answer "Toot, Toot" for Yes *(Letter T)*

This is similar to "Simon Says." All students stand; you ask a question. If the answer is "yes," the students answer "Toot, toot" and sit. If the answer is "no," the students remain quiet and still. The object is to have everyone, or almost everyone, seated by the end of the activity. (This is good for listening—and for exercise, too!)

Questions can be serious or silly. Here are some to get you started:

"Do fish swim?" *(toot, toot)*

"Do dogs bark?" *(toot, toot)*

"Do turtles fly?" *(silence)*

"Do phones ring?" *(toot, toot)*

"Do computers think?" *(silence)*

"Do cats use forks?" *(silence)*

"Do mice eat cheese?" *(toot, toot)*

Meet Barry Bear and the Bugle *(Letter B)*

Barry plays one note on the bugle, and it comes out sounding like "buh." Students may or may not be familiar with the bugle, a brass instrument, so make sure to have a picture available. (It is similar to the trumpet.)

Point out to students that this sound is made by first putting the lips together, filling up the cheeks with air, and then letting the air be expelled as the lips are opened. The tongue is at rest on the floor of the mouth. While the letter name sounds like "bee," the sound is closer to "buh."

Here is a verse to learn and to practice the sound of the letter *b*. You need to get the rhythm going:

The bugle blows *(Baton swings up.)*
The sun goes down
You hear the tune
All 'round the town.
Buh, Buh, Buh.

The bugle blows
The sun comes up
So wash your face
And pucker up.
Buh, Buh, Buh. *(Baton swings down.)*

Language Tongue Twister *(Letter B)*

Have some fun with the language and see if students can say these without getting their tongue twisted. It's fun, it's good exercise for the tongue muscles, and everyone's learning phonics.

Barry Bear boldly bit berries.

Bears blink when bees buzz.

Buster Bear buried buttered beans.

Meet Lyle Lion and the Lyre *(Letter L)*

Lyle plays one note on the lyre and it sounds like "uhl," whereas the name of the letter sounds like "el." The lyre (sounds like *liar*) is a stringed instrument of the harp family. In times long ago, it was used to accompany a singer or a reader of poetry.

Point out to students that this sound is made by placing the tip of the tongue on the ridge of the roof of the mouth, just behind the top front teeth. The lips are slightly parted, and the teeth are *not* together. The actual sound comes from the throat. Have students put their hands on their throats and feel the vocal chords vibrate while they make the sound and hold the note. (It feels like a motor humming—similar to the letter *m*. In fact, have students make a continual sound pattern of the letters *l* and *m [lll, mmm, lll, mmm]* and feel the shift that takes place in their vocal cords.) Also, notice how the tongue and the lips move when we shift back and forth from the *l* sound to the *m* sound. You can also repeat the word "elm," the name of a tree, over and over to gain practice shifting from the letter *l* to *m*.

Let's Hum Along! *(Letter L)*

Since the lyre was used as an instrument to accompany "lyrics" (words in poetry or song), have the students hum while pretending to pluck the strings of the lyre, as lyrics are read aloud by the teacher or a student. For vocabulary development, introduce and explain the meaning of the word *lyrics*.

Also, take a familiar tune and hum it rather than sing it. For example, hum "My Country 'Tis of Thee," "If You're Happy and You Know It Clap Your Hands," or "Twinkle, Twinkle Little Star." Have students suggest tunes they would like to hum.

Many people hum while working, so today during work time, you may hear a lot of humming. Encourage it as long as it is low and does not distract others.

Singing La-La-La with Lyle *(Letter L)*

To exercise the tongue and gain practice making the sound of the letter *l*, have students sing "la, la" instead of the words of familiar songs.

Our Voice Is an Instrument *(Letter L)*

It is important for students to begin to think of their own voice as an "instrument" that is capable of making many sounds. We can talk, sing, hum with our voice, and make it go way up high and way down low. We can make it sound sweet or make it sound gruff. Work with the voice in this way as you work with the ABC Marching Band Letters each month.

More Skill-Building Activities for Letters M, S, R, T, B, and L

Make Individual Letter Posters (M, S, R, T, B, L)

You will need poster paper, a felt-tipped pen, glue, and pictures or actual items that begin with the letter sound. Use the following procedure for all six letters, one at a time, during the month. Display the posters, then take them down at the end of the month and assemble them into a book. Here is a sample procedure using the letter "M,m."

Procedure: Have available five large pictures (for example, monkey, money, marbles, macaroni, man, and so on) that you have already cut from magazines that begin with the sound of the letter *m*. As you say the names, have children repeat them. Point out that the pictures begin with the sound of the letter *m;* use tape to attach the pictures to a large chart. Later, these can be pasted on by the students.

Repeat this procedure for all of this month's focus letters. Hang the posters at students' eye level so the children are able to go to the posters and say the words and listen to the sound the letter makes. Encourage students to bring in more items or find more pictures in used magazines
for the chart.

Let's Begin to Build the "Shopping for Letters" Routine *(M, S, R, T, B, L)*

Each day work with the letter posters previously mentioned. Here are some suggestions for doing this.

- Point to the pictures on the poster and have students say the *m-m-m-m* sound and the name of the objects fastened to the posterboard. This can be done as a whole-group activity. It reinforces the letter–sound relationship and the appropriate objects at a semi-concrete level.
- *"Shopping for Letter Sounds."* Go through a magazine to locate more pictures that begin with the sound of *m*. Cut them out and add them to the chart. Do this as a total group, then have children "go shopping" in magazines and follow this procedure on their own in their spare time. (Locate, verify the sound, cut, and paste to chart.)

Unpack the Shopping Basket *(M, S, R, T, B, L)*

The letter *m* has just come back from shopping. Have a wicker shopping basket or bag filled with several concrete items that begin with the sound of *m*, such as a mitten, macaroni, mask, mayonnaise, mustard, macaroons, mobile, and so on.

Take out the items one at a time. Say the sound of the letter *m (m-m-m-m-m)* and name the item. Can the letter keep it? Only if it begins with his or her sound. (For variation, after students are familiar with this letter–sound relationship, put several items in the basket that do not begin with the letter *m*. Oops! The letter has to return those items—they don't begin with the sound of *m-m-m-m-m*.)

Note: In general, the procedure described here is the one to follow for the letters you have selected for each month. Keep reviewing and practicing. Children thoroughly enjoy this and look upon it as play. You need to join in the magic of the child's world of play in order for the letters-of-the month to be a success. **A teacher of reading needs to have and to convey a sense of the magic and wonder of print.**

Hunting Through the House for Letters *(M, S, R, T, B, L)*

- Place an ABC Marching Band member (one that you have carefully colored) on the front of a large manila envelope. Let children fill the container with pictures they cut from magazines that begin with that sound. They can sort and categorize these daily.
- Have children color an ABC Marching Band member to take home. Then at home they can look for items that begin with that letter sound. Look in the kitchen, bathroom, living room, basement, garage, and so on. Have them report to the class the next day. Then, print the names of all of these items on a "Word House Chart." It may be helpful to put the shape of a house around the items listed by each student, along with the student's name on the chimney, so we can see where all of these items can be located. (See Reproducible Activity Pages for a Word House Chart.)

Yummy—Let's Snack with the Letters *(M, S, R, T, B, L)*

Students like to enjoy a snack while learning—and the ABC letters are always hungry—so you can link these two together if you choose.

Sometimes the size of a treat may be itsy, bitsy like a sample that we get at the supermarket. The important thing is to make the relationship between the letter and sound. A newsletter sent home to parents may be helpful here, as some may wish to donate food. (Also, be sure to check with parents for food allergies.) Some food suggestions to sample during September are:

M—marshmallows, M&M's®, melon, milk, macaroni

S—sip of soup, sandwich, strawberry, Snickers®

R—rhubarb, radish, raspberries

T—tomato wedge, Tater Tots®, toast

B—banana slice, berries, brownie

L—lettuce, lemonade, licorice, lollipop

The Bakery Shop *(M, S, R, T, B, L)*

Set up a make-believe bakery shop. Have six plastic bins or boxes with the "letters of the month" in each bin. Letters can be magnetic, cardboard, oaktag, written on paper, cube letters from games, etc.

Select one or two bakers (students) to be behind the counter, wearing a large chef's hat and apron. Customers can select "3 M's, please" or "2 R's and 3 T's, please." These are identified by the bakers or customer, bagged, and handed to the customer with the proper "Thank you" and "You're welcome, come again."

After two or three customers complete their business, empty the bags into the appropriate bins and begin again. (You may want to use pencil and paper for writing out the orders and for receipts. Play coins and a toy cash register can be added, and letters can be "purchased" depending upon the ability of the group.)

Variations:

- Change the bakers frequently (5- to 10-minute shifts).
- Add a toy telephone for phone orders (and talk about how one deals with interruptions of this nature).
- Add other props such as a calculator, a bell, and paper and pencil for marking sale items or specials.
- Simulate a "rush hour" where several students come in, all wanting service (and talk about how one conducts oneself appropriately in the store while waiting one's turn, and how it feels to be the clerk).
- Have the state inspector visit to note cleanliness, orderliness, and general demeanor of the bakers and customers.

Letter Shapes Look Yummy to Teddy Bears *(M, S, R, T, B, L)*

Each student receives a small ball of yellow, pink, or green play dough or plasticene. Pound and roll it into a flat letter shape. Then, using a toothpick, trace designs on the top. Display letters on a picnic tablecloth, with a picnic basket, and materials inside for setting up a table.

Students can bring in their teddy bears and set them around the display for a tea party. Also, students can introduce their teddy bears to the group when they join them for story time. Teddy bears might like to nap with their owners during rest time.

Teddies Like Storybooks *(M, S, R, T, B, L)*

For a story time treat, read the book *Ira Sleeps Over* by Bernard Waber. It is about a young boy who is planning to stay overnight at a friend's for the first time and wonders how to include his teddy. *Alphabears* by Kathleen Hague, with illustrations by Michael Hague, is a good addition to your alphabet study, since each ABC bear has an appropriate letter name. For another treat, read the series of stories about Eddie and his teddy, and a real bear and his teddy, by Jez Alborough entitled *Where's My Teddy?*, *It's the Bear*, and *My Friend, Bear*. A classic all-time favorite bear tale that children enjoy is *Blueberries for Sal* by Robert McCloskey.

Sing Along with the Focus Letters *(M, S, R, T, B, L)*

Distribute cards that contain the letters of focus when you are all together at circle time, or when you have a few extra minutes for instruction. To the tune of "Where Is Thumbkin?" you sing lead questions and the student who is holding the appropriate letter card sings out the answer. For example:

TEACHER: "Where is M? Where is M?"
STUDENT: "Here I am. Here I am." *(Student stands with letter.)*
TEACHER: "How are you today, M?"
STUDENT: "Very well, I thank you."
TEACHER: "Wonderful! Wonderful!"

Go through all of the focus letters. Then ask those students with letter cards to give them to someone else to hold and go through this singing routine again. Ask for students to volunteer to take the teacher role, or select one who seems quite adept for this job. On the last round, when the student answers to the letter name, the letter card can be deposited in a letter box for safe keeping. Toward the end of the month, make this material available during recess time so that children can select it as a free-time activity.

Sing Along with the ABC Marching Band Letters *(M, S, R, T, B, L)*

During Circle Time, distribute the focus-letter band members. You can point, with baton or ruler, to each letter printed on the chalkboard. The student who is holding that band member's letter calls out the SOUND that the letter makes, and can even simulate the sound as if the band member is "tuning" the instrument. In case students do not know the letter sound, they can stand with the letter card under their chin and call upon someone else to say it. Then they repeat it. Students can also simulate the playing of the instrument along with making the sound for a three-way visual–verbal–kinesthetic association.

The teacher's strong voice is an asset and may be essential for this letter–sound "tuning up" exercise.

M   mmm, mmm, mmm
S   sss, sss, sss
R   rrr, rrr, rrr
T   tuh, tuh, tuh,
B   buh, buh, buh
L   prolonged sound of *l*

Use the letter flash cards when lining up for lunch, special classes, etc.

Use the letter cards as a "drink ticket." A student must take a letter, say it, make the sound, get a drink, and give the drink ticket to another person who repeats this process. Students enjoy this learning activity and will ask to do it.

Band Music *(M, S, R, T, B, L)*

Go to your local community library in search of videos or cassette materials that feature band music. Select a leader and have students march around the room to the music. They can pretend to be playing a musical instrument. This is good exercise and a good activity for transition from one subject to the next.

Roll a Ball in Time to Music *(M, S, R, T, B, L)*

Have students sit in a large circle and roll a basketball or volleyball to one another, with music playing in the background.

Listen to Music Stories *(M, S, R, T, B, L)*

Obtain an audio-cassette copy of *Peter and the Wolf* by Prokofiev and play it for listening enjoyment. Students will begin to associate the sound of the instrument with story characters. Another audiotape is "Peter and the Wolf Play Jazz," with Jon Crosse. This ALA Noteable Recording (1990) presents a new approach to Prokofiev's tale; on the reverse side is "Cool Mother Goose Suite."

READING LINKS TO HOLIDAYS & SPECIAL EVENTS

Going to School Is a Special Event *(Language Development)*

Print the name of the school on the chalkboard. Have everyone repeat it and learn it. (Students say: "I go to _____ School.")

Print the name of the principal on the chalkboard. Have everyone repeat it and learn it. (Students say: "Our principal is Mr. (or Ms.) _____.")

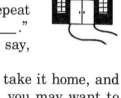

Print your own name on the chalkboard. Have everyone repeat it and learn it. (Students say: "My teacher is Mr. (or Ms.) _____."

Print the phone number on the chalkboard. Students say, "The school telephone number is _____."

Students can copy the information from the chalkboard, take it home, and study it for "homework." If this is a young beginning group, you may want to print the information and make copies. (See Reproducible Activity Pages for schoolhouse with school information.)

The "Practice Line-Up for Getting to the Door" as a Special Event *(Listening Skills)*

Students need to learn how to get from Point A to Point B in the classroom. One thing to practice is lining up at the door. This activity gives students practice in developing their listening skills. Have students stand, push their chair under the table, face the door, and follow the path you have designated at a walking pace that you have demonstrated. Here are some ways to line up at the door:

- All those who have the letter *g* in their first name.
- All those who have an eye color that ends with *n*, as in brown.
- All those who have an eye color that begins with *b*, as in blue.
- All those who are wearing something that begins with *r*, as in red. (This can be expanded to include *y* as in yellow, *o* as in orange, and so on.)

If time is running out and there are still many students left, you can say, "All of the good listeners at this table, please line up," and so on.

Hail, Hail the Gang's All Here! We're a Winning Team!

This is a good exercise in speaking, listening, and problem solving. Eventually reading and writing can enter into the picture.

To establish a team spirit for your classroom (and this is essential for working together), have the students select a name for their class. (The name can be selected from animals, birds, nature, patriotic symbols, or storybook characters.

Try to avoid the use of commercial sports team names.) Narrow the choices down to two or three names and then have a class vote by a show of hands or secret ballot. (You can help by selecting the name if these ap-  proaches aren't working.) Possible suggestions include: The Mighty Oaks; The (state, city, or school name) Win- ners; The Gold Medal Club; The Champs; The A Team; The Red, White, and Blue; "The Hungry Caterpillars"; and so on.

Next, We Need a Logo *(Reading Symbols)*

What's a logo? It's a symbol that represents some thing or some place. Have a variety of "symbols" available that you have found in magazines so that students can readily identify with the concept of a "logo." Usually, this is apparent in advertising.

A logo may be a visual picture; it can contain letters or numerals. If, for example, your class name is "The Bear Cubs," a bear would be an appropriate logo. Perhaps a bear wearing a cap with your room number printed on it would be appealing.

We "read" logos all the time. They're in our environment at gas stations, at the mall, on billboards, on automobiles, on bicycles, on T-shirts, on cameras, on crosswalk signs, etc. Have students be on the look-out for logos (become logo de- tectives) and be sure to bring up the subject another day very soon. (See Repro- ducible Activity Pages on environmental print, or logos.)

Logo Detectives at Work

Ask students to bring in samples of environmental print— such as paper cups, placemats, containers, and so on—that they get at fast-food restaurants. They can also bring in labels from cans, cereal boxes, and other food products. Set up a Logo Station and have students read the information. Some students do not think of knowing this information as "reading" in the usual sense. They are, however, reading symbols and making connec- tions to print. We live in a "print-rich" country.

Write an Experience Chart Story About the Class

With this activity, you are engaged in speaking, listening, writing, and read- ing. Use a very large sheet of paper or oaktag and discuss the following: the num- ber of students in your class, the school name, your room number, your class name, and your class logo. You do not have to write down every single word that is said, but rather, put it in abbreviated form. Once you have had your discussion, take the felt-tip pen and start printing. For example, it may go something like this:

TEACHER: "What grade are we in?" *(Students respond.)* "Okay, let's start with that." *(Print the following.)*

We are in _____ grade.

TEACHER:	"What school?" *(Wait for answer.)*
TEACHER:	"Okay. So far we have, '*We are in* _____ *grade at* _____ *School.*'"
TEACHER:	"Jessie said our class name, so let's put it in here."
TEACHER:	"Now we have, '*We are in* _____ *grade at* _____ *School. Our class name is THE LIBERTY BELLS.*'"
TEACHER:	"What else should we say? Yes, let's show our logo. Good idea, Elspeth. Would you like to select someone to help you draw it here when we finish? Good!"
TEACHER:	"Let's finish with our motto, which is _____ ."
TEACHER:	"Now, we need a title *(suggest or select one)*. Let's read it all together while I use the pointer and point to the words. Ready, here we go . . ."

Leave this experience story on display with the pointer readily available so that students can read it during recess or during free-choice time.

Extra! Extra! We Wrote a Story!

If you have a computer in the classroom, students can copy the experience story from the chart. A typewriter is also useful, and a copy can be made for everyone on the office copier. Or, you may want to have students print it on writing paper.

Students can take this home and be proud of their story. Have them use Rebus symbols whenever possible. (A Rebus symbol is a picture that stands for a word. For example, we see a picture of a bird and say "bird" rather than reading the word "bird.") It's another way to make a visual–verbal connection using symbols.

What a Photogenic Group

Have a camera in the classroom and take photographs of students at work and play. These can be put on display and students can write or dictate sentences to be placed under a photo that shows them in action.

Keep the camera handy in your classroom throughout the year. At the end you will have a grand record of the school year.

Variation: Toward the end of the school year, have students be the photographers of events going on in the classroom. Show them how to use the camera. If yours is too valuable, you might be interested in securing some of the box cameras that are designed for one-time use.

School Photos

Ask parents if you may have a school photo of each child for classroom use. Glue these to a long strip of oaktag. This can be displayed on the chalkboard and serve as a checklist for any number of things. It can be put on a sheet of paper and students can print their name after their picture as a sign-in sheet each day. It can be photocopied and used at your learning centers as a sign-up sheet and checklist. It can be photocopied, laminated, and made into a special book-mark for big books.

It's Grandparents Day!

During a designated time in September, some schools invite grandparents to spend an hour during the morning, or to bring their brown-bag lunch and eat with a group of students. They might like to read a story to the group. You might want to recruit volunteers to help individual students with reading or writing, or to enable willing grandparents to sign up for field trip duty or playground duty once or twice per month.

- Ask the grandparents to address a small envelope to themselves, and then collect them. During the month have the students select a worksheet or a picture to insert into the envelope, and send it home along with a note the child has written. (Check with the office to see if there is a budget for stamp money if grandparents live out of town, or check with the room mothers who often collect funds from parents.) Alert parents via your newsletter that correspondence for grandparents is coming soon.

- *Sign-Up Sheet.* Have grandparents sign in and also write down where they're from. Determine who came the shortest distance and who came the farthest. Lollipop prizes, balloon prizes, or ribbon prize badges are appreciated.

- During their visit, grandparents can be "observers" as the students go through their circle-time phonics games, read-aloud practice games, or writing lessons. It's a good opportunity for calendar review: The name of the month, the name of the day of the week, counting the numerals on the calendar, and so on.

- Be sure to have your camera handy for this special day. A group photo would be appreciated by all!

A Placemat at Grandparents' Table

Very often, children associate grandparents with food because of holiday get-togethers. Make a placemat using an 8½″ × 11″ piece of colorful poster paper. Have students glue a real paper plate in the center; draw a fork, knife, and spoon in the appropriate spot for a place setting. A small tissue that represents a paper napkin can also be glued to the mat.

Students can print a one-line sentence on the top of the mat that reads, "At my grandparents' table I like _____ ," or "_____ makes delicious _____ for me." The favorite food can also be drawn on the paper plate or made from construction paper. This makes a nice large greeting card at holiday time. A good storybook that shows relatives enjoying their time together is *The Relatives Came* by Cynthia Rylant, with pictures by Stephen Gammell.

Grandparents Like Storybooks

Grandparents enjoy listening to a good storybook and then hearing the students discuss the events. You might want to choose a book from the author-of-the-month study.

There are many enjoyable picture books available that include Grandmother or Grandfather as a main character. Here are some good book suggestions: *Grandpa's Slide Show* by Deborah Gould, with illustrations by Cheryl Harness; *Song and Dance Man* by Karen Ackerman, with illustrations by Stephen Gammell; *Chicken Sunday* by Patricia Polacco; *Grandfather's Journey* by Allen Say; and *Grandma's Cat* by Helen Ketteman, with illustrations by Marsha Lynn Winborn. *Grandma's Cat* is told in short rhymes. During the first half of the book, the young child pursues and pounces after a cat with a miss and a hiss, but then Grandma shows her how to go slowly, so that by the end of the story the language soothes us with "I bring a treat, He likes to eat, He tastes, he stays, I stroke, he plays . . ."

Labor Day Is a Special September Holiday *(Dictionary Skills)*

What does "Labor Day" mean? Use the dictionary to find the word *labor* and note that it refers to *work*. Turn this into a dictionary exercise. Show that the dictionary has words listed in alphabetical order. Start with *A,* and leaf through the letters slowly, calling them out loud until you get to the letter *L*. This procedure demonstrates the function of the alphabet for organizing material.

Labor Day is a national holiday set aside to honor workers, and usually marks the end of summer holidays—back to school, back to work. "We have many, many people who work hard to make our community a nice place in which to work and live. Let's name some of them and make a long list." Print the list as students are watching you. Call attention to beginning letters and sounds, certain letters within the words, ending letters, and so on.

Some good read-aloud books that involve people at work include *Mr. Grigg's Work* by Cynthia Rylant, with illustrations by Stephen Gammell (a happy postman); *Maxi, The Taxi Dog* by Debra and Sal Barracca, with pictures by Mark Buehner (a loveable dog who accompanies a taxi driver in a big city); and the unforgettable, Caldecott-award winner *Officer Buckles and Gloria* by Peggy Rathbun (school policeman). These three enjoyable favorites can provide a springboard for discussions about work, jobs, and career choices.

Two Jewish Holidays—Rosh Hashanah and Yom Kippur

A ram's horn, called a shofar, is blown to signal the beginning of the holiday. Rosh Hashanah is the New Year, and Yom Kippur means Day of Atonement. An excellent book to use as a resource for class activities or for information is *Menorahs, Mezuzas, and Other Jewish Symbols* by Miriam Chaikin, illustrated by Erika Weihs.

Celebrate National Pancake Day

You can do many activities during a day or spread out over a longer period of time, that include reading, with links to writing and mathematics.

Children's Books. Some appropriate read-aloud books for this topic include: *If You Give a Pig a Pancake* by Laura Numeroff, with illustrations by Felicia Bond; *Sam and the Tigers* by Julius Lester, with illustrations by Jerry Pinkney; and *The Pancake Boy, an Old Norwegian Tale,* retold by Lorinda Bryan Cauley. In this version the pig outsmarts the pancake by giving it a ride on its nose as they cross a stream. Since the poor pancake could go no farther, "this story can go no farther either." And that's the end of the pancake and the story.

A good companion book is the 1997 version of an old tale: *The Gingerbread Boy* by Richard Egielski. We're off on a merry chase through the city and underground in the subway and past a policeman in the park. Alas, there is the fox and the stream to cross "and the gingerbread boy was all gone."

Writing. Practice making the letter *p* as the beginning sound of pancake. Make a row of capital *P*, a row of lower-case *p*, and print the word *pancake*.

Print the word *pancake* on the chalkboard and have students trace over the letters.

Make a pancake-shape circular book. Have students print and illustrate it about their pancake experience.

Mathematics. Making pancakes in the classroom gives students an opportunity for dry and liquid measurement experiences, and for time and temperature awareness. You will need an electric frypan, mixing bowls, wooden spoons, plates, forks, and the following recipe.

A Pre-Mix Pancake Recipe

You need:

bowl	pancake mix (and necessary
mixing spoon	ingredients)
electric frypan	water
oil spray	strawberries, blueberries, and
spatula for turning	whipped cream *(optional)*
styrofoam plates, plastic forks	maple syrup

Procedure: Collect the necessary ingredients and follow the recipe on the pancake mix box. Serve only four students at a time. Use the strawberries, blueberries, and cream to make a face, or some may prefer maple syrup. Devour the pancake!

Crafts. Make a Pancake Person from construction paper. Cut a yellow or tan circle for the head. Use a red felt pen for strawberry eyes, a blue felt pen for a blueberry mouth, and a white crayon to make a whipped cream nose. Then make four strips of paper for arms and legs. Fold them back and forth (accordion-style) and paste them onto the head shape. Staple a string to the top so that the figures can be hung up from the ceiling and allowed to dance in the breeze. Or, use the Pancake Person as a puppet to help retell one of the stories that was read aloud, or to make a statement about the pancake experience.

Pancake Paper-Bag Puppet

Make a pancake puppet using a circular yellow cut-out shape from felt material. Glue this to the lunch-size paper bag. Also glue facial features from construction paper or felt. On the back of the bag, students can print the pancake recipe. Then have them slip the bag over their hand and have the puppet tell about his or her experience making pancakes.

READING LINKS TO WRITING

One of the major changes in reading/language arts instruction during the 1990s was the linking of reading and writing whenever possible. Children are encouraged to write at a much earlier age. They enjoy making up stories (invented spelling) and reading them aloud, sharing them with a partner or with the class, and making illustrations to accompany the story. Several reasons for the increasing awareness of print and media include the explosion in environmental print through the mediums of television, computers, newspaper ads, slick magazines, and an increase in advertising through catalogs and other junk mail sent to the home. Along with this is the number of books and magazines published expressly for children at a younger age and a greater use of picture books in schools. Children are exposed to quality art and writing when they are preschoolers.

Set Up a Writing Center

To facilitate the reading/writing process, set up a Writing Center in the classroom and eventually equip it with the following materials. It is best to go slowly, adding and deleting items as the months go by in an effort to maintain interest. The following is a starter list:

paper of different sizes
paper of different colors
paper of different textures
paper of different shapes
scissors
crayons
toy telephone
notepads
erasers
word processor and printer
    (if possible)
envelopes

thin-point pencils
thick-point pencils
pencil sharpener
black felt-tip pens
colored felt-tip pens
manual typewriter
typing paper
rubber stamps and pads
calligraphy pens

Ask parents to donate materials for the center. Many parents may have computer paper that has been aging on a shelf that they would be willing to contribute, or a box of envelopes, or pads of paper for making lists. List making is one of the first types of writing that children do if they see their parents or teachers making "to do" lists. Parents can also send in used greeting cards that children can cut apart and turn into their own creations.

The Jolly Postman Can Be in Charge of the Writing Center

Make a large cut-out of the Jolly Postman for this area. Use the popular, well-known book *The Jolly Postman,* by Janet and Allen Ahlberg, for the model or make your own version of a post office. You can project the postman image onto a large sheet of oaktag using the opaque projector. If you do not have this type of projector available, then make a photocopy of a page from the book showing the postman. From this copy, make a transparency. Then, using the overhead projector, project the transparency onto a very large sheet of heavy posterboard to make the postman figure.

Once you have the figure, paint it or color it with felt-tip pens. Cut it out and display it prominently at this area, along with the book. Children can enjoy the book on their own or with a partner. They like to read the mail that's contained in the book envelopes, and may get some ideas from it for their own writing. There are other *Jolly Postman* books as well.

Let's Make Lists

Children benefit from seeing parents and other adults writing because that shows it has value. Many people make lists, and your students can, too. Cut paper into strips, so students can make lists of the following:

groceries for the week: fruits, vegetables, meat, liquids, dessert

holiday presents to purchase

favorite meals in order from 1 (most favorite) to 5

clothing to wear

chores to do in general (the "to do" list)

things to tell Grandmother (or Grandfather)

"pet care" if someone is going to be pet-sitting

things to take on an overnight stay with a relative

games to play

their toys

favorite stories

winter sports and/or summer sports

things we find in the refrigerator

electrical appliances in the kitchen

procedure for coming to school

morning procedure at school

At the Writing Center, creative play becomes important as children pretend someone is calling in a telephone order (pizza with toppings, take-out food, and so on) for which they must make a list. The small pads of paper along with pencils facilitate the "taking down" of information—transforming speech into print.

We Can Make Circles and Sticks

Straight lines, slanted lines, and circular shapes are all important in the writing process. Students can practice making these at the Writing Center, and also follow dotted lines on paper. (See Reproducible Activity Pages.)

Lines and circles can also be made while standing at an easel. With a felt-tip pen, divide a large sheet of newsprint into fourths. Students can use the sections to make straight lines, diagonal lines, circles, and letter formations. For some children, small motor coordination develops more slowly, so they need to be able to write in large spaces (also true of art).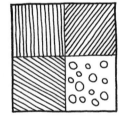

Let's Give Our Hands a Workout

Small motor coordination that enables a student to pick up a pencil and print with relative ease develops at different rates with different children. The small muscles of the hand can be strengthened by doing some of the following workouts at the Writing Center. (This will not speed up the development, but it will make for a firmer grip.)

- Put five coins (quarters) in a little bucket of dry rice and have students feel around (with their dominant hand) for the coins until all five have been located. Put the coins on the work area. Then put them back and try again.

- Put five different-sized coins in with the dry rice. Have students try to identify the denomination by size before they take the coins from the container. (This is also a good Math link.)

• Put a different small object in the bucket once every other day, and have students try to identify it before they take it from the container. (Use a small toy, eraser, paper clip, sponge letters, and so on.)

Sorting Letters

Put plastic letters in a container, or bag, and have students close their eyes, reach inside, and identify the letters by their shape. Then students pull out the letter shape for verification. As students pull the letters out of the container, they can line up the letters in ABC order. Have students keep track of which letter shapes are tricky and which letters are easy to guess. Have them verbalize why this might be so.

Portfolio—I Can Print My Name

This can be one of the first items that goes into each child's portfolio for the year. During the first week of school, give the student a sheet of writing paper with lines and a sharp pencil. Ask students to print their name (first and last, or just first) as best they can. Then collect the papers, label them "September," and put them in the portfolios.

Note: Do this during the first week of each new month, using the same procedure. You can use the same sheet of paper, or use a new one each time. Clip them all together as a record of the child's progress with the formation of letters. The gradual transformation provides a valuable developmental record. Students and parents like having a sample of the progress made during the year.

Use this portfolio information during conference time with parents throughout the year as a visual record of progress being made. Assure parents that it will be theirs at the end of the year.

During the last week of school, assemble this precious record, and write a cover letter to parents explaining that this is a record of a year's progress in manuscript printing. The student can write his or her own message underneath the teacher's message. Have students make a colorful cover for it, and staple it together for safe keeping. Many parents treasure this record, and keep it in a school box with a collection of children's work that is representative of the year.

It's Time to Print

Formal instruction in printing can be done with the entire group. Students will need lined writing paper and a pencil with a sharp point.

On the master copy, use a felt-tip marker to make a stroke or letter on the appropriate line. Reproduce this on the copier so that each student has one, which becomes a worksheet for the day. This can be done again and again

for upper-case letter practice, for lower-case letter practice, and for practicing and copying information from the chalkboard.

Letter Condominiums—Where Do the Letters Live?

When practicing letters, it is important to note that lower-case letters often take up the "first-floor" space, "upstairs space," "basement space," or combinations of spaces. Students need to get a sense of where these letters are located on the spaces provided. Make a giant-size piece of writing paper using the yardstick and felt-tip pen to help make the dark and light lines on kraft paper.

Make a game of it. The capital letters live on the first floor and upstairs (taking up the whole space between dark lines). The lower-case letters spread out and need more room both on the first floor and downstairs. Here are where the letters live:

First-floor letters: a, c, e, i, m, n, o, r, s, u, v, w, x, z

First-floor/upstairs letters: b, d, f, h, k, l, t

First-floor/basement letters: g, j, p, q, y

Fourteen of the lower-case ABC letters live on the first floor. Seven have a bigger condominium because they need space on the second floor. Five like to live on the first floor and have the basement fixed up, too.

Have students manipulate upper-case letters to determine if capital letters ever go into the basement. *(No)*

Have students manipulate letters to determine which capital and lower-case letters have the biggest condominiums, or three floors. *(Gg, Jj, Pp, Qq, Yy)*

In order to be able to learn to print well and with pride, students need to practice letter formation daily. It will pay off in the end when students learn that they can, indeed, gain mastery and control over the pencil. Just like a ball player who practices batting that ball, practice also counts in letter placement during the formative years.

READING LINKS TO MATH

Math Picture Books for Story Time

During story time, read a number book for enjoyment and for discussion. There are many lovely picture books on math-related topics that are available from the public library. Be sure to get several each month for your classroom. For a good start, work with the September author-of-the-month and read *1,2,3 to the Zoo* by Eric Carle.

Another fine author who works with concept books is Tana Hoban. Share her books, such as *Shapes, Shapes, Shapes* and *Circles, Triangles and Squares.* In her colorful, glossy book *26 Letters and 99 Cents,* you are working with the alphabet and with money.

Other enjoyable math counting books include *Count!* by Denise Flemming; *Counting on Frank* by Rod Clement; *Babar's Counting Book* by Laurent DeBrunhoff; *Miss Mabel's Table* by Deborah Chandra, with illustrations by Max Grover; and *My Little Sister Ate One Hare* by Bill Grossman, with illustrations by Kevin Hawkes.

After reading these books, place them in the Math Center for children to enjoy on their own or with a partner. Make sure to have many items for children to manipulate and count, such as buttons, paper clips, tiny sponge squares, nuts in shells, plastic bottle caps, jar covers, and so on.

Circles, Triangles, Squares, Rectangles

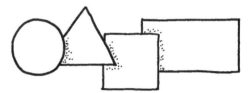

Most children by this time can identify a circle and a square, but are ready for all four shapes. Cut out huge, colorful shapes and hang them from the ceiling in different areas of the room, so children can brush up against them. Or hang them on the four classroom walls with identification name cards attached.

Meet under the circle for a special event, or meet at the triangle wall for a story. Keep reinforcing the names of the shapes. Another good book by Tana Hoban is entitled *So Many Circles, So Many Squares,* with photographs taken of the environment in which children find themselves.

Play a Math Shape Guessing Game

Ask the children to raise their hands if they know the answers.

- "I'm thinking of something in the room that you can see through and it's in the shape of a large rectangle." *(window)*
- "I'm thinking of something on the wall and it's in the shape of a circle." *(clock)*
- "I'm thinking of something we can twist and it's in the shape of a circle." *(doorknob)*
- "I'm thinking of something that we can sit on and it's in the shape of a square." *(chair seat, cushion)*

You can get this started, and then ask students if they are ready to try their hand at being the leader. The verbal formula is: "I'm thinking of something *(location, function)* and it's in the shape of a _____."

This can be played as a scheduled game, or you can use this game for teaching and reinforcement when there are two or three minutes to spare. It strengthens listening skills and visual awareness of one's environment.

Making Sense of the Calendar

Create a grid on a bulletin board for your September calendar. Have a method of keeping track of the days of the week on the calendar so that students get the idea that there is useful information in print. You can do this in a variety of ways.

- Have a grid for the month already filled in with numerals. Ask a student to cross off or color in the square each day to show the date.
- Have construction paper cut-outs to create an A,B pattern on your grid and apply one each day (for example, orange leaf shapes, green leaf shapes). Keep these in a container by the calendar. Every other day change the color for an A,B pattern). The date for the day can be written on the leaf shape for all to observe.

Is It "Today" Now?

Work with the concept of "today," which means "right now."

- Point to the date (numeral) for today. Say it. Have students repeat it.
- Point to the day of the week. Say it. Have students repeat it.
- Point to the clock. Say the time for "right now." Say it. Have students repeat it.
- Point to the numerals that represent the year. Say them. Have students repeat it.
- Summarize this information on the chalkboard. For example, this can be on the chalkboard prior to the discussion. Then read it, and fill in the information as children are observing:

    Today is _____ . *(Write in day of the week.)*

    It is September _____ . *(Write in numeral.)*

    Today we are going to _____ . *(Complete the short sentence with something you plan to do in class.)*

Let's Read Numerals

Numerals are symbols, just as the ABC's are symbols. Make a set of flash cards with numeral symbols from 1 through 10. Hold them up for students to say aloud together. Then, flash the cards for individual responses. (Add additional cards to 20, then 30, and so on, as the group appears ready to handle higher denominations.)

Let's Write Numerals

Print large numerals on the chalkboard and call upon children to trace them. Have three or four large numerals going at one time. After students trace over the numeral, have them say it aloud, then give the chalk to someone else. After several traces, erase the area and make a fresh numeral.

We Can Read Numeral Names

Numbers can be complicated for beginners. *Numeral* is the name given to the symbol, such as "1, 2, 3." Numbers are also represented as words, such as "one, two, three," or they can be represented by dots, such as ". .. ...." They also mean *how many* of something.

So, what does that tell us? It tells us that students need lots of practice with manipulating items, counting aloud, and associating the number we say with the numeral we write.

Make a set of semi-concrete materials for working with the numerals from 1 through 10. Using a felt-tip pen, divide an 8½″ × 11″ piece of colored construction paper into four equal parts. In one section, put the number name; in another, put the symbol; in another, put the appropriate number of dots (as on a die); and leave the fourth section blank. Laminate. Then have students put the appropriate number of manipulative items on the blank spot. This can be checked by you or a student assistant.

Do this for all numerals from 1 through 10 using different colors of construction paper for color coding. This will prove helpful for some beginners and for those who need additional practice.

This can be kept at your Math Center in the classroom, so children can work on it during free time.

Who's in Charge of the Math Center?

Since there is a storybook character in charge of the Writing Center, put a storybook character in charge of your Math Center. It can be someone from a math book, or it can be "The Very Hungry Caterpillar Math Center"—with a huge cardboard cut-out of a green, shiny caterpillar, always hungry for math information, prominently displayed here. The caterpillar can be in charge of the "Sign Up" sheet for certain activities during recess. Be sure to have the book *The Very Hungry Caterpillar* by Eric Carle on display at this area for children to enjoy again and again, after you have read it aloud to the class. (Other picture book characters can be selected as well.)

During the year, change the figure in charge of the Math Center. Children can help select a favorite character, and perhaps help with the tracing and coloring. If they are too young to have success with this project on their own, a parent volunteer or an upper-grade volunteer may be interested in helping. It's fun for all and keeps the area fresh.

Organizing a Math Center

A center is not used for presenting new material. It is used for review, reinforcement, or enrichment. A classroom of students needs an organized, daily math lesson. Since math is a skill that requires mastery, students do need lots of practice.

One place to begin is with manipulatives. These are concrete items or objects that students can hold in their hands so that they get a sense or a feel of a number.

Begin with counting. Purchase commercial counters or ask parents to help supply counters such as buttons, clothespins, old keys, nuts and bolts, nails, and so on. With very young children, begin by having them count from 1 to 5. Use a number line if it is helpful. Students can count out one nut, two nuts, three nuts, and so on, so that they have them in groups and can see that five are more than two.

In the beginning, it is best to have limited materials at any center. You can build it as time goes on.

READING LINKS TO SOCIAL STUDIES

We're One Big Happy School Family

Go on a walking trip around the school building. Gain permission (in advance) to take photos of the following school personnel at work (if you arrive at a convenient time): secretary, principal, custodian, nurse, cafeteria staff, speech therapist, school psychologist, librarian, art teacher, music teacher, physical education teacher, and any other school aides who help make the school hum with efficiency.

Take photos of the outside of the building and the classroom to finish the roll, if necessary, and then take it to a speedy developer, so that you will have the photos back in a day or two at the most. It may be possible to get two sets for the price of one.

Mount these colored photos on the chalkboard, and ask students to print with chalk underneath them (this allows for many erasures). Students can work in pairs or small groups to decide what to say for each picture, print it, and read it to the class.

Later, the photos and captions can be transferred to chart paper for a more permanent visual/written record. If you do have a duplicate set of photos and arrange the photos in another order, just think of how different the two stories could be.

Going off to school is not always a smooth and easy event in the lives of young children. A soothing read-aloud book this month is *The Kissing Hand* by

Audrey Penn, with illustrations by Ruth E. Harper and Nancy M. Leak. Mother Raccoon gives her son the present of a kiss on the palm of his hand and tells him that when he gets lonesome for home, to put his hand to his cheek and know that she loves him. This is a good book to share in your newsletter to parents.

Meet My Family

Have students use crayons to draw their "at-home family." Encourage them to take time coloring in shirts, pants, and dresses so that we can see the family all dressed up for this special picture. A sentence strip can be used underneath the picture to introduce the family members. Students can dictate the information or print it.

You will, of course, want the students to verbally share the information about their family (introduction of family members, names, pets, and so on) with classmates. Prior to this, it would be wise to have a discussion of families and how they differ—some families have a mother, grandmother, and the children; some families have a mother, father, and the children; and so on. There are various combinations of people who live together, and you want to make sure that all families are accepted. Be sensitive to each child's personal situation.

Picture Books About the Family

A number of family-oriented storybooks to read aloud during story time include the following: *Benjy and the Barking Bird* by Margaret Bloy Graham. When an aunt comes to visit the family with her pet parrot, Benjy the dog becomes jealous because the bird is getting all the attention. That's just the beginning!

At Daddy's on Saturdays by Linda Walvoord Girard, with illustrations by Judith Friedman, portrays the child of a divorced family. This author/illustrator team has another book, *Adoption Is for Always,* that could also be helpful.

My Mama Had a Dancing Heart by Libba Moore Gray, with illustrations by Raul Colon, tells about a loveable mother who enjoys movement and dance. The child grows up hearing her mother's words: "Bless the world, it feels like a tip-tapping, song-singing, finger-snapping kind of day." After reading this book, children could learn this phrase and say it each morning during Circle Time.

Wanted: Perfect Parents by John Himmelman is an amusing book in which children list all of the things that "perfect parents" would let them do, such as sleep on the roof, jump all over the furniture, paint pictures on the walls, and so on. But, at the end of the day, when they are tired, they list the most important thing parents can do (bedtime routine). For a language development activity, children could make a class list of their ideas for "perfect parents" and then make another list of the really important things that "perfect parents" do—the things that really count.

Shoes from Grandpa by Mem Fox is a good book to use for language development, rhyming, and memorizing. It's constructed in the same manner as *This Is the House That Jack Built,* so there are many opportunities for repetition. Use real items, or cut-outs, for the shoes, socks, skirt, blouse, etc., to help with the sequencing. Or, make the items from felt and recreate the story on a flannel board.

Helper's Chart—Read What You're Doing

The Helper's Chart can be a colorful and functional attraction in the classroom. For September, it could consist of a large cut-out of a tree with brown trunk and green top stapled or tacked to a bulletin board. Student names can be printed on bright red apple shapes and tacked to the tree. Job titles can be printed on yellow paper basket shapes at the bottom of the tree. When the student's apple lands in a particular basket, that means that person is in charge for the week.

"Read" the Helper's Chart together each Monday morning. Children can volunteer for these jobs, or you can make the assignments. Change assignments weekly, so that every Monday morning after the beginning exercises, attention is focused upon the business of maintaining the classroom environment. This builds a team spirit in the classroom.

What Can I Do to Help at School?

Some areas that need assistance are listed below. Think of managerial titles for each worker.

Teacher Assistants (office messenger, room helpers)

Flag Director (person who asks the class to stand, face the flag, place right hand over heart, and say the Pledge of Allegiance; then leads the singing of a patriotic song)

Door Greeters (select one boy and one girl to answer the knock)

Sink Captain (tidies up at the end of the day)

Chalkboard Chief (washes and erases board)

Floor Manager (in charge of inspecting floor at end of day after students have picked up excess "stuff" and put it in the wastebasket)

Librarian (straightens up book center)

Station Masters (different students in charge of tidying and straightening up the various curriculum centers)

Shelf Presidents (straighten material on shelves)

Wardrobe Stylists (select two to keep the coat area in order after arrival in A.M. and again after lunch)

Major General (keeps an eye on the end-of-the-day clean-up effort; a special hat and cane add to the authenticity of this role)

Even though, as a teacher of young children, it may be necessary for you to do many of these jobs over again after the students have gone home, it is important to have them play a role in keeping their environment tidy and orderly. The environment "sets the stage" for learning and "reflects learning going on," so it should be presented in an attractive manner.

Forming Friendships

An excellent read-aloud choice this month is *Wanted: Best Friend* by A. M. Monson, with pictures by Lynn Munsinger. This book links reading to the writing process when the Cat and Mouse are at odds. The Cat decides to write an ad to put in the newspaper, advertising for a new friend. Many animals answer the ad, but in the end Cat writes a note to Mouse to see if they can work things out. After the book, discuss the story and what it takes to be a good friend. Then focus upon friendships in the classroom.

A Social Studies Center

Often this center is a focal point for ongoing projects that relate to the curriculum. Students come here to work on skills such as vocabulary lists for a unit of study, or to create models from clay or other materials, depending upon the curriculum focus. Since there is much content to cover in a social studies curriculum, this is often a busy center. Some teachers do project work as a total class, and then students can individually work at centers in their spare time. Or they can work with small groups.

You will need to designate this space as a center. Push up a table to a bulletin board, and have the board serve as a colorful backdrop with a title. (If this is not possible, a folding board works extremely well as a backdrop.) Who will be the cardboard figure in charge? It's up to you and the class. You may wish to have a historical figure in charge (a past president, a past leader in his or her field) or a hero from a children's book who is either make-believe or real. Avoid commercial characters.

READING LINKS TO SCIENCE & HEALTH

The September Science Center

By all means, have an interesting Science Table or Science Center all year long. Change the materials in this area periodically to keep it alive with learning opportunities. Start small, and keep building.

Start off the year with "Signs of Autumn" since we will have a season shift during September, when some areas usually experience the first frost. What are the signs of autumn in your area? Bring in items from outdoors and have students bring them in as well.

Some permanent items for this center include the following:

microscope
magnifying glass
pencils and paper for recording
modeling clay
containers to hold items each month
books
magazines

Who's in Charge of the Science Center?

Since storybook characters are in charge of other areas in the room, you might want to have one here as well. You need a character who is inquisitive or curious, so take that into consideration when you make your selection.

Take this opportunity to introduce two new vocabulary words—*inquisitive* and *curious*. Say them one at a time, and write them on the chalkboard one at a time for students to see. What does it mean to be inquisitive? What does it mean to be curious? Let's check the dictionary. Do this process of checking the dictionary while children are observing.

For example, introduce the dictionary as *a book of words and what they mean*. Say, "It's in alphabetical order, and that's why we need to learn our ABC's. *Inquisitive* begins with the *letter i,* so I will leaf through these pages until I find it. A, B, C, D, E, F, G, H . . . ahhhhhhh, here it is, the letter I. I'll look for the word *inquisitive,* and here it is. This is what it says. . . " *(unusually curious, and inquiring, asks many questions, wants to know about things; eager to learn)*

Ask students to raise their hand if they are eager to learn and are inquisitive. Encourage them to do so. Good! Now, let's look up the word *curious.* (Follow the same procedure and do point out that the word "curious" was used to describe one of the traits of an inquisitive person.) Encourage students to be on the look-out for a storybook character (person or animal) who is inquisitive and curious. Perhaps that character can be in charge of the Science Center!

When the class selects the character, make a large cardboard replica of it and color it, cut it out, and place it in the area. (If, for example, the character becomes *Curious George* [series books by H. A. Rey], you can get fake fur at a fabric shop, cut it to the shape of the character, and glue it onto the cardboard.) Use real hats and clothing for your characters, if possible. Perhaps one of the monsters from *Where the Wild Things Are* would be effective here, or a huge dinosaur character.

Realia (Real) Items for the Science Center

Since autumn is in the air, with shorter daylight hours and crisper temperatures at night in most areas, we can note changes in the environment, and this is a natural subject to use to begin the year in your Science Center. Bring in abandoned bird nests (spray them with disinfectant first) for close examination.

Bring in nuts such as chestnuts, acorns, and buckeyes. How do they differ in size and color? Other items to include are:

teasels

cat tails

milkweed pods (enclose them inside a small plastic bag and
    enjoy the burst of seeds)

leaves of different shapes (classify them)

leaves that are beginning to change color

autumn flowers

seeds

seashells

other items native to the area in which you live

Healthy Snacks

Send a note home to parents about opportunities for them to contribute to Snack Time. (It's wise to keep an extra box of crackers for those children who forget, or simply get hungry.) Children can make a Rebus list of what a nutritious and delicious snack-time item would be for daily snack time. Here are some examples.

grapes   carrot sticks   apple   crackers

Caterpillars and Butterflies

As Eric Carle is the author-of-the-month—and *The Very Hungry Caterpillar* is a favorite book with young children—this may be a good opportunity to go one step beyond and take a closer look at caterpillars, butterflies, and moths.

Concept Development

1. A caterpillar is only one of the four stages in the life of a butterfly or moth. First is the egg, then the caterpillar (larva), then the pupa or chrysalis, and finally the moth or butterfly.

2. The process for the four stages of development has a name—metamorphosis. Have children say each of the five syllables after you: *met-a-morph'-o-sis*. Then glide the syllables together. Have students learn to say the word. Print it with green chalk on the chalkboard and draw the four stages.

3. Caterpillars look different and have different names. Some interesting names to learn are Woolly Bear, Bagworm, Green Grappler, Hickory Horned

Devil, and the Monarch. (An excellent picture book to use is entitled *Creepy, Crawly Caterpillars* by Margery Fack-lam, with illustrations by Paul Facklam. Children will enjoy looking at the illustrations and will become curious about the information.)

Concept Activities

1. Students can simulate—through movement—the four stages of development: (1) Curl up as an egg; (2) Wiggle out as a caterpillar, crawl, and chomp–chomp–chomp food; (3) Curl up again with head covered to simulate the chrysalis; and (4) Very slowly emerge as a beautiful butterfly, flap wings (arms), and fly in a circle or around the room. Be sure children know that they are to stop "flying" at an agreed-upon signal.

2. It's "Butterfly Day" at the easel. Put out the grandest purples, pinks, reds, oranges, and bright yellows. Have students first draw a huge outline with a black crayon or black felt pen. Then they paint designs on the shape. *Variation:* Have the students splatter paint, and then cut out a large butterfly shape.

A good resource book is *The Butterfly Alphabet Book* by Brian Cassie and Jerry Pallotta, with illustrations by Mark Astrella. Children can see 26 different butterflies from A through Z, and learn their unusual names, such as B—Baltimore Checkerspot, C—Cracker, D—Dogface, I—Indian Leaf, T—Transparent, and many more. Students will become curious to learn more about these amazing creatures.

Another excellent resource book is *The Butterfly ABC Book* by Kjell B. Sandved that contains actual photographs of butterflies. Look carefully and on the wings of those represented you can find an alphabet letter! Originally this was a Butterfly Poster, which received the Parents' Choice Award, and inspired the book.

Reminder: Help Your Body to Stay Healthy

Students need to learn to honor their body and their health. Eating the right foods builds strong bodies, bones. and teeth. Young children should be getting the necessary amount of sleep, from 9–11 hours daily. This is a good opportunity to send a note home to parents reminding them of the importance of sleep—and it may help them to get an unwilling child into bed at a reasonable hour.

LINKS TO
AUTHOR-OF-THE-MONTH

Author/Illustrator for September:
Eric Carle

In addition to recommending a wide variety of picture books for use during the month, we will also present ideas for doing an "Author Study" for each month. The authors have been selected from student favorites, and will provide many opportunities for language development, reading and writing, engaging in dramatic play, integrating the books into the general curriculum, and ideas for art projects and rhythms. Some students may use these stories as a "stem" and create, write, and illustrate a story in a similar vein.

It is highly recommended that students learn to tell a story by heart this month. It can be the same story for the entire group. There are means to assist the student, such as puppets, felt cut-outs, and so on. Then begin to see how much can be memorized and told without using any props. Along the way, make use of the tape recorder or video recorder as the students tell the story in a variety of ways. They can become storytellers and soon build up a repertoire of stories to tell—using facial expressions, hand gestures, and so on. Work with partners or in small groups and have students help each other. This is not a competition; it requires teamwork. Everyone can be a storyteller—it's a confidence builder.

The author/illustrator for September gets you off to a good start for the year. *Let's Read!*

***Walter the Baker* (New York: Simon & Schuster, 1995)** Everything is going well for Walter who has a shop filled with buns and rolls so good that the lines are long. Even the Duke and Duchess eat these delicious rolls for breakfast. But one day the milk spills and Walter substitutes water for milk, hoping no one will notice. Ah, but they do. Walter is about to be banished unless he can come up with a roll through which the rising sun must shine three times. What a challenge! Can he make it?

Activities to Accompany *Walter the Baker*

1. *Dramatic play.* Have an apron, big white chef's hat made from a white paper cylinder with tissue paper stuffed in the top, bowls, mixing spoons, measuring cups and spoons, sifter, and timer. You will also need a little pad and a pencil, and perhaps a toy phone. Children can set up a make-believe bake shop and take turns being Walter and the customers.

2. Set aside a learning station area and label it "Walter's Math Area" on a large baker's hat shape. Students can strengthen their math skills by measuring with teaspoons, tablespoons, and ounces and cups. Fractions can easily be introduced or reinforced by measuring *one half* a cup, etc. For working with dry measure, white sand works well.

For liquid measure, you will need a different area with large tubs, water, plastic measuring cups, and plastic containers of various sizes (quart, pint, half gallon). Students can gain experience measuring from smallest to largest amounts. Young children spill a lot of water because their coordination skills are just being developed, so have plenty of newspapers underneath the tubs.

Remember that clean up is important because Walter's shop has to pass sanitary codes—and the health inspector has sharp eyes! This calls for sponges, cloths, and a small mop.

3. *Problem solving.* Walter is challenged to come up with a roll through which the rising sun must shine three times. Use plasticene or salt dough to have children concoct shapes to meet the challenge. Walter called his shape the "pretzel." Have students taste real pretzels and then generate a list of descriptive words (adjectives) that can be printed on the shape of a pretzel. Encourage words by asking such questions as "Does it make noise when we eat it?" *(crunchy)* "Does it fall into pieces when we bite into it?" *(crumbly)* "What are those bumpy white pieces and how do they taste?" *(salty)*

4. *Word origins.* The word *pretzel* comes from the Latin word *bracchium,* meaning "arm." According to Walter, the pretzel was originally a simple bread eaten during Lent. Its shape is based on an ancient position for prayer in which the arms were folded across a person's chest and the hands were placed on opposite shoulders. Have students try *this* position as well as the position of the pretzel shape they create. For a good stretching exercise, they can twist their shoulders, arms, back, hips, knees, and legs to make body pretzels.

From Head to Toe (New York: HarperCollins, 1997) This is an action book. Starting from the head and working down to the toe, children are invited to move along with the animals. The "I can do it" refrain is a positive one for young children.

Activities to Accompany *From Head to Toe*

1. *Everybody listen . . . then move.* This book has a pattern to it. An animal is introduced, such as "I am a seal and clap my hands. Can you do it?" Children answer, "I can do it." So, from head to toe, children are moving body parts. This is good for body-part identification, as well as a good warm-up exercise. Get the rhythm of the words and the action going together.

2. *Let's move with the animals.* Try these movements: Penguin (move head), Giraffe (bend neck), Buffalo (hunch shoulders), Monkey (move arms), Seal (clap hands), Gorilla (thump chest), Cat (arch back), Crocodile (wriggle hips), Camel (bend knees), Donkey (kick legs), Elephant (stomp foot), Parrot (wiggle toe).

After children become familiar with the book, call out the name of the animal only (in order) to see if children can use the appropriate movement. If not, help them to remember by showing the book illustration.

When children become really familiar with this chant, call out the names of the animals backwards, from toe to head. Then try a random order.

3. *Eric Carle art paper.* Note the endpapers of the book—now those would make a colorful animal! Some of the animals in the book look like they may have been cut out from paper that was designed with fingerpaints. Using fingerpaints, each child can cover a large sheet of fingerpaint paper. Let it dry. Then, cut out both big and small shapes. Arrange them and then paste them onto another colorful background to create an animal. Add facial features with construction paper or felt-tip pen.

   Students can point to the animal body parts as you say them aloud—head, ears, eyes, nose, mouth, shoulders, legs, feet. Then continue with tail, claws, whiskers, antennae; have students add them if appropriate.

4. "Let's look at the animals in the book and see where they appear in the alphabet." Make a list. Now move alphabetically with the animals. This time the b—buffalo is first and the s—seal is last. Be alert! Three animals begin with the letter "c."

5. Where do the animals in the book live—in a forest, jungle, or sea? In what other ways can the real animal move? (swim, fly, prowl) What do they eat? Find some information books at the library and help your students learn more about these fascinating animals.

Today Is Monday (New York: Philomel Books, 1993) This is actually a song made into a picture book. The song is published at the end of the book. String beans, spaghetti, ZOOOP, roast beef, fresh fish, chicken, and ice cream . . . "Come and eat it up" is the familiar refrain, especially on Sunday for all the world's children.

Activities to Accompany *Today Is Monday*

1. Learn the verses and enjoy them! Children will be reviewing the days of the week with each verse, as it is done in a cumulative style.

2. For a tasty treat, try out the menu for the week: Monday (string beans), Tuesday (spaghetti), Wednesday (ZOOOP), Thursday (roast beef), Friday (fish). Have a tiny portion to taste (like the tasty sample portions distributed in grocery stores).

3. *Spread the good nutrition.* Make a copy of the song for each student and ask students to make a colorful menu illustration on the page as a reminder. Sing it together, and then send this home. Invite parents to plan a meal around one of the days of the week (or all of them if they can). Saturday is chicken day and Sunday is ice cream day.

4. Wednesday is ZOOOP day! On a large kettle shape, make a graph of the children's favorite soups. Begin by limiting the choices to three types of soup and have children choose one. Use cut-out shapes of soup bowls, and have children use felt pens or crayons to draw in the soup (for example, bright red for tomato, pale yellow for chicken noodle with white string glued on for the noodles, and lots of color shapes for vegetable zooop). A

taste of soup on Wednesdays might be something children will anticipate with pleasure.

5. The endpapers and the animals are vivid and patterned. Make some different Eric Carle paper by using fingerpaint and gadget printing. You will need large sheets of paper, tempera paint, and gadgets for printing—such as paper clips, small wood blocks, bottle caps, nail heads, etc. When dry, have students cut out shapes. Encourage students to exchange colors with their classmates. This adds a variety of texture, too, when creating one of the animals in the book.

***Draw Me a Star* (New York: Philomel Books, 1992)** On each page, the artist fulfills a request, such as "Draw me a sun . . . it was a warm sun." When the moon asks the artist to draw a star, we learn together how to draw an eight-sided star, along with a little chant from the author's German Oma (grandmother) to help us remember which way our pencil should go.

Activities to Accompany *Draw Me a Star*

1. *Paint Me a Sun!* You will need 12" × 18" sheets of construction paper in the orange and yellow sections of a mixed color pack. The variations in colors will pay off in terms of effective results. Students can put their initials on one side. Then they can use sponge painting (yellow, orange, red tempera paints) to give texture to the sun. When the paper is dry, guide students as they cut the edges off the four corners for a rounded look (this does not have to be a perfect circle). Cut the scraps into rectangular shapes for sunrays and paste them on the edges of the sun. These can be hung from ceiling lights all around the room, or hung from an overhead light in a section of the room for a sunny spot of pure sunlight.

   Put two or three bright orange pillows under your sunny area, and have students go through Eric Carle's picture books in search of the sun. They'll find a sun in every book; in this one, it is especially large. Include picture information books about the sun for students to look through. This helps to reinforce the sound of the letter *s* and strengthens location skills.

2. Notice the multicolored giant star in the book. Do the same as the previous activity, only start with white paper and use multicolors. When dry, cut out the star shape (perhaps using a pattern guide would be helpful). Then have a starry-night section hanging from your ceiling lights. Blue pillows can be added so that children can be comfortable in this area for silent reading. Books about the sky, clouds, weather, and stories about night can be located here.

3. *Science—Flowers in Bloom.* Take a clue from the bright, colorful fingerpainting paper to have students first enjoy the fingerpainting experience with one color. Another day, when paper is dry, have students cut giant flowers from them and make a mural all along one wall. Then take advantage of this opportunity to plant seeds in the classroom, or bring in a variety of plants to care for.

4. How do you draw a star? Eric Carle's Oma (Grandmother) has the helpful formula (listed in the back of the book). This enables the child to follow verbal and visual directions, and to gain practice drawing straight lines. A diagram is available so that the lines can be drawn while chanting, "Kri Kra Toad's Foot, Geese Walk Bare Foot."

***Have You Seen My Cat?* (New York: Picture Book Studio, 1987)** A little boy, out looking for his cat, finds all kinds of cats—big, little, striped, spotted. But none of these are his very own cat. He's in for a surprise when he finally does find his own cat.

Activities to Accompany *Have You Seen My Cat?*

1. Enjoy the story. Then go back over it and identify each of the cats. There is a picture key at the end.

2. On a chart, make a list of all the cats—lion, bobcat, panther, tiger, jaguar, and so on. These are all members of the cat family to which the boy's little pet kitty belongs. Make an illustration for each of the names.

3. Students can create their own Book of Cats, and use a variety of media for each cat.

4. The text is simple, with only two sentences repeated throughout the book. Students should be able to recreate this as a little picture book of their own during their spare time.

5. Make "Eric Carle" paper by brushing on a variety of paint colors with cloth or large brushes. Then, when that dries, use gadget printing. Cut up the paper into many pieces. Then piece together an interesting looking cat.

***Papa, Please Get the Moon for Me* (New York: Picture Book Studio, 1986)** Enjoy the wonder of this book as the pages go UP, DOWN, open up to a four-page spread, and then treat the reader to the wonderful folded page of the moon that is a pop-up design. Children are delighted with this book and want to experience it again and again. Papa is very busy trying to comply with Monica's request to get the moon for her. Call attention to the bold brushstrokes in the bright illustrations. And, of course, to the endpapers.

Activities to Accompany *Papa, Please Get the Moon for Me*

1. Have students retell the story in their own words, using their hands to show direction such as *up* and *down*. For the moon, they can make a big circle overhead with their arms. The story can be retold on a flannel board with felt figures and ladder pieces that keep going up and up.

2. Oh, those endpapers! In the hardbound edition, the endpapers are ablaze with stars of many sizes and colors—the sky is alive with them. Perhaps students can make a sky picture that is alive with star shapes that they have cut out from glossy magazine pictures. They can use these as their own endpapers for a book.

3. The phases of the moon come into play in this story. Readers see the moon *waning* and then *waxing*. These are new science vocabulary words for students.

4. Can students see a face in the moon when it is in full view? The profile view shows a face. This calls for a good discussion of just who this fanciful "man in the moon" might be.

5. Students can get ideas for future books that they might make by taking a look at the way the paper folds up, down, and horizontally to create a huge horizontal scene. The math concepts of *vertical* and *horizontal* can be reinforced by this book experience.

And Many More!

It is a delightful experience for students to do an Eric Carle "author study" because he is a prolific writer/illustrator and students soon recognize his style and enjoy his work. Get as many of his books as you can from the library in an effort to help students recognize the big, bright, bold art style.

One month—especially the busy month of September when you are just getting started—is probably not enough time for an Eric Carle author study, but he can be introduced so that students can enjoy his work throughout the school year. You can incorporate many of his books into your curriculum this month. Not only are the books enjoyable, but there is also a good deal to learn from them—which you can often turn into a lesson.

Here are more of the recommended books by this favorite of children everywhere, with some suggested activities.

The Very Hungry Caterpillar (various editions)

This extremely popular counting book, which is considered a modern classic, is familiar to most children by the time they reach grade school. Most all children have heard it at library story hours and in preschool settings. It has been made into a little board book for tiny tots so that they can have the experience of poking their fingers through the holes. It deals with the metamorphosis of a caterpillar into a chrysalis and then into a beautiful butterfly. Make felt shapes of items the caterpillar eats each day; the children can retell this story on the felt board. The story also offers good opportunities for food tasting, for the days of the week, the passing of time, and for poking small fingers through circles as an interactive experience.

Encourage students to make their very own caterpillar story book, but make it in the shape of a big butterfly! Students can paint the butterfly cover in the style of Eric Carle (gadget printing, fingerpainting); individual pages, done daily, can show what the caterpillar ate each day. Then retell the story. **(Check September's math section. This famous, busy caterpillar is recommended as the mascot for the Math Center.)**

The Very Busy Spider (New York: Putnam, 1985)

Create webs by gluing white yarn or string onto black background paper. Have students write a caption on a sentence strip and paste it along the bottom. Study web shapes and spiders in science books.

A House for Hermit Crab (New York: Simon & Schuster Children's, 1991)

Everyone lives in a house—even a hermit. This is an opportunity to introduce new vocabulary words to the students, and also to meet the underwater sea creatures.

1,2,3, to the Zoo (New York: Putnam, 1998)

Hop aboard a train with separate cars taking animals to the zoo, and count them on each page as they crowd into the cars. Then, when they arrive and all of the animals are let out, the children can search the page and locate them again.

The Grouchy Ladybug (New York: HarperCollins, 1996)

This bug got up on the "wrong side of the bed." (Introduce that phrase and explain that it means *grouchy*.) This is an excellent book for working with clocks and the passing of time. Can anyone really stay grouchy forever?

My Very First Book of Words (New York: HarperCollins, 1985)

This is one in a series of "first books." There are others about colors, numbers, shapes, heads/tails, etc. These books provide good visual teaching opportunities.

Enjoy the time spent with some of these experiences. Take advantage of the opportunity to teach and reinforce content information that relates to the various curriculum areas.

Help students learn the parts of a book, such as cover page, title page, dedication, spine, hard cover or soft cover. Eric Carle gives the reader an excellent introduction to the magic of *endpapers* that relate to the content of the book. Above all, help children to develop a love and appreciation for good books and to learn to handle them gently and with respect. Eric Carle helps us to do just that.

You can visit the official Eric Carle WebSite at: www.eric-carle.com or write to Eric Carle Studio, P.O. Box 485, Northampton, MA, 01060, to receive a colorful pamphlet showing the author's books along with a photo essay entitled, "How Eric Carle Creates His Art." This will be helpful for students. Also included is "The Caterpillar Express," an occasional newsletter.

A commercial book, *You Can Make a Collage,* is a simple how-to book that contains seventy-two different sheets of tissue paper designed by Eric Carle. (See bibliography.)

REPRODUCIBLE ACTIVITY PAGES

Marching Band—Letter M—Manny Mouse

Marching Band—Letter S—Sally Squirrel

Marching Band—Letter R—Rusty Rabbit

Marching Band—Letter T—Tootsie Turtle

Marching Band—Letter B—Barry Bear

Marching Band—Letter L—Lyle Lion

Word House Chart

Schoolhouse I.D.

Environmental Print

Getting Ready to Write

I Can Print My Name *(Portfolio Record Sheet)*

Children's Literature Activity Page—The Caterpillar Is Hungry for Information *(Eric Carle)*

Mm

© 2000 by The Center for Applied Research in Education

© 2000 by The Center for Applied Research in Education

© 2000 by The Center for Applied Research in Education

© 2000 by The Center for Applied Research in Education

© 2000 by The Center for Applied Research in Education

© 2000 by The Center for Applied Research in Education

Name _____

Word House Chart

Let's pretend we are hunting for items that begin with the letter that you print in the big square. Write or draw the items in each place. Work with a partner. Then we'll share this with classmates.

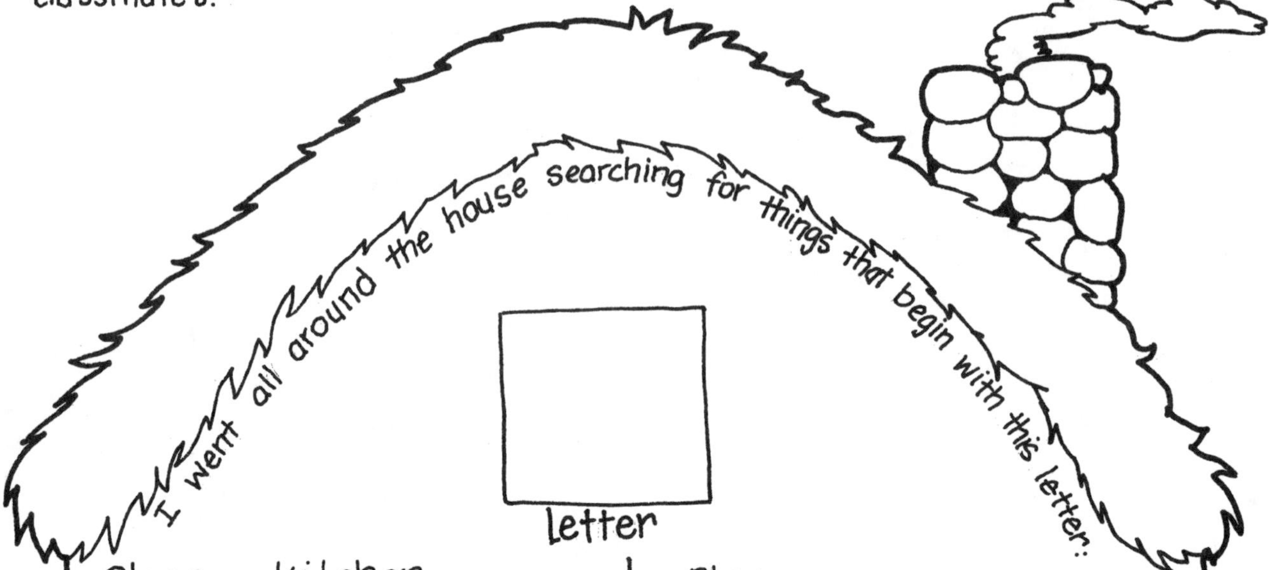

I went all around the house searching for things that begin with this letter.

letter

© 2000 by The Center for Applied Research in Education

Place: kitchen _____

1.

2.

3.

Place: _____

1.

2.

3.

Place: _____

1

2.

3.

Place: _____

1.

2.

3.

Name _____

I go to

_____
(school)

Our principal is:

_____

My teacher is:

_____

School phone number:

_____

© 2000 by The Center for Applied Research in Education

Name _____

Environmental Print

Print is all around us! Examine familiar labels from soup cans, cereal boxes, candy wrappers. Notice print and picture signs on your way to school. Then, design colorful labels for the following items.

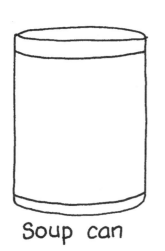

Soup can

bag of cookies

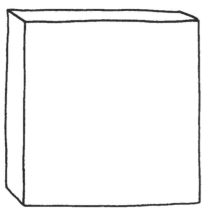

Cereal box

mug

shirt

I saw this sign outdoors.

© 2000 by The Center for Applied Research in Education

Name _____

© 2000 by The Center for Applied Research in Education

Getting Ready to Write

Slowly and carefully trace the lines in each square.
Then keep going until the space is filled.

I Can Print My Name

September	
October	
November	
December	
January	
February	
March	
April	
May	
June	

© 2000 by The Center for Applied Research in Education

Teacher Message:

This is a record of a year's progress in manuscript printing.

Student Message:

© 2000 by The Center for Applied Research in Education

Name _____

THE CATERPILLAR IS HUNGRY FOR INFORMATION

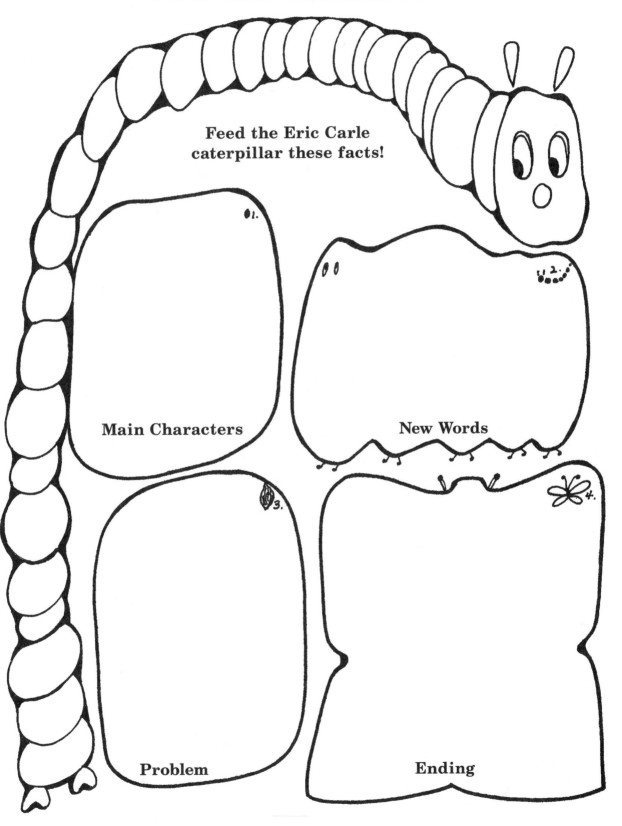

Feed the Eric Carle caterpillar these facts!

1.

Main Characters

2.

New Words

3.

Problem

4.

Ending

BOOK TITLE: _____

CHILDREN'S PICTURE BOOKS

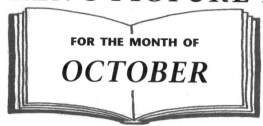

FOR THE MONTH OF

OCTOBER

Blacker, Terence. *If I Could Work.* **Illustrated by Chris Winn (Philadelphia: J.P. Lippincott, 1987)** This book sends out the message that work is fun, encouraging children to engage in dramatic play for a variety of careers, and to think about what they'd like to do as grown ups.

Brown, Margaret Wise. *The Little Scarecrow Boy.* **Pictures by David Diaz (New York: HarperCollins, 1999)** This book, originally written in the 1940s, has been given a new look by 1995 Caldecott Medalist David Diaz. The colorful reds, oranges, and yellows bring a touch of autumn to every page. This book was declared a *New York Times* Best Illustrated Book of 1998.

Greaves, Margaret. *Henry's Wild Morning.* **Pictures by Teresa O'Brien (New York: Dial Books, 1990)** Henry, the smallest cat in the litter, is out to prove himself today. He feels like a tiger, scampers up a tree after the birds, climbs too high and, despite coaching from his family, falls out of the tree. But he lands on his feet and is quite impressed with himself and decides to try it again. His mother has other ideas for Henry.

Harrison, Joanna. *Dear Bear* **(Minneapolis: Carolrhoda Books, Inc., 1994)** Katie is afraid of a bear that she says lives under the stairs. She tells her parents, and they help her to confront her fear by writing a letter to it. The bear responds. Letter writing is reinforced throughout the book, as Katie corresponds with the bear and deals with her fear.

Kraan, Hanna. *Flowers for the Wicked Witch.* **Illustrated by Annemarie van Haeringen. Translated by Wanda Boeke (New York: Front Street/Lemniscaat, 1998)** A gentle, humorous Dutch tale of an owl, a hare, and a hedgehog, and their misadventures when they meet up with a mildly wicked and misunderstood witch. This is one of a series. The title was originally published in the Netherlands as *Bloemen voor de boze heks.*

Rockwell, Anne. *Fire Engines* **(New York: E. P. Dutton, 1986)** A beginning book that takes an accurate look at fire engines and how they work. It is a good introduction experience for Fire Prevention Month with a quiet spotted dog family. (Simple text.)

Sheppard, Jeff. *Splash, Splash.* **Illustrated by Dennis Panek (New York: Macmillan, 1994)** One familiar animal after another falls into a lake. They all make sounds that are rhythmic when they splash ("quack, splash, quack, splash, quack") and children will be eager to join in the squeaking, mooing, and quacking.

Simmons, Posy. *F-Freezing ABC* **(New York: Alfred A. Knopf, 1995)** This book has a good letter–sound relationship as four animals—who are freezing in the "ar-ar-artic" cold weather—set out to find warmth. They are a complaining, shivering bunch, perhaps because it's "b-b-bitter c-c-cold."

Wildsmith, Brian. *Brian Wildsmith's Amazing World of Words* **(Brookfield, CT: The Millbrook Press, 1997)** The author has taken fourteen themes (such as space, desert, ocean) and given each topic a double-page spread. Each one contains a picture to examine, a border that has illustrations and word labels for many of the items shown in the picture.

Williams, Linda. *The Little Old Lady Who Was Not Afraid of Anything.* **Illustrated by Megan Lloyd (New York: Crowell, 1986)** A woman is returning to her cottage in the woods when she meets two big shoes that go CLOMP, CLOMP. "Get out of my way, I'm not afraid of you," she says. This continues when she meets pants that go WIGGLE, WIGGLE; shirts that go SHAKE, SHAKE; and so on. Children enjoy acting out this story with real props.

 # *OCTOBER*

OCTOBER GREETINGS! October is a magic month for learning! Things are well under way, the routine is established, and the classroom is beginning to buzz and hum with daily activity. If this is not happening in your classroom, take a step back and go more slowly. Do a great deal of review and repetition activities for reading this month.

Remember to praise children repeatedly for their achievement, effort, and progress. This provides encouragement for them and they will get the idea that praise is forthcoming when they make an effort. When they achieve results, they will be motivated to continue. Learning is not all "fun"—children need to know that much of it is hard work in the beginning. Also, they need reassurance for their efforts and know that they are noticed by you.

October's Focus on Reading. During this month you will be engaged in a wide variety of reading activities, and many will be suggested in this section. Specific skills to focus on are: (1) Review of the Alphabet Activities; (2) Words That Rhyme; (3) Ending Sounds in Words *(phonics);* and (4) The ABC Marching Band Vowel Letters of the Month—A, E, I, O, U.

Review of the Alphabet

Here are suggested activities for working with the letter–sound relationship of the ABC's (phonics). Continuing to master the alphabet and sounds is crucial for building excellence into the reading, writing, and spelling process. This can be done in a variety of ways.

ABC Flashcard Activities

Distribute alphabet flashcards to all students during circle time. *First,* have the students sing in unison "The Alphabet Song" as you point to each ABC letter card hanging above the chalkboard.

Next, sing the song slowly and have the children individually hold up the corresponding alphabet card as the song is being sung.

Then, collect the letter cards by having each child stand, one at a time, and call out the individual letter while holding it under his or her chin. Then, place it in a little basket (it can be called "Red Riding Hood's Basket" with a checkered cloth and a handle for easy carrying), and sit down. The letters can be collected in alphabetical order or in random order. (Do this at least two or three times per week, depending upon the needs of the group.)

The Cow Can Jump Over the Moon

Assemble a kit with a cut-out of a cow shape along with round, yellow flashcards (the moon). On each circle shape, print an alphabet letter. Make a pile of the moon shapes and have students turn them over one at a time. If the student says the letter correctly, then the cow "jumps over the moon." Have students work with a partner and keep track of how many times in a row the cow can jump. Keep practicing.

This can also be done with flashcards that contain review words that the students need to practice and learn.

To enjoy this activity even more, read the book *Moonstruck: The True Story of the Cow Who Jumped Over the Moon* by Gennifer Choldenko, with illustrations by Paul Yalowitz. The horse is in charge of training the 941-pound moon-jumping cows to flip up and over the moon that is 240,000 miles away! The horse also explains how Mother Goose came up with the phrase "the cow jumped over the moon."

What's on Your Page?

Have students work with a partner. Distribute a variety of ABC books and have them open to the "L" page and say the item or items found there. Then close the book, and open to the "E" page and repeat the procedure.

Students can print the words they find in a giant-size class alphabet book and make their own illustrations. Some excellent ABC books to use include *Ed Emberly's ABC* by Ed Emberly; *The Graphic Alphabet* by David Pelletier; *Allison's Zinnia* by Anita Loebel; *A, B, See* by Tana Hoban; *Wildflower ABC* by Diana Pomeroy; *Handsigns, A Sign Language Alphabet* by Kathleen Fain; *Navajo ABC, A Dine Alphabet Book* by Luci Tapahonso and Eleanor Schick, with illustrations by Eleanor Schick; and *DK Alphabet Book* by Lara Tankel Holtz, with illustrations by Dave King, which has hundreds of photographic images of A–Z objects.

ABC's of Hands

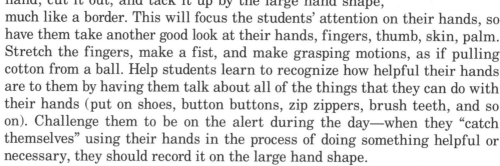

- Make a large construction paper hand shape and attach it to the bulletin board. Using a variety of colored construction paper, have each student trace his or her own hand. You or the student can print the student's name on the hand, cut it out, and tack it up by the large hand shape, much like a border. This will focus the students' attention on their hands, so have them take another good look at their hands, fingers, thumb, skin, palm. Stretch the fingers, make a fist, and make grasping motions, as if pulling cotton from a ball. Help students learn to recognize how helpful their hands are to them by having them talk about all of the things that they can do with their hands (put on shoes, button buttons, zip zippers, brush teeth, and so on). Challenge them to be on the alert during the day—when they "catch themselves" using their hands in the process of doing something helpful or necessary, they should record it on the large hand shape.

- You can list the alphabet along the side of the hand. Discuss what students have written or drawn on the hand shape, and then print the words alongside the corresponding letter. They don't have to be filled in order. You will need to be especially aware of the hand chart. When students are cutting or pasting, call it to their attention and have them fill in the chart. You may want to use Rebus illustrations also.

By going from the activity to the printed word, the student comes to see that the word or phrase can be recorded in print and read (decoded) over and over again.

- Here are some "ABC's of the Hand" activities in which children engage, and may help to get this project started: *(a) asking* (raise hand); *(b) bouncing* a ball; *(c) crushing* paper; *(d) delivering* a letter; *(e) erasing* chalkboard; *(f) folding* paper; *(g) grasping* a pencil; *(h) holding* a book; *(i) illustrating* a story; *(j) jumping* rope; *(k) kite* flying; *(l) lifting; (m) measuring* with a ruler; *(n) newspaper* folding; *(o) opening* a jar; *(p) petting* a cat or dog; *(q)* making the *quiet* sound with forefinger on lips; *(r) rolling* a ball; *(s) squeezing* a sponge; *(t) twisting* paper; *(u) umbrella* holding; *(v) voting* by hand; *(w) washing* hands; *(x)* making an 'x' in the dirt with a stick; *(y) yanking* yarn; and *(z) zipping* zippers.

Call out the alphabet letter and the information, and have the students use hand motions to pretend they are carrying out the activity. For a good guessing game, they can also make up their own hand activities to add to the list. A good picture book that focuses upon what hands can do is *Hands* by Lois Ehlert, which is in the shape of a hand.

ABC's of Hand Signs

Some teachers who are proficient in signing the alphabet are able to successfully teach children to do this at a young age. You can learn it right along with the alphabet letters. One excellent resource book for this undertaking is *The Handmade Alphabet* by Laura Rankin. In this interpretation of the manual alphabet, there is one large picture per page. Each one clearly shows the positioning of the hands for the letter and also gives a helpful hint by way of the illustration. For example, the *b* sign is surrounded by bubbles and the *c* sign has a cup dangling from the thumb.

As children become more proficient with the handmade alphabet, they can also use it as they sing songs.

ABC's of Sounds

A is for Ahhhhh!

B is for Boo!

C is for Crash!

Keep going, listening for sounds in songs, rhymes, nature—everywhere! Make a chart of these sounds.

A good ABC companion book for this activity is *ABC Drive!* by Naomi Howland. As you climb aboard this car-trip alphabet book, the pages are lively with activity in the city, in the country, and even at the seashore, so children can discuss the sounds they might hear on each page. This book is also a good resource for environmental print; it includes traffic signs, pavement signs, advertisements on trucks, and road signs. These signs are also displayed on the colorful book cover.

ABC's of Animals

Make an ABC Animal Book. Find pictures of animals in magazines that can be cut out, or pictures in ABC books that can be studied and drawn. Go through the book and classify the animals by those that live in the zoo, those that live in the wild, and "domesticated" animals (those that can live among people without hurting them). Take advantage of the opportunity to introduce the new word *domesticated*. "How many and what variety of domesticated animals live in our homes?"

Two good ABC books to help with this activity are the colorful *Bugs and Beasties ABC* by Cheryl Nathan and the dynamic designs of the large, cut-paper book *The Jungle ABC* by Michael Roberts.

Matching Capital and Lower-Case Letters

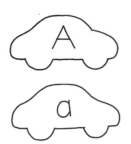

The ABC's sound alike but they don't necessarily look alike. In reality, we don't have just 26 letters of the alphabet to learn, but 26 upper-case and 26 lower-case, or a total of *52 letters*. Make a bulletin board parking garage with two levels and 52 automobile shapes. On one set of automobile shapes, print the upper-case letters; print lower-case letters on the other set. Students can move the cars up the ramp and "park" them (with thumbtacks) in the proper parking space that has been appropriately marked. These cars can be moved in and out of the garage. For variation, put alphabet letters on ticket-size slips of paper; students can pretend to park and pick up their car from the garage.

Capital and Lower-Case Twins

Some capital and lower-case letters look alike, or almost alike. The only difference is that one is bigger. This can be determined by looking at two sets and deciding which ones look alike. Hold up a *capital A* and a *lower-case a,* for example, and ask, "Are these two twins or almost twins?" The following letter-shape categories can be used:

The "twins" are: Cc, Oo, Pp, Ss, Uu, Vv, Ww, Xx, Zz

The "almost twins" are: Ii, Jj, Kk, Ll, Tt

Capital and Lower-Case Relatives

There are 12, or one dozen, upper- and lower-case letter "relatives"—that is, the capitals and lower-case letters do not visually look alike, nor do some remotely resemble each other. Get an egg carton and, from construction paper, cut out 24 egg shapes. Print the upper-case letters on one set and the lower-case on another. Then students can put them together in the proper egg slot.

The "relatives" are: Aa, Bb, Dd, Ee, Ff, Gg, Hh, Mm, Nn, Qq, Rr, Yy

Words That Rhyme

A Time to Listen to Poetry

During the week, be sure to include poetry when reading aloud. Soon the children will have favorite poems that they will begin to ask for. They'll learn them, say them along with you, and enjoy the rhythm and the rhyme. Two excellent poetry books to read aloud are *Hailstones and Hailibut Bones* by Mary O'Neill and *A Hippopotamusn't* by J. Patrick Lewis.

Note: A good teacher resource book is *Pass the Poetry Please!* by Lee Bennett Hopkins. It offers guidelines for teaching poetry and many ideas to encourage children to enjoy poetry.

Some Storybooks Are in Rhyme

Select books that have a rhythm and a rhyme to them—in addition to telling a good story—and use these during your story time. Talk about the words that rhyme, print them on a chart, and point out the similarities in the formation of the word endings of words that rhyme or "sound alike." Examples are b*unny*, r*unny*, f*unny* or c*op*, p*op*, t*op*.

Some good rhyming books to read aloud include any of the Dr. Seuss books, along with the enjoyable book *A House Is a House for Me* by Mary Ann Hoberman.

How to Memorize and Teach a Rhyme

Begin to strengthen memory by having students memorize short simple rhymes. They can do hand accompaniments along with the rhymes.

The steps to teaching a rhyme are:

1. You say it all the way through while children listen.
2. You say the beginning part of it while children listen. Then you all repeat it together.
3. You say the next part of it while children listen. Then you all repeat it together.
4. Start at the beginning again with you saying the part to be memorized so far, while children listen.
5. You and children say it together.

So we have the following speech pattern, where Teacher = T and Children = C:

T says entire rhyme, poem, or chant to be learned.
C listen.
T says line one.
C listen.
T and C say line one together.
T says line two.
C listen.
T and C say line two together.

Use this pattern until the rhyme, poem, or chant is completed. Then you say it once more while children listen; then they say it together. Do this daily until enough children learn the rhyme that they help you carry it. The children need your strong voice as leader throughout the process—and even after they have learned it. Be patient, for it takes time for the group to learn rhymes.

Some Favorite Nursery Rhymes

Use the T and C pattern as previously explained to learn these all-time favorites.

Peter, Peter, Pumpkin eater
Had a wife, and couldn't keep her.
Put her in a pumpkin shell
And there he kept her very well.

Roses are red
Violets are blue
Sugar is sweet
And so are you.

Twinkle, twinkle little star
How I wonder who you are.
Up above the clouds so high
Like a diamond in the sky.

Also, check the Mother Goose nursery rhyme books for short, simple rhymes like *Jack and Jill, Humpty Dumpty,* and many more. Most children need to listen to many rhymes before they can actually create rhymes.

Some New Rhymes for Listening and Guessing

October Days and Nights

Day

Orange as the sun
Blue as the sky
White as the clouds
That float up high.

Night

Orange as a pumpkin
Black as night
Yellow as a jack-o'-lantern
Shining bright.

Who Am I?

Greetings to you
On this Fall day.
"Are you coming
Out to play?" *(friend)*

I like to climb
High up in trees
Where I can "Meow"
And feel the breeze. *(cat)*

My color is red,
I like to shout it.
My siren is LOUD,
No doubt about it! *(firetruck)*

You see me hopping
At the zoo.
I've got a big pouch
And a joey too. *(kangaroo)*

I'm on a leash
And like to bark.
I warn of strangers
In the dark. *(dog)*

They carried a pail
To the top of a hill.
Down fell Jack
Then down fell _____ . *(Jill)*

Color Lollipop Rhymes

Distribute colored construction paper circles that are glued to kraft sticks. Say the rhyme and, as each color is called, students who are holding that particular color of "lollipop" can hold it way up high. In the beginning, as a helpful hint, you may want to use one set and hold up the appropriate color.

Red like a fire flick.
Red like a finger prick.

(those with red hold them high)

Orange like a crunchy carrot.
Orange like a squawking parrot.

(those with orange hold them high)

Yellow like a field of wheat.
Yellow like a cupcake treat.

Green like tree leaves.
Green like velvet sleeves.

Blue like the morning sky.
Blue like the baby's eye.

Purple like jelly.
Purple like jam.

Pink like frosting.
Pink like ham.

For several days, have a real lollipop treat of a different color. Some children may prefer to put them in their lunchbox or backpack to take home. Some eat them at school. Caution children not to eat them on the bus—if they save them, they must not be brought out until they get home. Remind students that "We never run with a lollipop in our mouth! We sit down and enjoy them." (Check with parents regarding sugar limits whenever serving sweets.) Colored cereal loops can serve as a substitute.

Speaking in Rimes

We speak of *word families* or *rimes* or *word clusters* or *phonograms* that sound alike. These are terms that refer to the same thing. It's a good way to introduce words that rhyme, and it also helps with spelling.

Here are some of the familiar ones to work with for starters:

–ab	–ack	–ake	–an
cab	back	bake	ban
dab	hack	cake	can
gab	jack	fake	Dan
jab	lack	Jake	fan
lab	Mack	lake	man
nab	pack	make	Nan
tab	rack	rake	pan
	sack	sake	ran
	tack	take	tan
	yack	wake	van
	Zack		

Procedure: Put the rime on the chalkboard and pronounce it. Have students repeat it after you. Then, from A to Z, sound out the alphabet letter before each rime. Does it make a word? Does it make sense by adding *only one letter* to the beginning of the rime?

For example, say "ab" and then, one by one, glide the alphabet letters to produce the letter joined to the "ab" sound while students listen to determine if a word is formed.

TEACHER: A ab. Does *aab* sound like a word? *(No)*
            B ab. Does *bab* sound like a word? *(No)*
            C ab. Does *cab* sound like a word? *(Yes)*
            D ab. Does *dab* sound like a word? *(Yes)*
            E ab. Does *eab* sound like a word? *(No)*

If a word is formed, print it on the chalkboard to make a list. Later, when working with blends, this same format can be used with the rimes.

Students usually enjoy working with the rimes. These can be left on the chalkboard for them to copy in their journals during spare time. You may wish to transfer them to a list, and even make a classroom book of rimes.

Children laugh and have a lot of fun with the language when they are engaged in this activity, as many silly words or nonsense words can be formed. This makes the activity lively and the learning enjoyable.

More Fun with a Silly Rime Story

Using the list of rimes that you generate, have students develop a silly story using the words in order. It gives them practice with beginning sounds and rhyming words, and they learn what the words mean and how they're used in a sentence. The children are learning and giggling at the same time, and they often have little difficulty remembering these stories.

The procedure to follow is for you to read the story and point to the rime so that children can fill in the necessary words in the silly story. Let's look at the **ake** list, for example, for a nonsense story that could go something like this:

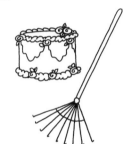

The _____ake Story

I am going to **bake** a **cake.** Not a **fake** one. It's a birthday present for **Jake.** He lives by a **lake.** I will mix the batter with a **rake.** When he sees this, he will say, "For heaven's **sake!**" Then he'll **take** it and **wake** everyone up.

Here's another!

The _____ab Day

Today Abby will take a **cab** to visit Grandmother. First, she'll put on a **dab** of hand lotion. Grandmother likes to **gab** and **jab** you in the ribs when she laughs. She calls her kitchen the **lab.** I'll go in there and **nab** a few cookies and tell her to put them on my **tab.**

Now the children can try a silly rime story. Here are some more rimes to work with: *age, aid, ale, am, and, ank, ate, ay, ean, ell, ess, ice, ick, ift, ike, ill, ink, oil, ome, ong, op, ot, ug, ull, ump, unt,* and *ut.*

Rime Time

You will need a paper plate and a long column of rimes. Make two slits in the plate and insert the list. Then have students gently pull the long list through and see how many of the rimes they can say. You may want to have each child make his or her own list.

Spin a Rime

You will need two paper plates (one large and one small) and a paper fastener. With a felt-tip pen, put rimes around the edge of the large plate, and print alphabet letters around the edge of the small plate. Center the small plate on top of the large plate and insert the paper fastener in the middle.

Then spin the inner plate around to see if sensible words can be made with the letters, taking one at a time.

Ending Sounds in Words

What's the End?

First, explain to the students that the *end* means the last one. In a story it means that the story is finished; it's over. (*Last, finished,* and *over* are all words that can be used to explain "end.")

"Words, like stories, have a beginning sound, an ending sound, and a sound (or sounds) in the middle. We're going to look at some that are last in the word."

The Sound of "ing"

1. Print the letters "ing" on the chalkboard and say "the sound ing as in ring."

2. Print a column or row that looks like this. Help and encourage students to create some rhyming *ing* words by filling in the first letter.

      _____ing   _____ing   _____ing

3. Erase those words. Next, make a column or row that looks like this and encourage students to add the *ing* sound.

      s_____   k_____   r_____

4. Next, print simple words and help students to say them. Then have them add the sound of *ing* at the tail end. Here are some starter words:

meet	beat	rush
go	fly	dry
walk	buy	try

Encourage students to use these words in sentences for practice. This can be a verbal exercise—no need to write it down at this point. Later, students may want to do some writing on their own using the *ing* sound.

Double "ing"

If students appear to be catching on to the previous exercises, you can go ahead with the double sound of *ing*. Otherwise, leave it for later in the months ahead.

      sing_____   ring_____   zing_____

Let's Meet "ng" Who Likes to Purr

This sound is made far back in the throat, and ends with the *hard g* utterance. The back of the tongue is on the roof of the mouth, and the sides of the tongue rest inside along the teeth. Have students encircle their throat with their fingers; when they say the *ng* sound, it's like feeling a cat purr.

Say these words, and have children say them after you:

sang, bang, rang

long, bong, song

lung, rung, sung

Later, when students are decoding words in a sentence and come upon the *ng* sound, you can encircle your own throat with your hand and remind the children that it's like a cat purring. They will begin to make the association.

The ABC Marching Band Vowel Letters of the Month— A, E, I, O, U

Information for the teacher: The vowels are "anchor" letters. They're used over and over again, and we rarely encounter words without vowels in the English language system. Sometimes the letter *y* (considered a consonant) will step in and function as a vowel, often using the sound of *long i,* usually at the end of a word (sky, try, why). This will be addressed when the letter *y* is introduced. The letter *w* very rarely steps in as a vowel, so we will not address it here.

To make matters more confusing for the beginning reader, the vowels are said to have two sounds—long and short—although several vowels have more than two. But we won't get into that this month!

While it is not the intent of these activities to have students learn vowel rules by heart, some programs do have this as a part of their instruction, and many teachers and students find them useful. They are especially useful later for spelling and for sounding out words.

Vowels Have Rules

Some of the more familiar rules that work fairly consistently are:

- When two vowels go walking, the first one does the talking (saying its long sound).
- Final *e* at the end of the word makes the vowel long.
- Use *i* before *e* except after *c*, or as sounded like *a* as in *neighbor* and *weigh*.
- Before adding *ed* or *ing* at the end of a one-syllable word that ends in *e*, drop the final *e*.

Note: It will depend upon your reading program and group as to whether you decide to introduce vowel rules this early in the year. At one time, vowel rules were not introduced until the end of first grade, but definitely in second grade. Vowel rules are also discussed in the December section.

Young students, especially from preK through grade 2, enjoy make-believe stories about the letters. If given a personality or the name of an animal, the alphabet letter stories work well in helping the young learner unlock some word clues. Vowels offer a special challenge. See the Marching Band members in the Reproducible Activity Pages. Note that each vowel letter plays either an instrument with more than one note (long and short) or two different instruments, some of which are make-believe.

Let's Strike Up the Band!

Use the same procedure that you used for the September letters. You assume the role of the bandleader with baton in hand: (1) say the name of the letter; (2) print the upper- and lower-case letter on the chalkboard; (3) introduce the ABC Marching Band member by name and tell what instrument it plays; and (4) model the sound that the letter makes and have students repeat it. As they repeat the sound, have the children note the role played by their teeth, tongue, and lips.

Note: Remember, after chants are practiced and learned, to hold the baton out in front horizontally until all students are quiet. Then raise the baton to have students say the sound; lower the baton with a swooping motion so that the sound will cease when your hand comes to a halt. Impress upon students that Marching Band members have to learn to be well disciplined.

Meet April Alligator and the Accordion *(Letter A)*

April Alligator plays the accordion. Her special accordion has two notes that she knows how to play. One is called "long *a*" and the other is "short *a*." Print the capital and lower-case letters on the chalkboard. The accordion is an actual instrument, with a piano keyboard along either side. Show a picture of one, and have someone come in to demonstrate one, if possible.

The long *a* sounds just like the beginning sound of April's first name—*a* as in April. The short *a* sounds just like the beginning sound in her last name—*a* as in Alligator (sounds like ahhhh). Demonstrate that when we say the long sound of *a*, the air is expelled from the back of the throat. Have students make the sound. Then demonstrate that when we say the short sound, or "ahhhh," the jaw shifts slightly and the tongue is at rest.

Have students put their hand to their throat and say the long and short sounds of the letter *a* back and forth, at least five times. Call attention to the fact that there is a muscle shift just under the chin. Some children may feel this more easily than others. Keep practicing.

Remember, you are the bandleader. The baton is in the horizontal position, and all eyes are on you. When the baton is raised, the students say the sound; when the baton is lowered, the sound stops.

Try Both Sounds on April's Accordion *(Letter A)*

Let's be on the lookout for these two sounds. They can appear at the beginning of the word, or anywhere else in the word, so be on the alert.

Tell students to try out both sounds when they come upon the letter *a* in a word, to see which one makes sense. Here are some words to list on the board to help get you started with the beginning sounds.

April Words (long *a*)	Alligator words (short *a*)
ace	agitate
acorn	after
angel	action
apron	apple
able	apricot

Which "A" Makes Sense? *(Letter A)*

Print a short phrase or sentence on the chalkboard. Underline the word that you wish to focus upon. Read the sentence, and try first the long *a* and then the short *a* sound on the focus word. Which one makes sense?

The dog ran *after* the ball. (long or short?)

The *apple* is delicious. (long or short?)

Is Spot *able* to jump? (long or short?)

Marking Long and Short Vowels *(Letter A)*

Show students that there is a method for marking both long and short *a* (as well as all vowels). You can call it the "line and cup" method.

Put a straight line above the vowel if it's long. Put a curved line above the vowel if it's short.

$$\bar{a} \qquad \breve{a}$$

April Alligator's Rhythmic Chant *(Letter A)*

Read this rhyme while students listen. Then, invite the children to join in. Use the rhyme repeatedly.

April Alligator   *(Bandleader: Lift up baton.)*
Likes to move
So swing your hips
Get in the groove.

With an **"a"** and an **"ah"**   *(chorus)*
   and an **"a, ah, ah"**
With an **"a"** and an **"ah"**
   and an **"a, ah, ah"**

She plays the accordion
And when she smiles
That accordion stretches
For miles and miles.

With an **"a"** and an **"ah"**   *(chorus)*
  and an **"a, ah ah"**
With an **"a"** and an **"ah"**
  and an **"a, ah, ah"**   *(Lower baton.)*

Make a Letter Poster *(Letter A)*

Print capital and lower-case samples of this letter on a piece of posterboard. Be on the lookout for pictures in magazines that begin with either the long or short sound of *a*. Have students cut them out and paste them on the posterboard.

Meet Emanuel Elephant with the English Horn and Eggaphone *(Letter E)*

Emanuel Elephant is the largest land animal in the Marching Band. He plays the English horn with his trunk and the Eggaphone with his two front feet while marching on his two hind legs. Emanual Elephant is quite an asset to the band, as we can see. The English horn is a double-reed woodwind instrument that is similar to an oboe. The Eggaphone is a make-believe instrument, made by Emanuel Elephant from a dried, hollowed-out purple eggplant shell, with twine stretched across it. He uses a twig for a bow.

The *long* sound of the letter *e* says the name of the letter. The sound is made in the throat: The lips and teeth are slightly parted. The *short e* is a sound that comes from farther back in the throat, and sounds more like "eh." Have students put their hand gently around their throat, and make the long sound and short sound of *e,* going back and forth. Have students note in a mirror that for the short sound, the mouth is slightly more open, but tongue and teeth remain in about the same position. The jaw gets a workout when going from "e" to "eh."

The Jaw Workout *(Letter E)*

"How do we know if the letter *e* is long or short when we see it in a word? We make the two sounds and give our jaw a workout." Students will need to be reminded to keep trying out both sounds when they encounter the letter *e* in words. There are other factors that affect the vowel sounds, but this is a place to begin.

Emanuel Elephant's Words *(Letter E)*

Make a list of words that begin with the long *e* (Emanuel) and the short *e* (elephant). Put them on an elephant shape. Have students add to the list. Here are some to get you started:

Emanuel's Words	*Elephant's Words*
even	egg
eel	entertain
Easter	elevator
eat	ever
e-mail	echo

Doing the Elephant Romp–Stomp *(Letter E)*

This can be done while students pretend to play the English horn with one hand and the Eggaphone with the other.

First, pretend to play the English horn with the left hand (fist) up to the mouth and with fingers pumping up and down. Second, pretend to play the Eggaphone by moving the right hand from side to side at waist level. Third, try to do the two at the same time. It takes a lot of coordination to work on this, so go slowly.

For the romp–stomp part, students can turn around while in place. They get practice with the long and short sounds of the letter *e*. Here is the rhythmic chant, as all eyes are on you. It's so quiet, you can hear a pin drop!

Emanuel Elephant	*(Bandleader: Lift baton.)*
Is our guy	*(Students play horn)*
He plays the horn	
With trunk held high.	
Doing the elephant romp–stomp!	*(Turn around.)*
Doing the elephant romp–stomp!	
"Eeeeeee, Eeeeeeee, Emanuel!"	*(Lower baton.)*
Elephant, Elephant	*(Lift baton.)*
Floppy ear	*(Students play Eggaphone.)*
Plays sweet music	
For all to hear.	
Doing the elephant romp–stomp!	*(Turn around.)*
Doing the elephant romp–stomp!	
"Ehhhh, Ehhhh, Elephant!"	*(Lower baton.)*

Meet Ivan Insect and His Icky Bug Wings *(Letter I)*

Although Ivan Insect is the smallest member in the Marching Band, he is very important. He plays two different sounds on his two sets of wings. He rubs one set of wings together to make the *long i* sound (which says his name) and rubs the other set of wings together to make the *short i* ("ih").

Many insects, like Ivan, have two sets of wings, so this role in the band can be taken over by swarms of others, even a tiny tick. With three pairs of legs and three body parts, insects are flexible and move quickly. So, Ivan can play many notes rapidly.

The long *i* says its name, "i." Note that the mouth is open, tongue is at rest, and then the mouth slowly closes. The sound comes from the back of the throat. The short *i* (sounds like "ih") is said with the mouth open, but not so wide. This sound also comes from the back of the throat. Have students put their hands under their chin, and note the shift in vocal chords as they shift from the long sound to the short sound at least five times. (This is similar to the jaw workout that was experienced with the letter *e*.)

Ivan Insect's Words *(Letter I)*

Make a poster with a variety of insects all around the border. Children can locate these in nature magazines, cut them out, and paste them onto the posterboard. Label two columns for long and short vowel words. Here are some to get you started.

Ivan's Words (long *i*)	**Insect Words (short *i*)**
ice	ill
ice cream	into
iron	it
island	if
iris	immediately

Ivan's Instrument Lesson *(Letter I)*

Since Ivan makes sounds by moving his wings together, he will assist students in making sounds with their body. The children will get practice with the numbers *six* (insects have six legs) and *three* (insects have three body parts).

Rub palms of hands together. (6 times)

Rub arms together. (6 times)

Rub thumbs together. (6 times)

Rub knees together. (6 times)

Rub ankles together. (6 times)

Rub elbows together. (6 times)

Click your tongue. (3 times)

Say long *i* (i, i, i). (3 times)

Say short *i* (ih, ih, ih). (3 times)

Ivan practices his sounds daily. How often do students practice saying their letter sounds? They can take a lesson from Ivan.

Three Body Parts and Six Legs *(Letter I)*

An insect has six legs and three body parts. Another name for insect is "bug." There are more insects than we can count. Some of the more familiar ones include the ladybug, bee, fly, wasp, and mosquito. (**Note:** A spider is not an insect because it has eight legs and two body parts.) Insects can be pesky because they bite or sting.

Sometimes the vowel letter *i* can be pesky because we don't know if it is making its long sound or its short sound. Encourage students to be like the hedgehog. Hedgehogs go after pesky insects until they catch them. So, students need to get the message to hunt down the pesky insects to see whether the letter *i* is making Ivan's sound (long *i*) or the insect sound (short *i*). A good book to use at this time is *The Icky Bug Alphabet Book* by Jerry Pallotta, with illustrations by Ralph Masiello.

Make an Insectivore Badge *(Letter I)*

Make a badge from construction paper with the words "I am an Insectivore." An insectivore hunts down insects until they are caught. Students can wear them only after they can *catch* or *say* the long *i* sound and the short *i* sound. If they can say a word for each, they can become an Insectivore Inspector.

Meet Olivia Octopus and the Oboe and Ocarina *(Letter O)*

Olivia Octopus has eight tentacles, and each tentacle has two rows of suction cups. She can play the oboe, a real woodwind instrument *(long o),* using one set of suction cups; with the other set she plays the ocarina. The ocarina is a real instrument, made from clay or even plastic, that has several finger holes. It is from the two rows of suckers that she makes the sounds for the marching band—the long sound of the letter *o* (sounds like its letter name) and the short sound of the letter *o* (sounds like "ahhh"). With her tentacles, Olivia also makes other amazing sounds with the letter *o*, but this will not be discussed at this time.

Have students note that when making the long sound, their mouth forms a circular shape, is open, and the sound comes from the throat. For the short sound, the mouth drops open even more, and the sound also comes from the back of the throat. Have students put their hand to their throat and, once again, give their jaw a workout as they shift from long *o* to short *o*.

The Word List of Olivia Octopus *(Letter O)*

Make a giant-size octopus from orange construction paper. The octopus has a large head and eight tentacles. Print the word list on the head shape, and exaggerate the circular shapes (letter *o*) along each side of the tentacles—one set can be blue, another set can be green. Use a blue felt-tip pen to print the words with the long sound of the letter *o*, and the green pen for the words with the short sound of the letter *o*. Here are some words to get you started.

Olivia's Words (long *o*)	Octopus Words (short *o*)
oatmeal	on
open	optional
okay	October
ocean	otter
over	occupation

Olivia Octopus Loves the Ocean Chant *(Letter O)*

This gives students an opportunity to practice the long and short sounds of the letter *o*. You say it first; then teach it to students, two lines at a time. Students can make flowing movements with their arms during the chant, as if swimming. Repeat it often.

Just say "ocean"	*(Bandleader: Lift baton.)*
and you know,	
Olivia Octopus	
is ready to go.	
Can she swim? Oh, oh, oh!	*(long sound of letter o)*
Can she dive? Oh, oh oh!	
Can she float? Oh, oh, oh!	
Push a boat? Oh, oh, oh!	
Does she like whales? Ah, ah, ah!	*(short sound of letter o)*
Does she like snails? Ah, ah, ah!	
Does she like shrimp? Ah, ah, ah!	
And lobster tails? Ah, ah, ah!	
Olivia Octopus! Rah, Rah, Rah!	*(Lower baton.)*

Olivia Likes Olives *(Letter O)*

 Do students like olives? Olivia sometimes brings in an olive treat, especially green olives. You can have an Olivia Olive-Tasting Party with an assortment of green and black olives (without pits). Make a graph of the children's favorites.

Olivia's Favorite Color *(Letter O)*

Olivia likes the color olive, especially olive drab. Print the word "Olivia" on the chalkboard and print "olive" just underneath, so that students note that many of the letters are the same. The name "Olivia" has four vowels and "olive" has three. Circle those that are the same.

Olive drab comes in various shades of greenish brown. Soldiers use it for their uniforms when they are camouflaged. Take the opportunity to introduce the new vocabulary words: *camouflaged* and *olive drab* (or *olive green*). "Is anyone wearing green today?"

Soon the leaves on the trees in many areas will no longer be green; they will be camouflaged with splashy bright and then drab colors. Encourage students to be on the alert for drab-colored leaves and bring them into the classroom for the Science Center. For a good picture storybook about a colorful elephant who rolls in berry juice to become drab, read *Elmer* by David McKee.

Meet Umbernella Unicorn and the Ukelele *(Letter U)*

A unicorn is a magical make-believe creature, shaped like a horse with a horn on the top of its head. This glorious creature prances in fairy tales and is pictured in tapestries and fabrics. It's no wonder that the unicorn would add a bit of glamour, stardust, and magic to the ABC Marching Band!

Umbernella Unicorn makes two sounds with the ukelele, a four-string guitar said to have originated in Hawaii. The sounds are the long sound of the letter *u* (sounds like its name) and the short sound of the letter *u* (sounds like "uh"). Since the unicorn is so mysterious, some claim that the sounds also come from the unicorn horn on top of its head. (See the Unicorn Read-Aloud Poem.)

For the long sound of *u,* the lips are puckered, the mouth is open, the tongue tip is pressing behind the bottom front teeth, and air is being expelled with a throaty sound over the top of the tongue. For the short sound of *u,* the mouth goes slack, the lower jaw drops, the tongue rests on bottom of mouth, and vocal chords shift to make a different throaty sound. Once again, have students gently hold their throat while they go back and forth five times with the two sounds. Note the jaw shift. Use a mirror so that students can see the shape of their mouth when making these sounds.

On the Look-out for Words *(Letter U)*

Make the posterboard word list look magical. Use a gold felt-tip pen for the long sound of *u* and a silver felt-tip pen for the short sound of *u.* The posterboard can be cut into a curved horn shape, and gauze or angel hair can be glued around the edge for a dreamy effect.

Unicorn Words (Long *u*)	Umbernella Words (Short *u*)
unite	uncle
university	under
universe	up
uniform	unlock
unique	unload

Let's Take a Look at "Under" *(Letter U)*

This is a good time to introduce the word "under" and to note that there are many words that begin with "under." We call these *compound words.* This activity provides an opportunity to use the dictionary to look up some words. Here are several to get you started.

underarm	undercover	undercut
undergo	underground	understand
undertake	underpaid	undershirt

On the Move with the Letter Bag *(Letter U)*

Begin with a cut-out of the letter *u* and call upon someone to be "It." That person is given the cut-out letter. Then, "It" must reach into the Letter Bag for a slip that contains directions as to where to put the letter. Each slip contains a direction, such as:

Place *under* stapler.

Place *under* the crayon can.

Place *under* the window.

Place *under* the magnifying glass.

"It" must read (with assistance) and follow the directions. Then that person calls upon another student to be "It." This time, the student has to read the directions, retrieve the letter, and place the letter in a new location. Then, that student calls upon someone else to be "It." Continue until each student gets a turn or until time runs out.

Another day, the letter *o* may be the focus and direction slips may direct students to put the letter *over* items. Use the letter *t* for on *top* of items. Use *l* for *left* of an item, *r* for *right* of an item, and *b* for *beside* an item, and so on.

The Unicorn Read-Aloud Poem *(Letter U)*

U is shaped like
   a tiny cup.
You can use it when
   you slosh water up.
U is an umbrella
   for you, my pet,
Turn it upside down
   so you won't get wet.
U smells like winter
   and glistening snow,
A U-turn takes you
   where you want to go.
The unicorn horn
   makes a long and short sound,
It says "U" on the tip
   and "uh" on the crown.

U is thoughtful,
  U is kind,
U says "thank you"
  and "I'll share mine."
If you want to dream
  of a unicorn
Say "u" and "uh" softly,
  and before the morn
A unicorn will prance
  right through your head
While you are snuggled
  safe in bed.

A Time to Eat, and a Time to Learn *(A, E, I, O, U)*

Serving good food to reinforce letter sounds is one way that helps students to learn. For vowels, try serving food that begins with the letter sound. If that's not possible, try for the letter in the middle of the word, or use props while serving the long or short vowels. Here are some helpful suggestions and a sentence to learn with the letter food. (For more vowel food suggestions, see the January section.)

A   Wear an **a**pron while serving **a**pple slices.
E   **E**at with your mouth closed when chewing **e**ggs.
I   **I**ce cream with **i**tsy-bitsy nuts on top tastes good.
O   **O**atmeal in **O**ctober tastes delicious.
U   It's a **u**niversal fact—pl**u**ms are y**u**mmy.

Time for Our Vegetable Vowel Crunch *(A, E, I, O, U)*

Have an assortment of cut-up vegetables—sticks, slices, wedges—for students to sample. Print the vegetable name on the chalkboard and have students name the vowels in the words. They can circle each one they find with chalk the same color as the vegetable.

Here are some food suggestions for starters: carrots (a, o); tomatoes (o, a, o, e); lettuce (e, u, e); cauliflower (a, u, i, o, e); broccoli (o, o, i). *Help students discover that the word "cauliflower" has each of the five vowels.* Even if it's an itsy-bitsy piece, make sure they eat their cauliflower to "help them learn the vowel letters."

It's a "Cauliflower Letter" *(A, E, I, O, U)*

Make a large white irregular shape from construction paper to represent a head of cauliflower. Place the letters *a, e, i, o,* and *u* on the cauliflower shape, with items that represent the long and short sounds. When students are having difficulty sounding out a word with a vowel sound, it might be helpful to refer to it as one of the "cauliflower letters."

It's a "Cauliflower Day!" *(A, E, I, O, U)*

Every day is a cauliflower day, because just about every descriptive word has one or more vowels in it. Have students list words that can describe a day, print them on a chart, and draw a circle around the vowels. Students can copy this for their journal. Here are some starters:

beautiful (e, a, u, i, u)   exciting (e, i, i)
wonderful (o, e, u)   magnificent (a, i, i, e)

See My "Colorful Cauliflower Clothes" *(A, E, I, O, U)*

Vowels are everywhere and we can't print words without them. We can take notice of them in the clothes and the colors that we're wearing. Have students come up with a list that describes the clothing they're wearing. Print them on the chalkboard and have children circle the vowels. Do some vowels appear to "work harder" than others? Here are some to get you started.

polka-dot sweater (o, a, o, e, a, e)   red sweatshirt (e, e, a, i)
green skirt (e, e, i)   yellow socks (e, o, o)
brown shoes (o, o, e)   striped dress (i, e, e)
bluegreen pants (u, e, e, e, a)   purple jumper (u, e, u, e)

It's a Cauliflower World *(A, E, I, O, U)*

The truth is that vowels do double duty in our language. You can list the continents, the 50 states, the names of flowers, the names of birds, the titles of books, the name of your school, the names of family members, and everyone's first and last names—you'll find the same five letters again and again.

The sooner students learn that they will meet these letters repeatedly, the more comfortable they will be when they see them. The vowels will be addressed each month because they are affected by other letters and make more sounds than just two. They play an important part in the reading and writing world.

How the Vegetables Learned to Read, or "Let's Hear It for the Cabbage Heads!" *(Read-aloud story rhyme)*

Read this again and again. Record it on a cassette tape so that students can hear it, learn it, and get the message that they need to learn to read. They can make up motions to go with the rhythm. (**Note:** Cauliflower and brussel sprouts are members of the cabbage family.)

One night, a cauliflower
  rolled into town
In a brand new shiny car.

It was green and white
  and glowed by the light
Of the moon that gleamed from afar.

The carrots were jealous,
  eggplants purple with rage,
'Cause that cauliflower could actually read
  every printed word on a page.

Yes, sir! Every printed word on a page.

The tomatoes were mean,
  their faces got red.
They shouted, "You're nothing
  but a, but a . . . cabbage head!"

The cauliflower sighed,
  "Well, that might be,
But why does that make
  you dislike me?"

The burly broccoli, strong and big,
  said, "Listen here, cats, he's cool. You dig?
He's got the skills that we all need . . .
  This cabbage head knows how to read!"

And so the vegetables got wise.
  They learned their ABC's,
They practiced reading every day.
  The celery stalks were pleased.

The cauliflower will help you, too,
  but you must do your part.
Practice reading every day,
  Learn the ABC's by heart.

"Cauliflower" uses all the vowels—
  A, E, I, O, U.
Some long, some short, some odd sounds, too.
  Now there's a tip for you!

Yes, soon you'll be reading,
  like the brussel sprouts, who said,
"Well, I can tell, it feels just swell
  to be a cabbage head."

Yes, sir. A well-read cabbage head.
Uh, humm!
An A-plus cabbage head.

READING LINKS TO HOLIDAYS & SPECIAL EVENTS

It's Fire Safety Week!

During this month there are various ways to make students aware of the dangers of fire. October presents an opportunity to take a field trip to a local fire station where students meet a fire-fighter, see the huge truck, and listen to the advice of the fire-fighter. If this is possible for your classroom, remember the follow up thank-you letter. This can be written, as a class, on large paper that is usually used for the experience chart stories. This gives students an opportunity to make pictures with red crayons along the edges. *Use a red felt-tip pen for the print.*

Introduce the words "Stop, Drop, Roll." Print them in 6-inch letters on the chalkboard. Have children get quiet and act out the words. It's not a time for gaiety; this is serious business.

Some communities are now having a Sunday Open House at the fire station. This provides an opportunity for children and their families to visit. Perhaps one could be arranged for your classroom. Discuss it with the principal and see if it is possible to include all of the primary classrooms.

Fire Reporting

Using a disconnected dial or push-button phone, teach children, or review for them, the purpose of "911." Then have a toy telephone available and demonstrate the appropriate procedure for reporting a fire.

Children need to learn that this number is used *only for an emergency*. They can practice saying their name, where they live (address), and the problem. Have a class checklist available, so that each student actually does go through this process early in the month.

Special Picture Books That Address "Fire"

I'm Going to Be a Fire Fighter by Edith Kunhardt helps children learn what it's like to do this work. Another is *Fire Fighters* by Norma Simon, with pictures by Pam Paparone.

Fire Drill Practice . . . Walk, Don't Run

You don't have to wait until a school fire drill to practice one—you can do it before and the day after, so that the class is alert and ready. Remind students that the primary aim of the fire drill is to get out of the building in record time while they walk swiftly and carefully. They do not go back for anything, they do not put anything away, they line up as quickly as possible, and they go to their designated place (check with the office regarding where your class should be located).

Take along your attendance book or cards. When at the designated area, call out each student's name as quickly as possible and have each answer, "Here." Then count to make sure all are present.

Make sure students know what to do if they are in the lavatory or another room of the school building when a fire bell rings. Are they near a different exit? How do they locate the class? What is the procedure for your particular school (or class)?

Students can draw a picture of the fire drill experience, take it home, and discuss it with their families. Then, encourage them to determine a drill routine at home.

"Exit" Here

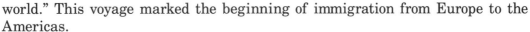

Chances are children have walked under many "exit" signs and are unaware of them. In case of fire, this is invaluable information. For an "October Exit Detective" experience, have students be on the alert for exit signs (environmental print) and tell where they find them. For example, where is the nearest exit sign at the movie theater? Where is it at the mall? Where else do they see the neon sign or the printed word "EXIT?" How many can they spot? (See Reproducible Activity Pages.)

Columbus Sailed the Ocean Blue in 1492

The fact remains that Christopher Columbus—with his ships and crew—did sail from the area that we now call Spain and landed in the Americas. From the European point of view, it was a new world. To the natives who lived here, of course, it was not new at all. In the days of Columbus, the country that "ruled the sea" did in fact "rule the world." This voyage marked the beginning of immigration from Europe to the Americas.

There are many picture books on Columbus that present the story from varying viewpoints. Two that you might want to consider are *A Picture Book of Christopher Columbus* by David A. Adler and *Columbus* by Ingri and Edgar Parin d'Aulaire. *Encounter,* by Jane Yolen, offers a different perspective.

Today's Explorers Are Star Sailors

The men and women who engage in Earth's space programs are today's explorers. They are delving into unknown territory—that is, unknown to Planet Earth.

Print the word "astronaut" on the chalkboard. Explain that *astro* means *star,* and *naut* means *sailor.* Today's explorers could be called "star sailors."

Contrast today's explorers with those of the days of Columbus in terms of how they travel, necessary clothing, and food.

Do space explorers ever get homesick? Read aloud *Commander Toad and the Voyage Home* by Jane Yolen, with pictures by Bruce Degen. The crew of Star Warts is thinking longingly of home, but something happens first.

Would You Like to Be a Star Sailor?

Make a large chart in the shape of a spaceship and print that question at the top. Draw a line down the middle of the chart. Print YES at the top of one column and NO at the top of the second column. Interview the students individually to see if they would go, or not go, and why.

Print their name under the appropriate heading with a brief description of their response. Then discuss the responses given by the group members.

Some children say *no* because "I don't want to miss my birthday." Others say *yes* because "I think it would be higher up than an airplane." Display the chart so that children can read it in their spare time. (Be sure to include the results in your newsletter to parents. A headline, for example, might be "Room 25 says YES to Neptune Visit.")

United Nations Day

The United Nations (UN) headquarters building is located in New York City. This organization has representatives from governments all over the world. Its aim is world peace. The UN has many committees, one of which is called UNICEF (United Nations International Children's Emergency Fund). This fund was set up to help children all over the world who are hungry or in need of clothing. Some children who go trick-or-treating at Halloween often take a UNICEF collection box with them. Does this happen in your school? Could it?

Happy Halloween!

"Trick or treat" is the familiar cry we hear on Halloween from children dressed up masquerading as ghosts, goblins, and other scary or fascinating creatures. Today it is a day for fun! Years ago it was a celebration that was associated with a religious holiday. The Halloween colors are orange and black, and the grinning jack-o'-lantern comes in all shapes and sizes. The Irish  brought this holiday to the United States. In Ireland, they didn't have pumpkins; instead they used gourds and hollowed-out beets to light their way on this dark night. The light served as a protection.

In Mexico, this holiday is referred to as the "Day of the Dead," a day in which families go to the graves of their ancestors to clean them and tend to the plantings. The families leave breads and other tasty treats for the departed relatives who are said to come back to visit on that night. At the end of the celebration—when the cemetery has been cleaned—the families open their baskets, spread their tablecloths on the ground, and have a meal in memory of their ancestors.

Halloween Rubaiyat

One familiar theme associated with Halloween stories is that of the haunted house. You will enjoy reading the *House of Boo* by J. Patrick Lewis, with illustrations by Katya Krenina. This story, done in rhyme, is called a *Rubaiyat*. This Halloween poem links the stanzas, which means that *the third line's end word is the major rhyme in the following stanza.* Robert Frost's "Stopping by Woods on a Snowy Evening" uses the very same rhyme format: AABA, BBCB, CCDC, etc.

First, read the book for enjoyment. Then, go back over the format and the rhyming words so that students will see that the author worked to get them to fit this pattern. Can they anticipate what the major rhyming words will sound like on the next page? (Example: *First stanza:* hill, mill, LIGHT, will (AA**B**A); *second stanza:* night, white, BOO, sight (BB**C**B); *third stanza:* new, two, ROW, blew (CC**D**C); and so on.

Halloween Music Activities

"Five Little Pumpkins"

Use hand movements to this familiar song's tune.

Five little pumpkins sitting on a gate *(hold up five fingers)*
The first one said, "Oh my, it's getting late." *(wiggle thumb)*
The second one said, "There are witches in the air." *(wiggle forefinger)*
The third one said, "But I don't care." *(wiggle middle finger)*
The fourth one said, "Let's run and run and run." *(wiggle fourth finger)*
The fifth one said, "Get ready for some fun." *(wiggle little finger)*

But, "ooooooOOOOOOO," went the wind.
And out *(clap hands)* went the light.
And the five little pumpkins, rolled out of sight. *(make circular motion with
    hand, over and over)*

"Five Little Mice"

Use the same tune and hand movements as for "Five Little Pumpkins" for this next verse.

Five little kittens sitting on a gate
The first one said, "Oh my, it's getting late."
The second one said, "There are mice by the gate."
The third one said, "I'd like one on my plate."

The fourth one said, "Let's run and catch the mice."
The fifth one said, "Now wouldn't that would be nice."

Repeat refrain.

"Five Little Witches"

Use the same tune and hand movements as for "Five Little Pumpkins" for this third verse.

Five little witches sitting on a gate
The first one said, "Oh my, it's getting late."
The second one said, "There are goblins in the air."
The third one said, "There are cobwebs in my hair."
The fourth one said, "I think I hear the bats."
The fifth one said, "Let's go and hide the cats."

Repeat refrain.

READING LINKS TO WRITING

Using Picture Books for Writing

Many picture books for the young learner are being printed that show the function and value of letter writing. One book to use this month is *Dear Mr. Blueberry* by Simon James. Emily thinks she saw a whale in her backyard pond and writes to the teacher for whale information. The story is in the form of correspondence back and forth between the student and teacher.

Dear Brother by Frank Asch and Vladimir Vagin connects the reading and writing process. Marvin and Joey find a packet of letters sent between their country mouse and city mouse ancestors, and learn about their family's past.

Other ways to use picturebooks for writing are: have students write their own ending to the story; change a last line in the story; or write a descriptive phrase or sentence of something that is shown in an illustration on the page but not mentioned in the story.

You might also use beginning information picture books. Have students explore the books, noting the pictures or photographs as well as the text, and then write a sentence about the book. This can be illustrated as well.

Writing Letters to Classmates

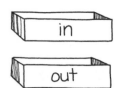

Children can write their own letters back and forth to each other in the classroom. Have an "in" and an "out" basket appropriately labeled. The "in" basket contains new letters, notes, or—in some cases—scribbles and pictures (student's beginning of correspondence) to be answered. The "out" basket contains the notes that have been answered. Students may need to get together to verbally help each other read the messages.

Letter Formations

In the Writing Center, have several laminated copies of alphabet letters so that students can practice by printing on top of the letters, using water-based colored pens. These can be wiped off and the copies used repeatedly. (See Reproducible Activity Pages for letter formation pages.)

Trace and Copy Letter Names

Print a copy of each student's name on lined paper. Laminate it. Keep these together in a container at your writing center or station. Students can locate their own name, trace it, and learn to print it. They can practice other names as well. (If they don't know the name, they are still getting practice with letter formation.)

Classroom management tip: If a child says, "That's my name!" when someone else is tracing it, listen to the tone of the voice. If they seem unhappy, assure the child that it is indeed his or her name and that he or she is being a good writing assistant by sharing the name. Encourage the child to join in. On the other hand, some children are pleased to note that their name is being traced by a classmate, and can be praised for their cooperative attitude.

Boo! Orange, Gray, Yellow, and Green Shapes for Writing

Encourage story writing on different colored papers that are cut into Halloween holiday shapes. Make a circular pumpkin shape in orange; a witch hat shape in dark gray; a cat shape in yellow; a ghost shape in green. Use orange and black felt-tip pens to enrich the experience.

Halloween Picture Books

Children enjoy hearing these fanciful stories; the illustrations are fun to look at, too. These kindle children's imagination for rich story writing of their own, and are reflected in their illustrations. Here are some to get you started: *Wobble the Witch Cat* by Mary Calhoun in which the cat is named Wobble because he shakes while riding through the skies on the witch's broom, hanging on for dear life. This is a reassuring tale because it shows that even a witch's cat can be afraid. Students can get some exercise after this by standing up and "shaking out" their fears.

Other books include *The Witch's Pig* by Mary Calhoun, with illustrations by Lady McCrady; *Which Witch Is Witch?* by Pat Hutchins; *Alice Nizzy Nazzy, The Witch of Santa Fe* by Tony Johnston, with illustrations by Tomie dePaola; *Wombat Stew* by Marcia Vaughn, an Australian tale that will inspire many recipes for this time of year; and *Arthur's Halloween* by Marc Brown. *The Little*

Old Lady Who Was Not Afraid of Anything by Linda Williams, with pictures by Megan Lloyd, inspires writing, storytelling, and reenactment of the story with real props.

Let's Write Spooky Stories and Recipes

Have the Halloween picture books on display after you read them so that students can examine them and spell certain words that appear in the books. A giant pumpkin shape made from construction paper and hung on the wall with "Halloween words" printed on as children request them can also help. Here is a starter list for your pumpkin wall:

abracadabra	spider webs	witch
pumpkin patch	boo	black cat
full moon	scarecrow	haunted house

Students can create not only stories, but rhymes, riddles, and recipes after listening to them. Read aloud to the children this month to help enrich their imagination and holiday writing. They can have a rich Rebus experience with this holiday writing as well.

Create the Atmosphere

Turn out the overhead lights and read aloud by holding a giant flashlight on the book! This makes for very good listeners who become writers, readers, and artists.

READING LINKS TO MATH

The Big Bright Calendar

The October calendar can glow with a big, bright orange pumpkin shape. Using black yarn, make the grid and the letters S, M, T, W, Th, F, S. Cut pattern shapes for the dates with the AAB pattern (cat, cat, broom; or moon, moon, star).

Apple Print Graphs

When making large graphs this month, have students record their vote with an apple print.

Another idea is to bring in a white sheet of kraft paper and have students make red apple prints all over it using red tempera paint. Use this as your party tablecloth at the end of the month.

Let's Read One to Ten

Introduce the written form of the numeral symbols by making a chart show-ing the symbol, the name, and a semi-abstract picture (or dots, stars, circles) as follows. Have flash cards for numerals and number names, as well as an assort-ment of manipulative materials so that students can recreate a concrete model of the one shown here.

1	one	*
2	two	**
3	three	***
4	four	****
5	five	*****
6	six	***** *
7	seven	***** **
8	eight	***** ***
9	nine	***** ****
10	ten	***** *****

Moon Landing Math Match

Use a pizza wheel shape for the moon and divide it into ten sections. Print one number name, from one to ten, in each section. Then, get ten clip clothes-pins, and glue construction paper wings and pipe cleaner antennae on them ("outer-space creatures"). Print a single numeral, from 1 to 10, on each one. Stu-dents can clip the outer-space critters onto the appropriate spot on the wheel (for landing on the moon).

This can also be done in the reverse order. Have the numerals on the wheel and the number names on the clothespin critters.

Speaking of Tens

October is month number ten, so review all of the names of the months for the year up to the present. Have students count aloud to ten, and write the numerals from 1 to 10.

Our hands have a total of ten fingers. To reinforce the concept of ten, have students hold out both hands in front of them, palms facing down. Start with the left hand and count to five (fold in the thumb first, then the forefinger, middle finger, and so on). As they count aloud from one to ten, students can bend a fin-ger for each numeral. When they reach ten, no fingers are extended.

Challenge: Unfold fingers and count backwards from ten to one. People have counted on their fingers for centuries. The term *digit* means number as well as finger.

Math Center Focus on Tens

Remember that nothing new is introduced in the Math Center. It is an op-portunity for review, reinforcement, and enrichment. Young students work best with manipulative items, but they do need a structured math program.

- Have a number of objects for counting in the Math Center. These can be purchased, or ask parents to send in items. Some counters include buttons, paper clips, pompons, pebbles, tiny seashells, leaves, and so on.
- Have flash cards from 1 through 10 on the table, face down. Students can turn over a card and count out the number of objects that represent that numeral. They can put these along a number line if that is helpful. Young students need repeated practice with this activity.

Numerals and Phonics

Print the numeral names from one through ten. Then take a look at the word, the beginning letter, and the sound that the letter makes (for example, two—t). You will find that from one through ten, all but two of the numeral names follow the beginning sound rules (that's 80 percent). (One and eight are exceptions.)

Pumpkin Seed Estimation

An estimate is a "best guess." Cut a rim around the top of a medium-size pumpkin (only you or another adult should handle the knife and then put it away). Children can help scoop out the insides, which contain the pulp and the seeds. Wash and rinse the seeds and put them on paper toweling to dry. Count them. Record the number and keep both seeds and pumpkin on display.

Next, bring in several pumpkins of varying sizes, from tiny to large, and line them up on the table. Have children lift them, handle them, and estimate how many seeds they contain. Have a blank sheet available for each pumpkin (number them) so students can print their name and their seed estimate.

On the appointed day, cut open the pumpkins (again, only you or another adult should handle the knife and then put it away). Repeat the procedure for scooping and counting. Help students to assess their estimation skills. What strategies did students use? Discuss this so students can learn from each other.

What Else Can We Estimate?

Try weather. "Let's say we've had six sunny days in a row. Do you predict sun or rain or _____ for tomorrow?" Record the information and check it the next day.

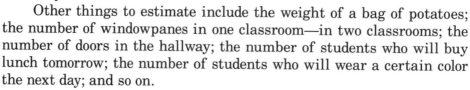

Other things to estimate include the weight of a bag of potatoes; the number of windowpanes in one classroom—in two classrooms; the number of doors in the hallway; the number of students who will buy lunch tomorrow; the number of students who will wear a certain color the next day; and so on.

Let's Read Aloud Some Good Math Picture Books

The Butterfly Counting Book by Jerry Pallotta, with pictures by Mark Astrella, has lovely pictures and counts by two's. Others include *1,2,3 to the Zoo* by Eric Carle; *Anno's Counting Book* by Mitsumasa Anno; *Inch by Inch* by Leo

Lionni; *Animal Numbers* by Bert Kitchen; and *We're Going on a Bear Hunt* by Michael Rosen, with illustrations by Helen Oxenbury.

READING LINKS TO SOCIAL STUDIES

Time to Learn About Our Pets!

Many students have a pet, or are familiar with pets in their own environment. Often, this depends upon where they live. A country environment and a city environment mean that we can care for a variety of pets. Encourage students to talk about their pets, the care of them, the names, and so on. Perhaps they can bring in photographs to share and display on a corner of the bulletin board. For students who do not have pets, ask them what city pet or country pet they might like to have some day.

A Closer Look at Cats

This is a good time to investigate pet cats, since the Halloween cat appears in newspapers, magazines, and highlighted stories this month. A cat, although independent, requires care and love for a long life.

Compare Yourself to a Cat

- *Teeth*. How many teeth are in a person's mouth? (Have students count their upper and lower teeth by running their tongue over them, not by using fingers.) How many are in the cat's mouth? (32) Cats need a mixed diet of soft and crisp (or hard) dry food, so that their teeth remain clean. How do people keep their teeth healthy and clean? *(By visiting the dentist, and by brushing and flossing daily)*

- *Sleep*. Cats require about sixteen hours of sleep per day! How many hours of sleep are we getting at night? What time do we go to bed? For primary-age children, the recommended sleep time is between 10–12 hours per night. (Be sure parents have that information in your newsletter.)

- *Coat*. A cat has two coats of fur: the fluffy undercoat and the regular overcoat. People have skin, not fur. But we can wear fur coats—preferably fake fur, except in areas where there is an abundance of animals and where people need the fur to survive during long, cold winters.

- *Sight/Sound*. A cat sees better than people, especially in the dark. A cat can hear sounds that people do not hear. They can hear you coming from a long distance.

Find information books on the cat at the library. Read storybooks about cats. Then, on paper cut into cat shapes, write a story about a pet cat or a storybook cat.

Cat Sayings

There are many sayings about cats. This exercise will aid in language development, as some children may not have heard these sayings. Here are some to get started. Discuss their meanings. A book of *Aesop's Fables* would be helpful here, as many of our sayings come from lessons learned in stories:

Curiosity killed the cat.

A cat has nine lives.

When the cat's away, the mice will play.

You are playing cat and mouse with me.

You're the cat's pajamas!

Cats and Dogs, Too!

It has been said that cats and dogs are enemies, not friends. Yet, they have been known to live side by side in the same household without any problems. Cats and dogs are the two most popular pets in our households. All dogs are descended from wolves, and the pet cats are related to the jungle cats. How many children in the class have pet dogs? Who would like to have a pet dog? What kind of dog?

Some Dogs Go to Work

Some dogs help us. There are Seeing-Eye dogs for the visually impaired and police dogs that sniff for the scent of missing people or sniff luggage at airports for goods that are being illegally transported. The Husky is a dog of the north that pulls sleds and helps with hunting. Farm dogs can do the work of many people; for example, the Australian kelpie helps round up sheep. In some countries, such as Costa Rica, guard dogs are chained to the rooftop to protect a home. These dogs are generally well cared for by the owners, but are ferocious when burglars come around.

Get information books about dogs at the library so that students can study the various breeds.

Some Dogs Go to School

For the dog who is having difficulty obeying its master's command, obedience school is often the answer. The dog learns to take commands such as "Sit," "Stay," and "Down." The owner, on the other hand, learns to be consistent in his or her signals to the dog.

Dogs aim to please, but they need to be well treated. They require good food daily and fresh water. They need to go outdoors at regular times. They like to be petted and brushed. They also like to see you coming home from school to greet them.

Have a discussion about dog care and gentle treatment of animals. Dogs, like people, know when they are loved.

Dog Sayings

Many sayings about dogs have crept into our language. We use them every day without giving them much thought. Again, many originate from fables, such as *Aesop's Fables*. For starters, say these, and talk about their meanings:

These are the dog days of summer.

It's a dog's life.

Going to the dogs!

Hot dog!

It's raining cats and dogs.

Comic Book Dogs and Cats

Many of the "funny papers"—or the comics section of the newspaper—have cat and dog characters. Have students cut these out, bring them to class, and introduce them to their classmates. This is an excellent opportunity for a student to give oral interpretation of a picture and text that usually contains humor. Put these in the Writing Center for inspiration.

Picture Books About Dog and Cat Characters

Using animals rather than people in picture books can teach much-needed lessons. They may also be read solely for the enjoyment of a good story!

Some good read-aloud books about cats are: *Horace* by Holly Keller, which deals with a spotted cat that is adopted by a striped cat family and doesn't feel like it belongs; *Mouse, Look Out!* by Judy Waite, with illustrations by Norma Burgin; *Come Out and Play, Little Mouse* by Robert Kraus, with pictures by Jose Aruego and Ariane Dewey; and the multi-ethnic *Mrs. Katz and Tush* by Patricia Pollaco.

Some good read-aloud books about dogs are: the *Spot the Dog* series by Eric Hill, such as *Spot's Baby Sister* and *Spot Goes to a Party*; *The First Dog* by Jan Brett; *Maxi, the Taxi Dog* and *Maxi, the Hero* by Debra and Sal Barracca, with pictures by Mark Buehner; and *Officer Buckle and Gloria* by Peggy Rathbun.

READING LINKS TO SCIENCE & HEALTH

It's Apple-Pickin' Time

Many students will be bringing apples to school for snack time because it is a healthy and delicious snack.

- *Color.* Let's compare apples. Have each student bring in an apple and note the color. Some are bright red, or yellow, or green, while others have a variety of these colors. Classify the apples by color. Put clean kraft paper on the floor and make an apple graph by lining up the apples vertically by color. Discuss this. How many of each? How can we make a picture of this? First demonstrate it using chart paper and crayons; then have students copy the information on a sheet of paper by forming vertical rows of colored apples. (They are going from concrete information to semi-concrete information, and are using symbols.) Students can print a title on their graph paper and print color names below.

- *Shape.* Some apples are round and elongated; some are round and pudgy; some are oval. When apples are put on a flat surface, some roll over and look lopsided. Since the children have had experience with making an apple graph by color, now they can get the kraft paper and put the apples on by shape, using the procedure mentioned above. Have students read the graph.

How Do You Like Your Apples?

List the many ways that apples can be made into different types of food, and have children note their favorite. For starters, there are apple pie, apple strudel, dried apple chips, apple cake, applesauce, apple butter, apple-flavored candies and

and ice cream, caramel apples, apple juice, and apple cider. Make apple-shape books with a stem shape on the top for a flip-top book. Use red, green, and yellow construction paper for the pages. Staple several pages together and students can draw and label their favorite apple treats. Then they can read their books.

Two good picture books about apples are *The Apple Pie Tree* by Zoe Hall, with pictures by Shari Halpern, and *Johnny Appleseed* by Aliki. For enjoyment, read aloud a fairy-tale favorite, *Snow White and the Seven Dwarfs,* to see the major role that an apple plays in this story.

If I Could Name an Apple, What Would It Be?

Apples have a wide variety of names. Some names refer to the place where they are grown, some are named after people, and some are named because of the way they look or taste. How do students think "Red Delicious" got its name?

The Baldwin and McIntosh apples are named after people who grew them. Other interesting names include Granny Smith, Jonathan, Rome Beauty, Cortland, Winesap, Northern Spy, and Ida Red. Ask students to be on the alert for names of apples in the grocery store.

If students could name an apple, what would it be? Have them cut out the apple shape on red, yellow, green (or another color) construction paper and print the name on it. Make a bushel basket shape from brown construction paper for the bulletin board, and pile the apples high.

We're Thirsty! Let's "Drink" an Apple

Apples are over 80 percent water! So pass out the apples, eat them, and feel refreshed and healthy. Have students notice that they are juicy and moist, not dry.

Demonstrate the concept of 80 percent by drawing a circle on the chalkboard. Then draw a line down the middle vertically and shade in half of the apple. Next, draw a line across the middle horizontally, and shade in one half of that, *plus* a little more. This visual picture makes the concept of 80 percent more understandable to the young learner.

The Science of Apple Growing

If you live in a part of the country where apples are grown, taking a trip to an apple orchard provides a good experience for seeing how apples are grown, learning about tree care, grafting, and the care of apples.

Some orchards, such as Lynd's near Columbus, Ohio, maintain an area of antique apple varieties. For example, Benjamin Franklin's favorite apple, called "Newton's Pippin," can be found there along with the "Lowery Sweet," cultivated in the state of Virginia in 1750 by George Washington's Uncle Lowery . Did you know that apples are still being developed? At Rutgers University in New Jersey, a new apple called "Sun Crisp" is a recent addition—and it's a bestseller.

An Orchard of Follow-Up Language Activities

After a trip to the orchard, there is much interest in reading about apples, making an experience chart story about the visit, writing thank-you letters, and planning and making a giant class mural of the day's event on which printed sentences describing the action taking place can be taped. You might want to have the students make the mural using only black, green, and red paints on a white background for a striking visual effect that spotlights the color red.

Bring on the Leaves and Nuts

It's time to note the changing colors of leaves from green to red, orange, yellow, tan. Encourage students to bring in pretty leaves that they find on their way to and from school, and at home in their yard. Display them.

Classify the leaves by shape. What are the leaf names that are familiar to your area of the country? Label them.

Also encourage students to bring samples of nuts that they find on the ground at this time of year. City students who may not have this opportunity as apartment dwellers will see, touch, and count acorns, chestnuts, buckeyes, and so on.

Autumn Pen-Pals

If you live in an area of the country that does not have nuts and beautiful leaves in abundance, this could provide a good opportunity for letter writing to a school far away with a request for samples. Check with the librarian or other teachers for addresses.

It's Harvest Time

Clear an area in your Science Center to make room for the abundance of pumpkins, squash, and other items that are harvested at this time of year. These can be brought in throughout October and November. (Also see November.)

Create an Apple Tree in the Classroom

Bring in a huge tree branch that has been rescued from the ground in a nearby park or wooded area. If this is not possible, create a tree on the bulletin board by using scrunched up brown kraft paper for trunk and limbs.

Students can make giant-sized red apples from construction paper and hang them from the tree with a bright green string. What's the occasion? It's just that time of year when apples need to be recognized for their nourishment value.

LINKS TO
AUTHOR-OF-THE-MONTH

Author/Illustrator for October:
Lois Ehlert

You and the children have a treat in store this month with the works of this author, who has several books on growing vegetables. If you're studying bird migration this month, you won't want to miss *Feathers for Lunch,* and *Nuts to You* is an excellent autumn book about squirrels.

All month you can enjoy the bright, bold colors in these picture books. Lois Ehlert uses collage, which means "to stick." She cuts shapes and puts the colors together in such a way that they look like paintings. You and your students can gain many ideas about making books from this author.

Let's take a look at some of the books by Lois Ehlert. Several of her books have Spanish text along with the English version, and the illustrations are influenced by pre-Columbian art. The students are in for a visual treat. *Let's read!*

Circus (New York: HarperCollins, 1992) This is made to look like a smaller book within a larger book, as if we're entering a big circus tent. The endpapers are colorful stars. Once the circus begins, we see many daring acts, and are treated to a visual display and colorful language. We take time for intermission, more circus acts, and then are invited to applaud at the end. Great show!

Activities to Accompany *Circus*

1. After reading the book, go back over it page by page to be reintroduced to the colorful characters of Hugo, the world's biggest elephant; Princess Lydia, who rides bareback; Fritz, the wonder bear; Samu, the fierce tiger; and others.

2. Now, let's pretend to be those characters. Get in a circle and amble like Hugo the elephant; ride a prancing horse like Princess Lydia by hopping on one foot with the other foot extended behind the body; become Fritz who has excellent balance and can ride his bike around the circle on a high wire; jump through a flaming hoop like Samu the tiger. There are also more opportunities for exercise and movement.

3. *Pucker up!* Bertha the parrot can whistle "Twinkle, Twinkle Little Star," so let's join her. Ready? Whistle the tune.

4. *A bright painting experience.* These illustrations are bright and bold, so let's take a good look at them. Have bright fluorescent-type colors at the easel for a week this month. Paint on any bold-color background except white or light gray.

5. On the first page of *Circus,* we only see the red–orange and blue–green stripes of the animal's tail. At the easel, or on large sheets of paper, have students outline and paint the rest of this striped cat.

   You might also have students make a black outline of a big cat. Have many paper strips of bright orange and vivid blue available, so that students can cut them and paste them on to fit the cat. (They may want to use two other colors, instead.) Get some ideas for shapes by taking a close look at Samu, the world's fiercest tiger.

6. Snack time can be called "intermission" after reading this book. Maybe a popcorn treat would be enjoyable today, especially during indoor recess.

7. Have children talk about their own experiences at the circus. Write about them. Draw the act that most appealed to them, and share it with the group.

Color Farm (Philadelphia: J.B. Lippincott, 1990) Children enjoy looking through this peek-through book's different shapes to view the animal on the next page. The book has a formula: Look through the shapes on three pages to discover the animal or bird face, and then on the fourth page the shapes are highlighted and named. Then this four-page sequence is repeated several times. (A good teaching book for colors and shapes that is done in a unique way.)

Activities to Accompany *Color Farm*

1. Go through the book and enjoy the colors, shapes, and design. Then return to the beginning. With this book it is important to show students how to turn the page—by the edges, *not* by poking fingers in the hole in the middle of the page, because it can tear the book.

2. As Lois Ehlert suggests, have students cut shapes and make some animals of their own, or recreate ones that are in the book.

3. On a 9″ × 12″ sheet of construction paper, cut out a shape that you can see through. Then have students create an animal around that shape. One day it can be a circle; then try a square, rectangle, oval, hexagon, and other shapes in the book.

4. Students can make a "My Little Shape Book." Use the information that is on the left page (or go through the book from back to front) to get an idea of the shape. Gently run the fingertips over the shape to feel it. (*Teacher:* Cut shapes that can be available so students can trace them for their shape book.) Be sure to label the shapes. Templates can be used also to make the shapes.

5. Once students make colorful creatures from *basic shapes*, they can use the basic-shape technique all year. When a student says, for example, "I don't know how to make a bird," remind them of the basic shapes. Look at a bird and see the oval body, the round head, the triangle beak, the rectangle legs, and so on. Create a mural of these colorful animals and birds, with a focus on basic shapes.

Feathers for Lunch (New York: Harcourt, Brace & Co., 1990) This story is told in rhyme, which adds to its charm. The cat is out looking for lunch, and since cats like to catch birds, this one is on the prowl. "He's looking for lunch, something new, a spicy treat for today's menu."

We're in for a treat as we meet up with twelve birds, all positioned near the plants or bushes that attract them. All the way through we can read "Jingle, jingle" which is the sound made by the bell around the neck of the cat. So, even though we may not SEE the cat, the bell tells us that it's nearby.

Try to get the hardbound edition—colors are brighter and the book jacket has a bird checklist. Both hardcover and papercover have a detailed glossary at the end for each bird.

Activities to Accompany *Feathers for Lunch*

1. *Bird study.* This book is a must for a unit on Birds, which often comes in the autumn along with Migration, and again in the springtime when birds are building nests. Go through the book and look for familiar birds in your territory.

2. *Bird watchers.* Set up a "bird watching" area by an outdoor window. You will need a feeder (with suction cups) that attaches to the window. Or, put a feeder in a tree outdoors. You can put bird books in this indoor area along with binoculars and chairs or cushions on a rug. Make a chart so students can keep track of birds that visit during the day. (It will take about a week or two to attract some birds, so be patient, and ask students to be quiet by the window and not to make any sudden movements.) Students get caught up in the spirit of bird watching and take it seriously.

3. *A bird mural.* When birds migrate, they gather in trees. Make a mural that shows a large tree (use twisted paper bags for the knarled trunk and branches, and bright sponge paint for leaves). Students can make colorful construction paper birds from basic shapes (circles, triangles, rectangles) and attach them to the tree. For print, you can have a checklist of who is moving out and who is staying for the season. Or, print a story on large chart paper about your bird-watching station.

4. "When you are outdoors on the playground, or when you go for a walk, listen for the birds. Can you hear them? See them? What color are they? Can any be identified?" Be on the alert and use magazines and books to help with identification. At the library you can often get cassette recordings of bird calls.

Growing Vegetable Soup (New York: Harcourt, Brace & Co., 1987) Call attention to the bright, bold colors typical of this author's work. The book could be called an "adventure story" because—although a garden takes planning—planting a garden is exciting and unpredictable. We meet the necessary implements for digging and the seeds, and watch the crops grow. It's a good book for autumn, which is harvest time. We see the ripe vegetables . . . "and we can grow it again next year."

Activities to Accompany *Growing Vegetable Soup*

1. This book cries out for you to make vegetable soup in the classroom. Bring in some fresh vegetables and have the children carefully wash them. Then, you (or another adult) can cut them up and put the sharp knife away. Children can place the vegetable pieces in the soup broth inside a crock pot. Set on "high" and cook for an hour.

   You can use canned vegetable soup as the stock, and add your vegetables to this mixture. Serve in styrofoam cups or bowls.

2. *A raw harvest.* Some of the vegetables we see in Lois Ehlert's illustrations can be eaten raw. Let's look for them—tomatoes, broccoli, and carrots are some. Sounds like a good opportunity for tasting a healthy snack.

3. The author has labeled each vegetable. That means you can make a Rebus chart of the vegetables. Children can copy the word from the book and print it alongside or under the illustration, just as the author has done.

   When you finish with the chart, you can make a graph showing the vegetables. Each student can put an X above his or her favorite.

4. French fries are a by-product of the potato plant. Do students know this? "There are many ways to fix potatoes. How many do you know?" Let's list

them: mashed, boiled, fried, baked, roasted. Potato dishes include scalloped potatoes and potatoes au gratin. A potato chip snack might help the children to think as they hunt through cookbooks.

5. Make a class cookbook. Invite parents to submit favorite vegetable dish recipes on a 3 × 5 card. Photocopy them, assemble, and staple together. Students can design a cover for "Growing Favorite Vegetable Dishes." This makes a nice take-home surprise.

Mole's Hill (New York: Harcourt Brace, 1994) Mole loves her burrow, which is situated near a pond. It's safe, cozy, and underground. But Fox wants a direct route to the pond and Mole's hill is in the way, so Fox says, "It must go." Mole finds a way to make the hill even bigger, and plants grass and flowers on it. Now it's so big that even Fox is willing to compromise. Rather than remove the hill, he asks Mole to dig a tunnel through it. She is happy with the settlement.

Activities to Accompany *Mole's Hill*

1. Read the story and discuss the concept of "compromise," which is how Fox and Mole solved their problem. How can children compromise in their daily life? We simply cannot always have our own way! Suppose we start with "food compromises." (having a chicken sandwich rather than a hot dog; having lemon–orange rather than chocolate ice cream; playing a different game in school rather than your favorite, and so on)

2. Note the way the author/illustrator has depicted the passage of time, with a two-page spread of graduated moon shapes using the colors red, yellow, blue, and green. Students can create their own lunar chart for the month, using this same artful technique.

3. The story is set in Wisconsin (stated in the back of the book), so the animals used are those indigenous to that area—fox, skunk, mole, and raccoon. How would the story animals change in your area?

4. The illustrations were inspired by two art forms of the Woodland Indians (stated in the back of the book). The exact geometric patterns seen in the book are ones traced by these Native Americans onto silk ribbons, cut out, and sewn to such clothing as shirts, skirts, leggins, and borders on blankets. Have students make a page of designs inspired by the book.

5. Students can make their own mole hill at the easel, and paint the beautiful landscape in the autumn season.

6. Ask, "What does it mean when we say 'to make a mountain out of a mole hill'?" (Language development)

Top Cat (New York: Harcourt Brace, 1998) Once again, we meet up with a cat. This one thinks he's in charge of things until one day a kitten arrives in a brand new box. The story is told in rhyme; for example, "Go away, cat! You've invaded my space. And I don't like your cute little face." But once the cat accepts the new kitten, the decision is made to "break in the cat" with the work that cats need to do around the house, such as "drink from the sink when company's there, dance on the table with the silverware." These two decide in the end to "share purrs." The book is done with bold collage forms. There is little red print throughout the book that tells us what sounds are being made. (Delightful!)

Activities to Accompany *Top Cat*

1. After the book has been read and enjoyed, go through it again and this time check the little red print. You'll find many words such as *purr, thump, scratch,* and *me-ow.* Make a list of these cat words. Then, talk about a Top Dog, or a Top Bird, or a Top Fish, and make a list of words that you might hear in that book. (Vocabulary)

2. Can birds be identified by the sounds they make? Who says "jay, jay" and who sings "o-ka-lee"? Let's find some bird books for the answers. Also locate a cassette recording of bird songs from the library and listen to them. Learn to identify the songbirds in your area.

3. Note that the endpapers are cat pawprints—four toes and the oval-shaped cushion in the middle. Students can make these shapes with a stamp pad and pencil erasers to use as cat stationery at the Writing Center.

4. The cats in the book are not named. Have each student tell what name he or she would give to the cats. Can the class vote upon its favorite name? This would involve "compromise," which was mentioned earlier.

5. If this book is used in October, tell what characteristics the cats would need to have in order to qualify as a good Halloween cat.

6. On the book cover is a bright red and green mouse hanging by the tail from the cat's mouth. This is whimsical, but, in real life, cats are excellent "mousers." Students need to know that farm cats do "good work" by catching mice in the barn, because the mice would eat the grain. Today, instead of "Duck, Duck, Goose," students can sit in a circle and play the run-and-chase game of "Cat, Cat, Mouse."

7. Use basic, simple shapes and a wide variety of paper (corrugated cardboard, wallpaper, prepasted paper, wrapping paper, and construction paper) to make unusual cats to hang on the classroom door. Make a sign, too: "Top Cats in Room _____." Explain that "top cat" means the best, and everyone should strive to be the best workers, best artists, best readers, and best achievers they can.

Moon Rope, Un lazo a la luna (New York: Harcourt Brace, 1992) This story is an adaptation of a Peruvian tale. Fox wants to go to the moon, but Mole does not. The two set off with a little help from a rope of grass and some birds. Mole slips off. Does Fox make it? Some people say they can see Fox in the moon at night.

The magnificent illustrations in this book were inspired by ancient Peruvian art designs. The artist used silver, since silver was used only for beautiful things—never as a medium of exchange. Text is in both English and Spanish.

Activities to Accompany *Moon Rope, Un lazo a la luna*

1. First read and enjoy the story. Point out to the students that the text is in both English and Spanish. The Spanish text is printed in silver. Also, many of the objects are silver. Make sure the students understand that this is because the ancient people from Peru used silver for beauty. Find Peru on a world map.

2. In the hardbound edition, call attention to the striking and colorful endpapers. They are a repeat design of squares of different colors, and a diagonal cut out of "stairs" of different colors. Give your students a design experience. Start with nine or twelve squares of four colors and paste them on a page. Next, use five or six squares and cut them on the diagonal line. Then cut the straight "stair steps" on the diagonal. Place one cut diagonal on each square—mix them around until they look right to the artistic eye. Then paste. Use the endpapers as a guide, but use different colors.

3. *The feeling of a good book.* This book "feels good" to the touch. It's large and glossy. Have students enjoy the feeling of the book and turning the pages carefully. It's an aesthetic experience for them, and one to be savored.

4. This artwork is inspirational. Point out the bright red backgrounds (solid) with green figures, orange eyes, and various shapes. Students can first use art scraps to practice making some bird and animal designs of their own. Then they can make a large cut-out from glossy paper and position it on a contrasting background color.

5. The artwork in the book was inspired by designs on jewelry, vases, sculptures, textiles, and architectural detail on buildings (information in the front of the book). Students might be inspired to work with clay or paint to create art objects.

Nuts to You (New York: Harcourt Brace, 1993) The hardbound edition has a circular hole in the cover so that you can see right through to the squirrel who is hiding in the treehouse with a nut in its mouth. The story, told in rhyme, is about the activities of a busy little squirrel who brushes past window boxes, climbs up the side of a brick house, eats from the bird feeder, and eventually gets inside of the house through a tear in the screen door. What gets the squirrel out? A shout of "nuts to you!" with nuts sprinkled on the ground are irresistible. At the back of the book is a section on "Squirrel Talk" with valuable information about squirrels.

Activities to Accompany *Nuts to You*

1. Once again, as with all books by Lois Ehlert, enjoy the sheer artistry and inventiveness of the book. Open the book cover and you will see two very tiny strips in the binding that contain the title and other information. Point this out to the students. Perhaps they can incorporate a similar technique into their book-making as the year goes on.

2. How can your students make brick endpapers or a brick wall? Note the endpapers at the back of the book. There is a brown background. Then

rectangular shapes of lighter brown and brick orange pieces, splattered with black paint, are cut and arranged on the brown background. Encourage students to keep this in mind for an idea of how to make something look just like brick when doing a mural, a poster, or even endpapers.

3. After enjoying the story, have the children go back through the book and note the squirrels. They are made from cut paper that the artist has created. Students can use watercolor wash to make gray splotchy paper, or use shades of gray tempera paint applied to the paper with a sponge. Then allow the paper to dry. Plan the squirrel shape: body, head, ears, front and back legs, and the bushy tail. The body parts can either be from the same paper or different types. Students can exchange bits of paper for ears and dramatic shade changes. Cut out the shapes and arrange them on a background or glue them together and place all of the class squirrels on a big bulletin board. They can be *next to, in, on top of,* and *under* a tree shape. The board can be labeled "Nuts to You" with cut-out letters and the author's name. Save room on the board for "Squirrel Talk" chart paper, and print squirrel information from the book in this area.

4. Caution students so that they do not feed squirrels, as they are wild animals. They may appear tame because they come close to us, but they have extremely sharp claws and teeth—and they do scratch and bite. Observe busy squirrels from a distance.

5. The tail of the squirrel is quite a wonder to behold, since it serves so many purposes. It's a blanket; an umbrella in rain or sun; and a balancing rod when walking along high wires and fence tops. This just might inspire students to write tales about the squirrel and its tail—good for exercise and dramatic play.

And Many More!

Lois Ehlert has other books also. Look for *Hands,* which is all about hands and is in the shape of a hand. Children can trace their own hand several times and make their own book. *Planting a Rainbow* is a colorful book about planting a flower garden. But that's not all! Lois Ehlert has many other books that would provide excellent learning opportunities as well as joy, for children. So, be on the alert for books by Lois Ehlert. She can make a worthwhile contribution to children's visual arts attempts this month and throughout the year. We're fortunate to have this quality of work for young children to examine, explore, and enjoy.

REPRODUCIBLE ACTIVITY PAGES

Marching Band—Letter A *(April Alligator)*

Marching Band—Letter E *(Emmanuel Elephant)*

Marching Band—Letter I *(Ivan Insect)*

Marching Band—Letter O *(Olivia Octopus)*

Marching Band—Letter U *(Umbernella Unicorn)*

The Cat In The _____at Hat

Zack Is Squirreling Away Words *(ab, ack, an, ake)*

Word Family Holiday *(ig, ell, ink, op, ut)*

Look for Exit Signs

ABC Blast Off!

Become a Vowel Detective

Cabbage Head Reading Chant

Children's Literature Activity Page—Create a Spanish Mola Design
   (Lois Ehlert)

© DCW 99

© 2000 by The Center for Applied Research in Education

Aa

© 2000 by The Center for Applied Research in Education

© 2000 by The Center for Applied Research in Education

© 2000 by The Center for Applied Research in Education

© DCW99

© 2000 by The Center for Applied Research in Education

Name _____

The Cat in the __at Hat

This cat wants to fill up her hat with words that rhyme with <u>cat</u> and <u>hat</u>. How many words can you make?

_____at

_____at   _____at

_____at   _____at

_____at

_____at   _____at

_____at   _____at

© 2000 by The Center for Applied Research in Education

Name _____

Zack is Squirreling Away Words

Zack likes words that rhyme. Help him hide four words in each word family. backpack. He can dig them up and use them all winter.

Zack's Backpack Service

© 2000 by The Center for Applied Research in Education

ab

_____ ab
_____ ab
_____ ab
_____ ab

ack

_____ ack
_____ ack
_____ ack
_____ ack

an

_____ an
_____ an
_____ an
_____ an

ake

_____ ake
_____ ake
_____ ake
_____ ake

@DCW99

Name _____

Word Family Holiday

These five word families - ig, ell, ink, op and ut are going on a trip. How many words can you help them pack into each suitcase?

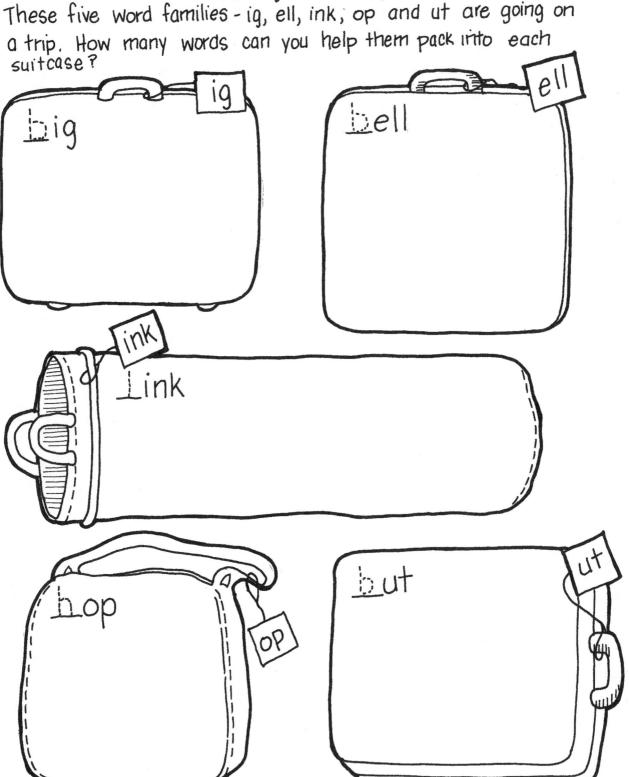

big

ig

bell

ell

ink

Link

hop

op

but

ut

© 2000 by The Center for Applied Research in Education

Name _____

Look for EXIT Signs

Fire Prevention Week is in October. Winfield Bear wants you to locate EXIT signs.

In the spaces below, show where you found an EXIT sign.

1 school

2 school bus

3 _____

4 _____

© 2000 by The Center for Applied Research in Education

Name _____

ABC BLAST OFF!

This space shuttle is ready to blast off. First, the explorer must write his ABC's in the correct squares. Can you help? Use your pencil and work slowly.

© 2000 by The Center for Applied Research in Education

Name _____

BECOME A VOWEL DETECTIVE

Sam Sparrow is looking for
missing vowels (a, e, i, o, u).
You can help. Print the appropriate
letter on the spaces below.
Sam says "Thank you."

1. __ct__b__r
   This is the name of a month.

2. T____sd__y
   This is a day of the week.

3. n____n
   This is a time of day.

4. s__n
   This is a weather word.

These are number names:

tw__   s__v__n

f__v__   __n__

____ght   n__n__

© 2000 by The Center for Applied Research in Education

CABBAGE HEAD READING CHANT

One night a cauliflower
   rolled into town
In a brand new shiny car.

It was green and white
   and glowed by the light
Of the moon that gleamed from afar.

The carrots were jealous
   eggplants purple with rage
'Cause that cauliflower could actually read
   every printed word on a page.

YES, SIR! Every printed word on a page.

The tomatoes were mean
   their faces got red.
They shouted, "You're nothing
   but a, but a . . . cabbage head!"

The cauliflower sighed,
   "Well that might be,
But why does that make
   you dislike me?"

The burly broccoli, strong and big
Said, "Listen here, cats, he's cool. You dig?
He's got the skills that we all need.
This cabbage head knows how to read!"

© 2000 by The Center for Applied Research in Education

And so the vegetables got wise. They learned their ABC's,
They practiced reading every day. The celery stalks were pleased.

The cauliflower will help you, too
   but you must do your part.
Practice reading every day.
   Learn the ABC's by heart.

"Cauliflower" uses all the vowels—
   A, E, I, O, U.
Some long, some short, some odd sounds too.
   Now there's a tip for you!

© 2000 by The Center for Applied Research in Education

Yes, soon you'll be reading,
   like the brussel sprouts who said,
"Well, I can tell, it feels just swell
   to be a cabbage head."

YES, SIR! A Well-read cabbage head. UH, HUMM! An A plus cabbage head!

Name _____

CREATE A SPANISH MOLA DESIGN

Lois Ehlert, author and illustrator, writes many of her books in English and Spanish and likes pre-Columbian art. Here is a stitched mola design of a gato (cat). Molas consist of many layers, and often only a rim of color can be seen.

Color each rim a different color. Then use layers of construction paper designs and glue them onto the gato (cat).

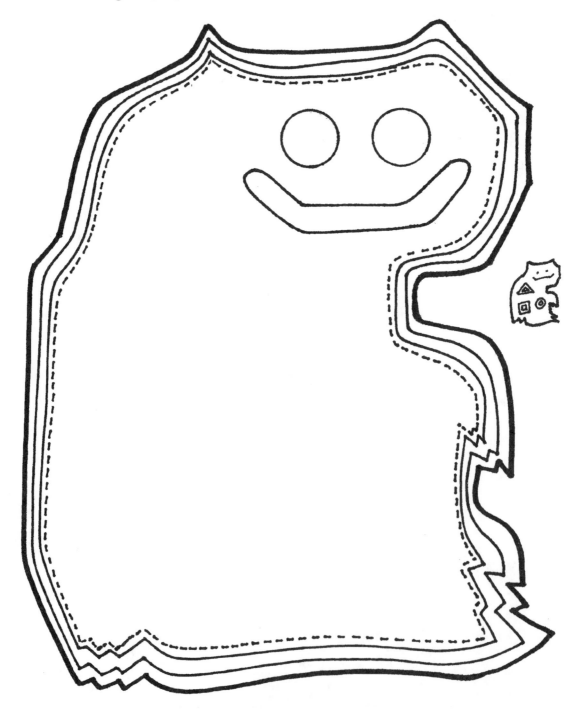

After practicing on this page, use felt and glue, or stitches, to make a cloth mola.

© 2000 by The Center for Applied Research in Education

CHILDREN'S PICTURE BOOKS

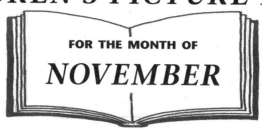

FOR THE MONTH OF
NOVEMBER

Brenner, Barbara. *Group Soup.* **Illustrated by Lynn Munsinger (New York: Viking, 1992)** This story on values is one in a series from the Bank Street College of Education. Hungry rabbits hurry home for dinner only to find out that Mama Rabbit has been called away and they have to collaborate to make the soup. (Reminiscent of other soup tales such as *Stone Soup.*)

Bruchac, Joseph. *The Circle of Thanks: Native American Poems and Songs of Thanksgiving.* **Illustrations by Murv Jacob (New York: BridgeWater, 1996)** This is a collection of poems retold by Abenaki writer Bruchac, and illustrated by Cherokee painter Jacob. The book contains additional information about the poems and the culture from which it originates.

Brusca, Maria Cristina and Tona Wilson. *When Jaguars Ate the Moon: And Other Stories About Animals and Plants of the Americas* **(New York: Henry Holt, 1995)** A collection of folktales that are native to the Americas. The book is arranged alphabetically by plants and animals—from anteater to zompopo. Many of the animals will be unfamiliar, so you may have to hunt down some information in the library once you get a look at the watercolor illustrations.

Cook, Joe. *The Rat's Daughter* **(Honesdale, PA: Boyds Mills Press, Inc., 1995)** Who could possibly be worthy enough to marry the daughter of the elegant Father and Mother Rat? In a retold version of an old tale, the search is on.

Cowley, Joy. *Gracias, the Thanksgiving Turkey.* **Illustrated by Joe Cepeda (New York: Scholastic, 1996)** Miguel has a special attachment to Gracias, a turkey that makes it to the Thanksgiving table—but not as the main course! This humorous story about a loving Latino family is set in New York, and intermingles well-known Spanish words and expressions.

Goble, Paul. *Iktomi and the Coyote, A Plains Indian Story* **(New York: Orchard Books, 1998)** Coyote is outwitted once again when this trickster convinces a pack of prairie dogs to line up for dinner—but he intends the pack to be his dinner. Also in this series are *Iktomi and the Ducks, Iktomi and the Buffalo Skull, Iktomi and the Buzzard,* and many more. This can be an author/Native American study in itself for November.

Keller, Holly. *The New Boy* **(New York: Greenwillow, 1991)** The lesson to be learned in this story is that it's tough to be the newest person in the class. Milton goes through a troublesome initiation period. Then, when another new student arrives, Milton is no longer the new student.

Millman, Isaac. *Moses Goes to a Concert* **(New York: Farrar Straus Giroux, 1998)** Moses is deaf, as are his classmates, so when they go to a concert, they hold balloons in their laps to feel the vibrations. We learn that the percussionist in the orchestra is also deaf. She meets with the children and allows them to try out all of her instruments. (Joyful eye-opener.)

Modesitt, Jeanne and Johnson, Lonni Sue. *The Story of Z* **(New York: Picture Book Studio, 1990)** The letter Z, at the very end of the alphabet, feels overlooked and unappreciated, so decides to leave the alphabet. Suddenly many words don't make sense. Children beg to go to the *oo* to see the *ebras,* and planes *ig ag* across the sky.

Moon, Nicola. *Lucy's Picture.* **Pictures by Alex Ayliffe (New York: Dial Books, 1994)** It's a day for art when Lucy finds the scrapbox. This is a good introduction to collage via this little girl, who creates a picture at school for her grandpa. An ordinary painting just won't do for him.

NOVEMBER

NOVEMBER GREETINGS! There's a chill in the outdoor air in many parts of the country, and that makes it possible to concentrate on indoor activities. During this month the classroom should begin to be enriched with more independent activities for skill review and reinforcement, even though total-group or small-group instruction continues. Children can be encouraged to work on review and reinforcement activities during free time as well as during indoor play period. Also, review the material already taught from the beginning of the school year.

November's Focus on Reading. During this month you will be engaged in an ever-increasing variety of reading activities. Specific skills to focus on, in addition to your regular program, are: (1) More Phonetic Awareness of Symbol–Sound Relationship with the Alphabet; (2) Sight Words—The First 100 Words; (3) Environmental Print; (4) Rebus Reading and Writing; and (5) The ABC Marching Band Letters—C, F, N, P, W.

More Phonetic Awareness of Symbol–Sound Relationship with the Alphabet

Acrostics with the ABC's

This month let's work with the alphabet in a different way. First, take a short word such as "cold" (since the days are getting colder in many areas) and print it *horizontally* on the chalkboard. Then demonstrate to students how you can write the word "cold" *vertically*. After you have done that, have students think of words or phrases that describe the autumn season.

NOTE: First, students need exposure to acrostics in large groups. Then many have success working with a partner or in small groups.

Here are some examples:

Corn stalks
Oh, it is cold!
Look at the blue sky
Don't forget your mittens.

No more robins
Outside my window on a
Very cold morning.
Everything is frosty.
My cat is indoors
By the warm heater.
Even the icicles have long
Runny noses.

A good picture book to read aloud to the students to help get you started is *Autumn, An Alphabet Acrostic* by Steven Schnur, with illustrations by Leslie Evans.

An Alphabet Feast

This is the month for soup! We can make "stone soup"—read one of the picture book variants of this story and reenact the story. "What will we put into the vegetable soup, and what letter of the alphabet does it represent?" Make a list on the chalkboard or on chart paper, and have students make an illustration of the item.

You will need a crockpot, scrub brush, a knife (only you or another adult handles the knife), a large spoon for stirring, a clean stone, soup stock, water, styrofoam cups, plastic spoons, and a ladle.

If you do not want to have a knife in the classroom, then cut up all of the vegetables before bringing them to school, or ask parents to donate cut vegetables in plastic bags. Another option is to purchase frozen or cut vegetables at the supermarket. The soup stock, along with the scrubbed stone, can either be canned vegetable soup or bouillon cubes, with plenty of water to make a clear broth.

Some vegetable choices are: diced potatoes, carrots, frozen peas, frozen corn, and a little bit of onion for flavor. If the soup looks too watery after an hour, add a can of crushed tomatoes. While this is not exactly making soup "from scratch," it is the next best thing, and many students have never seen soup being made except from a package or a can. The aroma from the crockpot fills the classroom all morning (1–2 hours) and makes for a comfortable feeling. For lunch, ladle it into styrofoam cups or cereal-sized dishes. It's good with bread or crackers, and a beverage of water or juice.

An Experience Chart Story to Accompany Our Soup-Making

Here's where the reading and writing connection comes in. Get a large piece of chart paper or brown kraft paper and tape it to the chalkboard. Along with the students, review the process for making the soup and print it on the chart.

When doing an experience chart story, you are working from an experience common to all students, so they are all involved. When talking about the procedure and this special event, listen to what the children say and then synthesize it. You do not have to print on the chart what every student says but, rather, a summation of the discussion.

It can go something like the following example:

TEACHER: **"We just went through the process of making our soup! What did we do first?"** Encourage a discussion of the procedure for washing the vegetables, washing the stone, putting the vegetables into the pot, pouring in the water.

TEACHER: **"Okay. It sounds like we have a good story beginning. Our opening sentence can be, '*Today we made harvest soup.*'"** Print this on the chart or chalkboard. Call attention to the letters and how they are formed. Say, for example, "d lives upstairs and downstairs," "soup begins with the same sound as Samantha's and Sheridan's names," and so on. This commentary helps keep the students engaged while you are modeling the printing.

TEACHER: **"Next, we need to name the vegetables that went into the soup. What are they?"** Print on the chart the following, using a different color, as students recall the ingredients: *'We used carrots, potatoes, celery, beans, peas, corn, and a little onion.'*

TEACHER: **"Did we just throw them into the pot or did we wash them or cut them? Let's talk about how we did this."** After a discussion, print in a different color: *'First, we put a stone in the bottom of the pot, just like the story. Next, we washed and drained the vegetables, and put them into the pot. Then, we filled it with water.'*

TEACHER: **"How long did it take to cook?"** After a discussion, print in a different color: *'The soup cooked for two hours and it smelled delicious.'*

TEACHER: **"When it was ready, what happened?"** Encourage discussion and print in a different color: *'We ate it all up!'*

TEACHER: **"Let's think up a title for our experience chart story."** Encourage short titles, then print one at the top and underline it.

TEACHER: **"This is a good story. Let's read it together."**

THE TASTY HARVEST SOUP

Today we made harvest soup. We used carrots, potatoes, celery, beans, corn, and a little onion.

First, we put a stone in the pot, just like the one in the story. Next, we washed and drained the vegetables, and put them into the pot. Then, we filled it with water.

The soup cooked for two hours and it smelled delicious. We ate it all up!

TEACHER: **"We changed colors** (or alternated colors) **every time we changed to a different part of the story, didn't we? We have 1, 2, 3, 4, 5 different colors. That means we have five parts to our story. Now we need some volunteers to illustrate the story and make a border all around the edges. Raise your hand if you haven't done that for us yet. Would you like to do it today during indoor play time?"**

Using the Experience Chart Story

Keep this chart story up for a couple of weeks and encourage students to read it during their play time or free-choice time. Students can copy it, or you can copy it on 8½″ × 11″ photocopy paper and make multiple copies so that each student has one. Then they can illustrate their own page and create their own border.

Another idea is to print the story on chart paper the first time, then print it on chart paper again (after students go home). Cut it up into parts or sentence strips, and have students match these parts with the original story sentences or paragraphs.

Have props available so that students can reenact the experience, using the chart story as a guide. They'll enjoy this and be reading at the same time. Also, have a copy of a book version of *Stone Soup* available so the children can reenact that favorite story as well.

A Picture Book to Help with a Feast

An excellent resource ABC book for the occasion is *Alphabet Soup, A Feast of Letters* by Scott Gustafson. First, the book begins with a letter written by Otter, who decides to have a pot-luck soup party, and shows the letter being mailed. (The function of print is reinforced here.) This book is rich with alliteration for each letter. For example, "Bear was the very best baker who baked the most beautiful breads . . . braided bread and brown bran muffins, buttermilk biscuits and buttery buns . . ." This book will add to the joy of your ABC feast of letters.

Stone Soup Versions

A new version of *Stone Soup,* retold by Heather Forest and illustrated by Susan Gaber (Little Rock, AR: August House, 1998), portrays the title with twisted and shaped vegetables. The author's note reminds the reader that this European folktale has many versions. In France, the travelers are soldiers. In Sweden, the traveler is a tramp who uses a nail, and in the Russian version, an ax is the soup starter. They all teach the lesson of cooperation and sharing.

Guessing Game ABC's

"I'm thinking of something that begins with the letter 's.' It has a bushy tail and scampers up and down tree trunks. Raise your hand if you know the answer." *(squirrel)*

Students are ready for this guessing game. The one who is called upon to guess is the next one who is IT. If students are not able to guess by the clue given, ask for another clue. You may have to confer with the one who is IT for some possible ideas.

A good ABC book to assist with this activity is *It Begins With an A* by Stephanie Calmenson, with illustrations by Marisabina Russo.

More ABC Autumn Puzzlers

Have a word—such as turkey, pilgrim, Indian, pumpkin—already in mind, but the students do not know the word yet. An example for the word *turkey* would be to say, "I'm thinking of something that begins with the *t* sound. It has a very hard shell. What is it?" Students give the "thumbs up" sign if they think they know. Give more clues so that more thumbs go up. When the student who is called upon responds correctly, print or write that beginning sound, in this case the letter *t,* on the chalkboard while students print it on a little square of paper. Then go down to the next line and give the clue for the letter *u*, and so on.

Rules: Remember to give the thumbs-up sign to be called on, and do not call out the answer OR the final word. (If someone should call out the letter, ignore it and go on, to send the message that this is not how we proceed. If it happens again, remind students of the rules. If it continues, give that student or students time-out from the game while the rest of the class continues.)

The following is a puzzler sample:

T something that begins with *t* that moves very, very slowly *(turtle)*

U something that begins with the short sound of *u,* and you hold it over your head when it rains *(umbrella)*

R something that begins with *r,* with long ears and a twitchy nose *(rabbit)*

K something that begins with *k* that unlocks the door *(key)*

E something that begins with the short sound of *e* that is a good breakfast food *(eggs)*

Y something that begins with *y* that you can use to knit a sweater *(yarn)*

This autumn phonics puzzler spells a complete word in the vertical position. If students think they know the word before all of the clues have been given, have them print the word on their paper, fold it, and hold it to their cheek as a signal. Continue with the game until all of the clues have been given.

This game can also be played so that each answer to the puzzle is complete and separate from the rest. Examples:

something that begins with *p* and is orange and round *(pumpkin)*

something that begins with *b* and flaps its wings and flies *(bird)*

something that begins with the *s* sound, and you can cut with them *(scissors)*

Line Up Alphabetically by First Name

Explain to students that they will line up in ABC order using their first names. Call out the names and have students form a line. When the line has been formed, have the children look to the right and to the left to see who is next to them. Then have them say their letter, and sit down alphabetically.

Next, just call out the letters, slowly, in order. Have students line up. You may want to say, "Calling letter A," or "If your name begins with A, line up," and so on.

Line Up Alphabetically by Last Name

Use the same procedure as for the first names, except now students are working with their last names. The students will have a different person on the right and left of them, so they will need to take note. The change of neighbors helps keep this exercise lively.

Line-Up Scramble

Once students become familiar with where they are in the line-up, you can do a variation by saying, "First Name. Students A through E. Line Up." They will go to the designated spot and must find their place in the line-up. Students are physically involved in this active—somewhat noisy—activity, but they enjoy "playing the game" while they are learning.

Variation: Use the same format, but this time work with boys only or girls only. Make two lines—one in front and one in back. "Ready? Go!"

Outdoor Playground Challenge

Ask everyone to get in line. Then say, "Now rearrange yourself in ABC order by first name."

Ask boys to get in one line and girls in another. Then have them rearrange themselves in ABC order, by first name, within those two lines.

Next, have them rearrange themselves in one long ABC line by first name. Then rearrange the line by last name.

Do this outdoors where children have space to move about and you don't have to be concerned with the volume of sound.

More ABC Picture Books

Some good books to check out at the library to reinforce letter–sound relationships are *City Seen from A to Z* by Rachel Isadora; *Anno's Alphabet* by Mitsumasa Anno; *Animalia* by Graeme Base; and *So Many Bunnies* by Rick Walton, with illustrations by Paige Miglio. In this book, the bunnies from A–Z live in a shoe and are named in alphabetical order where they sleep. The book, done in pastels, has a quiet feeling and would be good to read after a noisy activity.

On the other hand, a good ABC book to use either indoors or outdoors is *The Hullabaloo ABC* by Beverly Cleary, with illustrations by Ted Rand. After it has been read aloud, examined, and enjoyed, students can act out the story—page by page. It calls for shouting "Hello!" and making sounds such as pigs grunting, donkeys calling hee-haw, cows mooing, tractors putt-putting, and so on. It's a barnyard romp through the alphabet—and then time out for a rest.

Sight Words—The First 100 Words

The following list is called *The Instant Words: First Hundred.** They are the most common words in our English language, and are ranked in frequency order. The first 25 comprise about one-third of all printed material. The first 100 make up about half of all written material. So students must learn to recognize these words *instantly* and to spell them correctly as well.

---

*Source: Fry, Edward Bernard, Ph.D.; Kress, Jacqueline E., Ed.D.; and Fountoukidis, Dona Lee, Ed.D. *The Reading Teacher's Book of Lists,* 3rd edition. West Nyack, NY: The Center for Applied Research in Education, 1993 (1-800-288-4745).

Words 1–25	Words 26–50	Words 51–75	Words 76–100
the	or	will	number
of	one	up	no
and	had	other	way
a	by	about	could
to	word	out	people
in	but	many	my
is	not	then	than
you	what	them	first
that	all	these	water
it	were	so	been
he	we	some	call
was	when	her	who
for	your	would	oil
on	can	make	its
are	said	like	now
as	there	him	find
with	use	into	long
his	and	time	down
they	each	has	day
I	which	look	did
at	she	two	get
be	do	more	come
this	how	write	made
have	their	go	may
from	if	see	part

Common suffixes: s, ing, ed, er, ly, est

Working With the "People" Words in the 1–25 Instant Words

Ask for a student volunteer to lie flat and still on a sheet of kraft paper. Then, two other students with black felt-tip pens can trace around the student. Use felt-tip pens and construction paper to add clothing and facial details. Glue on yarn for the hair.

On a standard-sized sheet of construction paper, print all of the names from the list (1–25) that "stand for" someone's name, or that are used instead of someone's name. These words are: *you, he, his, they, I, we, your, she, their, them, her,* and *him.* (They are called pronouns, but students don't need that information at this level.) Put this paper on the front of the figure and leave it there for a whole month, so students can see it and work with the words. Point out that we use these words to help make our language flow more easily. For example, instead of using a person's name over and over again, we have "substitute words." Print the following sentences on the chalkboard for students to see the substitutes for names.

Mary can run.	Mary can run.
Mary can run fast.	*She* can run fast.
Mary's mom can run, too.	*Her* mom can run, too.

Then read them aloud, and point to each word or use a marker under each sentence. Read the left column first, then read the one on the right. Ask students, "How many times did we read the name 'Mary' in the first column?" *(three)* "How many times did we read the name 'Mary' in the second column?" *(one)* Point out that in place of the word "Mary," we used "she" and we also used "her." Circle these two words, and tell students that we will meet up with them again and again, so we have to make every effort to learn them by heart.

Follow the same procedure for the male gender:

Warner can run.	Warner can run.
Warner can run fast.	*He* can run fast.
Warner's dad can run, too.	*His* dad can run, too.

More Work with People Words (1–25)

Make up additional phrases that show the use of the other "substitute people" words, instead of saying the person's name over and over again. Print this on a kraft paper chart made from the outline of a person, but leave the details (clothing and face) blank. Display it in the room so that students can look at it and read it in their spare time. This assists the visual learners and all learners.

You run.	*Your* mother can run.
He can run.	*She* can run.
His dad can run.	*Their* dog can run.
They like to run.	See *them* run.
I like to run.	*Her* dog can run.
We all run.	

Note: Some of the activities used for Instant Words 1–25 can be done with the second 25 words, then the next set, and finally the last set.

Stick Out Your Tongue and Say "Th"

There are four *th* words in the first 1–25 list. *Th* can be voiceless as in the words *thank, think, throw, thunder, thistle. Th* can be a voiced sound also, as in the words *this, that, them, there, their, the, then.* For both the voiceless and voiced words, the tip of the tongue is held under the top teeth. Exaggerate this motion so that students get the idea.

The Motor-Boat Sound

For the voiced sound of *th,* have students lightly encircle their throat with their hand, stick out their tongue, and make the sound that they hear at the beginning of the word *the.* They will feel the vibration.

Tell students that whenever they see a word that begins with the letters "th," they can try it both ways—voiced and voiceless to see which one makes sense to them. (During silent reading time you will often see students gently clutching their throat and making the motor-boat sound as they attempt to sound out the words in print.)

Looking for Ways to Group the First 1–25 Instant Words

- Words can be grouped by number of letters (the words "I" and "a" in the first column say their name, and have only one letter).
- Words can be grouped by common beginning sounds.
- Words can be grouped by people, places, things.

The Word Wall

Many teachers have a large sheet of paper in the classroom that covers a portion of the wall. On this sheet they write words that students ask about during the day, or new words that they are introduced to during story time, and so on. Soon, the word wall has many words on it. Some teachers have the words on the wall in a random pattern, and some use the alphabet to systematize the words.

Make sure that the instant words are included on the word wall. Use different colored felt pens for them. Draw a circle around them. Put a star in front of them. But do single them out as being important.

Memorizing Is Important

When a student learns something by heart, or by rote memory, and keeps practicing this skill, it serves as a foundation for learning more complex things later, because neural connections are made in the brain. Have students learn to spell the words on the 1–25 list by rote memory, and then move on to other words.

"Say the word, spell it aloud while looking at it, close your eyes, spell it again. Then say it, spell it aloud while looking at it, cover the word, and print it." Check the work. Students can work with partners so they can help each other.

Environmental Print

What Is Environmental Print?

It's the print that is in our surroundings. We see print on billboards, street signs, grocery store windows, gas station pumps, restaurants, menus, and while walking along at the shopping center or mall. We see bright and bold neon signs, and some with flashing lights that send messages. We have newspapers, magazines, and books in our home, and flyers and junk mail are hung on our doorknobs. People wear T-shirts with print and drink beverages from mugs that have print. We are bombarded by print in our environment, both outdoors and indoors—and that is what has come to be called environmental print. Encourage students to "read" it rather than walking right on by.

Start Saving Junk Mail

This is a great resource. Ask parents to send it in, too. Keep it in a big basket by the door. Children can open up the letters, their very own mail, and try to make sense of the print and the accompanying pictures. They can cut out the colorful letters and pictures for chart illustrations and Rebus books. They can circle letter shapes that they recognize.

Environmental Print "Homework"

Give students an assignment. Have them copy four samples of environmental print that they have seen over the weekend. They can print the word or draw the accompanying picture or logo. Chances are they will see a great deal more than four, so have those who can, turn over the sheet and keep going.

Start a Menu Collection

Go to a variety of restaurants and ask the manager to donate a menu for your classroom. Some are glossy and have brightly colored pictures to accompany the items. Children enjoy "reading" the menu and can make their own as well at the Writing Center. They also serve as props and add to dramatic play for children who want to set up a play restaurant. This facilitates the language arts—reading, writing, speaking, listening, and the visual production of a menu.

Bring on the Brochures

While on a trip, when you stop at a roadside rest area where there are brochures, pick up one of each for your classroom. Other good resources for brochures are many local hotels and motels, auto clubs, and your city or area Chamber of Commerce. Children can pour over these and be exposed to a wide variety of places to visit right in their very own area. How many words can they read? Do the pictures help? They can design a brochure for their city, or local zoo, or for their school.

Rebus Reading and Writing

Working with environmental print leads naturally into Rebus symbols. Rebus symbols are pictures that "stand for" or represent something, so that we "read the pictures."

Let's Read Logos

A logo is a common Rebus symbol that is familiar to all. Many restaurants have a logo. Are there any in your area? Talk about the subject and then have students be on the lookout.

Do you have a sports team in your city or state? Chances are they have a logo printed right on their shirt or hat. What is it?

The United States has two major political parties, each with a logo. One is an elephant and one is a donkey.

"Where else can we find logos?"

We Can Read Rebus Stories

Several good Rebus picture books that can be borrowed from the library include *The Little Red Riding Hood Rebus Storybook* retold by Ann Morris, with illustrations by Ljiljana Rylands, and *Mother Goose Picture Riddles, A Book of Rebuses,* adapted and illustrated by Lisl Weil. One illustration in this book that would challenge students to come up with their own symbols is as follows:

Diddle, diddle, dumpling, my _____ John

Went to _____ with his _____ on.

_____ _____ off, and _____ _____ on,

Diddle, diddle, dumpling, my _____ John.

An updated 1994 version of Mother Goose rhymes is entitled *Mama Goose, A New Mother Goose,* collected and retold by Liz Rosenberg, with illustrations by Janet Street. *The Other Mother Goose,* by poet J. Patrick Lewis, is also a treat. These could challenge students to create new Rebus symbols.

We Can Write a Group Rebus Story

It's November, the time for Autumn Festivals and Thanksgiving Day. Write a group November story and include such pictures as: leaves, trees, Pilgrims, Indians, turkey, drumstick, pumpkin pie. To help get you started, here is a sample that can be printed with a felt pen on a large turkey shape. (Also see Reproducible Activity Pages.)

Title: _____

November is the _____ month of the year.
The _____ on the _____ have
turned bright colors of red and orange.
Soon it will be Thanksgiving Day. The
first Thanksgiving Day was celebrated
by the _____ and _____ .
It's a time to be thankful for a harvest of
good food.
We like _____
and _____ .

My Thanksgiving Rebus Book

Students can make mini flip-top books. They can print the words "I am thankful for _____" on each page, and then fill in the blank with a picture that they draw or one that is cut from a magazine. The children can read and share their books in class and at home with their family. Also, they can make a card in the shape of a turkey and add feather shapes to the bird. On the feathers, print words of those things for which they're thankful.

Silly Rebus Stories

Have a variety of word cards and picture cards available so that children can compose silly sentences. (*Example:* The pumpkin pie ran after the dog.) This makes children laugh and enjoy some playfulness with the language while they are gaining experience with words and reading. For some children, it helps to make the process of reading less threatening.

Back to the Bakery

Carry over the bakery experience from the previous month. You might want to "open the bakery" for only a week, but it will be helpful.

Students enjoy the delicious smells from the bakery, so if you have the opportunity you can bake bread easily in the classroom using an electric bread machine. If you don't have one, perhaps another teacher has one that you can borrow, or a parent may be willing to either loan one or come to the classroom, demonstrate the process, and get a loaf of bread started. You can enjoy the aroma all morning and then eat it.

This approach can be used each month to signal that the ABC Bakery is in operation once again.

The Chefs and the Consumers

Students can take turns being the chef/clerks and the customers, or consumers. Introduce the new word *consumer* to the students, explaining that it means *buyer*.

This month, the ABC specialties are coils of clay that have been rolled into the shape of the letters *c, f, n, p,* and *w.* Have an abundant supply so that students can "purchase" them. (This can be integrated with math in terms of *how many,* as well as *addition and subtraction with money,* and integrated with writing by making colorful signs for the products as well as writing out receipts.)

A Letter Poster

Print the capital and lower-case letters for this month on an 8½″ × 11″ sheet of colored posterboard. This will require five papers for the letters *c, f, n, p,* and *w.* Two more will be needed for a total of seven, since the letters *c* (with hard and soft sounds) and *f* (which is the same sound as that made by the letters *ph*) will require two papers. Students can cut pictures from magazines that represent the letter sound, or draw items on the paper.

The ABC Marching Band Letters—C, F, N, P, W

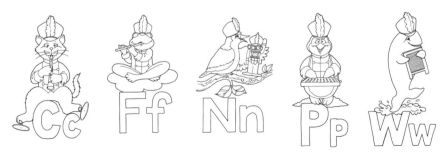

See the Marching Band members in the Reproducible Activity Pages.

Meet Cindy Cat with the Clarinet and Cymbals *(Letter C)*

Cindy Cat, the alphabet letter that is third in line, is the clarinet player in the ABC Marching Band—but that's not all! She is versatile and plays the cymbals, too. Take this opportunity to present the new vocabulary word *versatile,* which means having more than one use or function.

When clever Cindy Cat (call attention to the hard and soft sounds of her first and last names) is not playing the clarinet (hard sound as in the letter *k*), she is playing the cymbals (sound of *s* as in the word *sweet*).

The clarinet is a woodwind instrument with a reed mouthpiece. The cymbals are a pair of brass plates (concave) that are either struck together as percussion instruments, or used singly and sounded by being hit with a drumstick. Locate a picture of each instrument to show the students.

- *Soft C.* This sound is made by putting the top teeth directly on the rim of the bottom teeth, parting the lips, and letting the air be expelled from the mouth through the teeth. This makes the hissing sound.
- *Hard C.* This sound is made like the letter K. It is a voiced, gutteral sound from the back of the throat. The mouth and teeth are slightly open and the tongue is at rest on the floor of the mouth.

Clarinet Words and Cymbal Words *(Letter C)*

Let's be on the lookout for words that belong in each sound category. Make two lists. Illustrate the words or cut out pictures from magazines and paste them onto the poster to give a visual clue. Here are some to get you started:

Clarinet Words (Cat)	Cymbal Words (Cindy)
cactus	Cecil
corn	Cecelia
cave	cedar
cupboard	Cinderella
cotton	city

The City Cat/Country Cat Chant *(Letter C)*

This is a chant you can say with a sing-song voice as you encourage students to sway back and forth (like a cat moving). Students can bend their arms at the elbow and let the wrists go limp, like cat's paws. With this chant, students have an opportunity to hear and say both the soft and the hard sound of the letter *c.* (See Reproducible Activity Page.)

Cindy likes the city
    With tall skyscrapers.
She can climb up fire escapes
    And read newspapers.
Her city sound is a
    definite hissssssssss.
If she lived in the country
    It's the city she'd missssssssssss!

Heeerrre City, City, City Cindy.

This kit-cat likes the country
   With fields of yellow grain.
She can walk in the road.
   She can play in the rain.
Her country cat sound
   Is shared with Cousin "K."
She sings it out clearly
   In the light of the day.

Heeerrre Country, Country, Country Cat.

City, City, Cindy—Country, Country, Cat,
Tell me what you think of that? MEOW!

How Do We Know If a Letter Sound Is Soft or Hard? *(Letter C)*

We don't know, so, that is why students need to be encouraged to try both sounds when they meet the letter *c* in a word. This takes time and practice. Repeating the chant will help. Make a cassette recording of the verse so that students can listen again and again.

Food Fit for a Calico Cat or a Cerise Cat *(Letter C)*

Calico (hard c) and cerise (soft c, pronounced sir-EESE') can help us with food and colors.

Calico is a spotty mixture of colors; cerise is a shade of purple. Let's see what foods we can eat that have the hard 'c' as in calico and the soft 'c' as in cerise, to help reinforce these two sounds. Perhaps the food can be served on a calico tablecloth. Here are some ideas:

Calico Food (mixed colors)	Cerise Food (purple)
mixed Jell-o™ cubes	plums
scrambled eggs and ham	grapes
marble cake	grape juice

Meet Philip Frog and the Flute *(Letter F)*

Philip Frog, the sixth letter in the ABC Marching Band line-up, plays the flute, an instrument that makes a high-pitched sound and is in the woodwind family. It has finger holes and keys on the side.

When making the sound of the letter *f,* instruct students to put their top teeth on their bottom lip and blow air out of their mouth. The tongue is at rest. When the palm of the hand is put in front of the lips, students can feel the air being expelled and making a windy, hissing sound.

Philip the Frog and the Ffff Mix-Up *(Letter F)*

"Life is not always easy for Philip Frog. He gets confused with letters and sounds." (*Note:* This is reassuring for some students.) "Let's listen to the following story, and find out how he got mixed up and how his best friends helped him."

Philip Frog and the "Fffff" Mix-up

Each time the ABC Marching Band practices, the bandleader has them do what is called a "warm-up" exercise. Here's how it works. The bandleader calls out the alphabet letters in order. "A," he calls, and the animal answers. "B," he calls, and the animal answers, and so on. When each band member answers with his or her instrument sound, that's how the leader can tell if they are all there and if they are all in tune.

One day, Philip Frog was late for band practice because he overslept and missed the ferryboat. The bandleader was tapping the baton for attention and starting to call the roll.

"I wonder where he can be?" asked his best friend H.

"A, B, C," the bandleader called out slowly.

"He was late yesterday," said another friend P, "and he can't be late again or else."

"Or else what?" asked H.

"D, E," the bandleader called out slowly.

"Or else he will be kicked out of the band," said P.

"F" the bandleader called out slowly.

The letters P and H both sighed together at the very same moment and it came out sounding like "Ffffffffff"—just in the nick of time!

"G, H, I," the bandleader continued until he got to the letter Z.

Well, that was a close call. Philip Frog was twenty minutes late, and every time the flute was supposed to be heard, his friends PH sighed and you really couldn't tell the difference. The frog had been saved by his buddies.

To show how grateful he was, *to this day* Philip Frog still shares his sound with his two good friends, P and H. You still can't tell the difference when you HEAR it, even though they don't look alike when you SEE it. So, whenever you see "ph" side by side, put your top teeth over your bottom lip and blow—and you too will sound just like "f." Now try it! "Ffffffffff."

The End

Practicing with "F" and "Ph" *(Letter F)*

Say four words in a row, emphasizing them equally, and have students repeat them. Can they tell which one starts with the letters "ph"? No, not when they HEAR them. Then print the same words for them to SEE. Do they look alike? No. (Sound alike—yes; look alike—no.) Emphasize that point. Also, encourage students to say the sound of "f" when they see "ph" together. Use these words:

feet	four	phantom	feather
funny	phone	favor	fish
photo	full	found	football

"Ph = F" Headbands and More Practice *(Letter F)*

Print on the chalkboard this formula: "Ph = F." Explain to the students that this sign (=) is called the equal sign, and means "the same as." Have students print it on a construction paper headband and then measure, staple, and wear it. Tell students that the letters "ph" can appear at the beginning of a word, in the middle of a word, or even at the end of a word. Then print these words on the chalkboard, one at a time. Say them and circle the letters "ph" with different colored chalk. Students can be called upon also to draw the circle around the letters *p* and *h*.

Here are some sample words to use:

elephant	telephone	telegraph
pharmacy	photograph	phony
rephrase	alphabet	Ralph

Philip Frog Gets Mixed Up, Too *(Letter F)*

Call attention to the fact that <u>Ph</u>ilip <u>F</u>rog uses both the "Ph" and the "F" in his name. ***Important:*** *The students should know that the reason he was late for band practice was that the ferryboat ride left from Philly Hill—and not from Filly Hill, where he was waiting. People tend to get those two mixed up if they don't know how to spell them.* <u>*Remember, "PH = F" when we HEAR it, even though it looks different when we SEE it.*</u>

For students who are having some difficulty with letter–sound relationships, it is reassuring to know that they are not alone.

The "GH" Connection Sounds Like "F" Sometimes *(Letter F)*

"We've already seen that the letter *f* is generous because it lets two other letters (ph) use its sound. But wait, as if that generosity isn't enough, the letter *f* also lets letters *g* and *h* get together and make music sometimes. Thus, we have the sound of *f* in words like *enough, tough,* and *rough.* Have students be on the alert for the "gh" connection, usually found at the *end* of words. (**Note:** There are many exceptions to the "gh" combination, such as in the words *ghost* and *eight,* for example. So addressing this in detail at this time will depend upon the group. Save it for later in the year if they're not ready yet.)

A Variety of Forks *(Letter F)*

The word *fork* begins with the sound of *f,* and there are several meanings for this word. This word presents an opportunity for you to instruct children that a word can have more than one meaning. We have to look at the context in which it is used, or whether or not it is used in a "saying" in order to understand its meaning.

> fork: a utensil for piercing, scooping, serving, or eating food
> fork: a separation of branches in a tree
> fork: a separation in the road
> fork: a truck that lifts heavy items
> fork: a saying, such as "fork it over"

Distribute a blank sheet of paper to students. Have them fold it in half (vertically) and then fold it in half (horizontally). They can print the letters "Ff" at the top of the page. Then have them choose four of the forks to illustrate on their page. Be sure to label them. (This is good practice with the letter *f* in terms of language development and forming the letter.)

Speaking of Food *(Letter F)*

It always helps reinforce a letter if food that begins with that letter can be served. Here are some possibilities for the letter *f*. Always check with parents for allergies before serving food morsels.

fudge	French pastry	fried cake (doughnut)
fritters	fruit	frosty (milkshake)
figs	fruitcake	fruit cup

A Colorful Letter Poster *(Letter F)*

Have students search through magazines for items that begin with the letter *f*. Students can cut them out and paste them on the posterboard. Display this prominently in the classroom. Then have students use it as a prop for playing a guessing game.

They can say, "I'm thinking of something that begins with the sound of 'f' and it is very hot. *(picture of furnace)*

Since the pictures, or answers, are already in view, this makes the game easier for students with special needs who can use the visuals for reinforcement and review.

Good Read-aloud Books About Frogs *(Letter F)*

Students will enjoy the adventures of the *Frog and Toad* series by Arnold Lobel; *The Tale of Mr. Jeremy Fisher* by Beatrix Potter; *The Frog Princess* retold by J. Patrick Lewis, with paintings by Gennady Spirin; and *The Mysterious Tadpole* by Steven Kellogg.

Meet Nanny Nuthatch From Nottingham
Who Plays the Nutcracker *(Letter N)*

Nanny Nuthatch from Nottingham is the 14th letter of the alphabet—and our oldest marching band member. Nanny is 99! But Nanny can keep up with the best of them as she plays the nutcracker. Most people use the nutcracker to crack open hard nut shells, but Nanny Nuthatch from Nottingham learned to play the nutcracker as a little girl, and she can make it say the sound of the letter *n* which is "nnnnnnn." For our purposes, the nutcracker is a make-believe instrument.

Note: *Actually, the nuthatch—a real bird—is sometimes called the "nut hatchet." This is because a nuthatch can wedge a nut under the bark of a tree and crack it open with repeated tapping of its bill. So, in this spirit, we have the bird playing the nutcracker in the band.*

Demonstrate for students how to make the sound of *n*. They are to place the tip of the tongue on the ridge of the mouth roof that is behind the top front teeth. The mouth and teeth are open slightly, and the sound is made from the back of the throat. The prolonged sound resembles a hum.

Nanny Nuthatch Likes Nuts. Do You? *(Letter N)*

Bring in a small metal nutcracker and a variety of mixed nuts with shells. Students can work the handles to crack open the nuts and eat the nutmeat inside. (**Caution:** Be aware of any allergies your students might have!) This squeezing activity is good for small motor development and helps students to gauge the necessary amount of hand pressure needed to crack nuts. Some hard-shell nuts that work well are: walnuts, pecans, almonds, and Brazil nuts.

Students can make the prolonged sound of the letter *n* while they are cracking nuts—and sound just like Nanny Nuthatch from Nottingham, sometimes called the nut hatchet.

Nanny Nuthatch Wants an Introduction *(Letter N)*

Nanny is a very proper bird. If you were to meet her, she would say to you, "Hello, I'm Nanny Nuthatch from Nottingham. Who are you?" She has good manners.

She would expect you to say your first name, last name, and where you're from (either the city or the street). For example, "I'm Marlo Furnstein from Seattle" or "I'm Harley Brown from Sims Street."

Call upon a volunteer to play the part of Nanny. Five other students stand in line. Nanny can say her line and the five students can take turns answering with their line. Then, call upon another volunteer to play Nanny, and five more students can be introduced.

A handshake or a nod of the head would be in order after each student introduces himself or herself. After this, encourage children to use their good manners daily.

Nanny Nuthatch Is a "No-Nonsense" Bird *(Letter N)*

Now that Nanny has been introduced as a disciplined bird and a proper bird, the Nuthatch reproducible page can be used as a stick puppet or double puppet that will help with classroom management. She can leave notes and messages for the students. She can speak directly into your ear so that you can then relay messages to students, such as, "Nanny is trying to read and it's too noisy in here. She says to settle down, please" or "Nanny says she's on the look out today for good workers and she'll reward them at the end of the day . . . hmm. Wonder what Nanny has in mind?" (Good workers can have their name printed on a chart or chalkboard, or they can receive a hand stamp, sticker, or a badge to wear.)

Nanny Nuthatch Says "No" to Negligence *(Letter N)*

What is negligence? Explain to students that this is a new vocabulary word and it means "being careless." Discuss how some people don't have concern for others or for belongings, or for keeping a classroom looking attractive and neat. What can be done about this to keep Nanny happy?

Make an "N" Poster *(Letter N)*

On a sheet of colorful construction paper, list the upper-case and lower-case letters "N,n." Have students search through old magazines for pictures of items that begin with the sound of this letter. Cut them out and paste them on the paper. Students can use these for letter-guessing games.

It's November *(Letter N)*

November is the ninth month (another "n"). Have students work with a partner to see how many little words they can make from the long word "November."

Abbreviations *(Letter N)*

"Nov." is the abbreviation for the month of November. On the chalkboard, or on a chart, go through each month and print the abbreviation for the name of the month.

Print the abbreviation for the days of the week.

"How many other ways do we abbreviate items in the classroom or names of food that we eat? Let's think about it and talk about it, because abbreviations are used to a great extent in our world."

Meet Peter Penguin and the Piano *(Letter P)*

Peter Penguin represents the 16th letter in the ABC Marching Band line-up. Peter plays the piano, which has a keyboard. When a key is pressed, it strikes a hammer that vibrates the strings. It is referred to as a member of the percussion (striking) family and also the stringed instrument family. Peter's piano is a mini-piano that has straps that go over each arm, and one that goes around the waist.

As a "stand alone" letter (not together with "ph") the sound that we hear from Peter is at the beginning of the word *pencil*. Encourage students to put their lips together, fill the inside of their cheeks with air, and blow out the air with a puh-puh-puh sound.

Peter Plays a Powerful Piano *(Letter P)*

Make up silly or meaningful sentences that focus upon alliteration, or repetition of words that begin with the letter *p*. Here are some to get you started:

Peter plays a powerful piano.
Peter plays a pretty piano.
Peter plays a purple piano.

Popcorn popping sounds like p-p-p.
Polly parrot perches on the porch.
Peas are plentiful at parties.

That's "Poster" With a "P" *(Letter P)*

Make a poster with the letters "P,p" (upper case and lower case) written in the top left corner. Then have students look through colorful magazines to find pictures of items that begin with the letter *p*. Have students cut them out and paste them on the poster. Use this as a tool for guessing games.

That's "Poetry" With a "P" *(Letter P)*

Some poetry books that children will enjoy hearing you read aloud include: *Zoo Doings, Animal Poems* by Jack Prelutsky, with pictures by Paul O. Zelinsky; *Riddle-icious* by J. Patrick Lewis, with illustrations by Debbie Tilley; *My Cat Has Eyes of Sapphire Blue* by Aileen Fisher; *Hailstones and Halibut Bones* by Mary O'Neill; and the very popular *Where the Sidewalk Ends* by Shel Silverstein. (April is Poetry Month so you will have more activities at that time.)

Pease Porridge Hot, Pease Porridge Cold *(Letter P)*

Remember the nursery rhyme, "Pease porridge hot, pease porridge cold, pease porridge in the pot, nine days old"? In honor of the letter *p* you can make and serve a simplified version of this porridge with the following recipe, using frozen peas. Your students can memorize the verse, too.

You will need:

one chopped onion	crockpot
1 tablespoon butter	spoon for stirring
1 cup chopped celery chunks	ladle
2 cups frozen peas	styrofoam cups
6 cups water	plastic spoons
salt and pepper	

Procedure: Add all of the ingredients together in the crockpot and put on high setting. Let cook for about 1½ hours, or until steaming. Mash the peas. (Bits of ham can be added during the last half hour.) Serve warm.

Make a Patchwork Quilt *(Letter P)*

Cut out a large shape of the letter P from heavy cardboard. Glue patches of material on it either in formation or in random order (crazy quilt). On each patch, students can paste a piece of paper that contains a word that begins with the letter *p*.

I'm Going to Pack Peter's Pouch *(Letter P)*

Play this verbal game, which is a variation of several others. Have students say, "I'm going to pack Peter's pouch and I'll put a _____ in it." The word has to begin with the sound of *p*. Accept all answers that begin with the letter, no matter how silly. This is an enjoyable way to practice the letter–sound relationship.

Pack Rats—Beware! *(Letter P)*

Along about this time of the year, it is a good idea for students to do an extra special job of cleaning out their desks or cubbies. This might be a good time for Peter to help the pack rats sort out their papers and take them home. (Some teachers allow time for this every other Friday afternoon so that students don't get into the pack-rat habit.)

Peter Piano Loves Pizza Dogs *(Letter P)*

Pizza has been consistently voted as the #1 favorite food for lunch by school-children throughout the U.S. With a toaster oven you can make your own pizza dogs and have an enjoyable treat.

You will need:

pizza sauce (qt. jar)	toaster oven
pepperoni slices	large spoon (for spreading)
mozzarella cheese pieces	paper napkins
hot dog rolls (cut in half)	oven mitt

Procedure: Separate the hot dog rolls. Each student gets a top or a bottom, which serves as the crust. On that roll, students (a) spread pizza sauce, (b) sprinkle mozzarella cheese on top of sauce, and (c) place pepperoni slices on top. (**Note:** *You or another adult handle all oven responsibilities.*) Bake at 350 degrees until cheese begins to melt. Remove. Wrap in a paper napkin. Enjoy. (You can bake about 4 or 5 at a time.)

Meet Wally Whale and the Washboard *(Letter W)*

Wally Whale represents the letter *w* in the ABC Marching Band, which is the fourth letter from the end, or thirtieth from the beginning of the alphabet line. Wally Whale plays the washboard in the band. Actually, the washboard is a type of percussion instrument that has a corrugated surface of metal. (Long ago, women used washboards, soap, and a water tub on washdays. The washboard was used to help scrub dirty clothes.) Wally Whale found the washboard in the ocean. It was probably tossed overboard from a ship. He learned to play it. He is an environmentalist.

Model the sound of the letter *w*. Point out to students that it is made by puckering the lips, blowing out air, and uttering a sound in the throat that sounds like "wuh." Have them put the palm of their hand in front of their mouth so that they can feel the air being expelled.

Print the upper- and lower-case letters on the board. (Note that they look more like a double "v" than a double "u." In any case, both sides are even.)

Who, What, When, Where, Why *(Letter W)*

When Wally Whale wants to practice his special sound of the letter *w*, he puts the palm of his hand up in front of his mouth (not touching) and feels the air being expelled as he slowly says: "Who, what, when, where, why" at least three times. It is a "warming up" exercise for the sound.

This "5W" format can be used when reading or writing a story. *Who* are the story characters? *What* is the story about? *When* does it take place? *Where* does it take place? *Why* did this story take place?

Print these five words on a big shape of the letter *w*. Perhaps it will help children learn them, since they are designated as "sight words" and need to be memorized by heart.

Wally Is Looking for Water Words *(Letter W)*

Since Wally lives in the ocean, he likes to use the dictionary to look up names or words that use "water" because the words begin with Wally's "w" sound. Students can help Wally find these words. They can be printed on a large paper shape of a whale and illustrated by students. Here are some to get you started:

waterboy	water ballet	watercolor
water cooler	waterfall	water hole
water lily	watermelon	waterproof

Wally Is Looking for Good "W" Food to Eat *(Letter W)*

Students always enjoy eating something that begins with the letter sound they are learning about. Some of Wally's favorite foods include:

wheat crackers	whole wheat bread	wheat cereal
wax beans	water chestnuts	walnut

Wally's Wash Day Chant *(Letter W)*

Even a whale has washing to do—at least Wally does! He gets out the detergent, the washtub, puts it on a wash stand, and uses his washboard on wash day.

It's good practice for his "w" sound. Students can learn this, verse by verse, and simulate the up-and-down scrubbing movement on the washboard.

Wally likes to
  wishy, washy
  wishy, washy
  wishy, washy
Wally likes to
  wishy, washy
'Til he's all washed up.

Wally's clothes are
  washable
  washable
  washable
Wally's clothes are
  washable
'Til he's all washed up.

Wally likes the
  wash and wear
  wash and wear
  wash and wear
Wally likes the
  wash and wear
'Til he's all washed up.

Please help Wally
  wishy, washy
  wishy, washy
  wishy, washy
Please help Wally
  wishy, washy
'Til he's all washed up.

The Wally Whale Word Scramble *(Letter W)*

Wally likes nine of his relatives very much. These whale names can be listed on the chalkboard: blowhead, blue, gray, humpback, killer, narwhal, right, sei, and sperm.

Then make another list and mix up the letters. Have the students draw a line from the correct mix of letters to the mixed-up letters. (Students are gaining practice with letter recognition with this exercise.) Example:

narwhal - - - - - - - - eis
sei - - - - - - - - -   larwanh

See Reproducible Activity Pages for a word scramble.

READING LINKS TO HOLIDAYS & SPECIAL EVENTS

Children's Book Week—Looking for Readers

There is an entire week during November devoted to children's books and a focus upon reading. In the United States, we are fortunate to have over 5,000 picture books printed yearly for young children.

In your November newsletter to parents, extend an invitation for them to come to your classroom to read a story aloud this week.

Some districts have a schoolwide or districtwide effort to invite people from the community to read to students. Get permission from the principal, and then send letters to businesses, colleges, and such community workers as firefighters, police officers, news reporters, and even the mayor. Invite them to read a story aloud to your class. Everyone enjoys this experience.

It's American Education Week

For this week, some schools have day programs, while others have evening programs for parents, where they visit their child's classroom and listen to a talk given by the teacher. Some schools have had success with pot-luck suppers, where they eat and then informally visit the classroom with the whole family. Either way, make sure students are made aware of the golden opportunity that they have for learning. (In some third-world countries, there are extremely limited facilities for learning—no supplies, no paper, no books. Children—and parents—should know this.) Send home a monthly newsletter describing what's taking place in the classroom.

Let's Start an Education Timeline

If you haven't already done so, this is a good time to reflect on what your students have done so far this year. Have an 8½″ × 11″ sheet of paper, variety in color, for each month of the year. Put the name of the month at the top. Eventually this timeline can hang at eye-level across the front or side of the classroom. Students can gain a sense of past time, present time, and future time from this visual representation.

Go back over September events that took place in your classroom, including national holidays and class birthdays. This is where you can prompt students and jog their memory. Then talk about what happened in the classroom during the month of October.

Next, decide which of these items gets a place on the class timeline. The month can be divided into beginning/middle/ending, or the actual dates can appear at the bottom and text can be added. Students can illustrate the event.

It is a good idea to give students twelve sheets of blank paper so that they can make their own timeline of school events. They can copy the one that is on display in the classroom, or they may wish to add events on theirs that the class voted to delete. They can make a folder for it and give it a title. At the end of each month, be sure to review the items and place them on the timeline. In some classes, this is done throughout the month. When done, you have a grand record for the year of events that were important for all. (Some students prefer to work on their own timeline throughout the month; on some days they do it as an alternative to story writing or journal writing.)

Veteran's Day

Celebrate this day by having students make an extra effort to learn the pledge of allegiance to the flag. Learn a patriotic song today, and begin to sing it daily during opening exercises. "Veterans are men and women who defend our country—it is because of them that we can live in freedom." Students need to be exposed to this point of view at an early age and to begin to learn to be grateful. This is a difficult concept for many young children.

On a more concrete level, ask students to gather information at home about someone in their family who may have served in the armed forces. Was it the army, navy, air force, marines, coast guard, or other? Have them bring in a photo to share, if possible.

Children need to know that men and women are working in jobs to protect us. It is the responsibility of the school to promote Veteran's Day as an important part of our history. This is a time to renew efforts to learn the pledge of allegiance.

Pledge of Allegiance

I pledge allegiance
to the flag
of the United States of America
and to the republic
for which it stands,
one nation under God,
indivisible,
with liberty and justice for all.

Do a Flag Survey

Have students be Patriotic Detectives and see where they can locate Old Glory (another name for the flag) flying outdoors in the community. Each time they spot the place, have them remember the location (store, public building, post office, gas station, and so on) and record it on the survey sheet. Many teachers have found that McDonald's restaurants, public buildings, and some gas stations have the most flags.

The red, white, and blue flag—a symbol for our country—flapping in the breeze in November against a bright blue sky is a lovely sight. Perhaps students can go on a letter-writing campaign for even more flags to be flown in their community. Talk it over.

National American Indian Heritage Month

The richness of this culture can be conveyed through picture books to read aloud. Some suggestions are: *Everybody Needs a Rock,* and *I'm in Charge of Celebrations* by Byrd Baylor, with illustrations by Peter Parnall; *The Girl Who Loved Wild Horses* by Paul Goble; and two trickster tales by Gerald McDermott, *Raven* (Pacific Northwest) and *Coyote* (Southwest).

Native Americans Are Storytellers

In this culture, the stories of the people and the lessons to be learned are passed down by word of mouth, which is referred to as storytelling.

- Emphasize storytelling this month by *telling* rather than reading a story. Then have students retell the story.
- Use puppets to have students retell stories that have been read in the classroom so far this year.
- Use the flannelboard to have students reenact stories with the felt props that you make available.
- Use real items to serve as props. Have them lined up in a row so that students can be helped to remember the sequence of the story.
- Native Americans used their hands to communicate. For example, a *deer* was described by holding hands to the side of the head for antlers; *heart* was described by holding a fist to the heart area. Students can think up hand signals for words like *rain, sun, tree* and use them with storytelling. A good resource book is *Indian Signals and Sign Language* by George Fronval and Daniel Dubois (New York: Wings Books, Random House, 1978).

Many Tribes—One People

The Native Americans are grouped in many different tribes, often depending upon where they are located. Here are some names, by no means all, to learn. Print them on the chalkboard, and have students arrange the four names in each group (I, II, and III) in alphabetical order. This will familiarize the younger students with names and give practice in alphabetical order. For older students, find out more information about these Native Americans at the library, and find names of other communities.

I	**II**	**III**
Shawnee	Sioux	Blackfeet
Navajo	Algonquin	Seneca
Apache	Blackfoot	Huron
Onondaga	Hopi	Maumee

The topic of Native Americans is also addressed in November's "Links to Writing," "Links to Math," and "Links to Social Studies."

Time for Thanksgiving

You need to stress that this time of year is set aside not just as a day off from school, but as a day to give thanks for our country, our freedom, for good health and friends, and so on. With young children who are not used to dealing with abstract concepts, begin at a concrete level—right where they are. Focus upon and give thanks for what they have, not just what they want.

"Let's have a discussion of 'things money can't buy' that we're thankful for; things that make us happy." Some starter ideas are:

my baby brother sleeps through the night

my dog licks my face when I come home

my mother's spaghetti and meatballs

my dad plays ball with me

my Grandma Carol hums when she's in the kitchen

my Aunt Holly's brownies

my baby sister got better after having a bad cold

my Grandpa had an operation and feels good

there is no fighting

The Thank-You Tree

Make a classroom chart in the shape of a large tree, with brown corrugated cardboard trunk and a green leaf top. Then give each student a leaf shape of orange, or red, or yellow construction paper. The students can write their thankful message on the leaf and tape it to the tree.

"We should also be thankful for products that come from trees." Encourage students to bring in items to hang on a bulletin board tree. Hang items in groups, such as paper products, fruits, wood products, seeds and nuts, plastics, rubber, and so on. This makes a dynamic classroom bulletin board.

READING LINKS TO WRITING

Print With Natural Items

In days long ago, people did not have fancy pens and pencils for writing. Students need to know that people long ago used plant stems, the sharp end of bird feathers, and pointed sticks for writing. They dipped them into writing fluid (ink) that they made, often from the juice of berries.

Turn Back the Clock in the Writing Center

Set aside a portion of the Writing Center with items from nature. Show students how to print words, letters, names, pictures, and stories on sheets of brown kraft paper with gently torn edges to resemble tree bark. This will create curiosity in the classroom about the process of writing.

Many students will find that it is awkward to print with a stick, while others may do surprisingly well with this natural item. Do not put everything out at once; do this gradually throughout the month. Have students wear a smock.

Some items to include:

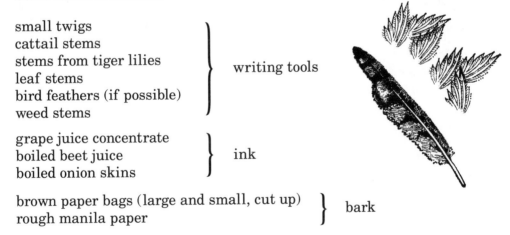

small twigs
cattail stems
stems from tiger lilies
leaf stems
bird feathers (if possible)
weed stems
} writing tools

grape juice concentrate
boiled beet juice
boiled onion skins
} ink

brown paper bags (large and small, cut up)
rough manila paper
} bark

Use Picture Writing

Have a sample of Native American Rebus pictures—pictures that represent a word—in the center. (See the Reproducible Activity Pages.) Students can create stories using these special symbols. Here are some samples:

sun   home   rain

A good resource book is *Talking Hands,* written and illustrated by Aline Amon.

Use Picture Writing on Rocks and Stones

Students can collect and bring in small, smooth rocks and stones. Then, using the natural writing items, they can print their name on the rock. Perhaps the rock can be painted first with tempera paint.

Make Pamphlets

Have a variety of pamphlets available so that students can see them, what they contain, and how they are folded. The children can be motivated to create a pamphlet for Children's Book Week or for American Education Week. Work in partners or teams of three so that the jobs can be shared.

READING LINKS TO MATH

Change the Calendar

This month, and every month, devote a large bulletin board space to the calendar. Make a giant turkey shape so that the head and neck, tail feathers, and legs go right off the space and onto the wall. Then use the body of the turkey as the grid for the days of the week and for the dates. Make yellow construction paper corn kernels with numbers. Students can sift through the kernels, locate the date, and "feed the turkey" all month long.

What Day Is It?

Give each student a calendar grid page for the month of November. The numerals can be filled in, or this can be done as a class activity. For math concepts, ask them to do the following on the grid:

"Color today pink."
"Color tomorrow green."
"Color the last day of the month violet."
"Color yesterday red."
"Color the first day of the month orange."

Let's Make a Tally of Number Letters in "November"

Print the word NOVEMBER vertically on the chalkboard. Then tell students you want to find out how hard those eight letters in the word "November" have to work when spelling out number names from one through ten.

Hold up the number name "one." The letters *o, n,* and *e* are all put to work, so after the N in NOVEMBER, make one straight stick mark; after the O, make a straight stick mark; and after the E make a straight stick mark. (These are called "tallies.")

It will look like this:

```
N  |
O  |
V     |
E  |
M
B
E
R
```

Hold up the number name "two." The letter *o* is put to work, so place another tally mark after the O.

When you finish, the November number-letter tally should look like this:

```
N  | | | | |            5
O  | | |                3
V  | |                  2
E  | | | | | | | | |    9
M
B
*E
R  | |                  2
```

*All tallies for the letter E were placed after the first showing of the letter.

Add up the tallies. Let's have some "math talk" about November. Which letter worked the most? the least? Was there any November letter that didn't have to work at all for this activity?

Some students may want to do this with SEPTEMBER and OCTOBER, or other months and come up with a different tally. Eventually, make a graph of the months and then one general graph that includes all of the information. Students are gaining experience by locating letters and recording numerals.

Interview the Month of November

Have two students represent the month of November. They can conduct a news conference and call upon students to ask them questions about their month. Students can ask factual questions, such as:

How many days are there in your month?

On what day do you begin?

On what day do you end?

How many Tuesdays are there in your month?

Do you have a holiday that falls on Thursday? If so, what is it?

How many full weeks are in your month?

Math Manipulatives From Nature

For math problems this month, become a nature detective. Select items from nature that can be used for simple addition and subtraction problems. Collect nuts, pebbles, shells, twigs, seeds, leaves, etc. Be sure to keep several natural containers to hold and classify the items. What can a natural container be? Grapevine baskets and other rough baskets, for starters.

Counting to Ten on Hands

Children make a fist on each hand and then raise their fingers one by one, beginning with the right hand, in the following manner:

Right Hand

#1—raise little finger on right hand

#2—raise little finger and ring finger

#3—raise little finger, ring finger, and middle finger

#4—raise little finger, ring finger, middle finger, and pointer finger

#5—raise little, ring, middle, and pointer fingers and thumb so that all fingers are extended

Keep the right hand in that position. Now move on to the left hand, which is in the shape of a fist:

Left Hand

#6—extend thumb so that both thumbs meet

#7—extend thumb and raise pointer finger

#8—extend thumb, pointer finger, and middle finger

#9—extend thumb, pointer, middle, and ring fingers (this one takes some practice)

#10—all ten fingers are extended, thumbs are touching

READING LINKS TO SOCIAL STUDIES

An ABC Picture Book for Native American Study

A good picture book and an excellent resource is *Many Nations, An Alphabet of Native America* by Joseph Bruchac with illustrations by Robert F. Goetzl. This book shows a variety of activities in 26 different communities. You can list the types beginning with Anishanabe artists, Blackfeet riders on horses, Chocktaw stickball players, Dakota storytellers, and 22 more to round out the alphabet.

The Four Corners

A concentration of Native Americans are in the "four corners" area of the United States. This is the area where corners of the states of Arizona, Utah, Colorado, and New Mexico meet. On a large map of the United States, have students locate these states. On kraft paper, make a large outline of the United States shape. Then, make smaller shapes of these four states, cut them out, label them, and place them on the map where they belong. The rest of the map will be blank, but during the month it can be filled in with names of Native American communities, or factual information, or designs that students find in picture books or information books (designs on pottery, jewelry, and so on). Make an attractive border inside the map with Native American designs and symbols.

Create a 3-D Dwelling

In the classroom, construct a native dwelling that is large enough and sturdy enough so that students can crawl inside or underneath and read. This can be done using an outdoor umbrella as a base. Drape an extra large piece of burlap over the umbrella top to serve as a roof. This can be decorated with student-made shapes and designs. Or, drape burlap over a card table and display the book selection on top.

Put pillows on the floor and have a selection of good books available for browsing or reading. Some suggestions include: *Indian Chiefs* by Russell Freedman; *The Girl Who Loved Wild Horses* and *Love Flute* by Paul Goble; *Coyote* and *Raven* by Gerald McDermott; and *Brother Eagle, Sister Sky,* a tale retold and illustrated by Susan Jeffers. By browsing through these books, students will gain a feeling for the designs and colors used by many of the Native American communities.

This activity offers an excellent opportunity to study the different types of Native American dwellings.

It's Harvest Time—Give Thanks

One of the reasons for harvest festivals the world over is to give thanks for the bountiful fruits and vegetables from the earth. Have the students discuss Thanksgiving customs and the dinner menu at their home. How is this special holiday celebrated?

Plan a holiday menu as a class. Bring in the newspaper and make a list of the items that would need to be purchased for a family of four or six (or however many the class decides). Then have students go through the ads, simulate the purchase of the items, and figure out the cost of Thanksgiving dinner.

The Corn Belt

In the United States, corn is grown mainly in a cluster of states that we call the "corn belt." Use the map of the United States and have students locate the following states that make up the corn belt: Illinois, Indiana, Iowa, Kansas, Minnesota, Missouri, Nebraska, Ohio, and South Dakota. You may want to tell this information to students or send them to the library to locate the nine states that make up this belt. Have students read the map to determine where their state is in relation to the corn belt.

Puzzle Maps USA by Nancy L. Clouse (New York: Henry Holt & Co., 1990) is an excellent resource book. In this book, the state shapes are shown as colorful kites high up in the sky, or are worn as clothing, or are put together to make the larger shape of a horse or a boy walking his dog. Cut out the shapes of the states you're working with (the four corners or the corn belt) and make a picture puzzle. This book is also available in Spanish, *Mapas rompecabezas de los Estados Unidos.*

An Abundance of Corn

Corn was known only to the people native to the Americas when Christopher Columbus arrived. Corn became the gift from the new world to the old. There are several types of corn:

- dent—field corn, mainly used to feed animals
- flint—like dent, but grown only in South America
- Indian—multicolored kernels, used mainly for decoration at harvest time
- flour—colored kernels (blue) to make tortillas and chips
- sweet—the most common type eaten by people; the sooner it is eaten after it is picked, the more sugar it contains; soon the sugar changes to starch and the corn becomes tough
- popcorn—the most popular snack food
- waxy—used to thicken food and to make starch

Have a display of Indian corn in the classroom during November, along with other harvest vegetables. (See Science & Health links.)

Print the names of the corn on a large sheet of construction paper in the shape of an ear of corn. Then, on the chalkboard, print only the partial word. Students can search for the correct letters to print in the blanks. For example:

p _ c o _ n   _ a x _   _ e _ t

An excellent resource book to have available in the classroom is entitled *CORN IS MAIZE, The Gift of The Indians* (New York: Harper & Row, 1976). This Let's-Read-And-Find-Out Book is written and illustrated by Aliki.

Our Responsibility to the Veterans

"Let's give thanks for the freedoms we enjoy in this country. Many people fought and gave their lives or their time so that we might enjoy these freedoms. Our form of government is unique in all the world. We owe the veterans a debt of gratitude."

For young children, link freedom with responsibility at a personal level. "In class, for example, when we have 'choice time' that gives us the freedom to choose what we can do, within limits. When we do choose to do some things, with it go certain responsibilities. Let's talk about freedom to choose and the responsibility that goes with it, right here in our classroom." Print the following on the chalkboard or on chart paper.

Free Choice Time	Responsibility
Painting at the easel	Cleaning up
Selecting a game with pieces	Picking up pieces and putting the game back
Building with blocks	Returning the blocks
Selecting a book from the Book Center	Returning book carefully, and setting others up that tipped over
Playing a game	Being a good sport and following the rules

Aw, Gee! Adults Don't Have Rules, But Do They?

Some students seem to think adults impose rules on them, but adults don't have any rules for themselves. Start with what students are familiar with, and talk about the fact that adults follow *many* rules. These are some to get the discussion started:

Traffic rules: light signals, signs, speed limits, etc.

Paying for goods: parents buy food, clothing, shelter

Paying for services: parents pay electricity bills, gas bills, water bills

Civil behavior: when standing in a line (you can't push to the front); in restaurants (you can't shout and run around); in theaters (you don't talk out loud and disturb others)

Recipe for Peace

The class can create its own recipe for peaceful living in the classroom. Ingredients can include items such as:

5 cups of "thank-you"

4 cups of "please"

3 tablespoons of "excuse me"

3 pints of "you're welcome"

The children can decide how to mix, blend, add, and share the ingredients.

A Recipe for a Pleasant Day

On colorful construction paper shapes, print words such as "thank you," "please," "excuse me," "you're welcome," "I'm sorry," and so on. Put a big pot and mixing spoon in the center of the room or circle. Everyone gets a shape to put into the pot, stirs it, turns to a neighbor, and says, "Have a good day today, _____." That person, in turn, says "Thank you, _____."
        (name)   (name)

Recipe for Cornbread

There are many math opportunities for measurement and time/temperature, and for sharing something that the group has made. You will need a toaster oven or access to a stove. (**Caution:** Used only under adult supervision!)

Ingredients:

1 cup all-purpose flour   1 well-beaten egg
3 teaspoons baking powder   1 cup milk
1 teaspoon salt   ¼ cup melted shortening
1 cup yellow cornmeal

Procedure: Sift together all dry ingredients. In another bowl combine the egg, milk, and shortening. Then pour the liquid mixture into the dry mixture. (Everyone gets a chance to mix.) It will have a lumpy consistency. Fill a well-greased pan ¾ full. Bake for 15–20 minutes at 450 degrees. (*Note:* A prepared corn muffin mix can be used instead.)

READING LINKS TO SCIENCE & HEALTH

A Harvest of Science Investigation

The Science Center for the month of November can be an investigation station. Have a microscope available. Students can examine kernels of corn under the microscope, draw them, and label them.

In addition to the Indian corn, have an array of other vegetables that can be on display in the classroom and then taken home and used, such as the squash family members—acorn, butternut, hubbard, turban, and so on. Slice one or two so that students can examine the inside, both with a magnifying glass and under the microscope. Draw a diagram and label the parts.

Make a booklet for keeping this information. Use a 12″ × 18″ sheet of colored construction paper, fold it in half, and have students decorate it for their November harvest study.

Time for P-P-P-Popping Corn

Today, corn can be popped in the microwave oven or air popped in the classroom using a popcorn machine. Popcorn is delicious and nutritious—and eating it plain helps to clean and polish one's teeth.

Popcorn dates back over 5,000 years ago in Mexico. There were no microwave ovens or popcorn poppers then, so Indians would hold the ear over the fire or throw the kernels into an open fire to pop it. Some would throw the kernels into a clay pot filled with hot sand and they would pop out.

For a good story and for more information, read *The Popcorn Book* by Tomie dePaola.

From Seed to Sprout

Make a diagram on a chart showing the progression "from seed to sprout" of various plants and flowers. Introduce the book *Jack's Garden* by Henry Cole, *Tops & Bottoms* by Janet Stevens, and *Your First Garden Book* by Marc Brown.

What's the Difference?

Have students dramatize the planting of a seed (digging a hole, gently setting the seed inside, covering with dirt, watering the seed). Then, students become the seed by getting into a crouched position, and then slowly awakening, stretching, poking an arm right through the ground, and slowly, slowly standing up tall. For contrast, have the children dramatize the popping of popcorn in a see-through popper (getting out the popper, measuring the butter, measuring the corn, filling the popper with corn, covering it with a lid, and plugging it in). Then they become the seed by getting into a crouched position and—when they warm up—they POP right up!

Ask the children, "How were the actions different? Which ones were done slowly and which swiftly? What was taking place here?"

Design a Birdfeeder

Bring in materials from home and design a birdfeeder. Then try it out on a tree branch, filled with popcorn seeds. Does it attract birds? Why or why not? Would different seeds work? Try it.

Let's Problem-solve This One

"How can we make popcorn of different colors? Will liquid coloring work? What about dry coloring? Will it stick best if the corn is buttered or natural? Let's experiment."

Weather Changes

Display a large monthly graph in the classroom, on a corner area of the chalkboard, that shows pictures (or cut-outs) of sun, rain, snow, wind, clouds. Then each day, at the same time, decide what symbol will be represented for that day and have students either put an "X" on the grid or draw in the symbol. This gives information about the weather for the month at a glance.

Clothing Changes

"Some animals naturally grow additional fur to keep them warm through winter. But people can't do that. So, to keep healthy and fit, as the weather gets colder, let's have a discussion about what appropriate clothing we would wear." *(sweaters, mittens, hats, long trousers, appropriate footwear)* This is something to note in the monthly newsletter for parents.

Also, students can make a "Booklet of Autumn Fashions" showing the changes that will need to be made in clothing. Have available an assortment of swatches of different types of material, so that students can cut out the shape of a sweater. They can paste it on the book page and draw themselves into the picture. Do the same for mittens, boots, jackets, and long trousers.

With more clothing coming into the classroom, make sure children hang them in their cubbie or on their hook, rather than just tossing the clothing in a pile. This calls for stepped-up responsibilities for those helpers in charge of wardrobe.

LINKS TO AUTHOR-OF-THE-MONTH

Author/Illustrator for November: Patricia Polacco

Patricia Polacco is a gifted storyteller and artist. She has a knack for quickly engaging the audience with her words and the colorful folk art illustrations in her books. One can gain additional information about the story, the people, and the setting by examining the pictures carefully after enjoying the text. Some of her earlier works are set in Russia. The stories she tells have a warmth that children and adults can sense, and they have an underlying message that is skillfully conveyed.

This author/illustrator has won many prestigious awards for her work. She lives in Michigan, where a meteor once landed in the yard, and that gave rise to the storybook *Meteor.* When she visits schools to talk with children, she takes a piece of the magic meteor with her in a little box and has children touch it and make a wish that will not affect others personally, and it can't cost money. She also shows students the quilt that is featured in her popular book *The Keeping Quilt,* which deals with generations of a Jewish family. Many of her stories are intergenerational; that is, they deal with children interacting with older adults in a positive way. We see this in *Mrs. Katz and Tush* and *Thundercake.* Also, the stories are multi-ethnic, since two of her childhood friends were African Americans, and we meet them in *Chicken Sunday.* A respect for Jewish tradition—as well as for learning and teachers—runs through several of her books.

Everyone falls in love with her Babushka. You are in for a treat from this storyteller! *Let's read!*

Chicken Sunday (New York: Philomel, 1994) This is a touching story about three children who want to get gramma Eula Mae a new Easter hat that she so admires in Mr. Kodinski's shop window. Pooling their resources, the children go to the shop, but their arrival is untimely, and they are blamed for throwing eggs that have just splattered his door. Gramma believes that they didn't do it, but now they have to convince Mr. Kodinski if they want to get that hat in time for Easter. They discover an inventive way to achieve their goal.

Activities to Accompany *Chicken Sunday*

1. First, read the story for the sheer enjoyment of the wish, the problem, and the solution that brings everyone happiness in the end.

2. Revisit the story, page by page, and "visit gramma's house" with its real photographs and colorful tablecloth, and the items served for Chicken Sunday. Visit the house of the little girl with the Russian icons.

3. This is a perfect invitation to make "Pysanky" eggs or a version thereof. A simple solution, since the actual pysanky method involves hot wax, is to bring eggs to a boil, allow them to cool, have students decorate them with wax crayon, and then submerge them in commercial egg dye. If you choose to make the dye for the eggs, a few suggestions are to use water in which onion skins were boiled, or grape juice, berry juice, or beet juice. Be sure to wear smocks. Refrigerate the eggs and take them home the next day in a little carton (decorated milk carton).

4. Listen to the language. Mr. Kodinski says, "Chutzpah, you have Chutzpah!" (pronounced HUT spa) It means that you have courage. Ask students when they have shown courage.

5. Listen to more of the language. Gramma's voice is described as being like "slow thunder and sweet rain" when she was singing. Engage students in a

conversation of just what such a lovely voice would sound like, when someone sings from their heart.

6. Make hats and have a tea party. Even Mr. Kodinsky wears a hat. Students
   can create hats from paper plates, netting, ribbons, artificial flowers, and
   so on. Use hats that have been donated for the dress-up and dramatic play
   areas, and reenact the story. (Lemonade can be served from the teapot.) Select background music and play it for the tea party.

7. Ask students this question: "When was the last time you did something nice
   for an older person for the sheer joy that you knew it would bring that person? These children in the story did not want anything in return. Let's foster this attitude and see if we can do a good deed for our own gramma, or
   mother, or relative. Why? Just because." Then have the children come back
   and talk about it at a designated time.

Rechenka's Eggs **(New York: Philomel, 1988)** This story is set in Russia. Babushka
lives alone in a dacha, a little house in the country. She's known for her egg painting,
and is aiming for first prize at the Easter Festival in Moskva (Moscow). One day when
she is outdoors, she finds an injured goose and nurses it back to health. She names
the goose Rechenka. But one day the goose accidentally overturns the basket of beautiful eggs and all is lost. But the next morning there is a surprise awaiting Babushka in
the basket that she has fixed up for the goose. "A miracle!" she cries. There is one
more major miracle to go before the story is over. (A tale lovingly told.)

Activities to Accompany *Rechenka's Eggs*

1. Go through the book and enjoy the story, and then revisit Babushka's house
   with its colorful quilts. Revisit Moskva (Moscow) and compare the colorful
   rendition of the Kremlin with actual photographs of the Kremlin that you
   can find in other informational books about Russia. This is called "artistic
   license"—the author has given the beautiful buildings a warmth, design,
   and color just for the story. Students might want to try this technique.

2. Make colorful eggs using 12" × 18" manila paper. With a black crayon, create the oval shape. Then create the egg designs and color them in with
   bright colors. Press hard on the colors so that all spots are filled. Next, use
   a watercolor wash (orange or red or blue) over the egg. Allow this to dry.
   Then cut out the oval-shaped egg. Make a paper basket for the bulletin
   board and pile it high with these large, colorful eggs.

3. Retell and reenact the story. Use a head shawl, a chair, a basket, and a
   stuffed (paper) goose. What song will children sing to soothe the injured
   goose?

4. Make a colorful goose using the same technique referred to in activity 2, or
   have students paint a goose at the easel with brown, white, black, and tan.
   The geese can be displayed on the same bulletin board as the eggs, or on the
   door with a title. They can also serve as a prop that children hold up to help
   them tell the story. Rebus story pictures on the back can help, too. Since it's
   November, these birds and the story can fit in with a unit on bird migration.

***Babushka's Doll* (New York: Simon & Schuster, 1990)** In this delightful turn-about tale, Natasha wants her busy grandmother to do things with her and for her NOW. Grandmother has to go to town but before she leaves, she takes a little doll off a high shelf and tells Natasha the time is right for her to play with the doll. When Grandmother leaves, the doll comes to life and is very demanding—and even more rambunctious than Natasha! Grandmother returns just in time to comfort the girl and to put the doll back on the shelf—but not before the doll gives a wink to Babushka. Natasha, on the other hand, "turned out to be quite nice after all."

Activities to Accompany *Babushka's Doll*

1. Reread the story and enjoy the pictures. Take note of how hard Babushka works with the laundry tub, old pump, and hanging up the clothes by hand. Discussion questions: "How would life be different for her if she had modern equipment? Does this give a person more time for other things?"

2. Have students reenact this turn-about tale. What props will we need?

3. What other stories have we read where the dolls or animals come to life? (*The Nutcracker; The Velveteen Rabbit; The Gingerbread Boy;* and so on) If students are not familiar with these stories, this might be a good time to read them and make some comparisons. Students can listen to music from *The Nutcracker Suite.* Have them close their eyes and envision the toys coming to life and dancing.

4. Have students write a story about a toy or doll that comes to life and does not behave well. There will have to be a satisfying ending to the tale.

***Thunder Cake* (New York: Philomel, 1990)** This is one that students want to hear again and again. Babushka helps her granddaughter get through a day that promises a good thunderstorm by deciding they'll bake a thundercake. She gets the child's mind off of the sounds of crashes and bangs by having the granddaughter fetch items for the cake. Babushka gives the child a formula for counting so she can determine how close the storm is. While waiting for their cake, Babushka tells the little girl how brave she is. Then as they sit before an open window with the dark storm and roaring thunder outside, the little girl and Babushka just smile and eat their thundercake. (The recipe for My Grandma's Thunder Cake appears at the back. Why the tomatoes? For moisture, says the author.)

Activities to Accompany *Thunder Cake*

1. Go back through the book and note the designs and textures on the fabric. Perhaps students can make some paper that looks like these folk prints using gadget printing.

2. Copy the formula for determining how far away a thunderstorm is. Then someday the students might be able to use it.

3. If possible, bake the Thunder Cake in the classroom. This is a good hands-on math experience with measuring, counting, timing. If you don't have an

opportunity for this, make sure that a copy of the recipe goes home with each child (it's in the back of the book). Perhaps parents will try this at home. Someone might even volunteer to make one for the next class celebration.

4. Discuss bravery. Grandmother thinks the girl is brave and tells her so. A good question for students is to have them determine how they might overcome fears (night fears, storm fears, etc.).

5. Students can reenact this story through dramatic play, and help the girl (and themselves) to confront fear.

The Keeping Quilt **(New York: Simon & Schuster, 1988)** In this story, The Keeping Quilt is passed along from generation to generation. It is made from the clothing of family members who came to this country as immigrants. This quilt is used for a variety of things: as a tablecloth, as a wedding huppa, as a wrap for new babies born into the family. Throughout the book the quilt is in color, whereas the rest of the book is in black and white. A tenth-anniversary edition of this book was published in 1998 to bring the readers up to date on the family.

Activities to Accompany *The Keeping Quilt*

1. This calls for quilt making, so have students design a classroom quilt. You can use white material squares and fabric crayons. Students can make self-portraits and print their names at the bottom. The quilt can be sewn together with a colorful border, just as in the book.

2. For a different type of quilt, use brown or white butcher paper. Students can paint an animal or tree or a figure, inspired by the quilt in the book, directly on the quilt in scattered fashion. Make the scalloped edge from paper designed by the class, or use wrapping paper.

3. *Companion books on quilts.* There are many books about quilts, and this would be a good time to get them to read to students. Make a chart comparison for the books, listing the main characters, the setting, the uses for the quilt, and so on. Some good storybooks that contain quilts include *The Patchwork Quilt* by Valerie Flournoy, with pictures by Jerry Pinkney; *Eight Hands Round, An ABC Book of Quilts* by Ann Whitford Paul, with illustrations by Jeanette Winter, is extremely helpful to students for making designs; *The Quilt* by Ann Jonas; *My Grandmother's Patchwork Quilt, A Book and Pocketful of Patchwork Pieces* by Janet Bolton (with actual pieces for students to trace onto cloth and sew); and *The Seasons Sewn, A Year in Patchwork* by Ann Whitford Paul, with illustrations by Michael McCurdy. A good resource book for the teacher is *Stitching Stars, The Story Quilts of Harriet Powers* by Mary E. Lyons.

4. Invite a quilt maker to class to discuss this process and demonstrate how it is done. Perhaps the quilt maker could "set up shop" in the classroom for a whole morning, so that students would be able to observe in small groups. Some children might be inspired to try quilting or needlework.

5. "What is your family history?" Students can interview parents to learn about their ancestors. Perhaps a figure or design representing each person could be colored (or painted), cut out, and pasted to an individual Story Quilt done by each class member. The top of a large page could be used for the quilt; the bottom could contain the text, which explains the quilt.

***Mrs. Katz and Tush* (New York: Bantam Books, 1992)** This is the story of an unlikely couple—an elderly Jewish widow who is all alone and a young African American boy named Larnel who lives in the same neighborhood. To ease her loneliness, he suggests that she take in a kitten. She does so on the condition that he will help her, as she's never before had a pet. So, as she teaches him about Jewish traditions and holidays, they find that they have quite a lot in common. (A touching intergenerational story.)

Activities to Accompany *Mrs. Katz and Tush*

1. Go through the story and list the expressions as well as the words that Mrs. Katz uses to describe Jewish holidays.

2. The story is also centered around a cat. How many students have a pet cat? Does it look like the one in the story? What did they name their pets and why were the names chosen? That calls for some "storytelling."

3. Have students list their holiday traditions for the upcoming season. How do they vary from home to home? What "traditions" do students particularly enjoy? Which ones would they like to take part in?

4. Write a story, true or make-believe, about how neighbors help each other, such as when a pet is missing, when a child gets lost, and so on.

And Many More!

A festival of Patricia Polacco stories could go on all month—and beyond. There are many other interesting stories she has written, including: *Just Plain Fancy*, the story of an Amish girl who would like to wear some colorful clothing; *The Bee Tree*, a celebration of learning how to read; *My Rotten Redheaded Older Brother; Meteor;* and *Pink and Say* (for older readers). Don't forget to read *The Trees of the Dancing Goats* next month in celebration of the Christmas/ Hanukkah season.

Keep a chart of these magical stories, and have students fill in the information that includes: Title, Characters, Setting, Plot (action), Theme (the story message), Ending. Students can select their favorites and give them "starred reviews."

If you ever have the opportunity to have this author visit your school, you are in for a treat! The author has the gift of being able to make a connection with the audience in person, as well as through the delightful books that she creates.

REPRODUCIBLE ACTIVITY PAGES

Marching Band—Letter C (Cindy Cat)

Marching Band—Letter F (Phillip Frog)

Marching Band—Letter N (Nanny Nuthatch)

Marching Band—Letter P (Peter Penguin)

Marching Band—Letter W (Wally Whale)

November Highlights Concentration

The City Cat and Country Cat Chant *(Letter c)*

Wally's Wash Day Chant *(Letter w)*

The PH = F Bake Shop

Sunny Side Up and Scrambled Words

The "Instant People" Words *(Sight Words)*

Autumn Rebus Pictures and Words *(Rebus)*

Children's Literature Activity Page—The Comparison Goose *(Patricia Polacco)*

©DCW99

© 2000 by The Center for Applied Research in Education

© DCW99

© 2000 by The Center for Applied Research in Education

© 2000 by The Center for Applied Research in Education

P p

© 2000 by The Center for Applied Research in Education

© 2000 by The Center for Applied Research in Education

Ww

NOVEMBER HIGHLIGHTS
CONCENTRATION

Look carefully at the squares that highlight special events during the month of November. Learn what goes together as you color them. Cut the squares on the lines. Place them face down on a grid. Turn two over to see if they match. If they do, set them aside. If not, put them back and try again. This game can be played with two players. The winner is the player with the most matching cards. When finished, reshuffle the cards and play again!

© 2000 by The Center for Applied Research in Education

Name _____

THE CITY CAT AND
COUNTRY CAT CHANT

Learn this chant. It has both the soft sound (city) and hard sound (country) of the letter "c." Move back and forth like a cat. What color will you choose for the cats?

Cindy likes the city
    With tall skyscrapers.
She can climb up fire escapes
    And read newspapers.
Her city sound is a
    definite hisssssssssss.
If she lived in the country
    It's the city she'd missssssssss!

Heeerrre City, City, City, Cindy.

This kit-cat likes the country
    With fields of yellow grain.
She can walk in the road.
    She can play in the rain.
Her country cat sound
    Is shared with Cousin "K,"
She sings it out clearly
    In the light of the day.

Heeerrre Country, Country, Country, Cat.

City, City, Cindy/Country, Country Cat,
Tell me what you think of that? MEOW!

C C C

© 2000 by The Center for Applied Research in Education

Name _____

WALLY'S WASH DAY CHANT

Learn to say Wally Whale's chant as you help Wally do the wash. You can pretend to rub, scrub, and wring out the wash. Learn the sound that the letter "w" makes. Color Wally a happy color.

Wally likes to
 wishy, washy
 wishy, washy
 wishy, washy
Wally likes to
 wishy, washy
'Til he's all washed up.

Wally's clothes are
 washable
 washable
 washable
Wally's clothes are
 washable
'Til he's all washed up.

Wally likes the
 wash and wear
 wash and wear
 wash and wear
Wally likes the
 wash and wear
'Til he's all washed up.

Please help Wally
 wishy, washy
 wishy, washy
 wishy, washy
Please help Wally
 wishy, washy
'Til he's all washed up.

© 2000 by The Center for Applied Research in Education

THE PH = F BAKE SHOP

Philip Frog is getting mixed up. The *Ph* in Philip sounds just like the *f* in frog. Today Philip Frog could use your help at the bake shop. He needs to make new signs, and his head is spinning!

Here's what you can do. Get your pencil. Place the letter "f" or "ph" on the lines. Use the dictionary for help.

Color everything so that it looks delicious! Thank You!

© 2000 by The Center for Applied Research in Education

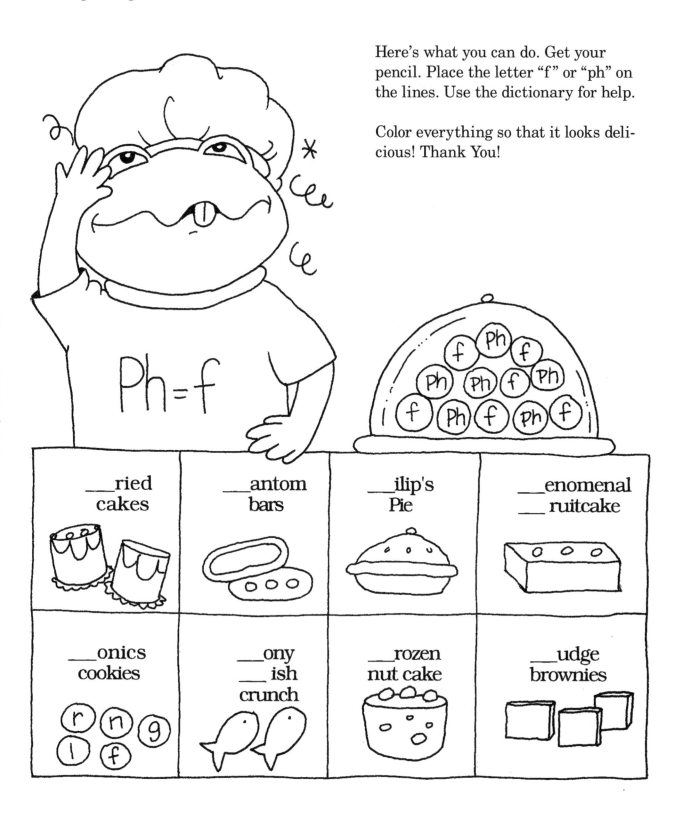

___ried cakes

___antom bars

___ilip's Pie

___enomenal ___ruitcake

___onics cookies

___ony ___ish crunch

___rozen nut cake

___udge brownies

SUNNY SIDE UP AND
SCRAMBLED WORDS

Match the words on the left side with the scrambled words on the right side. Look carefully at the letters. The first one is done for you. Color the eggs a sunny yellow.

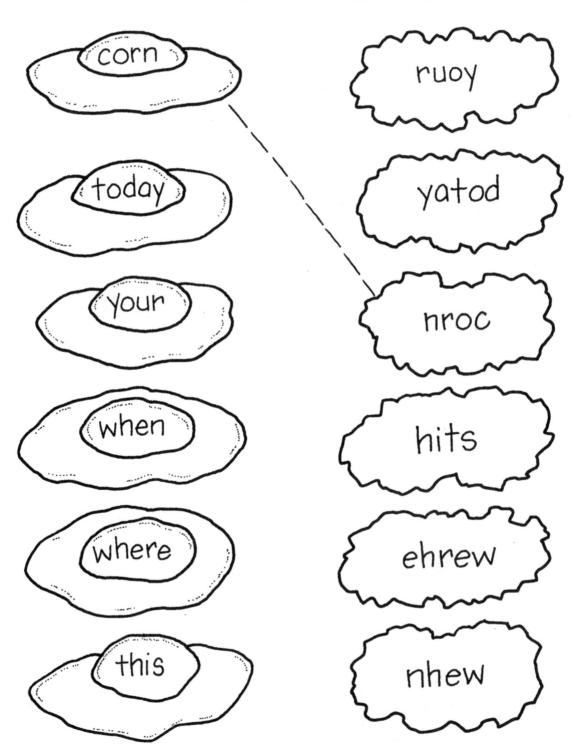

© 2000 by The Center for Applied Research in Education

© 2000 by The Center for Applied Research in Education

THE INSTANT PEOPLE WORDS

These words are from the first 100 Instant Words. There are *ten* people words. Find them. Circle them. Learn ALL of these words by heart. Work with a partner.

Name _____

you   she   his   we

I   he

the   and

the   of   your   in

is   her   that   be

my   it   was   for

are   as   him   with

Hi, Bill.
How is Bill?
Where is Bill going?

You need to
work on the
"people words."

Bill

AUTUMN REBUS PICTURES AND WORDS

Identify and color the pictures. Learn the words. Then, cut them on the lines. Arrange them into a "sentence starter." Write and draw your sentence. How many can you make?

the	thanks	dinner	on
in	day	fun	peace

© 2000 by The Center for Applied Research in Education

THE COMPARISON GOOSE (PART 1)

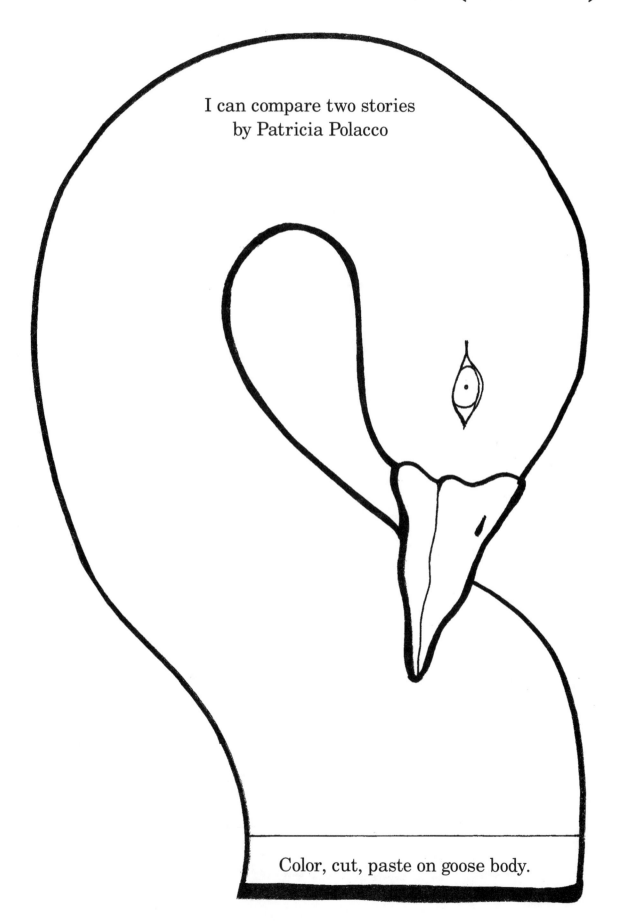

I can compare two stories
by Patricia Polacco

© 2000 by The Center for Applied Research in Education

Color, cut, paste on goose body.

THE COMPARISON GOOSE (PART 2)

Name:

Fill in book information.

Title	Characters	Setting	What's the problem?	Ending	Rating

© 2000 by The Center for Applied Research in Education

December

CHILDREN'S PICTURE BOOKS

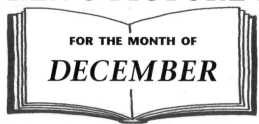

FOR THE MONTH OF
DECEMBER

Fleming, Denise. *Lunch* **(New York: Henry Holt and Co., 1992)** It's time for lunch and this little mouse is famished, eating everything in sight until he can't eat another bite—that is, until dinnertime! (Big, bright, bold figures and colors for children to enjoy with a minimum of text.)

Garten, Jan. *The Alphabet Tale.* **Illustrated by Muriel Batherman (New York: Greenwillow Books, 1994)** A guessing game with the ABC rhymes. On each page is a tale of an animal, along with a verse, and the reader must turn the page to find out to which animal the tale belongs. This book makes learning fun.

Hague, Michael. *The Perfect Present* **(New York: Morrow Junior Books, 1996)** It's Christmas Eve and Jack Rabbit wants to buy his sweetheart something special from Big Bear's Toy Shoppe. When he finds a playful-looking kangaroo, the kangaroo bounces out of the door before it can be wrapped up, and the merry chase is on. There are four double gatefolds that open into winterland panoramas. (A tender story with gorgeous illustrations and endpapers, too.)

Howard, Elizabeth Fitzgerald. *Chita's Christmas Tree.* **Illustrated by Floyd Cooper (New York: Bradbury, 1989)** Chita is the daughter of one of the city's first black doctors. The setting is Baltimore and the joyous occasion includes getting the Christmas tree with Papa. Chita and Mama bake cookies, relatives come, and finally it's Christmas.

Joseph, Lynn. *An Island Christmas.* **Illustrated by Catherine Stock (Boston: Houghton-Mifflin, 1992)** In this book, Rosie is busy helping her mother and Tantie, her aunt, prepare the traditional black-currant cake, sorrel drink, and soursop ice cream for the holidays.

Kimmel, Eric. *The Chanukkah Guest* **(New York: Holiday House, 1990)** A side-splitting tale of a little old woman who is preparing potato latkes for dinner guests, including the rabbi. A lazy, hungry bear sniffs the delicious aroma and comes to the door. Bubba Brayna, the grandmother with failing eyesight, mistakes the bear for the rabbi—and the fun begins. Children will ask to hear it again. Also look for *The Magic Dreidels* by this author.

Lewis, J. Patrick. *The Christmas of the Reddle Moon.* **Illustrated by Gary Kelley (New York: Dial, 1994)** An original tale inspired by the works of Thomas Hardy. Taking place on the moors, two children set out late in the day to deliver presents, but stay too long and get caught in a snowstorm. Legend has it that Wee Mary Fever, a woman who lives nearby, has magic powers. She takes in the dazed and frightened children, and somehow they are transported to their own home, safe and sound. It's a puzzler!

McKee, David. *Snow Woman* **(New York: Lothrop, Lee & Shepard, 1987)** It's a great day to build a snowman, but two children with "politically correct" parents are reminded that it's a *snowperson*. They end up building a snowman and a snowwoman, but the next day when they've melted, they leave the language behind and have fun building a bear.

Pinkney, Andrea Davis. *Seven Candles for Kwanzaa.* **Illustrated by Brian Pinkney (New York: Dial, 1993)** A bright, colorful book that gives the reader a good feeling about this African American celebration in December. There is information in the book that will be helpful to students concerning the purpose and intent of the holiday.

Sabuda, Robert. *The 12 Days of Christmas, A Pop-Up Celebration Book* **(New York: Simon & Schuster, 1996)** This book is most special for children, because the timeless song of the 12 days of Christmas come to life through pop-up engineering that the artist has designed to twist and turn, go around in circles, and create marvelous three-dimensional structures. It is a lavish treat for all!

DECEMBER

DECEMBER GREETINGS! This is an exciting month for students, with the expectation in the air of holiday festivities. It's also a good opportunity for integrating reading and language activities into other areas of the curriculum. In so doing, with children's stories, you maintain a focus upon the main idea, the setting, main characters, and secondary characters.

Although students will have met the alphabet repeatedly, it is still necessary to focus upon single letters, and you need to keep up that effort during the month. The ABC Marching Band continues to be introduced with helpful activities for young learners, designed to provide a special emphasis upon phonics. This month you'll maneuver your way through a page of print by noting the *reading road signs,* much as a car would maneuver through traffic. *Let's read!*

December's Focus on Reading. Specific skills to focus on, in addition to your regular structured reading program, are: (1) More Phonemic Awareness with the Alphabet; (2) Guided Reading Activities; (3) Reading Road Signs; (4) Root Words and Endings; and (5) The ABC Marching Band Letters—D, H, J, K, and G.

Because of changing weather in some areas, it is necessary to spend more recess time indoors. Rather than experiencing mayhem, structure the indoor recess and include reading skill games. Tell students what their options are, and have them volunteer to spend recess time doing a particular activity. Many of these activities can be reading activities.

Plan Together for a Typical Recess   Students wait for all assignments to be made before they begin. For example, you can say, "Who would like to take the big pointer and 'play school' with the letter posters?" (assign two or three); "We have room for two or three at the bakery center to buy ABC letters. Who are they?" (assign two or three); "There is room for two people at the easel. Who has signed up?" (check the sign-up list and assign two students); "The flannel board can handle two people to retell stories. Who are they?" (assign two or three) "Room for two people at the jigsaw puzzle table. Who is interested today?" (assign two) Keep doing this until all games and activities are assigned. Then when you ring the bell, it's time to begin; when you ring it again, it's time for clean up. *(This can be so successful that many students prefer indoor recess and look forward to it.)*

More Phonemic Awareness with the Alphabet

An ABC Tale

There is ample opportunity to associate letter–sound relationships with the cumulative refrains in the read-aloud book *Bearsie Bear and the Surprise Sleepover Party* by Bernard Waber. In this book, it's a cold and snowy night; just as Bearsie Bear is going to sleep in his warm bed, there's a knock at the door. It's

Moosie Moose who wants a warm bed for the night. These two are eventually joined by Cowsie Cow, Piggie Pig, and others. Everything is fine until Porky Porcupine joins them. Ouch! What then? (Stop at this point and have students predict the ending, or the sequence of events to follow. What would they do?) Read on. This is a good story for children to reenact in dramatic play. It also provides an opportunity for phonics association with the animal names.

The Letter Delivery

Students can be assembled on the floor in front of the chalkboard or seated at their desks for this total-group experience. Use a small toy truck and put as many letters inside as will fit. Then ask a student to pretend to be the driver and make a letter delivery to the class. One by one, call upon a student to help unload the truck by removing a letter. Then discuss the letter—the shape, lines, whether it is a capital or lower-case letter, the sound that it makes, and any words they know that begin with that sound.

Follow this procedure until all of the letters in the truck have been delivered. Letters can be cardboard with magnetic tape backing for placement on the chalkboard or a magnetic board. Or, work with a flannel board and cut-out letters that have Velcro™ glued to the back.

Variations: Change the letter delivery daily, so different letters will be discussed. This will assist the students with their writing as well. Also, a letter can be delivered inside an envelope; the person who removes the letter has to describe it while others try to guess the letter.

The Missing Letter

Place all of the alphabet flash cards except one along the chalkboard ledge. Students have to discover which one is missing. When they know, they can print the letter on a small piece of paper, turn it over, and wait for further instructions.

The cards can be placed in a row in the traditional ABC order. For beginners, this is best.

For advanced readers, place the letters in random order and have them search for the one that's missing.

We Know Who's Missing, But Now What?

"Well, we're off on our own for awhile with a missing letter. For the next ten minutes, we will not be able to use that letter . . . after all, it's missing!" Determine three or four ways in which we cannot use the missing letter. Examples are:

- for someone's name
- for the month or for day of the week
- for the teacher's name, principal's name, etc.

D_c_mb_r

Have students make up a silly sentence and omit the missing letter. For example, missing letter is D, so we will have to say, "This is the month of _ecember."

Names to substitute are: _avi_ for David; _onal_ for Donald; _an for Dan. Derek becomes _erek, and Dominic becomes _ominic. For girls, you will need to say _aphne for Daphne; _onna for Donna; _anielle for Danielle.

Look around the classroom for names of items that you will have to change. This causes a great deal of attention to be focused upon the letter and its sound, and heightens visual awareness. Children delight in looking for words they cannot say today—so this is a good time to use the _ictionary.

Eventually, the missing letter must be found (in a bottom drawer, underneath the sink, in a wire basket on a shelf, or in the teacher's coat pocket).

Two good picture books to read for this type of activity are *V Is for Vanishing, An Alphabet of Endangered Animals* by Patricia Mullins and *The Disappearing Alphabet* by Richard Wilbur, with illustrations by David Diaz.

"I'm Meeting the Man in the Moon for a Munchy, Then I'm Off to the Big Dipper for Lunchy"

Distribute the ABC cards (space shuttle tickets) to students and rev up the engines. All aboard! Students say, "I'm going to the moon and I'm going to take a/an/my. . . . " (The item must *begin* with the letter sound they have in their hand, which is their ticket to the moon.) After they name something, they can deposit the card in a bucket labeled "The Big Dipper." If a student has difficulty, he or she can check with visual pictures that are on letter posters and cards around the room. They can also get help from a fellow traveler.

On another journey, students must select an item that *ends* with the letter sound on their ticket.

Variation: Students can do this exercise on paper. Fold the paper in half, and then in half again. This will provide four spaces. In the first space, print the upper- and lowercase letter that is on the "ticket" and draw something that begins with that letter. In the three remaining spaces, they can print the letters that come right after their ticket letter. Then they can draw and label an item in each space for that letter. Students can compare information as a total group.

Guided Reading Activities

The Space on the Page—A Guided Tour

This month use the overhead projector for an awareness of white space, or blank areas on a page of print. Also use big books or picture books to help with this awareness.

You need to direct students' attention to the fact that the print does not run in together. A page of print can be compared to a super highway or a well-designed park—everything has a place. In the case of print, there are spaces between words.

There is an indented space for a new paragraph (new thought). The left side of the margin usually has a straight space and the right side of the page has crooked or wobbly space, depending upon where the words stop and start.

On the first page of a story, there is a title "centered" on the page. Point this out and note the space before and after the title.

Point out that there are white spots or *spaces* between certain letters. When you see clusters of letters together, that's what is known as a *word*. To reinforce the concept of a word, have students come to the big book and cup their hands around a word, or come to the overhead projector and run their finger under a word. What is a word? A unit of sound that has meaning.

Sentences Have Spaces

Take a simple sentence and print it on the chalkboard. Say it and point to the letters and spaces. Then print the same sentence with no space between the words. For example, **Today is Tuesday** can be printed as **TodayisTuesday.** When you say "Today is Tuesday," it is said at a slower pace because of the white spots between the words. ("When we listen, we can't *see* the white spots. When we read, we do see them.") **TodayisTuesday** looks like it has run in together with no place to stop, so we would say it faster.

Print additional sentences on the chalkboard. First, model it correctly and then run all of the letters together. Can students figure out where the spaces should be? Here are some simple sentences for beginning readers.

Ruth can play ball.	Ruthcanplayball.
Misty is tall.	Mistyistall.
Anthony likes pizza.	Anthonylikespizza.

This exercise should help with word-attack skills. Students need to work on one word at a time—rather than on the whole sentence at once—until they gain some proficiency with reading.

Also, when printing words they can use their finger to make a space between words. Place the finger on the page and put a tiny dot to the right of the finger. Then begin at the dot for the next word.

More Guidelines With Markers

Give each student a reading marker. Cut up a page of construction paper and give each student a piece of paper about the size of a 4-inch ruler (about the size of a bookmark). On a page of print in a familiar story, have students do the following with their marker:

- Put your marker under the word that shows the name of the girl.
- Put your marker under the name of the frog.
- Put your marker under the name of the boy.

- Put your marker under the word that tells _____ .
- Put your marker under the first word on the page.
- Put your marker under the last sentence.
- Put your marker under the word "and."
- Put your marker under the first sentence and, with your pointer finger, trace along under each word (left to right).

Read to Find Out

Give students a purpose for reading. Beginning readers can be asked to, for example, "Read until you find out who is at the door," or "Read to find out why the mouse has such a surprised look." Instruct students to raise their hand when they know; they must not shout it out. "Let your neighbor discover it, too."

The Guided Reading Lesson—A Group of Readers

Work with a small group of students that is of similar ability. Perhaps the students are going through a basal reader text together or a short story that will give them little difficulty. These are the steps to follow:

1. Assemble the students in a group, while other students are gainfully occupied and quiet. (Their turn comes soon with their peer reading group.)
2. Review vocabulary words. Introduce new vocabulary words, whether in a list or in a sentence on the chalkboard. Point to commonalities about the words: same beginning sound, a familiar name, a pattern to the words, and so on. Then say them together.
3. Motivate the students for the story. Say, for example, "Today we are going to read a story about a boy who lost his dog, and ended up being glad about it! That sounds a bit strange, doesn't it?" or "In our story today, a most unusual thing happens."
4. Distribute materials (books or story). Students open them to a particular page. Read the title and discuss the pictures on the page with the students.
5. For each page, you will say one of the following prior to silent reading:
   - Read the page to find out . . .
   - On this page we'll learn why . . .
   - You will meet an old friend on this page.
   - When you find out the secret, don't say anything. Put your bookmark in your book and close the book.
6. Discuss the story along the way (for younger students) or after several pages (for more advanced readers). The story can be discussed factually, or students might want to predict what will happen next.
7. Decide what parts need to be read aloud. This gives you an opportunity to observe the readers and the strategies they use and need to learn.

- Ask for volunteers, "Who would like to read this part?"
- "Let's each read a paragraph on this page, starting with Lamar."
- Do some of the story as choral reading

8. Discuss the story fully at the end and student reactions.

9. Provide ways to enrich the story. (Choose one. Draw a picture, diorama, clay sculpture, make puppets for reenactment, letter writing, skill page, and so on.)

Guided reading groups can meet daily, or three times each week, for 20 to 30 minutes. What are other students doing during this guided instructional time? They can be working in various Learning Centers, or working on activities from #9 above that pertain to their own reading, or working on assigned work for the day, or writing in their journal, or reading, and so on. They are NOT playing. Have a place for them to deposit their finished work, or collect it at the end of a productive morning.

Reading Road Signs

Driving Your Way Through a Page of Print

Just as road signs are important for a driver, the "road signs" in print are important for a reader and a writer. Make a big traffic-signal shaped chart in the classroom with these signs and the title "Reading Road Signs." Have students think of Rebus shapes to help them identify these signs and draw them on the chart.

 . *Period.* This is the first "road sign" that jumps out at the reader because it is used more than any other signal on the page. It's repetitious. It stands out. It's like a red light. It means put on the brakes and STOP.

 , *Comma.* This means pause, or slow down, and then start right up again. It's like a yellow flashing light.

 ! *Exclamation point.* This driver is blowing the horn . . . LOUD! When you see this sign, you make your voice sound louder. (It can be joy or fear or surprise or anger.)

? *Question mark.* This sign means that someone does not know and is asking a question. It can be likened to the driver who is asking for directions. Usually when you meet this sign in print and read it aloud, you raise your voice at the end.

 " *Quotation marks.* These signs indicate that someone is talking. They come at the beginning and at the end of what the person is saying. They wrap around speech like a bumper wraps around a car. The traffic cop who is directing traffic says, "Stop!" and then blows his or her whistle and says, "Go."

'*Apostrophe*. This sign can mean a short cut. For example, *I am* becomes *I'm* and *she will* becomes *she'll*. When you take a short cut, you cut out some of the letters. Just like when you take a short cut in a car, you cut out some of the streets or miles.

The apostrophe can also mean possessive. That is, it shows ownership, such as Anna Louise's coat or TJ's jacket. Yesterday's newspaper means that the news belongs to that day. Whose car is it? It's Tanya's car.

Yesterday's Newspaper Is Today's Road Map

Students can go through a page of print in search of the signs previously described. On one page, just make a tally of the periods. On another page, circle the commas. On another page, draw a circle around the exclamation points, and so on.

Bring on the Junk Mail

How do advertisers use these signs? Examine want ads and glitzy mail that is received from the post office or that someone hangs on the doorknob. Find the reading signs.

Proofreading

By using these signals, students will be able to self-correct their written work in a new way. They are gaining a knowledge of punctuation marks and a useful strategy. (See Reproducible Activity Pages for skill building.)

Root Words and Endings

How Do We Indicate More Than One? (S)

Usually by adding the letter *s* to a root word. Give students practice with this on the chalkboard. Have them add the suffixes. Notice that in words that end in a consonant, the letter *s* can be added.

run—runs   stop—stops   S
click—clicks   pull—pulls

A Variety of Endings (S, ED, ING)

For most root words you simply add the endings, such as:

laugh—laughs, laughed, laughing   ing
sigh—sighs, sighed, sighing
plant—plants, planted, planting

Change "Y" to "I" and Add "ES"

Children have to learn this rule by heart. Here are some examples. Give students ample opportunity to do this on the chalkboard as a whole-group lesson. Use individual skill sheets for practice.

sky—skies   try—tries
fry—fries   cry—cries

The Root Word Train and the Caboose

The caboose is the last box car on the train—it brings up the rear. The caboose factory makes a wide variety of endings. In addition to the single *s*, there is the *ly, less, ed, ing,* and others. While the root word may remain the same, the caboose attached to the end can vary. Here are some examples:

LY	LESS	ED	ING
slow	care	join	go
slowly	careless	joined	going
month	thank	rain	slow
monthly	thankless	rained	slowing

Beginning students need an abundance of practice with the endings, but once they are able to sound out the "caboose" endings, it makes for smoother reading. Some students are still working on this at the end of their primary school years, whereas others have mastered it and gone on.

The ABC Marching Band Letters of the Month— D, H, J, K, G

See the Reproducible Activity Pages for the Marching Band members.

Meet Dolby Dog and the Dulcimer *(Letter D)*

Dolby Dog plays the dulcimer in the ABC Marching Band. The dulcimer is a real instrument with strings of varying lengths that are stretched over a wooden sound box It can be played by plucking or by striking it with a padded hammer.

The sound that this instrument will make for our marching band is the sound of the letter *d*, which is similar to "duh." To make this sound, the tongue is pressed against the ridge on the roof of the mouth, just behind the front teeth. The tongue is pushed and then released at the same moment that air is expelled from the back of the throat, thus giving us the sound.

Have students put their hand to their throat while making the repeated sound of *d*. Note that the sound can also be felt with the hand.

Dolby Dog Has a Dew Claw *(Letter D)*

dewclaw

Dolby Dog plays the dulcimer with his dew claw. What is a dew claw? It is the small claw at the side of the paw of a dog (or cat). It is said to be called a "dew claw" because the claw does not touch the ground, but is high enough up that it only meets the dew on the grass. Introduce the new term to students, but caution them to be careful not to play with the paws of their real cats or dogs, as they are very sensitive. Take a "look but don't touch" approach.

Doing the "Dolby Doo, Dah" *(Letter D)*

With this chant, students make the letter D in the air, and gain practice with the sound of the letter D before each of the vowel sounds. As always, you demonstrate the sing-song pattern and students follow.

(Bandleader: Raise baton.)

Raise your hands and make a straight line *(arms overhead)*
   Doo, Dah! Doo, Dah!
Raise your hands and make a half-moon *(arms arched)*
   Doo, Dah! Doo, Dah!
Now, after me, repeat this tune: *(teacher sings notes)*

Doo, dah	(Doo, dah)
Day, oh!	(Day, oh!)
Dee, dee	(Dee, dee)
Di, di	(Di, di)
Doe, doe	(Doe, doe)
Dew, dew	(Dew, dew) *(Bandleader: Lower baton.)*

Once more, and clap your hands when you say the chant. Ready, go.
Once more, and raise left foot, right foot as you say the chant. Ready, go.
Once more and swivel body left and right from the waist (continuously) as chant is called out and repeated. Ready, go.
THEN, end it in unison, going from normal voice to whisper and eventually to just mouthing the words with no sound. Ready, go.

(Bandleader: Raise baton.)

Thank you, Dolby,
   for the   *(normal voice)*
   Dolby Doo, Dah!
   Doo, Dah! Doo, Dah!

Thank you, Dolby,
   for the   *(softer voice)*
   Dolby Doo, Dah!
   Doo, Dah! Doo, Dah!

Thank you, Dolby,
   for the   *(whisper)*

Dolby Doo, Dah!
Doo, Dah! Doo, Dah!

Thank you, Dolby,
   for the   *(mouth the words, no sound)*
Dolby Doo, Dah!
Doo, Dah! Doo, Dah!

                                   (Bandleader: Lower baton.)

Dolby's Dogteam of "D" Words *(Letter D)*

Students have been introduced to the vowels *a, e, i, o, u* and Dolby Dog likes to team up with them to make words. Since he's the leader, and they're second, they're called his *dogteam words*. This has worked very well. "How many can you think of, locate in the dictionary or pictionary, and then learn to spell?" Here are some words to get the dogteam started, using the long vowel sounds:

da	*de*	*di*	*do*	*du*
day	dear	dice	doughnut	duplex
danger	develop	dike	dome	dune
daily	deep	dine	dose	duty

Dolby's Favorite Dairy "D" *(Letter D)*

Dogs like to eat and Dolby is no exception. However, since he is a make-believe dog, he will eat almost anything that comes from the dairy. He says words like "delicious" and "dandy" when he eats good food.

On a poster or bulletin board, put a cut-out of a milk container to represent "dairy." Then have several pieces of yarn extending from the milk carton to pictures (or real containers) of dairy products that you tack or paste to the surface. Here is a list of dairy foods that students could try. (**Caution:** Be sure to check for allergic reactions before serving food.)

cottage cheese	cream
milk	cheese
yogurt	

Meet Holly Horse and the Harmonica *(Letter H)*

Holly Horse plays the harmonica. The harmonica is a real instrument and is also called the mouth organ. It is a small, rectangular instrument that has a row of air holes. It can be played while inhaling or exhaling along the edge of the row.

Holly Horse has the sound of "huh." This letter sound can be made by parting the lips and teeth and expelling air from the back of the throat. The tongue is at rest. The vibration of the vocal chords can be felt by gently touching the throat.

Gutteral Sounds *(Letter H)*

There are several sounds made with the mouth in a similar position, such as *k, c* (hard sound), and *g* (hard sound).

Students can make these sounds with their own natural voice instruments by repeating "kuh," "guh," and "huh" *(k, g, h)*. Have the children look in the mirror and note that, on the outside, their mouth stays the same. Have them repeat these sounds and note that the tongue is at rest and the mouth does not move—sounds come from deep in the throat.

Which Letter Am I Sounding? *(Letter H)*

Students can make a game of the "kuh," "guh," and "huh" sounds. Have one student leader stand facing three students with three letter cards and say one of these sounds. Students guess the sound by writing down one of the three letters. The leader verifies the guess by flashing the card. Then shuffle them and say one sound again, using the same procedure.

Next, have flash cards with a series of two of the sounds, such as "kuh" and "guh," or "huh" and "kuh." Follow the same procedure. Eventually work up to a set of flash cards that shows all three letters and have the students work with these.

This is good practice for sounding the letters, making sound associations by listening, and writing the shape of the sound.

On the flash cards, it may help to have picture clues or photographs from magazines, such as kitchen, ketchup (k); goat, garden (g); and horse, hammer (h). In this way, students are guessing a word rather than a sound.

At Work and Play With Holly Horse *(Letter H)*

A horse is a powerful animal that can be hooked up to wagons or carriages, and can be trained to pull a great deal of weight. Look for pictures in magazines of horse-drawn carriages. Is there one in your town? Have students been pulled in a horse-drawn buggy?

Someone who can work for long periods of time is often referred to as a *workhorse*. Students can pretend to be a workhorse and get all of their work done today. Get a silent timer or one that rings. Set it on an individual's desk to see how much he or she can accomplish when the child sets his or her mind to it and stays on task. Many students enjoy this challenge. It can affect work habits for students who have difficulty staying on task, or who have ADD.

In addition to work, Holly likes to play horseshoes. An indoor version of this is the "beanbag" basketball floor game. You will need a wastebasket and a beanbag. Have students stand a certain distance from the wastebasket (or hoop or actual basket) and toss the beanbag (underhand) so that it lands in the container. Students score one point for each basket and keep on going until they miss. Then it's the next student's turn. This is a popular indoor game during rainy-day recess time.

Holly Horse likes to compete with Lyle Lion. So you can have the *h* team and the *l* team, and score points for the animals. That makes it a team sport and takes the pressure off an individual student.

Holly's Thirsty for a "Horse's Neck" *(Letter H)*

A horse's neck is an old-fashioned drink that students will find refreshing. Fill a see-through pitcher with ginger ale and ice cubes. Then cut up lemon slices and orange slices. Add cherries (and other fruit). Pour into small glasses and enjoy this refreshing drink.

Language Enrichment with Holly Horse *(Letter H)*

There are many expressions in our language that use the word "horse." Introduce students to these expressions and explain what they mean. Knowing these enriches students' awareness of the variety of uses for language. It also enriches their written expression. Print the following on cards and have students match them.

Expression	Meaning
get a horse	get a move on
a horse of a different color	that's a different matter
horse laugh	loud laugh
hold your horses	slow down
straight from the horse's mouth	not a rumor
horsing around	playing vigorously
beating a dead horse	no hope of success

The "H" Poster *(Letter H)*

Make a colorful poster from construction paper by placing the capital and lower-case letters (H,h) in the upper left corner. Then have students search through magazines for colorful pictures that begin with the sound of the letter *h*. Students can cut them out, paste them on the poster, and label them.

Meet Jarvis Jaguar and the Jingle Bells *(Letter J)*

Jarvis Jaguar is the ABC Marching Band member that represents the sound of *j*. Jarvis plays the jingle bells, a cluster of bells. The bells, or even a single jingle bell, are considered an instrument used in a real band or orchestra.

The sound of *j* is made by clenching the teeth and expelling air from the back of the throat with a gutteral sound, while jutting the lips forward. Be sure to have a mirror handy so students can observe their mouth while making this letter sound.

Playing the Bells *(Letter J)*

Most students will be familiar with jingle bells because they are prevalent at Christmas time. A jingle bell is round, often silver, and has a small metal ball inside that makes a sound when you shake the bell. The bell is not solid; it usually has decorative holes to allow the sound to escape. (Harness bells used on a horse are a form of the jingle bell, only they are larger and with a deeper tone.)

These small bells can be purchased in craft stores. Students can link several together on a piece of yarn and shake them in time to music.

Variation: Make several sets of bells for wrists and ankles, and have different students take turns wearing them as everyone marches around the circle during music and rhythm time. Many familiar holiday tunes use the words "jingle bells" in the lyrics.

Eating With Jarvis Jaguar *(Letter J)*

Jarvis Jaguar loves jam and jelly on crackers. During the week, you can offer a different jam or jelly treat each day (strawberry jam, peach jam, raspberry jam, plum jelly, grape jelly, and so on).

Link the snack time to math each day. Make a Jam and Jelly Graph on a large jar shape, and have students vote on their favorite kind at the end of the week.

Additional foods to enjoy that begin with the sound of the letter *j* are: juice, Jell-o™, jellyroll, and jelly doughnut.

Plasticine "J" Doughnuts *(Letter J)*

Make "doughnuts" in the shape of the letter J. Roll out a coil of plasticene and turn it up at the bottom edge, toward the left. Dot it at the top with a circular shape made from construction paper. That circular dot is a "secret code" and is sending a message. It tells the student's favorite jam from three choices; for example, a red dot for strawberry, a purple dot for grape, and an orange dot for marmalade.

The Jaguar "J" Jingle *(Letter J)*

When Jarvis says "jeh"
   it means one thing.
Give me jelly
   and I will sing!

(Bandleader: Raise baton.)

JEH, JEH. JEH, JEH, JEH.
JEH, JEH. JEH, JEH, JEH!

(Ring bells in time with chant.)
(Lower baton.)

When Jarvis says "jah"
   it means one thing.
Give me jam
   and I will sing!

(Raise baton.)

JAH, JAH. JAH, JAH, JAH.
JAH, JAH. JAH, JAH, JAH!

(Lower baton.)

When Jarvis has jelly
   in his belly.

(Raise baton.)

He jumps for jam
   saying "Thank you, Ma'am!"

JING, JING. JING, JING, JINGLE!
JANG, JANG. JANG, JANG, JANGLE!   (Lower baton.)

A Read-aloud Book for Jarvis *(Letter J)*

The favorite this time of year is *The Polar Express* by Chris VanAllsburg. A bell figures prominently in this tale. Read it aloud and have a discussion about the story.

Meet Kerry Kangaroo and the Kettle Drum *(Letter K)*

Kerry Kangaroo from Kalamazoo plays the kettle drum. This is a real instrument, made from brass or copper, and shaped like a kettle with a parchment top. For the make-believe marching band purposes, it fits snugly into the kangaroo's pouch and there is no difficulty lugging it around the marching field. The drum can be played by striking or tapping it with the hands or with a drumstick.

The sound of the letter *k* is made by parting the lips and teeth and expelling air from the back of the throat. The edges of the tongue are resting along the top of the back upper teeth. Students can put their hand up to their mouth and feel the air being expelled from the lungs as this sound is made. Then move the hand to the throat, gently, and feel the vocal chords in motion as the sound is expressed. (Also, have students gently rest their hands on their upper abdomen so they can feel movement as the air is expelled.)

Your "Walking Instrument" Needs Care. If you have not already done so, focus upon the fact that students can make sounds and music with their own voice, which is an instrument. The lungs (air) play a big part, but so too do the voice box, tongue, lips, and teeth. Boys and girls are a "walking instrument" and should take good care of themselves.

This calls for a discussion of care of teeth, good mouth hygiene (brushing and flossing), eating a variety of foods from the various food groups, and getting plenty of rest.

Do, Re, Me, Fa, So, La, Te, Do. To help illustrate that the voice is indeed an instrument, have students sing up and down the scale (after you have modeled it). Then sing it with the alphabet letters; with the alphabet sounds. For example:

do	re	me	fa	so	la	te	do
A	B	C	D	E	F	G	H
I	J	K	L	M	N	O	P
Q	R	S	T	U	V	W	X,Y,Z

Cindy and Kerry Are "Kissin' Cousins" (*Letter K*)

Remember Cindy Cat who represents the two sounds of *c* and plays the clarinet and cymbals? Well, she and Kerry are "kissin' cousins."

Note that *kissin'* begins with the letter *k* and *cousins* begins with the letter *c*. This calls for the introduction of this new term, which means *relatives*. Cindy Cat and Kerry Kangaroo make the same sound, which is "kuh."

For language development and some experience with the repeated sound of the letter *k*—as well as the hard sound of *c*—have students repeat these sentences after you. Then they can practice making up some sentences for Cindy Cat and Kerry Kangaroo.

Kerry Kangaroo likes ketchup (or catsup).

Kerry Kangaroo can carry a kyack.

Kerry Kangaroo can kick a rock.

Kerry Kangaroo can fly a kite.

Kerry Kangaroo has a lock and key.

Print these sentences on the chalkboard and have students circle both the letter *c* and *k* in the sentence.

Where Do You Hear the Sound of "K"? (*Letter K*)

The *k* sound (and hard sound of *c*) can appear at the beginning, middle, or end of words. Have students listen carefully to each word and hold up their pointer fingers if they know where the sound of *k* is made. When called upon, they answer either "beginning," "middle," or "end."

ankle	king	duck	sank	kitten
pucker	luck	kiss	kettle	second

Let's Brew Some "K" Words (*Letter K*)

From construction paper, cut out a giant kettle. Print "K,k" on the bubbles coming out from the top. Have students look for magazine pictures of items that begin with the sound of the letter *k*, cut them out, and paste them on the kettle.

Letter Formations (*All Letters*)

Just as a marching band makes different formations all over the field, so too do letters arrange themselves in different positions to make words. Young children may understand this analogy if you use magnetic letters on a magnetic board, and move them around to make different words.

For example, "no" can be spelled backwards to make the word "on"; "net" becomes "ten"; "pin" becomes "nip"; and so on.

A good read-aloud book to increase the challenge of this activity is *Word Wizard* by Cathryn Falwell. This book, through the use of a magic spoon, helps young Anna to move the letters in the word "shore" so that they make the word "horse" and to make "ocean into "canoe."

Meet Ginger Goat and the Glockenspiel *(Letter G)*

Ginger Goat is the seventh band member when the band is marching in ABC order. She plays the glockenspiel (pronounced GLOK en speel, or GLOK en shpeel). It is a German word that means "playing bells."

The glockenspiel is played by striking the metal bars with two light hammers. This is perfect for Ginger Goat, because with one hammer she can play the soft sound of *g* (as in *ginger*) and with the other hammer she can play the hard sound of *g* (as in *goat*).

The soft sound of *g* (sounds like "gee") is made by pursing the open lips, putting the top teeth over the bottom teeth, and making the "gee" sound in the throat while expelling air. The hard sound of *g* (sounds like "guh") is made with the mouth slightly open, the teeth apart, with the "guh" sound coming from the throat while expelling air. Thus, both sounds are made in the throat. Have students place their hand to their throat and feel the shifting of their jaw and vocal chords as they move back and forth between the hard and soft sounds of *g*.

Make a Word Chart *(Letter G)*

On a colored sheet of construction paper, make a goat shape. Then make two columns for Ginger Goat's words. Here are some to get you started:

Ginger (soft "g")	Goat (hard "g")
ginger ale	good
Gibraltar	get
geranium	girl
germ	gift
general	gate

Make a "Toast" With Ginger Ale *(Letter G)*

Often people toast to good health, happiness, a good trip, or a happy vacation while they are seated around the table. Your class can have its own "toast." First, pour the ginger ale into small plastic glasses and model the procedure for toasting: make a "here's to" statement and take a sip of the ginger ale. Give children some time to think about what a good toast would be, and go around the circle and have them say it aloud. Accept all honorable suggestions. This would go well with any occasion by changing "here's to" to "give thanks for" and supplying new thoughts and ideas.

Perhaps this is the first time that some children have engaged in the procedure of "toasting" and they may not be able to think of anything on the spur of the moment. A discussion beforehand—with a variety of suggestions—would be helpful. Children can also choose to make the same toast that someone else has already said if they can't think of another.

Many "here's to" suggestions can take us outside of the classroom and into the community. For example, here's to:

- the good work done by our firefighters
- the crossing guard at the crosswalk
- the bus driver who gets us safely to school
- the truck drivers who work through the night
- the mail carrier who delivers our mail

Eating With Ginger Goat *(Letter G)*

To reinforce the two sounds of the letter *g,* here are some food suggestions. Print them on the chalkboard in scrambled order (not classified) and have students put a *circle* around the soft sound of *g* words and a *square* around the hard sound of *g* words. Here are some to get you started:

> grapes, German chocolate cake, gelatin,
> gingersnaps, gingerbread, gumdrops

After this has been done, have a soft *g* and a hard *g* treat all set to be served.

Ginger Goat's Chant *(Letter G)*

Ginger the goat
  has a brand new coat
And it's made of gingersnaps.

When Ginger the goat
  wears that brand new coat
The gumdrops are aghast!

They're jealous, you see,
  'cause they're so gummy
And Ginger's coat has class.

But, you know goats,
  they love to eat
And Ginger ate her coat!

She ate the gumdrops
  one by one—
They slid right down her throat.

They did!
They slid right down her throat, GUH, GUH.
There are no more gumdrops.
No more coat. GUH. GUH. JUH. JUH.

READING LINKS TO
HOLIDAYS & SPECIAL EVENTS

Christmas, Hanukah, Kwanzaa

Print these words vertically on the chalkboard and have students work with a study buddy to create a greeting, a sentence, or a poem using the first letter as the beginning of the phrase. (*Note:* Hanukah can also be spelled as Hanukkah, Hanukka, or Chanukkah.) Have holiday books handy so that students can locate words in them. For example:

Cheery greetings
Holiday ribbons
Real mistletoe
Ice and snow
Santa is coming
Trumpets sounding
Merry days
Almost here
Shouts of joy!

potato
latkes

Happy faces
All the family is here
Now is the time to light the candle
Uncle Carl is humming
Kisses and hugs, and good food
All is right!
Hearts are glad.

Kids are all dressed up
We are sharing
And making promises
Now is a good day
Zap! goes the match
And another candle glows
All is well for we are together.

Christmas Symbols Around the World

Point out to students that the Christmas holiday is celebrated the world over. There are many symbols common to this holiday. Use these symbols when making greeting cards and for holiday Rebus stories.

bells   holly   evergreen tree

wreath   St. Nick   reindeer

candles   fireplace   chimney

Felices Pascuas, Merry Christmas!

For Americans, St. Nicholas is another name for Santa Claus, but St. Nicholas actually was a Bishop who lived thousands of years ago and wore red robes. The red is still associated with the American creation of Santa Claus, "born" in the 19th century. Legend has it that St. Nicholas (from Turkey) enjoyed giving gifts in secret, and that segment of the story has been kept alive—the Santa who comes during the night while we're sleeping and leaves presents. This bringer of gifts is known by different names, but "Merry Christmas" is said in many languages all over the world. Here are some to learn:

Feliz Navidad (Mexico)	Felices Pascuas (Spain)
Glaedelig Jul (Norway)	Kala Christ Ougena (Greece)
Buon Natale (Italy)	Joyeux Noël (France)
Frohliche Weihnachten (Germany)	Wesolych Swiat (Poland)

How Would You Draw Santa Claus?

Dr. Clement Moore's poem "Twas the Night Before Christmas" was written for his children in 1822 and later published. The poem inspired Thomas Nast, cartoonist, to draw a picture of Santa Claus. He showed Santa in his workshop with a sleigh and reindeer, stockings hung by the fireplace, and a Christmas tree close by. The right jolly *little,* old elf was done in pen and ink. Later, in the 1920s, Santa Claus was changed from black and white to color in the ads done for Coca-Cola™.* He had rosy cheeks, bright red suit, buckled belt, knee-high boots, and became a *large,* old elf.

---

*Source: Duden, Jane. *Christmas* (New York: Crestwood House, 1990). This book is one in a series of holiday books.

Read the story poem to students and have them draw a Santa Claus scene that they see in their head, as the story is read. Then make some comparisons with classmates.

For pleasure, read aloud the story again from the 1998 version of *The Night Before Christmas* by Jan Brett. Notice the fanciful use of border scenes and border information in her drawings. Perhaps students could begin to incorporate the border concept into their work. Have other versions of this story poem available so that students can see how illustrators perceive things differently, just as the students did with their classmates. *The Grandma Moses Night Before Christmas, Poem by Clement C. Moore* gives the reader a primitive, New England view of this night.

Hanukah, the Festival of Lights

This is a special Jewish holiday.** It's celebrated because long ago the Jewish people wanted to worship one god, but the Syrians worshipped many Greek gods and goddesses. The Syrians destroyed a Jewish temple of worship. When the pure oil was found to light the candle, there was only enough for one day; however, the oil burned for eight days! That is why Hanukah is celebrated over a period of eight days.

Today in Jewish homes, the *menorah* (or candleholder) holds eight candles, with one in the middle from which all others are lit. The extra candle, the ninth, is called the *shammash*. The first candle is lit at sundown when the holiday begins. Each night another candle is lit; by the eighth night, all candles are burning brightly.

On the first night children receive money, which they call Hanukah gelt.

Spin-the-Dreidel Game

Children take turns spinning the dreidel while a timer is running. The dreidel that spins the longest wins. Then the children start over again.

Another Dreidel Game

This is one variation of a dreidel game. You will need the dreidel and nuts for each child. First, each child puts one nut in the center of the table. Then, each player spins the top. When it stops, what letter is showing? To score:

nun—worth nothing
hay—player gets half the nuts
gimel—player wins all the nuts
shin—player must add a nut

gimel   hay   nun   shin

**Source: *Jewish Holidays* by Margery Cuyler illustrated by Lisa C. Wesson. (New York: Holt, Rinehart, Winston, 1978).

Kwanzaa Celebration and Its Symbols

This African American holiday season was developed in California in the 1960s so that African Americans could have their own special holiday at this time of year. "Kwanzaa" comes from the Swahili word meaning *the first fruits* of the harvest.

These are the symbols of Kwanzaa and what they stand for:

- **kinara** (kee-NAR-ah)—This is a candleholder for seven candles, standing for the family background. One candle is lit each evening. A black candle is in the middle to represent skin color, three red candles on one side represent struggles, and three green candles on the other side represent the future.
- **mkeka** (m-KAY-kah)—This straw mat represents the foundation on which all else rests.
- **muhindi** (muh-HIN-dee)—These ears of corn stand for the children of the family. One ear of corn for each is placed on the straw mat. Apples, nuts, and yams can also be added to remember the harvest from the earth.
- **matunda** (ma-TOON-dah)—This is fruit placed in a basket to represent the bountiful harvest. Bread is sometimes added.
- **kikombe cha umoja** (KI-kohm-bay cha oo-MO-jah)—This is a cup that represents "unity."
- **zawadi** (za-wah-DEE)—These are the gifts that children receive for the hard work they have done during the year. (In Africa, children are not allowed to ask for gifts; they do not make a wish list, for example, but are grateful for what they receive.)

Activities for Each Day of Kwanzaa*

- *First day.* Greet family members. Be together. The greeting is "Habari gani" (hah-BAR-ee GAH-nee) which means that someone is asking "what is new?"
- *Second day,* "Kujichagulia" (koo-jee-cha-goo-LEE-ah). Learn your family traditions and the traditions of your ancestors.
- *Third day,* "Ujima" (oo-JEE-mah). Time to do something together in the family; perhaps fix up or clean.
- *Fourth day,* "Ujamaa" (oo-jah-MAAH). Save coins all year and buy a gift that *all* of the family can share, not just one person.
- *Fifth day,* "Nia" (NEE-ah). What is your strength? What is your purpose in life?

*Source: *Seven Candles for Kwanzaa* by Andrea Davis Pinkney, pictures by Brian Pinkney (New York: Dial, 1993).

- *Sixth day,* "Kuumba" (ku-OOM-bah). Devoted to creative endeavors. Make up a rhyme, a song, a poem, or paint a picture.
- *Seventh day,* "Imani" (ee-MAHN-ee). Express faith that good things will happen in the future. Then enjoy a good harvest meal.

Make a Kwanzaa Booklet

Each student will need seven blank pages and a folded cover. Have children illustrate their covers. On each page, they print the word that describes the activity of the day. Then students can draw a picture that pertains to them and that concept.

READING LINKS TO WRITING

The Writing Center this month can be made to look inviting by changing it weekly with the addition and deletion of objects that represent the symbols from different holidays. Some parents may be willing to donate items for this purpose. Having the actual items at hand may inspire students to be more detailed in their writing.

Keeping a Journal

This month encourage students to keep a special journal in which they write their good deeds and kind actions toward others. This spirit of kindness and respect toward others is rewarded in all of the special holidays spotlighted this month.

Students should be able to write a kind deed for each day. Discuss some of the things that would be considered helpful in the classroom, at home in the family, on the way to and from school, on the weekend, and so on. The idea is to do good for others, not just for the reward of a material gift, but because it should begin to make students feel good. It's a habit that needs to be cultivated.

Story Starters

Some students are successful with "story starters." One technique is to paste an attractive picture (magazine, paper) at the top of a lined sheet of paper and to write the first sentence. A good story starter is just that; it leads right into the action. Make sure the lines go with the picture. Some include:

- "Just as Feliciano was sitting down to eat, there was a soft knock at the door . . ."
- "Terry heard footsteps in the basement, and then a thud . . ."
- "Rooster was ready to crow to welcome the new day, but when he reached for his bright red comb, it was missing . . ."

The TV That Wanted to Go Out to Play

A good story starter discussion is about a TV set that is tired of being indoors all the time. It wants to see trees, walk through the park, feel the rain and snow on its face, and do all the things that boys and girls do. It wants to play! One day it just gets up, unplugs itself from the wall, and runs outdoors to freedom. Have children discuss this possibility. Where could it go? What could it do? This calls for a story! Students can work independently or with a study buddy. (See Reproducible Activity Page.)

Make Shape Books

Use a holiday shape. Cut out at least four shapes and staple them together for ready-made books. Students can select a shape, print the holiday symbols on the shapes (front and back), and label them.

Encourage Creative Writing

Have students create their own stories. Encourage them to invent the spelling because it can be checked later. The point is to get the flow of the story on the page—*not* get caught up in the mechanics at this point. Encourage them to cross out a word or to erase, whichever makes them more comfortable. (Sometimes when students erase, they go right through the paper, so teach children how to erase. Teach the gentle back-and-forth motion, and use soft art gum erasers at the Writing Center.)

Ask for a Typewriter Donation

In your newsletter to parents, ask if someone has an old typewriter no longer in use. Would they be willing to donate it to the classroom for a week or two this month?

Some students are successful with type, and like the looks of it. There are white liquids for erasures. Using a typewriter for a second draft is often a good idea.

One thing about the typewriter is that it's slower than working on a computer, especially if it's a manual machine. This is good for the student who is typing word lists because he or she needs to concentrate on each letter.

Computers at the Writing Center

Many schools are in the position of having a computer, or several computers, in classrooms. Some classrooms do not have computer access; rather, the students go to a general computer center or to the library.

Students can experiment with different fonts, different letter sizes, different commands such as "cut" or "copy" or "paste" for shifting print. The computer is an excellent tool for facilitating the writing process once students are familiar with the mechanics. There are several fine programs available. (See the media specialist in your school district for information and supplies.)

Be on the Lookout for Number Writing

Have a discussion with students about how we use numbers in our daily life, and when it is that we see people writing numbers on paper. Some responses may include:

- writing a phone number
- writing a house number and street address
- writing a ZIP Code to address an envelope
- writing a check
- writing a grocery list
- a waiter writes numbers on an order pad
- a sales clerk writes numbers on a sales slip

Have a supply of "sales slips" available for writing. Have a toy phone at the Writing Center so that students can take orders and write down numerals with the order.

Use the telephone book as a resource for looking up phone numbers and street addresses of familiar places in the community. Start your own Yellow Pages.

READING LINKS TO MATH

Number Word Names

Students need to learn the number word names by sight. Make flash cards so that the numeral and number word appear on the same side (for example, **1 one**) and have students make their own set. They can begin to practice memorizing these words, or continue if they are already working on the words from one through ten. Phonetic clues for beginning sounds are helpful.

Make a set of flash cards that fold in the middle. On one side, write the numeral. On the other side, write the number name. Students can work in pairs to gain practice. The one who is acting as "teacher" has the answer, and can give hints and assistance to the one who is getting some practice. Then they switch roles. Since students learn in different ways, they may be learning just as much in the "teacher" role as their partner.

The Big Countdown

Vacation comes near the end of December. Make a banner of numerals from 1–10, with the numeral 10 being the day before vacation time. Then each day students can highlight a numeral or cross off a numeral for the big countdown. This can be done within the calendar also.

A Calendar for December

Continue with patterning for the numerals. Cut out an evergreen tree shape (Christmas), a dreidel shape (Hanukah), and a candle shape (Kwanzaa). For this month the pattern is ABC, ABC. The background shape of December can be rectangular, with a great big ribbon at the top, so that December looks like a giant gift.

You Can Count on These

Provide a new variety of manipulatives in the Math Center so that students can gain more practice with counting. Gather objects and ask for donations of empty film cylinders, nuts, stickers, colored paper clips, cotton tips, and so on. You can purchase circular plastic chips by the hundreds, as well as other commercial counting materials in various animal shapes.

Students can work with worksheets or flash cards that give directions, such as "one + six = _____." They have to learn to *read the plus and minus signs.* Flash cards can become more challenging on longer strips with problems such as "one + five − two + ten − six = _____."

one + six = ___

Flannelboard Stories Using Math

Have students use flannel or felt shapes to reenact stories that require counting, so that they have to say the numbers as they tell the story. A good starter story for size and number relationship is *Goldilocks and The Three Bears.* Another story that requires counting is *Snow White and the Seven Dwarfs.* Snow White, for example, could set the table for the seven dwarfs.

Also, students would have fun with the award-winning picture book *My Little Sister Ate One Hare* by Bill Grossman, with illustrations by Kevin Hawkes.

Numbers in Our Environment

Have a discussion with students about where they see and read numbers in the home, in school, when they're on the bus looking out the window, when they're in a car looking out the window, when they're at a store, and so on. Encourage them to make such responses as "gas pump," "billboards," and "sale prices in windows."

Next, begin to collect magazine pictures that show *environmental math.* Some samples include: bus number, advertisement, postage stamps, shoe sizes, clothing sizes, numbers on tickets, numbers on toys, and prices on items. Eventually make a scrapbook of "Numbers We See Every Day, Even When We're Not Looking."

READING LINKS TO SOCIAL STUDIES

We Are Explorers

The first two weeks of December are an interesting time to go on a field trip that takes you to the center of your city or town. Plan carefully. Are you out to see the decorations and special holiday displays? Do you plan to see them as you pass by on your way to a particular destination? Are there statues or fountains that are special to your area that you will want to point out to students?

As the teacher, your first step is to get permission from the principal for your trip. Plan in advance in terms of the date and time. When permission is granted, start making preliminary inquiries about your destination spot. If you are going to one specific location, talk to a person who is responsible for setting up field trips for school children, and be sure to get that person's name. Meet and plan with that person. Contact your room mothers for three or four parents to travel along on the bus. Send permission slips home well in advance, and have them returned in advance.

Some Possible Destinations to Explore

There are interesting places to visit in your town or city that fit in with your curriculum.

If you are studying community services, you can visit one of the following:

police station	post office
capitol building	television station
newspaper building	government building

If you are studying community culture, you can visit one of the following:

art gallery	museum
planetarium	science center

If you are studying community businesses, you can visit one of the following:

bakery	ice cream factory
grocery store	factory (other)

If you have a lively theatre arts program in your area, investigate the possibility of going to a dress rehearsal of one of the following, either at the city or college level:

symphony rehearsal	musical rehearsal
choir rehearsal	band rehearsal

Put on Your Visiting Manners

Set rules and regulations with the class well before the trip. If students know what is expected of them, they will have a better time and will profit from the trip. There are expectations for behavior on the bus, as well as at the point of destination. Some things to do are:

1. Establish hand signals so that students will know when they are to be quiet and listen for directions.

2. Make sure everyone has a partner and that they hold hands in line and when walking.

3. Practice lining up once or twice before the day of the trip, in the order that students will line up on that day.

4. Have students look at their partner and know who it is.

5. Have them look at who is in front of them, and who is behind them.

6. Carefully spread out the students so that all of the behavior challenges are not in the same cluster.

7. Put parents in charge of a set number of students, for that time when the group divides into subgroups.

8. Give parents a list of the names of students for whom they are to be responsible. Count them.

9. Give each student an identification card. Decide if this will be worn around the neck or pinned on. It should have the student's name, the school, and the school phone number.

10. You should carry a class roster, school name/address/phone number, and a cellular phone (or coins for a pay phone) should it be necessary to call the school.

11. In case of a health emergency, always call the school first for input from the principal and school nurse. They, in turn, may call parents if that is necessary. If time is critical in a health emergency, the school still needs to be notified as soon as possible.

12. You sit at the front of the bus (you need to give directions, maintain eye contact by facing students, and so on). A responsible parent is at the rear.

13. You can have a whistle on a string, worn around the neck. This is a way to get attention when everyone needs to be given instructions. Don't overdo it, however.

14. Take juice snacks along in self-contained cardboard containers. This is a treat for the return trip.

15. Be sure to count students each time you move from place to place. Rely upon parents for their part in counting.

Let's Learn While We're Looking Out the Window

Students can have maps and a pencil with them, so that they can trace their route along the way while on the bus. Statues, fountains, specific buildings can be circled on the map as they pass by.

Look for environmental print. Students can list some of the many examples and keep the others in mind to list when they return to the classroom.

"How many varieties of doors do we see? What do the shop windows look like? How many people are wearing hats?"

The reason for pointing out these things beforehand and as you go along is that some students need to be given an extra reminder that they're on a learning adventure—*not* just looking at the bus seat in front of them.

Discuss the Trip Before and After

Since you, as teacher, will have set up the trip and hopefully had the opportunity to visit beforehand, you can explain what students will be seeing on their tour.

Use the K,W,L (Know, Want to Know, Learned) technique. Make a chart with three columns and label it as follows:

What We Know	What We Want to Know	What We Learned

Use the chart before and after the trip.

More Planning for Success

- Make sure students line up and visit the bathroom before taking off on the trip.
- Establish appropriate clothing to wear.
- Take snack food along.
- If you will be missing lunch at school, request that all students bring a bag lunch (name on outside of bag) and eat lunch at a designated location OR on the bus on the return trip.
- Take a bag of kitty litter along with you in case someone gets sick and vomits on the bus (sprinkle it on top).
- Take large baggies along for "bus-sickness" (just in case).
- Take a camera along for color prints.
- Plan songs to sing on the return trip.
- Plan a candy treat for the return trip.
- Students are often tired and quiet when they return to the classroom from a trip, so have a rest period with soothing music.

Our Classroom Went on Wheels Today

"We learned a lot and we saw a lot when we took our trip today." Establish this with the students, since that is the purpose of the trip—an educational adventure. "Where did we see ramps for people in wheelchairs or for the elderly?"

- Use the K,W,L chart referred to earlier.
- Have students draw pictures of their trip.
- Write an experience chart story about the trip.

Follow-up Activities

- Write thank-you notes to people at the destination (send pictures and drawings, too).
- Write thank-you notes to helpful parents.
- Make a class mural.
- Make a sequence chart of the day (timeline).
- Design a postcard of a place seen on the trip.
- Make a travel brochure of the city sights.
- Use the developed photographs for story writing. The stories can be photocopied and made into a book, right along with the photos.

Children's Books to Read Aloud

Now that you have returned safely and settled down for a few days, read *Big Anthony: His Story* by Tomie dePaola. In this book about Strega Nona's assistant, he travels from city to city in Italy. Knowing Big Anthony, of course, there's bound to be trouble, but he does get to visit some interesting sites. Another book about traveling is *Bridges Are to Cross* by Philemon Sturges, with illustrations by Giles Laroche.

Making a Class Mural or a Picture

When making a mural or picture of the city, think "vertical." Give students a long, thin sheet of paper. Have them start planning (drawing with chalk) at the bottom third of the page or mural. That's the street level. That is where they can plan the action—people, cars, buses, bicycles, taxi cabs, dogs, cats, sidewalks, storefronts.

The middle third is the upper floors of buildings, restaurants, lots of skyscrapers, gargoyles, and signs that show advertisements or names of buildings. You might even see some treetops and the tops of statues here.

The top third is the very tiptop of the tallest buildings and air traffic such as birds, airplanes, a helicopter, a hot air balloon. You can also see clouds, the sun, or big snowflakes.

When the mural has been planned, the children can develop it by using cutout construction paper items. (If this method is chosen, you get into the concept of *overlapping* in art.) You can do the whole thing as a photo montage, with magazine pictures, or you can plan it with chalk and then paint in the forms with tempera paint.

An excellent book that gives the feel of the vertical city is *Town and Country* by Alice and Martin Provensen. It also gives the horizontal feel of the country.

Sky Scape/City Scape, a book of poems about city life, selected by Jane Yolen, with illustrations by Ken Condon, gives various city perspectives.

Note: If you plan to travel on a field trip in autumn or in spring, use this section at that time. Students across the country take school visits during every month of the year, so use it when it is valuable for you.

Cooking Up Holiday Recipes

Cooking in the classroom involves reading, math, and science. It is also a good social activity. Children are learning by doing, watching, and observing. Later they can write stories about their activities, or write it in a journal, or make a picture journal of the experience. (Cook with another adult, if possible, and have the camera handy.)

We Can Make Potato Latkes

You need:

8 potatoes, grated	mixing bowl
2 eggs	electric frypan
1 grated onion	vegetable oil
1 tablespoon flour	mixing spoon
dash of salt and pepper	plates and forks

Procedure: Mix all ingredients together. Everyone gets a chance to mix (after washing hands). Drop by large spoonfuls into an electric frypan that has been coated generously with vegetable oil or spray. (Children stand back as you do the cooking with an adult assistant.) Fry on both sides until brown. (Add more oil as needed.) Serve with applesauce.

Yummy French Toast

You need:

1 egg	mixing bowl
⅓ cup milk	electric frypan
1 tablespoon sugar	spatula
½ stick margarine	tongs
½ teaspoon vanilla	mixing spoon
jam or maple syrup	
6 slices white bread (cut diagonally)	

Procedure: Break egg into a bowl and add milk, sugar, and vanilla. Beat until frothy. Put electric frypan on medium heat, and melt 2 tablespoons butter. Dip bread into egg mixture (use tongs) and place in frypan. Fry until lightly golden brown, then turn over with spatula and fry other side. Add more margarine as needed.

Serve with jam or syrup and a sprinkling of confectioners sugar on top.

Sweet Ghana-style Doughnut Balls

You need:

1 egg	mixing bowl
½ teaspoon salt	electric frypan
3 tablespoons baking powder	plastic gloves
½ teaspoon nutmeg	mixing spoon
1½ cups warm water	paper towels
3¾ to 4¼ cups all-purpose flour	
vegetable oil	

Procedure: Combine egg, salt, baking powder, nutmeg, and sugar, and stir well. Add water and stir. Fold in flour so dough is stiff and slightly sticky. Put on plastic gloves. Flour hands and then roll dough into tiny balls the size of pecans. Then heat an inch of oil in a frypan. Carefully place balls in oil and fry until brown (about three minutes). Remove, drain, serve warm. Makes about 36 sweet doughnut balls.

Holiday Pretzels

You need:

4 cups flour	mixing bowl
1 egg (separated)	mixing spoon
1 pkg. yeast	flat cookie sheet
1 teaspoon sugar	pastry brush
1 teaspoon salt	
1½ cups warm water	
red and green edible glitter	

Procedure: Dissolve yeast in warm water. Add dry ingredients and mix together. Form dough into flat shapes (can be a letter shape). Brush with egg white. Sprinkle with salt. Bake at 425 degrees for 10 to 15 minutes. Sprinkle with edible glitter.

Easy Moo-cow Hot Chocolate

You need:

3 or 4 quarts of chocolate milk	saucepan
miniature marshmallows	hot plate
	styrofoam cups
	ladle

Procedure: Place chocolate milk in saucepan and heat on low. When steaming, pour or ladle into cups. Add marshmallows. (If this isn't easy enough, you can also warm the chocolate milk in a crockpot. Now, *that's* easy!)

READING LINKS TO SCIENCE & HEALTH

Simple Machines

There are several categories of simple machines that include the wheel, screw, lever, and wedge. Print these categories on the chalkboard or on a chart. Once students catch on to what these tools are, the children seem to locate them in a variety of places.

Remember, a simple machine has *at least one* moving part and *helps* people do work. Have real samples of each of the following. Here are a few of the simple machines, or tools, you might find in the classroom:

- **Wheel**—casters on TV cart or art cart; pencil sharpener; toy car's tire; toy wagon
- **Screw**—used to fasten back of clock onto face; fasten switch-plate cover to switch; fasten seats of chairs to frame
- **Lever**—scissors; a can opener; anything used to help pry open a can
- **Wedge**—a solid triangular shape that could be used to prop open a door; prop open a window; or used to push under a table or chair to make it level (a knife is a wedge)

Classroom Tools of the Trade

Look around the classroom at all of the materials to help us learn. These are called 'tools of the trade.' Some of these learning tools include: books, pencils, paper, rulers, and computer.

Have students make a giant-size list of all the tools of the trade for learning in the classroom. You might want to categorize the list by subject matter or areas of interest in the classroom.

School Tools of the Trade

Look around the building and list all of the tools of the trade that a school needs to run a smooth operation. Take into consideration the office, cafeteria, gymnasium, computer center, art room, music room, and other areas of learning at school—both inside and outside.

Community Tools of the Trade

The people in our community have their own tools of the trade. For example, a *dentist* has a *drill, pick, mirror,* and *scraper.* A *roofer* has *nails, hammer, roof shingles,* and *ladder.* Have the students list the people in the community who are contributing members and try to discover their tools of the trade. Some members who contribute are as follows, but there are many more:

firefighter	nurse	mayor
police officer	physician	editor
landscaper	technician	reporter
crossing guard	florist	hotel manager
airline pilot	lawyer	bookkeeper
window designer	waitress/waiter	chemist
candy sales clerk	orchestra leader	fast-food server

Perhaps students can look through the Yellow Pages of the telephone book for assistance with tools of the trade. They may even find the tools first, and work backwards from that point.

Machines Make Things Easier for Us, or Do They?

How would you explain an escalator to a talking animal who has just landed from a storybook—kerplunk!—right in the middle of your town or city? How would you explain how to use a drinking fountain, or a telephone, or a revolving door?

Read the classic children's book *The Story of Babar* by Jean de Brunhoff. In this tale, Babar the elephant visits the city and has to be reminded that the elevator is *not* a toy.

This might be a good opportunity for some creative writing. Perhaps a talking animal might decide that machines that are useful to people are really toys, and keeps getting things all mixed up. Help! We need some education here!

Some Machines Are "Out of Date"

The new vocabulary term for being out of date is *obsolete*. The steam shovel, for example, was replaced by a modernized machine. Read the classic children's book *Mike Mulligan and His Steam Shovel* by Virginia Lee Burton. Bring in items from home that are now considered quite changed or even obsolete. Inviting an antique dealer to visit with some examples would be ideal.

A discussion of how kitchens have changed—with microwave ovens for fast food and modern refrigerators—would be a good place to begin. Ask students to interview their grandparents for some information on this topic.

Also, the biggest revolution of all is the computer! Not only has it replaced the typewriter, but it is replacing the way people shop and do business from their homes.

From Pony Express to E-Mail

The Pony Express* lasted only eighteen months, although most people think it was longer than that. The trail ran from St. Joseph, Missouri to San Francisco,

---

*Source of information: *National Geographic,* Vol. 158, No. 1, July 1980, "A Buckaroo Stew of Fact and Legend, The Pony Express," by Rowe Findley.

and the trip took ten days. In order to make his schedule, a rider had to average ten miles an hour. Horses were changed at stations along the route, and the riders had to be on the alert for Indian attacks. Since parts of the ride were dangerous, there was a famous poster that advertised for riders: "WANTED—young, skinny, wiry fellows not over eighteen. Must be expert riders, willing to risk death daily. Orphans preferred." Some famous riders were "Buffalo Bill" Cody and "Wild Bill" Hickock.

The Pony Express got Abraham Lincoln's Inaugural Address to California in only seven days. A record! What happened to the Pony Express? It became obsolete. It was replaced by the telegraph, which got messages along wires in only seconds. The wires pretty much follow along the route of the old Pony Express trail.

Today, people get news via newspapers, magazines, television, and computers. They also have access to e-mail right in their home. This was not always so. You can now send a message to anywhere in the country, or in the world, in a matter of seconds. Make sure students are aware they are right in the middle of a "communications change" (revolution) and that, within the next decade, many more differences will occur in our lives because of the Internet and its vast communication potential.

We Need Good Scientists

Research scientists are always looking for ways to do things faster and more efficiently. Science is an exciting field, and you need to help students foster an attitude of respect, curiosity, and anticipation for the challenges ahead.

In order to become a good scientist, students need to begin to do the following: examine things closely, define problems (inquiry), make hypotheses, explore, analyze data that they gather, reach conclusions, check them.

Many scientists in early life had hobbies. Do students have a hobby where they are collecting and learning? This might be a good opportunity to have a hobby chat, and get some students moving along that path. How about coin collecting? stamp collecting? rock collecting? leaf and bark examination? seashell collecting?

Scientists Play a Big Role in Our Health

Research scientists are working every day on finding cures for diseases. Impress upon students that even as they are learning, so too are scientists. "The reason we get 'shots' is that scientists have discovered ways to prevent us from getting certain diseases." Scientists and medical doctors work on body organ transplants, spinal cord injuries, and other major health concerns that people have. Some students may become interested in getting library books on health, the way the body functions, and the challenges ahead that people face in this area. They may want to play a role in that area some day. (Many successful people in this area attribute their early interest to a teacher who encouraged them and guided them during the early school grades!)

Ring a Bell for the Future

Bring in a little bell. Sit in a circle and demonstrate for students how you'd like them to ring it. The idea is to circulate the bell around to each group member, have the child ring it and tell what he or she is glad to know about, and then something he or she would like to learn more about. This sets up a positive attitude toward learning. (For example, "I'm glad I know how to _____ , and I want to know more about _____ .)

LINKS TO AUTHOR-OF-THE-MONTH

Author/Illustrator for December: Jan Brett

This author/illustrator is a good choice for December because many, though not all, of her books take place in snowy settings and deal with holiday themes. These books are colorful, happy, and bright.

One thing Jan Brett is known for is the borders that surround the pages of her books. As she has explained, she has so many ideas for the illustrations that they spill over onto the borders, so the reader is treated to more designs and information along the edges of the book pages. (Check *The Mitten* for especially clever use of borders.)

This prolific author has her own website, which you can access at *www.jan-brett.com* and receive a teacher's pack, bookmarks, and so on. If you write to her at her studio address, you are apt to get a packet of information that contains a newsletter about the current book she's working on; sometimes you are sent a photo, an activity page, or even masks that will help students reenact some of the stories. The address is: Jan Brett, 132 Pleasant Street, Norwell, MA 02061.

Since Jan Brett likes hedgehogs, look for Hedgie in most of her books. We're in for a treat this month, so *let's read!*

***Annie and the Wild Animals* (New York: The Trumpet Club, 1985)** A delightful story in a winter setting about a little girl whose pet cat, Taffy, has disappeared. Annie, lonely for company, takes corn cakes out to the edge of the woods each day to feed the animals, but each one in turn is too grumpy or too mean or far too big. Finally, the corn cakes run out and the animals return to the woods as spring approaches. Annie, alone again, suddenly sees Taffy the cat emerging from the woods—and she is the proud mama of three friendly kittens. Annie will not be lonely again.

Activities to Accompany *Annie and the Wild Animals*

1. Ask students to identify the wild animals, one by one, as you revisit the book.

2. Let's look at borders. How do the borders reflect what is going on on the double-page spread? The first border reflects winter clothing and the second border features Taffy the cat. Here are other picture clues:

   • Notice how the border at the bottom of the page alerts the reader to the animal that will appear next on the scene.

   • Find the cat in the borders. Where is the cat spending her time? What information do the readers know that Annie still doesn't know? *(Cat has kittens.)*

   • How can we tell by the changing border that spring is on the way? *(Robins begin to appear.)*

3. Have students begin to illustrate their stories and pictures with borders. Begin with simple designs at first; then work in subject matter that goes with the picture or story.

Trouble With Trolls (New York: Scholastic, 1992) This book has a Scandinavian setting. A young girl decides to visit her cousin on the other side of Mount Baldi with her dog, Tuffi. It takes all morning to walk up the mountain, and no time at all to ski down the other side.

But this day, there is trouble with trolls—they want Tuffi! The young girl keeps outsmarting one troll after another by giving them articles of clothing, until she finally runs out of things to do at the top of the mountain where they are gathered for her dog. It is then that she gets an inspiration—and all of her clothes back—as well as a safe trip down the mountainside with Tuffi.

Activities to Accompany *Trouble With Trolls*

1. Throughout this story at the bottom of the page, there is activity underground. The entire page is bordered by the outdoor scenery until we check out the bottom and about one-fourth of the way up each side. It shows the underground home of the trolls and a hedgehog that gets inside. Page after page, watch the adventures going on indoors as well as outdoors.

2. Students can write story text for the underground story, which is almost a wordless picture book accompanying the main story. They can describe the home, what made them leave, and then the activity of the hedgehog. They are free to write their own ending.

3. The story is set in Norway. Locate this country on the map. Note the Nordic designs on the girl's clothing, the skis, the Swiss chalet. Perhaps students can design socks, sweater, or mittens in a similar style.

4. Notice that these story trolls have pointed heads with white hair, pointed ears, large feet, and a twisty tail. Their clothing is patched. At the easel, students can create their own version of a troll, or use these same characteristics.

5. The girl "outsmarted" the trolls. (This may be an opportune time to introduce that new vocabulary word.) That was clever. This would be a good story to do as a play. Try it.

6. Write a story about another encounter with these trolls and the way they could be outsmarted another day.

***Beauty and the Beast* (New York: The Trumpet Club, 1989)** This retold tale of *Beauty and the Beast* has lovely, detailed illustrations. In this book, all of the people in the household are vain and revere beauty; thus, a curse is put upon the entire household. They all appear as animals, and the beast is a wild boar. The story is the familiar tale. The household continues to run, and the costumes are beautiful. The peacock, a sign of vanity, appears on almost every page. It is a visual treat.

Activities to Accompany *Beauty and the Beast*

1. Read the story—the students will enjoy it. Find other versions of this same familiar tale and make a comparison of the illustrations. See how one illustrator depicts a scene as compared with another artist's rendition.

2. The beautiful, swirling, purple cabbages that Beauty is holding on page 3 invite students to paint. Use glossy paper and a variety of purple and violet shades. Then take a fine cloth and make the inside ridges by wiping away some of the paint. When it dries, use a fine black felt-tip pen to outline the edges of the swirling cabbage head.

3. "We're getting a great deal of information in visual form with this book. For example, in the middle of the book we see tapestries (murals) hanging on the castle walls. Look closely! The figures in the tapestries depict the people as they once were before they were turned into animals. In the foreground, the matching action shows us what they look like now." Students need to be made aware of this, as they may not notice it on their own.

4. Examine the messages above the murals. They are: "Be Guided by Your Heart's Gratitude," "Do Not Trust to Appearance," and a foreshadowing of what is to come in the mural, "Courage, Beauty." What do students think these messages mean? Talk about the idea of a motto to live by.

5. Students enjoy going through the book page by page to find the peacock that represents "vanity," or from what the household once suffered. "On many pages we find the peacock, so be on the alert. Can you find the peacock vase? When do we last see the live peacock and not just the feathers? What does this mean?"

6. Note the silhouette of Beauty and the Beast. This is one page done entirely in black, with a gray background and a sliver of a crescent moon. Ask students what type of music they would select to play in the background for this particular scene if it were a movie or video. Encourage students to give the silhouette art form a try. They often find success by first sketching out an item and then cutting it out. It should be simple at first. Have students experience success with a border design, and perhaps a simple vase of flowers.

7. When the magic spell is broken by the power of love, the servants—as well as the Beast—turn back into people again. Be sure to note this on the second to last page. What music do we hear in the background? How grateful they must be to Beauty who broke the spell. How will they show this gratitude? Will they change? Have they learned a lesson? What is the lesson?

***The Mitten* (New York: G.P. Putnam's Sons, 1989)** This is an adaptation of an old European tale set in the Ukraine. A boy named Nicki gets a new pair of mittens, which his grandmother has just knitted, and promptly goes out into the wintery outdoors and drops one. The delightful story goes on to show how, one by one, animals come to explore the mitten and crawl inside. Of course it expands until even a bear wiggles inside. It can't seem to hold another creature, so when a mouse comes along, the mouse settles on the bear's nose, which causes the bear to sneeze—and the animals scatter in all directions! The mitten comes falling into the boy's hand from the sky, and when he takes them home to Grandmother, they surely don't match.

Activities to Accompany *The Mitten*

1. Read the story and enjoy it. Chances are students will want to hear it again and again, for it quickly becomes a favorite.

2. By now the children are somewhat familiar with this author/illustrator's borders, but this book holds a surprise for the reader. Each page in the book is a double-page spread, so a mitten shape appears at both the left and right sides of the page. The visual picture in the mitten on the left shows what has gone on in the story, while the picture in the mitten on the right shows the reader what is to come next. Students are thrilled with this discovery!

3. Try this. The students as artists can draw one scene from a story, any story, and enclose it with an artistic border. Have them create a space to the left and right of the main picture, and show what came before this and what will happen next. Students may want to select *The Mitten* or a favorite fairy tale. Talk about what shape they will use that goes along with their story.

4. Do artists rush? No, artists take their time to create a drawing. Jan Brett is known for her attention to detail. In one of her newsletters, she mentions that it takes her one hour to do one inch, so it takes about a week just to do one page! This is excellent information to pass along to students. There is no rush! Slow down!

5. The very last page of the book shows Grandmother looking at the two different mittens. There is no text on this page, but Grandmother has a perplexed look. Have students write text for this last page on a mitten shape. Then compare endings.

***Berlioz the Bear* (New York: G.P. Putnam's Sons, 1995)** A Reading Rainbow book, this is an adventurous tale about a group of animals that is on its way to give a concert. Berlioz, the bear, is having a difficult time trying to get his stubborn donkey to pull the wagonload of musicians and instruments. Again, we are entertained and informed by extra material in the borders that shows the animals gathering for a gala ball in a village square. The animals arrive by climbing the side borders and set up tables for the party, while more people continue to climb the side borders. While this is going on, the musicians are featured in the middle of the page trying to get to the square. When they finally arrive at their destination, a strange sound is coming from the bear's cello. It's certainly not the notes that he is intending to play. What is creating this sound? Read on.

Activities to Accompany *Berlioz the Bear*

1. Read the book and enjoy it. Then return and examine the illustrations carefully for all of the little details. Students can begin to make their drawings more detailed. Start with animals and detail for fur. This can even be done at the easel once the big painting is dry. Go back and add strokes with a finer brush for whiskers, eyelashes, stripes, little hairs on paws, and so on.

2. Identify all of the animals and instruments in the book. Read other books in which music plays a role, such as *The Bremen Town Musicians,* a tale from the Brothers Grimm, and compare the stories.

3. What do these instruments sound like? Ask the children's librarian for help in finding an audio cassette or CD available in your library that will enable the instruments to be heard.

4. The buzzing bee is making the noise. One suggestion from the promotional material on this book is for the students to listen to "The Flight of the Bumblebee" and imagine the bee in the cello.

5. Jan Brett tells us that her husband, who plays in the Boston Symphony Orchestra, was the model for the bear character. Perhaps students can use a real model from their own life and make that person into a hero/heroine in a fairy tale setting.

***The Night Before Christmas, A Poem by Clement Moore* (New York: Scholastic, 1998)** Done in Jan Brett's style—with magnificent borders that are filled with the sights, sounds, smells, and joys of Christmas—this book provides the reader with a visual treat. In this version, Santa's little elf helpers are extremely merry and have fun playing with the toys while Santa is inside making his deliveries. The attention to detail is magnificent.

Activities to Accompany *The Night Before Christmas, A Poem by Clement Moore*

1. Read the book and enjoy the pictures. Then go through the book again, this time inspecting the pictures as everyone enjoys them.

2. Have students draw themselves sleeping and the detailed "visions of sugarplums" dancing above them. "In this book there is a swirl of gingerbread cookies, candies, canes, and wonderful goodies of all colors, so let's take our cue from the illustrator when we draw our own visions." What will students include?

3. Inspect the borders. "What information can we learn from these?" Note the "shapes within the shape" of the border where illustrations are displayed.

4. Make a "Find It" challenge sheet. See if students can locate certain items and tell the number of the page on which it appears. For example, "Where is the elephant bank with Scott's nametag? Where is the present marked for Kayla?" Have students make up their own challenge sheets; other students can search for the visual clues.

5. "How many different ornaments can we name on the beautiful Christmas tree?"

6. "Let's draw and design our own stocking to hang by the chimney with care."

7. If students should ask for Rudolph, let them know that this is the original version of the poem. Rudolph was added to a much later version of Santa and his reindeer, when a song about him became a commercial hit. So Rudolph belongs in the song version.

8. Enjoy the book *The Twelve Days of Christmas,* beautifully illustrated by Jan Brett, as a companion piece to this book.

And Many More!

Jan Brett has additional works to her credit. Other books written or retold and illustrated by her are *Fritz and the Beautiful Horses; The First Dog; The Owl and the Pussycat;* and *Goldilocks and the Three Bears.*

Sometimes artists do illustrations for books that are written by others. This is called "collaboration." Jan Brett (illustrator) and Eve Bunting (author) have collaborated on the following books: *The Valentine Bears* (February); *St. Patrick's Day in the Morning* (March); and *The Mother's Day Mice* (May), among others. You won't want to miss them.

Encourage students to do some collaborating in the classroom. One student might write a story, while a partner draws a picture or two for it.

Enjoy this author/illustrator's talents and contribution to children's books. Remember to write to her as a class for an enriching letter-writing experience.

REPRODUCIBLE ACTIVITY PAGES

Marching Band—Letter D (Dolby Dog)

Marching Band—Letter H (Holly Horse)

Marching Band—Letter J (Jarvis Jaguar)

Marching Band—Letter K (Kerry Kangaroo)

Marching Band—Letter G (Ginger Goat)

Reading Road Signs *(Punctuation Marks)*

Word Ending Bubbles *(s, ed, ing)*

The TV That Wanted to Go Out and Play *(Story Starter)*

Holiday Gift Bag Puzzle Words

The K W L Planner

Learning On A Field Trip

Children's Literature Activity Page—I Just Love Borders *(Jan Brett)*

©DCW99

© 2000 by The Center for Applied Research in Education

© 2000 by The Center for Applied Research in Education

Jj

© 2000 by The Center for Applied Research in Education

© 2000 by The Center for Applied Research in Education

G g

© 2000 by The Center for Applied Research in Education

© 2000 by The Center for Applied Research in Education

Name _____

READING ROAD SIGNS

These are important "road signs" when you are driving through a page of print. Learn to spot them. Follow their directions.

STOP SIGN

SLOW DOWN. YELLOW IS FLASHING.

LOUD. DRIVER IS BLOWING HORN.

PULL UP. DRIVER IS ASKING DIRECTIONS.

TALKING. "Stop" and "Go."

SHORT CUT.

STOP! Draw a line from the words to the "short cuts" below. Use each short cut in a sentence.

she will	they're
I will	she'll
they are	I'll
we are	I'm
I am	we're

Name _____

WORD ENDING BUBBLES

Edith Elaine Elephant is blowing double bubbles through her trunk. OOPS! She forgot the word endings! You can print either s, ed, or ing in the spaces at the end of the root words to make a new word. How many sentences can you make with these words?

© 2000 by The Center for Applied Research in Education

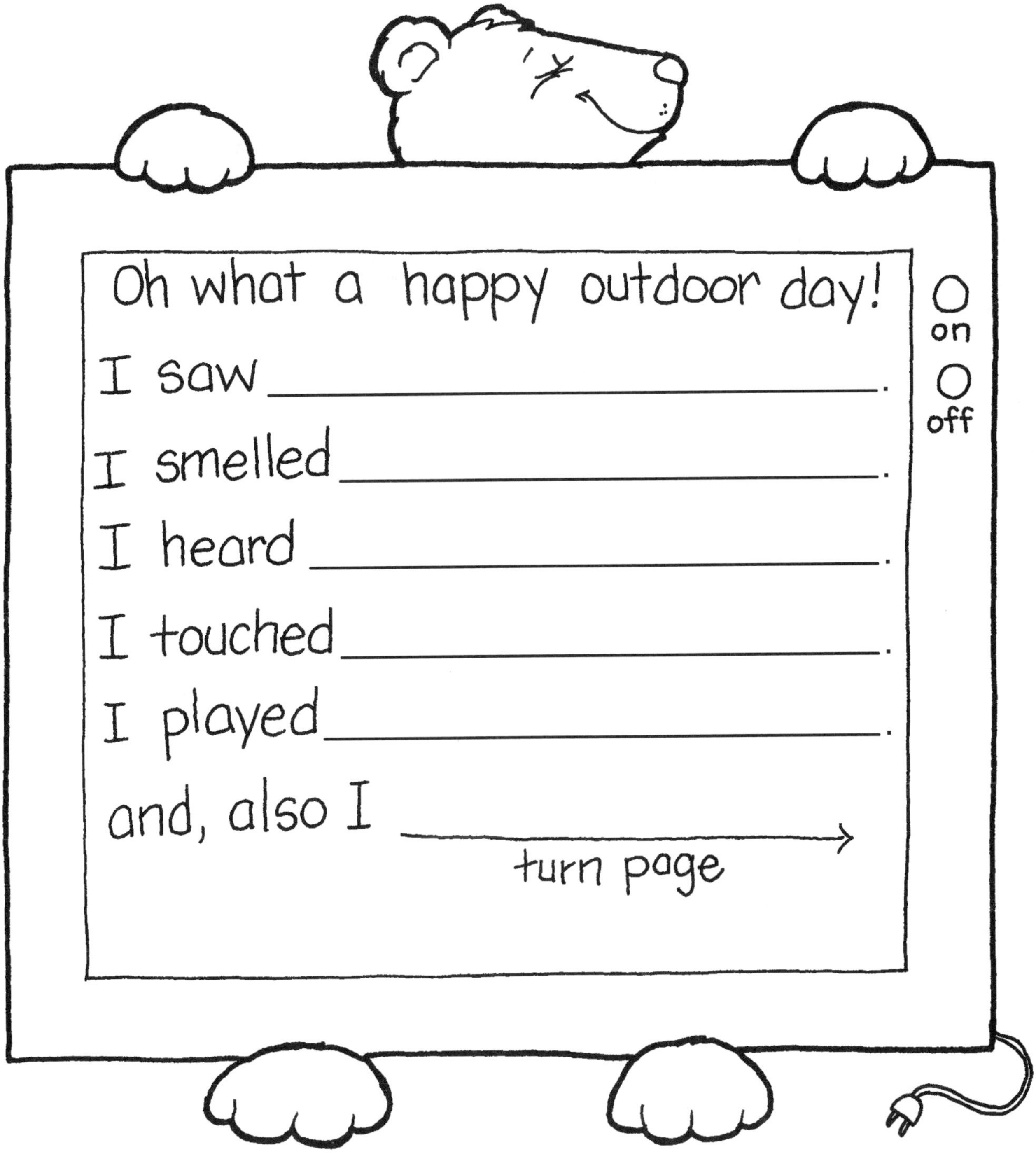

© 2000 by The Center for Applied Research in Education

Name _____

THE TV THAT WANTED TO GO OUT AND PLAY

Terry the TV Teddy wished for the day he could go outdoors and play. He needed some exercise! You can write a story about Terry Teddy's day off when his wish came true and he went out to play.

Oh what a happy outdoor day!

I saw _____.

I smelled _____.

I heard _____.

I touched _____.

I played _____.

and, also I _____→

turn page

on

off

Name _____

THE K W L PLANNER

Even the fox doesn't know everything! When he wants to learn something new, he writes on the planner. Try it.

K —What I Know
W—What I Want to Know
L —What I Learned After I Studied

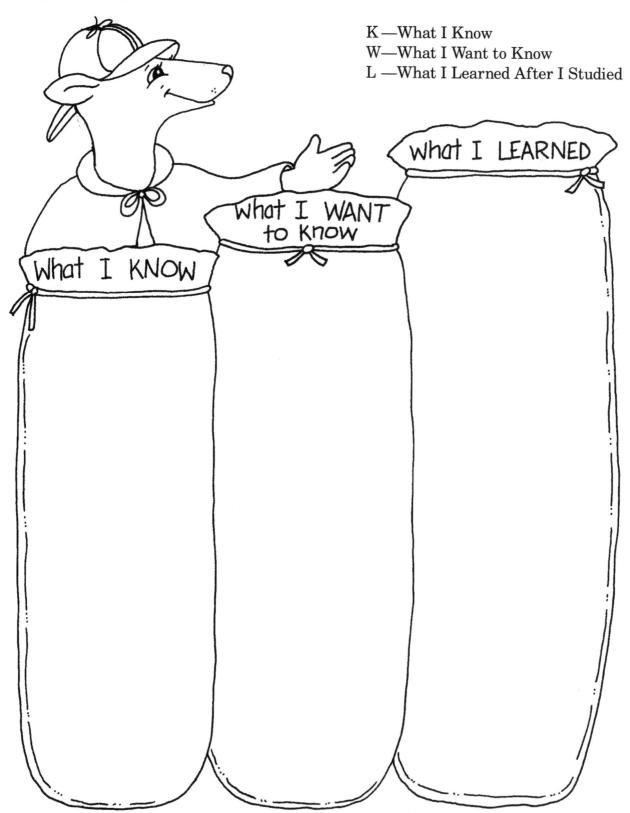

what I LEARNED

what I WANT to know

What I KNOW

© 2000 by The Center for Applied Research in Education

BOOKMARKS

Name _____   Name _____

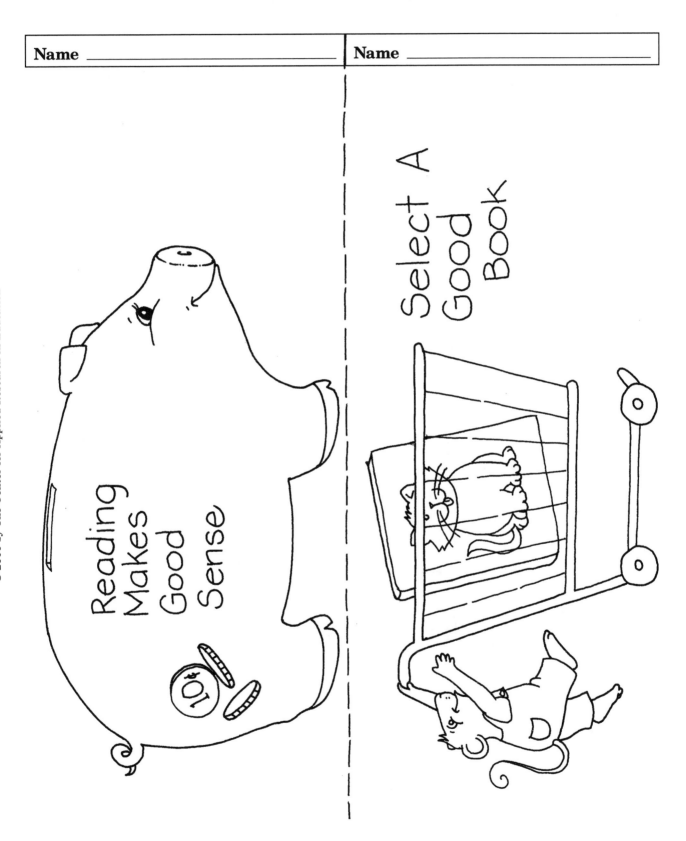

Reading Makes Good Sense

Select A Good Book

© 2000 by The Center for Applied Research in Education

LEARNING ON A FIELD TRIP

Record your findings in the school bus when you return from your field trip.

We saw these examples of environmental print.

I liked this best.

I learned this.

Field Trip to:

ABC HONK

© 2000 by The Center for Applied Research in Education

© 2000 by The Center for Applied Research in Education

I JUST ♡♡♡♡ BORDERS

Name

Select a book by Jan Brett. In the space below, draw your favorite part. Then, draw or print more story information along the borders. Can your classmates guess the story.

January

CHILDREN'S PICTURE BOOKS

FOR THE MONTH OF
JANUARY

Egielski, Richard. *Buz* **(New York: Scholastic, 1995)** This book has huge illustrations and very little text, so it is a good selection for the beginning reader. It's also a good book for this season because it's about a boy who swallows a bug with his morning cornflakes. The doctor shines a light in the boy's eye, tells him he "caught a bug," and gives him some pills to get rid of it. So now, the chase is on through the body. Buz finally swims out of the boy's ear. But guess what? *Buz* has caught a bug and has to go to the bug doctor!

Emberley, Rebecca. *City Sounds* **(Boston: Litttle, Brown & Co., 1989)** An inviting book that encourages readers to join in as they listen for city sounds and imitate those that are represented. A glossary of sounds appears at the end.

Florian, Douglas. *A Winter Day* **(New York: Greenwillow, 1987)** Snowflakes and pancakes, a winter day, cold and gray. Simple text, with large bold print, that rhymes. The illustrations provide many opportunities to discuss both indoor and outdoor winter activities.

————. *A Year in the Country* **(New York: Greenwillow, 1989)** A delightful picture book that begins with January and ends with December. The same scene is depicted throughout on a double-page spread, with only the name of the month at the top. Colors—as well as the activity of people and animals—change throughout. (Excellent for language development, as there is no written text.)

Jordan, Martin and Tanis. *Amazon Alphabet* **(New York: Kingfisher, 1996)** Explore the Amazon region for unusual animals—from Agouti to Zorro. The bright realistic paintings give us a close look at unusual animals and make the ABC's come to life in this extraordinary world.

Melmed, Laura Krauss. *Little Oh.* **Illustrated by Jim LaMarche (New York: Lothrop, 1997)** A Japanese woman spends her evenings folding origami. Imagine her surprise when one origami doll comes to life and becomes like a daughter. The doll wants to see the outside world, gets lost, and is returned by a helpful crane to a happy reunion.

Musgrove, Margaret. *Ashanti to Zulu, African Traditions.* **Pictures by Leo and Diane Dillon (New York: Dial Books, 1976)** The author, who has lived and studied in Ghana, introduces the reader via the alphabet to 26 aspects of African culture by depicting something important to each. This book shows the richness of the vast continent in text and in the art work.

Pinkney, Brian. *The Adventures of Sparrow Boy* **(New York: Simon and Schuster, 1997)** Henry has a paper route and always enjoys reading the front page. Then he reads the comics and "The Adventures of Falcon Man." Along the route Henry's bike almost collides with a sparrow and he's thrown skyward as Falcon Man, and rescues the little sparrow who is grounded. Henry doesn't come down until he's finished with his paper route. Done in action-packed comic book style, with scratchboard art technique, this book has high appeal for the reluctant reader.

Wheeler, Bernelda. *Where Did You Get Your Moccasins?* **Illustrated by Herman Bekkering (St. Paul, MN: Pemmican Publications, 1986)** Jody's kindergarten classmates admire his new moccasins and ask where they came from. His "kookum" made them. Children ask about that and learn that "kookum" is his word for "grandmother." This leads to more questions and answers. (A good multicultural awareness book.)

Young, Ed. *Seven Blind Mice* **(New York: Philomel, 1992)** This is a tale of seven different colored mice who find a strange "Something" by their pond. Each day a different mouse goes to find out what it is, and comes back with a different conclusion. Finally, on day seven they make a grand discovery. (Good for reviewing colors, the days of the week, and for a discussion of getting all of the facts before making a decision.)

JANUARY

JANUARY GREETINGS! It's back to school again after the winter break and that means one thing . . . time for review. Review the material from September through December each day, in addition to introducing new material. Some materials that were used for instruction purposes can now be put on the shelves so that students can use them during their free-choice time or during indoor recess time.

Students are usually quiet when they return after a long vacation, so make an effort to point this out to students and let them know that this is the atmosphere you are expecting. It's a good time to review the rules and perhaps rewrite some. It's a time for you to "tighten up the strings" and let the students know that we are all here to work and learn. The holiday is over . . . let's get busy. If students understand the purpose of school, they are more apt to meet expectations. *Let's read!*

January's Focus on Reading. During this month you will be engaged in a variety of reading activities. Specific skills to focus on are: (1) Time for Review; (2) Assessment; (3) Building a Story Background; and (4) The ABC Marching Band Letters—Y, Q, V, X, Z.

Time for Review

Let's Review

Whenever you come back from an extended vacation, you need to take time to review. So this month, reread the ABC Marching Band letter stories and work with the rhymes and chants. The first week back to school is an excellent time to do much of this. Students can bend, twist, reach, march backwards, march by side-stepping, make sharp corner turns, march forward, and get some much needed exercise during the indoor days.

Review All Letters and Sounds

Do this by singing the ABC song, pointing to the letter and calling upon someone to identify it. You can also distribute the ABC flash cards and play the "Calling All Letters" game. The student holding the letter A is first, and comes up and stands in line *or* places the card on the chalkboard or in a pocket chart. When all the letters are there, divide students into two groups and have them do *echo speaking* with the ABC letters in a row. For example, Group One says "A"; Group Two answers "A." Group One says "B"; Group Two answers "B," and so on.

Review Sight Words

You, no doubt, have a list of *sight words* or words that need to be learned by heart. You can place these in the classroom on a large heart shape, entitle it

"Love at First Sight," and have students identify them. Students can make a copy of these sight words.

Make a Word Study Box

Have each student bring in a recipe-size box and a packet of 3 × 5 cards. Make tabs for the inside and label them "Words I Know" and "Words I Need to Study." The object is to have the "Words I Know" section expand. Also keep adding new words to study, so that the first section can continue to expand. When students are looking for something to do (or say that there is nothing to do), direct them to work on their study box of words. For the "Words I Know" section, students can put the words in ABC order or categorize them in different ways. The words to study can be said, written, covered up, written again, and checked. Students can work with a partner on this section. In other words, there is *always* something to do in the classroom!

Review or Reteach the First 100 Instant Words*

Earlier in this book you were introduced to the first 25 Instant Words, so by the end of December it's possible that you have worked through the first 100. If this has not been feasible for your group, review the first 25, and go on now to the second 25 so students will learn 50 words. Then progress to the next 50, so students will know the first 100 sight words. The Instant Words are listed here again for your reference:

1–25	26–50	51–75	76–100
the	or	will	number
of	one	up	no
and	had	other	way
a	by	about	could
to	word	out	people
in	but	many	my
is	not	then	than
you	what	them	first
that	all	these	water
it	were	so	been
he	we	some	call
was	when	her	who
for	your	would	oil
on	can	make	its
are	said	like	now
as	there	him	find
with	use	into	long
his	an	time	down
they	each	has	day

*Source: *The Reading Teacher's Book of Lists, Third Edition.*

I	which	look	did
at	she	two	get
be	do	more	come
this	how	write	made
have	their	go	may
from	if	see	part

Review the First 100 Words and Go On to the Next 25

Put each group of five words in alphabetical order. Make up a silly sentence using the groupings. Give students an opportunity to write them. They could be included as spelling words. They are listed here for your reference:

over	new	sound	take	only
little	work	know	place	year
live	me	back	give	most
very	after	thing	our	just
name	good	sentence	man	think

Review Writing and Forming Letters

Work as a group, or in small groups, or have students work individually during January to sharpen their letter-formation skills. Make those lines straight. Make the circles round. Encourage students to take their time with writing—the object is not to rush through and be the first one done. Display exemplary papers. Display papers that show improvement. Students need to see not only *you* modeling good print, but also the work of fellow students. This serves as a motivation to improve.

Check to see how students are holding their pencils. The thumb, index finger, and middle finger are important to this process. Remember that left-handed students need to turn their paper in the opposite direction as that of right-handed students.

Reread Some of the Favorite Stories of Children

Go to the library and get some old favorites that children really enjoyed last autumn. Bring them out, read them again, and have students enjoy them all over again. Remember, the children are almost half a year older now—a long time at this age.

Review and Rewrite Classroom Rules

Check the rules. Do they apply to your classroom now? Do some fit, but perhaps new ones need to be added? Do you need more specific ones now that the learning centers may be busier? Perhaps rules for each center can be established and posted at the spot.

Remember to let students know how many children can be allowed at a center at one time. Do you have the sign-up sheet in full view? Many of the center rules can be attached to the figure of the animal or person in charge of the center. Sometimes a "bubble" shape can be attached to the character so it looks like that character is thinking or saying the rules. (*Reminder:* Centers are for review, reinforcement, and enrichment. The students do not go there to meet up with brand-new material that requires instruction and, consequently, your attention. By now, the centers can be running without your constant assistance.)

Review with Reproducible Activity Pages

Go back through this book and use some of the activity pages that were used earlier in the year. This serves as good review and reinforcement. The results of assessment this month will be helpful in selecting the activity pages. Sometimes students don't even remember having done the pages, and do much better as the year goes by.

Have Students Review Directions on Tape

Remember the directions that you recorded on tape last September? Some students may benefit from listening to them again.

Time to Freshen Up the Classroom

Take a good look around the classroom. If the student name tags are dog-eared, cut oaktag strips and make new ones. If labels posted around the classroom look a bit frayed, replace them.

Make sure that all signs of December holidays are gone. (This should be done before the students return to the classroom—*not* on the first day back.)

Have January bulletin boards that reflect "learning going on here." Link them to the curriculum areas.

Time for a New Helper's Chart

Make snowman cut-outs and print the job titles on them. Cut out red hats—one for each student. Students can print their name on the hat. When their hat is on top of the snowman, they are in charge of that duty this week. Change hats every Monday.

Time for a New Calendar

During morning circle time, many teachers gather the group around the calendar for the review and planning for the day. Have your calendar ready to go with a dark blue background, snowflakes around the edges, and a grid made from white strips of paper. Print JANUARY across the top and the letter for each day of the week.

To continue with the patterning for the dates, use snowmen and shovels, or snowball shapes and triangular pine-tree shapes.

Time for Discussion

Who is in charge of the various centers that you have around the classroom? "Do we want the same storybook characters in charge or do we want to make some changes?" If children vote for changes, this is a good month to make new large cardboard figures because, in many areas, a great deal of time will be spent indoors during recess. Students enjoy becoming involved in this type of art activity at that time.

Give Students Choices

If you have planned ten or fifteen minutes into your schedule for review, give students a choice of reviewing one skill or another. This can be done by having three review skill activity tickets in a bag. Call upon someone to come up, reach into the bag, and read the activity to be reviewed.

Provide a five-minute review time with a partner. Students can choose the skill they wish to work on.

Assessment

Time for Assessment

Once you have the reviewing well under way, students will begin to get back into the rhythm of school again. During the second and third weeks in January, you will need to take stock of where each student is and record the progress.

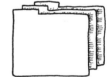

Prepare an assessment sheet for each student. If there are 27 students in your classroom, for example, you will need 27 record sheets. Some of the information you will want to know is:

- Can student print first and last names and demonstrate this? (Put a sample in the student's portfolio.)
- Can student identify the capital and lower-case letters?
- Can student point to the lower-case letter that matches the upper-case letter of the same name?
- Can student read a line of print that you have prepared?
- Can student read an entire paragraph?
- Can student read an entire page with few errors?
- Does student demonstrate some knowledge of "word attack skills"? (Is student using letter–sound relationships?)
- Can student retell a story in his or her own words?
- Does student exhibit good listening skills?
- Does student exhibit good speaking skills?
- Does student ask appropriate questions for the material presented?
- Does student get right down to work?

- Does student enjoy story time?
- Does student contribute to the class in a positive way?
- Does student work carefully?
- Does student willingly participate in reading activities?
- Does student come to school rested and eager to learn?

(See Reproducible Activity Pages for two prepared lists for your use.) Feel free to add your own information to this list. Some of the above skills may need to be worked on continually throughout the year.

Small Group Shift

This may be the time to rearrange instructional groups. Or it may be the time to refer students for additional remedial help if they are having difficulty. Sometimes, you can plan to meet daily for just ten minutes with two or three students at a time for some additional skill building. This can be helpful to them.

What's in the Portfolio?

During the previous months, if you have not been collecting sample work for student portfolios, now is a good time to do so. If you have been collecting work, now is a good time to decide what stays and what goes because folders can get quite full. Meet with small groups and have the children go over their portfolio material and decide what they would like to keep in it for the record. Some may want to do some of the work over, and this is a good indoor recess activity. If it's a valuable record, staple the new effort on top of the earlier work.

And the Message Is . . .

Review Time

What you are trying to do in January is to set the stage for review, assessment, and further learning in the classroom. Planning is the key. Being ready each day is what teachers owe to children.

Building a Story Background

Read Independently and Silently

Give students time to browse through books and then later share with peers the information they get from the text and illustrations. But, during this silent reading time, no one is talking or moving about—they are just enjoying books. Everyone can select a book from the library table and look at it. Initially, students may only be able to sustain this activity for five or ten minutes (depending upon age and maturity level of young children). Build gradually to a longer time period.

Children are gaining experience with books, turning pages, getting information from pictures and print, and some get a feeling that they are actually reading the whole book. This is good, as the success from this experience is helpful for children who can read independently as well as those who need more of a familiarity with books.

Be sure to ask, "What book did you read today, Jamal?" or "Did you select a good book to read today, Ernestine?" in an incidental way. This gives the message to the child that *of course* he or she can read.

Build a Story Background

Read aloud to children each day. Remember to build a story background before reading. This can be done in a variety of ways. For example, you can say:

"Let's look at the cover of this book to see who we will meet in the story."

"Does this look like a city story or a country story as we see these pictures? What makes you think so?"

"Do these endpapers give us a hint about the story? If so, what?"

"Today we are going to hear a story about . . . (a girl who lost her dog, for example, or a boy who is going to the dentist, a mom driving a taxicab, etc.)."

Build Your Expectations Into Story Time

Sometimes you want to discuss the story with students as you go along, sometimes the schedule allows time for students to talk about their experiences as you go along, and sometimes it's a good idea to just listen to the story and then talk later. Lay the ground rules for the students, and explain them for today . . . now. Students can handle the changes if they know what is expected of them. This also makes the experience more enjoyable for everyone.

Often the storytime can be used as a teaching experience after the story is enjoyed. Discuss the main characters in stories, the main idea (story message), and the setting. Once again review the title page, the author/illustrator, and the way the illustrations give meaning to the words. The words also give meaning to the pictures; they work together for a visual–verbal connection.

Make a Finger Chain

When a group of students is gathered together on the floor for reading time, the children need to be in control of their own bodies. Storytime is not a time for poking, tapping, or motioning to a friend. Ask students to:

- Cross your legs.
- Make a finger hand chain. (That is, instead of folding their hands, make a circle with the thumb and forefinger of the left hand. Then make an open circle with the thumb and forefinger of the right hand, interlock it with the left-hand circle, and clamp it shut. Fingers are at rest.)

- Lock your lips.
- Keep your eyes on the teacher (or speaker).

Make a Story Diorama

Select a favorite story and create a scene from it using a box, construction paper to cover the inside and outside, and materials and real items for the inside. Items for inside the diorama scene from the story may also be made from plasticine or modeling clay. This story diorama can serve as a backdrop as students retell the story.

One large diorama can be made by the class, or students can work in small groups to make several. Some students continue to do this on their own, where they create one at home and bring it in to share. This should be encouraged!

The ABC Marching Band Letters of the Month— Y, Q, V, X, Z

Note: January is the last month that will introduce the letters via the ABC Marching Band. (See the Reproducible Activity Pages.) There has been quite a bit of rhythm and rhyme—and hopefully laughter and learning—with the letters. If the group is so inclined, keep using a marching band cassette tape and march around the room on a daily basis because young children need the exercise, especially during the winter months.

Certainly by this time, the students have worked with the ABC's quite extensively. The following is intended to provide a special focus upon these letters, and to round out the band.

Meet Yazoo Yak and the Yo-Yo *(Letter Y)*

Yazoo Yak plays the yo-yo. A yo-yo is not an actual instrument; it is a toy. But in the ABC Marching Band, Yazoo Yak has transformed it into an instrument. He took two round spools and stuck them together; then he wound yarn around and around between them. With a flick of his hoof, Yazoo learned to wind and unwind the yarn, which creates the sound of the letter *y*.

The letter *y* sound is like "yah" in the word "yak." The sides of the tongue push alongside the inside of the upper side teeth, and the jaw drops down as air is expelled from the throat, through slightly parted teeth and lips. Have students gently touch the throat to feel the vocal chords vibrate.

The Kuh, Guh, Yuh Car Start-up *(Letter Y)*

The letters K, G, and Y like to get together and practice. One thing they do is something your students can do. Look in the mirror and repeat "kuh," "guh," and "yuh" repeatedly. Have students notice that the tongue gets a workout, but the lips and teeth stay perfectly still. The repeated sound of "kuh, guh, yuh" sounds like a car motor that won't start. Here is a little verse to practice along with these gutteral sounds:

(Bandleader: Raise baton.)

The car just stopped,
   it wouldn't go.
I tried to start it,
   but it said "no."

Kuh, guh, yuh. Kuh, guh, yuh. Kuh, guh, yuh.

I stepped on the pedal,
   and turned on the key.
Now come on, car,
   won't you ride with me?

Kuh, guh, yuh. Kuh, guh, yuh. Kuh, guh, yuh.

We got some gas and
   poured it in the tank.
And Yazoo Yak
   gave the starter a yank!

"Yaaaaaaaaaaaaaah." *(Hold this sound for as long as you can without taking a breath. It's the sound of the motor running.)*

(Bandleader: Lower baton.)

Glorious Yellow Food *(Letter Y)*

Yazoo Yak likes to eat almost every food that is yellow in color, because yellow starts with the letter *y*. To assist with this sound, students can enjoy a "taste of yellow" party. Here are some possible foods: banana, apple sauce, yellow apple, lemon Jell-o™, lemonade, lemon pudding, lemon sherbet, lemon drop, lemon yogurt.

Make a Yazoo Yak Poster *(Letter Y)*

Form the letter "Y" in the middle of an 8½" × 11" sheet of construction paper using big loopy yarn. Then glue yarn pieces out from the letter and put circles on the ends to represent the yo-yo. Have students cut pictures from magazines that begin or end with the sound of "y" and paste them on the yo-yo's.

Bring in a real yo-yo for the class, and have students practice with it on the playground.

Yazoo Likes Rhyming Words for Spelling *(Letter Y)*

Yazoo Yak was named after a river in Mississippi, but he has trouble spelling it. The following is a little chant that was shared with young children—in sing-song fashion—by Louis Harbater of New York City, many years ago. Children today will also enjoy it. Get the rhythm going; it makes spelling fun. Ready, go:

How do you spell Mississippi?
An M and an I and an SSS
And an IPPI and a PIPPI
And THAT'S how you spell Mississippi!

Two others that Louis Harbater enjoyed chanting with children are as follows:

How do you spell Chicago?
A chicken in a car
And a car can't go
And That's how you spell Chicago.

How do you spell New York?
A knife and a fork
And a bottle and a cork
And That's how you spell New York.

(*Note:* These three rhymes are printed with permission from (retired) Judge Maurice Harbater, Supreme Court, New York, NY. Both Judge and his father, Louis, enjoyed working with children in Boy Scouts. The judge's wife, Marilyn Harbater, has had much success working with developmentally-delayed children when she dons her clown outfit and gazes into their eyes.)

And Sometimes "Y" *(Letter Y)*

The vowel letters are a, e, i, o, u "and sometimes y." Often the letter *y* will step in and pinch hit for the long sound of the letter *i*. Print a list of examples on the chalkboard, have students circle the letter *y*, and say the word so that they hear the long sound of *i*. At the same time, let students know that this is not always so. They need to be on the alert with these tricky letter sounds.

sky   buy   try   why   cry

Meet Quinella Quail and the Quill *(Letter Q)*

One thing students have to learn right from the start is that the letter *q* rarely appears in a word without *u* right alongside it. Together they make the "kwa" sound. This sound is made with a gutteral glide. It begins in the back of the throat with the sound of *k*. Then lips are pursed and the air is blown out of the mouth *(wa)* as the vocal chords vibrate. Be sure to have students observe themselves in the mirror for this complicated sound combination.

Quinella Quail plays the quill in the ABC Marching Band. The quill is an actual instrument, like a flute. It is often referred to as a *musical pipe* that has a hollow stem. Think of a quill feather, with the main shaft being hollow, and air blown into the stem, while fingers cover and uncover the holes that have been cut into the quill.

Doing the Gutteral Glide–Slide! *(Letters Qu)*

Quinella plays
  the musical pipe.
The pitch is high,
  the sound is ripe.
Now let's join hands
  Stand side by side

And do the Gutteral Glide–Slide   *(Move sideways, by sliding the feet.)*
And do (Kwa)   *(Students move in unison in one*
The gutteral (Kwa)   *direction for the "glide–slide" while*
Glide (Kwa)   *saying "kwa.")*
Slide (Kwa)

Then repeat the chant and movement again.

The Queen of Quackers Has Invited the Quail to Tea *(Letters Qu)*

The Queen has invited
  the quail to tea.
Oh what a great party
  this will be!
You see, the Queen
  wants to hear the quill.
For her it will be
  quite a thrill.

The Queen likes to swim
  just before tea,
And quack a honking
  melody.
"Quack, Quack! Quack, Quack, Quack!"

By the sound of this song
  if we are in luck,
We're going to guess
  That the queen is a d_____!   *(Have students fill in the word "duck.")*

Select the "QU" Word *(Letter Q)*

Read these sentences to the students one by one. Have students select the "qu" word that makes the most sense (context clue). When they think they know which one is correct, have them raise their forefinger as a sign.

Carmen likes to work when it's _____.   (quail, quill, quiet)

Grandmother is stitching a new _____.   (quid, quilt, quick)

Did you ask a _____?   (quite, quack, question)

It's now time to _____.   (quit, quota, quotation mark)

Complete the Word *(Letter Q)*

Make a set of flash cards that have *qu* printed on them. Distribute them to several students. Next, set up along the chalkboard a set of word endings (in some cases, they are rimes) that you have printed on a set of flash cards. Call upon a student to put the *qu* card in front of the word card, say the "kwa" sound, and then glide into the letters to complete the word. You will need the following starter cards:

ill	ilt
ack	ick
it	een
estion	ail

Meet Vulcan Vulture and the Violin *(Letter V)*

Vulcan Vulture plays the violin in the ABC Marching Band. The sound of the letter *v* is made by parting the lips, resting the top front teeth on the bottom lip, and expelling air while making a gutteral sound in the throat.

The violin is a real stringed instrument played with a bow. This five-stringed instrument has sometimes been called a fiddle. A larger version of the violin, with a lower sound, is called a viola.

The Vulture Is Voiceless *(Letter V)*

The vulture has a speech problem—it doesn't make a sound. Birds often use their calls to determine their territory, but a vulture has no territory. It is a "carrion" bird—nature's clean-up bird—and goes where it is needed.

It is fitting that the sometimes mournful sound of the violin would be played by the vulture. Vulcan is sad that people throw things on the ground and mess up the environment. He likes things neat and tidy. This might be an opportunity to work this message into the clean-up duties both during and at the end of the day.

Vulcan Is Putting Together an ABC of Vegetables, Fruits, and Condiments *(Letter V)*

For the letter *v*, Vulcan selected *vinegar*, the condiment (new vocabulary word) that you sprinkle on salad. Have students see how many foods (or food-related items) they can come up with to make the complete alphabet. Find pictures in magazines. Make a big book of delicious food for some ABC practice.

Vulcan Is Going on a Voyage *(Letter V)*

A voyage is a journey, and Vulcan needs to pack his suitcase to get ready to go away for two weeks. Students can pretend to do the same thing. Start with an ABC list; as items are named that can go along (in a suitcase or in carry-on luggage), print that word after the letter. "What is essential?" "What is not essential?" "What is too big to take?"

Vulcan Needs Help With Vocabulary *(Letter V)*

"Vocabulary" can be an accumulation (list) of spoken or written words. For this activity, deliberately put words on the chalkboard that are misspelled. (These are from Vulcan's paper.) Have the students look for the errors and try to help Vulcan by correcting the words.

Vulcan Needs to Make a Study List. Do You? *(Letter V)*

From the words used above, students can see that Vulcan needs to practice. Have students make a list of their own words that they need to study. Help the vulture strengthen his memory!

Meet X-ray Man and the Xylophone *(Letter X)*

X-Ray Man plays the xylophone in the ABC Marching Band. The xylophone is an actual musical percussion instrument consisting of a row of wooden bars, graduating in size from small to large. It is played by striking the bars with a mallet.

This letter itself makes two distinctly different sounds: the first says its name, or "eks," and the second takes on the sound of "zee." It's tricky; there is no rule for it. The "eks" sound can appear at the beginning (as in *x-ray*) or at the end of a word (as in *fix*). The letter is not used a great deal, but is important when it appears.

When saying its name, or "eks, the mouth drops open, the teeth are parted, the tongue pushes against the bottom front teeth, the sound "eh" comes from the back of the throat, immediately followed by a crashing sound of *k* in the back of the throat, and rapidly followed by the top front teeth resting on the bottom front teeth as a "s-s-s-s" sound escapes from between the teeth. All of this takes place rapidly.

When saying the second sound, as in the letter *z,* the top front teeth rest on the bottom front teeth, and the throat emits a gutteral sound. Students can feel the sound by placing their hand gently on their throat.

"X" Marks the Spot for the X-ray Man *(Letter X)*

Familiarize students with the saying "X marks the spot." The letter "X" is often used on forms directing people where to sign their name. It is used in theatre performances as a mark on the floor to show actors and actresses where to stand. It is used on treasure maps to show where the hidden treasure lies, and so on. Write "X Marks the Spot" on the chalkboard and have an assortment of the letter "X" taped around the classroom for directions. For example, an "X" in front of the doorway means "line up here."

Who Is This X-ray Man? *(Letter X)*

Here is a chant that you can read to the students again and again. It is aimed at demonstrating the double sounds of this letter. It is deliberately designed to be playful, as are so many rhymes, so that students will relate to the fantasy and learn at the same time. (For example, the initials for Elmer K. Spaghetti are EKS, which is one sound of the letter *x.*)

Meet Elmer K. Spaghetti,
  the X-ray Man.
He makes two sounds
  for the ABC Band.

He's very fussy and
  doesn't eat baloney.
He gobbles up spaghetti
  and he loves macaroni!

And he says his initials
  whenever he can.
So that's why we call him
  the "EKS"-ray man!

"Eks, eks, eks-ray man!"

Now, the X-ray Man
  can also say "zee."
He plays the xylophone,
  you see.
When you cross his path
  during day or night,
Say "eks" or "zee,"
  one is bound to be right.

- Practice saying "eks" five times. *(Hand play: Place right hand over left hand, and chop the sound five times.)*

- Practice saying "zee" five times. *(Place the left hand over the right hand, and chop the sound five times.)*
- Practice alternating "eks" and "zee" ten times. *(At the same time, alternate the left and right hands that are making chopping motions for the letter.)*

Can You Hear It? *(Letter X)*

Read a sentence that uses a word with the letter *x* in it and one that does not. Ask students to listen for the sound of the letter *x*. If students know whether the word has the "eks" or the "zee" sound, have them cross their two arms to make the letter *x*. That serves as a signal that they want to be called on.

You can hear it in xylophone, but not in telephone. What is it? *(zee)*

You can hear it in extra, but not in electric. What is it? *(eks)*

You can hear it in x-ray, but not in freeway. What is it? *(eks)*

Let's Work With Our Own Initials *(Letter X)*

Elmer K. Spaghetti's initials are "EKS," which make the sound of "eks." Have students print their first, middle, and last initials and sound them out. How many make a word? How many sound like a letter name? Make a name tag, wear it for a day, and sound it out. This gives students practice with phonics. For example:

Patti Alice Newton (PAN)

Jason Andrew Morgenstern (JAM)

Sarah Marie Burke (SssMmmBuh)

Meet Zachary Zebra and the Zither *(Letter Z)*

Zachary Z. Zebra is the marching band member who plays the zither. The zither is a real instrument with about 30 to 40 strings stretched over a flat sounding box. It is plucked with the fingertips, while being held in a flat position.

The letter *z* is made by parting the lips, placing the top front teeth on the bottom front teeth, and pressing against the back of the bottom front teeth with the tip of the tongue, while air is expelled through the throat (growling sound) and from between the teeth, thus making the hissing sound. It is a voiced letter, so children can feel the vibration of the sound by touching their throat.

Practice With The Letter Sound *(Letter Z)*

Read the chant. Students make the sound of the letter *z:*

Z plays the zither
    z, z, z
The vacuum cleaner hums his sound
    z, z, z
The sleeping giant snores his sound
    z, z, z
The yellow jackets buzz his sound
    z, z, z
The hummingbirds hum his sound
    z, z, z
Can you make his sound?
    z, z, z

More Practice With Razzle, Dazzle *(Letter Z)*

Since this letter is the last letter of the ABC Marching Band, it can be introduced with a flourish. Get the rhythm going for this chant; students can keep the beat by swaying shoulders back and forth. Read it first from beginning to end, then have students move in time with the chant.

WELL, here he is,
    our Zither Z.
He's the razzle, dazzle boy
    of our letter family.
He's at the end,
    Z closes the door.
And now you know
    what letters are for.

We sound them out
    and get excited
'Cause words come out
    when they're invited.

So take a lesson
    from razzle, dazzle Z
And practice every day.

Before you know it
    your effort will show it—
You'll be a READER. Hurray!

You will! U-huh! Yes, sir!
You'll be a reader today! Z-z-z-z-z-z.

Students can use black and white crepe paper streamers to wave in the air for this chant, which represent a zebra's stripes.

Spelling Program

If you do not have a spelling program, begin one now. A good place to start is with the rimes (word families). For young students by the age of seven, they can be in a formal spelling program with spelling exercises throughout the week that require practice and memorization. Use this as a guide:

Day 1. List spelling words for the week on the chalkboard. Say them; spell them aloud. Look for patterns in words. Students can copy them from the board.

Day 2. Students write their spelling words three times. After they write them twice, encourage students to cover up the word to see if they can master it the third time.

Day 3. Students write each spelling word in a simple sentence and underline it. You can have a skill sheet that has been prepared, or students can copy from the chalkboard. On this day, you may give a test so students can determine how well they are doing and which words they need to study. This activity motivates some students to get down to the business of learning the words by rote memory.

Day 4. Put scrambled spelling words on the chalkboard or on a skill sheet that you have prepared. Students unscramble the words and write them. They can work with a study partner today, whereby one student says the words and the other student spells them. Take turns.

Day 5. Give the spelling test. Distribute half sheets of writing paper. Students put their name and the date on the top two lines and then number the paper from 1–8 (number can vary). Then, when everyone is ready, begin in this manner: Say the spelling word; use it in a sentence; repeat the word. Speak distinctly.

Papers should be corrected the same day for immediate feedback. Sometimes students will study words they missed over the weekend, thus getting two scores for the test but the first score remains as well. Sometimes teachers have students exchange papers for correction, but not as a regular practice.

READING LINKS TO HOLIDAYS & SPECIAL EVENTS

Happy New Year

"On January 1, we celebrate the new year. The last page of the calendar is turned over and we begin anew." Students can discuss what they need to work on during the year. What subject is going to get special attention from them? What classroom behavior do they all need to work on?

On a bell shape, which indicates "ringing in the new year," have students print the numerals 1, 2, 3. Then have them fill in what they plan to work on. At the end of the first week, have them give themselves a star for the skill they worked on the most, a + for the one they worked on next, and a − for the one that didn't get their attention. That way, during the next week, they can focus upon the item that didn't get the attention and aim for balance.

New Year Customs

"Put your best foot forward" is a common phrase. It means that we will try to do our best, with a good attitude. Place a small rug inside the classroom door that has a gripper non-slip backing. When students step on the rug to come into the classroom, it can serve as a reminder that they are to put their best foot forward in their "house of learning" and to bring their indoor voices and a cheerful attitude for learning. This helps to set the tone in the classroom.

Have students stand in a circle, hands on hips, and put their foot forward and back (twice) as they repeat this pledge. On the last line, they jump ahead and back twice, before they sit down.

TEACHER:	What do we do when we come to school?
STUDENTS:	We put our best foot forward, our best foot forward.
TEACHER:	How do we work together each day?
STUDENTS:	We put our best foot forward, our best foot forward.
TEACHER:	What do we do when it's time for play?
STUDENTS:	We put our best foot forward, our best foot forward.
TEACHER:	So, what do we do when we come to school?
STUDENTS:	We put our whole self forward, our whole self forward.

Then children sit down and assume the position of attention—feet flat on floor, hands held together on desk, back straight, lips locked, eyes straight ahead. When you are satisfied with the "inspection," you say, " At rest"; students relax their body and show that they are ready for what comes next.

Musical Birthdays

This month we celebrate the birthdays of two famous composers: Wolfgang Amadeus Mozart and Franz Schubert. At the public library, obtain CDs or cassette recordings by these composers, and play them this month during rest time.

Students can also paint pictures with these composers' music playing in the background. Fingerpainting in time to the music can be peaceful . . . exciting . . . rhythmic.

Recent studies in the late 1990s have indicated that listening to music by Mozart can increase a person's IQ by making new connections in the brain. Is this so? Well, it's worth a try. Explain to students that while they are resting, they are recharging their learning batteries at the same time.

Humanitarian Day

Talk about what it means to be a "humanitarian." This is someone who is concerned with others, who is helpful, who does good deeds for others.

Have a class discussion about this quality. Make a list of words that would be helpful in describing a humanitarian.

This might be a good day to declare "please," "thank you," and "excuse me" as very special words. "We can each keep a tally of how many times we have the pleasure of saying these words to someone today. Wouldn't these words make our cafeteria workers pleased? And the bus driver? And the teacher? And all class-mates? And parents?"

It's a Happy Birthday Month

January celebrates the birthdays of several famous and important people:

Jan. 1—Betsy Ross

Jan. 15—Martin Luther King, Jr.

Jan. 17—Benjamin Franklin

Jan. 18—A.A. Milne (creator of Winnie the Pooh)

Be sure to highlight these dates on the monthly calendar.

Celebrate With Betsy Griscom Ross

Since students will not be in school on this date (January 1), be sure to celebrate later in the month. Students can use red, white, and blue paints at the easel (for a week) making designs, flags, or an actual picture.

Students can pretend to be an assistant to Betsy Ross, and create symbols and new designs made with red, white, and blue colors. This will come in handy next month, February, because President George Washington has another request for Betsy G. Ross—and students will be included!

Celebrate With Martin Luther King, Jr.

Martin Luther King, Jr. wrote a famous speech in which he told of the dreams he had for his people and for the world. It has been referred to as his "I Have a Dream" speech.

Perhaps students have a dream for the world. This calls for a discussion and some speechwriting, even if it is only a statement. Students can work to memorize their speech and give it before the class on the anniversary of King's birthday.

The speech rehearsals could be videotaped, played back for the class, and critiqued in a serious manner. Suggestions would be welcome, such as "maybe you should pause right here"; "Raise your hand up right here"; "Smile here"; or "Look very serious here." Anyone who chooses to do his or her speech over again, with gestures, can ask to do so at this time. Remember, the audience needs to be attentive and to applaud at the end. Perhaps one or two students standing at the side can be appointed to come forward and shake the hand of the speaker at the end.

Hand-in-Hand Necklace

Have students trace their hands and cut them out. These can be on colorful sheets of paper (green, orange, tan, white, yellow, red). Turn the hands with fingers facing downward and print the phrase "We work hand in hand" on the hands. Use a hole punch on the hands (at the wrist end) and string a colorful piece of yarn or ribbon through the holes. Wear the necklace with pride.

Celebrate With Benjamin Franklin

Many hardware stores, variety stores, libraries, buildings, schools, and even products have been named after Benjamin Franklin. Have the children look for these names in the town. Look for them in the Yellow Pages, too. How many can be located in the area? List them.

Benjamin Franklin, the Leather Apron Man

Ben Franklin was a "Leather Apron Man," a name given to tradesmen, for they wore an apron made of leather to protect their clothing. He worked in a printing shop, and enjoyed reading books and newspapers. He formed a book club, after work, for tradesmen who wanted to discuss the books that they had read. It was called "The Leather Apron Club." Perhaps students from the class can form a "Leather Apron Club" and meet weekly or bimonthly in the classroom for lunch and book discussions with you. Decide in advance what the topic of discussion is to be. This is a serious book discussion time, a treat—*not* playtime. (Limit the number of students, and meet more often if needed so that everyone gets a turn.)

Celebrate With Winnie-the-Pooh

Have a Pooh festival. List all of the characters. Write down a word that describes each one. Have students retell, in their own words, something they liked about a story of Winnie-the-Pooh.

Have swatches of material available—from rough burlap to smooth satin, and others in between. Have students feel the materials and put them in order from soft to rough; put them in order according to how they think Winnie might order them. If students differ, have them tell why. What words describe these textures? What material would the different characters select for a new shirt?

Have swatches of printed material, calico, checks, stripes, and so on. Encourage students to select fabric combinations for a new shirt, overalls, and scarf for Winnie and/or the other characters. (Combinations will differ.)

READING LINKS TO WRITING

Headings Are Important

If you have not yet established that a heading is to be put on all written work that is to be turned in, now is the time to do so. What do you, as teacher, expect on a heading? For younger students who are using wide-lined paper, use the first two lines for first and last names, and the second two lines for the date. Students can begin written work on the third set of lines.

For older students working with smaller lines on paper, some teachers have students print or write their name at the left on the first line and the date at the right on the first line. On the second line, students print or write the subject at the left and the day of the week at the right. Why? So that students are not scribbling their names anywhere on the page.

This is a formal writing procedure. Students need to learn that writing requires a certain amount of repetition and self-discipline.

Name Date

Name   Date Subject   Weekday

Let's Freshen Up Our Writing Center

For the new year, have new pencils and some new felt-tip pens at the Center. You will also need a fresh supply of colored pencils. (The used, knubby stubs can be put in a small container for use later.) Obtain several individual pencil sharpeners and soft erasers (at an art supply store).

A new supply of paper, cut into different shapes, is also an impetus to writing. For starters, circular shapes for snowballs or a circular snowman shape might bring forth some wintry prose or poetry.

We Can Write Cinquain Style

Cinquain, pronounced sin-KAIN, has a set formula for the poetry. First, have a lesson with the entire class and do some writing together. Only after that initial introduction should cinquain be introduced at the Writing Center as reinforcement, review, or enrichment. At the Center, students should not be dealing with new learning. You need to provide some independence for them here.

After the whole class lesson, create a poster for the Writing Center, but don't put any words on it. The visual message is important. Select a black background, cut out rectangles from a bright color, and display this format.

This visual impact serves to remind students of the actual formula (shape) that has already been taught. It can also be spelled out as follows, so that it serves as a review:

Line 1: topic word
Line 2: two descriptive words about topic
Line 3: three words that end in "ing" that describe topic
Line 4: a four-word sentence about topic
Line 5: a *sensational* wrap-up word

Cinquain example by a second grader:

Mom
Nice, pretty
Running, smiling, driving
I love my mom.
Fabulous!

Cinquain example dictated by a first grader:

Frog
Bumpy, green
Jumping, swimming, hopping
See it jump high.
R-r-ribbit!

Younger children may have more success if they work as a total group and then in groups of two or three. Select the groups so that more able students can help those who are still in the process of learning the formula.

Some of the younger students may only have success with this after working individually with the teacher, who can elicit descriptive words from the child. Looking through colorful picture books with bright illustrations seems to help elicit descriptive words. Be sure to have some at the Writing Center.

Celebrate National Handwriting Day

"Let's practice, practice, practice our writing this month so that we show great improvement."

Have students place their best handwriting sample in their folder, as they do every month. They have the opportunity to add to it or to delete any items any time. After all, their aim is to improve during this month.

Have several small chalkboards and erasers at the Writing Center so that students can practice their letters and sentences.

Let's Look for Pen Pals in Another Classroom

Arrange with another teacher in your school district to have students correspond with one another by mail. In this way they will work hard to do their best. The children can start with a letter of introduction that tells something about them, their hobbies, their family, and what they like best about school. A class photo can be taken and eventually sent to the pen-pal classroom; hopefully, that class will do the same.

Later in the year, it would be a good experience to arrange to meet the pen pals for a field-trip lunch. (Be prepared, because when this happens young children often get quiet when they meet their pen pal in person.) Make a list of possible topics the children could talk about before you meet, such as pets or something exciting that is going on in your classroom.

Introducing the "Pen Name"

Benjamin Franklin used the pen name of "Silence Dogood" when he wrote stories, but didn't want anyone to know that he wrote them. (Actually his older brother ran the printing shop for which Benjamin worked and his brother would not publish young Benjamin's stories, so Benjamin submitted them under a pen name and was published!) Have students select a pen name for themselves.

- Set up a "Suggestion Box" in the classroom. Have students submit suggestions for the classroom under their pen name.
- Set up a "Dear Abby" box in the classroom. Have students submit letters under their pen name, and you can answer. (*Note:* Be prepared for possible letters that reveal personal problems. Have a system in place to handle this possibility.)

READING LINKS TO MATH

Counting by Ten's

Benjamin Franklin was the tenth son born into his family. So let's work with counting by 10's this month—maybe Benjamin Franklin can help us. First, since he liked to read, let's learn to read these number names by heart:

one	six
two	seven
three	eight
four	nine
five	ten

Make ten flash cards with the number names written on them. On the other side, write the numeral. Have students study the spelling of the words (start first with 1 through 3), and then work with a partner. The partner can hold up a card with the numeral showing. The student has to (depending upon the student's development) write the beginning sound, write the first two letters, or write the word.

Using the same cards, show the written number name and have students write the numeral for which it stands.

Work with two columns: one has the numeral on one side, and the name on the other. Have students link up the corresponding names and numerals.

Work with three columns: one has the numeral, one has the number name, and one has a square with dots (like a die). Students can do a three-way link.

Jumping Rope, Bouncing Balls, Rolling Balls by Ten

- Have students jump rope while counting by ten. How far can they get? (10, 20, 30, 40, 50, 60, 70, 80, 90, 100 . . .)
- Have students bounce a ball, counting by ten. How far can they get?
- Have two students bounce a ball back and forth to each other while counting by ten. How far can they get?
- Have two students roll a ball back and forth to each other while counting by ten. How far can they get?
- Sit in a circle and roll the ball to one another. The first person starts the roll; the person to whom it is rolled calls out "ten." Then "ten" must roll the ball to someone else who will call out "twenty," and so on. When students get to "one hundred," start over again with "ten."

Betsy Ross Flag Math

Have a short math lesson using the American flag. You can do the following:

- Count the number of red stripes.
- Count the number of white stripes.
- Count the number of stars.
- Count the total number of long stripes and short stripes.
- Measure the length and width of the flag.
- Measure the length of the stripes.
- Measure the blue field in relation to the flag.

Using strips of red, white, and blue paper, students can make paper chains. Using the information above as a blueprint, recreate the flag on a bulletin board.

Reading and Math—"QU" Is Found in a Quarter

Since you are working with the letters "qu" this month, examine the coin called a quarter. Explain that in this case, the quarter means ¼ of a dollar. It takes four quarters to equal one dollar.

Have students look for other examples of quarters in the classroom. For example, there might be four windowpanes in the door window, or four cupboard doors in a row, or four file drawers in a cabinet, and so on.

Another way to show quarters is to work with fractional parts that are labeled. Each of the four pieces must be the same size, or equal. Take two rectangular strips of paper of the same length and size. Put one aside. Take the second, fold it in half, and then in half again. Cut along the folds. Place each of the four pieces (quarters) on top of the rectangle that is the same size. Label each as ¼, which means "one of the four pieces." The same can be done with rectangles of different lengths. It can also be done with circular pieces. (*Note:* Fraction manipulatives are commercially available.)

READING LINKS TO SOCIAL STUDIES

What Do People Do to Get Ready for Winter?

You have already discussed clothing and the fact that people wear heavier clothing in winter. Have a discussion of how people in some areas must "winterize" their homes. (Storm windows are put up, lawn furniture is stored, the water hose is brought inside, awnings are taken down, plants are brought indoors, boats are stored, and so on.) Explain that this will vary depending upon in what area of the country people make their home. Even if students live in apartments, it is important for them to know that homes do get winterized.

Students can divide a sheet of paper in half and draw a whimsical picture of a house in summer wearing sunglasses, with the windows wide open and a garden hose and flowers in the yard. Then, on the other half, draw a house in winter wearing a hat and scarf; show the bare tree branches and snowy yard. The children can write a descriptive sentence about each.

What Do Animals Do to Get Ready for Winter?

Introduce the term *hibernation*. Some animals sleep during the winter in caves, or burrow underground, or swim down and dig underground beneath pond water.

Bears hibernate, with the females often giving birth to twin cubs during this time. Bears eat and gain a great deal of weight before hibernation, and then use their stored food (fat) during the hibernation period. They come out slim and hungry.

Some animals change fur color (rabbit) or get spots in winter (deer) so that they can be camouflaged in wintry weather.

Have the class make a giant diagram with tempera paint on a tan or gray background. First, do the sketching with chalk; then later fill it in with paint. Divide the paper in half with an irregular line depicting hills. The bottom half can be devoted to what is going on *under* the ground; the top half can show what is going on *above* the ground. The rabbit, spotted deer, and squirrels (as well as domestic animals) can be seen above the ground, but the bear is asleep in a cave underground. Who or what else is underground sleeping? Include several trees, showing the roots underground. In the tree branches, paint birds that stay in the area. Put cotton balls in the sky for a snowy-day effect as the finishing touch.

Healthy Outdoor Sports

"We can enjoy being outdoors as long as we are properly dressed. There are many sports in which we can engage, so that we get exercise over the winter months. Outdoor sports can include: ice skating, sledding, making snowforts and snow people, tobogganing, skiing, ice hockey, and ice fishing."

Remind students that for health and safety reasons, they are to always get parent permission for involvement in outdoor sports. Also, they should be reminded to always play with a friend (or friends) and in areas where they can be seen.

Protection in the Outdoors

Discuss with the students what people need for protection around the country when they are in the following places: (1) at the beach, (2) in the desert, (3) on a camping trip, and (4) in a snowstorm. Take four large sheets of paper and cut them into the following shapes: giant beach ball, enormous sun, giant tent, and a big snowman. On these shapes that represent the four settings, have students draw protective clothing or items needed. If you prefer, students can cut the pictures from magazines and paste them on the appropriate shape.

Go on a Footprint Walk

Be on the alert for prints in snow. On rainy days, prints appear on dry cement or brick areas (dog prints, cat prints). Birds (and squirrels!) make telltale marks around bird feeders. Take the magnifying glass, sketch pad, and pencil along.

Who's Our Classroom Visitor?

Bring a box into the room and place it in a prominent spot. Cut out footprints from black construction paper and tape them to the floor leading to the box, and up the side of the box. The curious students have to determine what animal is in the box. They can write creative stories or factual stories about the animal. The prints can be changed throughout the week.

Potato Footprints

Students can find books on animal prints in the library and see if they can make a match. Have students draw a footprint for a particular animal on a potato half. (**Caution:** You or another adult will cut around it.) Then students can draw a picture, using the potato print to make the border.

Also, take a sheet of 8½″ × 11″ construction paper and fold it into thirds each way. (You will end up with nine squares.) Students can use the potato print for some of the squares, and draw in the animal in the rest of the squares. Animal facts or stories can be written on a paper and attached to the back, or to the bottom of the page. This also makes an attractive quilt pattern when displayed.

Winter Snowflake Mural

For a nice winter touch to the room, you will need dark violet or blue background paper for the bulletin board. You will also need white tempera paint, lacy paper doilies, and black construction paper. Have students, wearing smocks, dip lace paper doilies into the paint and make an imprint on the paper to create a glorious sky. With the black construction paper, create bare trees for the lower foreground; they appear as dark silhouettes. Put the doilies on the branches for snowflakes. Make sure that the trees form an irregular line along approximately the bottom third of the mural, so that the sky is the major focus. Black letters can be added at the top for a title. Student poetry about winter can be framed and hung in the sky area.

READING LINKS TO SCIENCE & HEALTH

Chart the High and Low Temperatures for the Month

Each day, use the newspaper or weather report to record the high and low temperatures for the day. Record this on graph paper so that, at the end of the month, the data has been collected and graphed at the same time. Discuss the results. "What was the highest temperature? the lowest? What days were average?"

Weather Sayings

Collect an assortment of weather sayings and check them out on your weather graph to see if they are correct, for this month at least. (Examples are: "Red sky at night, sailor's delight; red sky in morning, sailors take warning." "If the snow sounds crunchy underfoot, it means it's a very cold day." "The weekends are always the worst weather days.")

Weather Predictions

After a week of recording weather temperatures, have students predict or estimate what they think the temperature will be for the next day. An estimate is a "best guess" based on the data at hand. If a storm is forecast, the temperature may be lower. If you're in for a stable period, the temperature may change very little, and so on. Point this out to students. Listen to the noon weather reports for an update and for tomorrow's estimates. (If the temperature has been in the 40's all week, for example, and the weather reporter is saying it's going to be mild, then you know a student is not getting the concept if he or she predicts that tomorrow will be "20." So independent work is needed with estimators who are way off.)

Snow and Temperature Experiment

Lay a thermometer on top of the snow for 30 minutes to get a reading. Record the temperature (Rebus style too). Next, find a snowdrift, dig in, and place the thermometer on the ground. Bury it with snow. Wait 30 minutes. Uncover it and get a reading. Record it and compare. (It should show a warmer temperature the second time because snow acts as a blanket for the earth. We speak of a "blanket of snow.")

Of course, if you live in an area with no snow, then you can do some experiments using crushed ice.

Winter Weather Around the World

Check the local, national, and world weather news. An excellent resource is the weather map on the back page of the first section of the newspaper *USA Today*. Here are some activities you can do:

- Compare temperature and weather in three cities around the world for one month.
- Note the color coding on the map and map legend. Distribute three sheets of construction paper—red, blue, yellow. Determine with the students which one would be the hottest, coldest, and in between. Each day, for one week, distribute these three colors and say: "I'm looking for the coldest day of the year! It's so cold, the polar bears are freezing!" (The person with the white paper comes to the front of the room. Continue until the three colors are called in. You can do this with more colors, depending on the group.)
- Find your state and the coldest city.
- Find the coldest and warmest spots in the country.
- Find "weather words" in the news, such as *hurricane* and *avalanche*. Look up their meanings.

Make an ABC Newspaper Book of Weather and Weather Terms

The local and national newspapers will be very helpful here. Use news photos, words, and phrases from the pages to make a class ABC book of weather and terms associated with weather.

Snowblindness

The effects of the bright sun on white snow can result in eye pain and squinting, so avoid this condition. In the Arctic, people must wear wrap-around glasses with small slits, so that only a portion of the light comes through. This protects their eyes.

Make a pair of glasses using a rectangular shape of construction paper. Cut small slits instead of eye holes. Staple string on both sides of this eye mask and tie string at the back of the head. Look through the eye slits. It narrows the field of vision, while protecting the eyes. What do students see that they didn't notice before?

Picture Books With Snow

Read *A Snowy Day* by Ezra Jack Keats and look for dark and light contrasts in the book. Then, for a book with blustery, windy, blizzard-like conditions in the swirling illustrations, be sure to read the tale about Ol' Man Winter in the book *Is That You, Winter?* by Stephen Gammell. Make a comparison of the illustrations in these two snowy books. Also compare the print.

Ice Explorers

If applicable, bring in an icicle from outdoors, and have it be the focus of attention at the sink area. Observe the way in which it melts and the different color (density) of the ice as it melts.

Make ice cubes and observe the same as above. Also, ice cubes can be put into a glass of warm water and a glass of cold water to determine which will melt first. Have students make predictions, and then check their accuracy.

LINKS TO AUTHOR-OF-THE-MONTH

Author/Illustrator for January: Marc Brown

Author/Illustrator Marc Brown has created the character named Arthur, who is an aardvark. This animal, who lives in an animal family, has all of the problems and delights that any young boy growing up in a family with a little sister, a mother, and father would have. The Arthur character is very well known and loved by children, and can be seen on his own PBS television show. Marc Brown has written over twenty books in the Arthur series; each one is called "An Arthur Adventure."

In addition, this author has written and illustrated a second series featuring D.W., Arthur's little sister, as well as more than 100 other books for children. We always learn something from Arthur, and have fun doing it. So, *let's read!*

Arthur Writes a Story (Boston: Litttle, Brown & Co., 1996) Mr. Ratburn, Arthur's teacher, has given the class a creative writing assignment. The sky's the limit.

Students can write about anything that is important to them, so Arthur decides to write about his pet dog. However, when he reads the story to his sister, D.W., she thinks it's boring. So he changes it. Next day, he reads it to a friend who influences his thinking in another direction, and so it goes. In the end, he has written a completely different story. When he reads it before the class, and throws in a little song and dance, the class reacts with stone silence. Mr. Ratburn asks Arthur how he happened to write the story, so he tells the story of his pet dog, which everyone likes. He gets a gold sticker from Mr. Ratburn, who expects him to write it all down by Monday.

Activities to Accompany *Arthur Writes a Story*

1. Read and enjoy the story. Then go back and read what Mr. Ratburn has printed on the chalkboard on the very first page. He gives three suggestions for story writing: (1) Have a beginning, a middle, and an end. (2) Use details. (3) Be creative.

   Can students write a one-page story using that formula? How do you explain #3? What does it mean to "be creative"? Some students don't know. So this may require some further discussion about using colorful words, illustrating the story with an unusual medium, and letting your imagination go to work for you. "Don't copy what someone else has done, but make it different" is often a good motto. Students can try it.

2. "When we read a story and get feedback (what another person thinks of the story), how do we know what to do with it? Do we change our own work every time we read it aloud to someone different? Did Arthur's sister give him good story-writing advice? Let's think about these questions and discuss it."

3. "The teacher said, 'Write about something that is important to you'—and Arthur did. He wrote about his pet dog. How did he get sidetracked? Let's trace the steps so we can avoid them."

4. Have students tell about the best story they ever wrote. "Let's try to write another good one."

5. Check the illustrations and the inside of Arthur's house, especially his room. Notice that he has a table for writing, a lamp, a pencil container filled with pencils, paper, and so on. Do students have a special spot at home that they can call their own where they can do this kind of work? Also, check the illustrations in Arthur's classroom and note how they compare with the students' classroom.

Arthur's Baby **(Boston: Litttle, Brown & Co., 1987)** When his parents tell Arthur that they have a surprise for him, Arthur immediately thinks of a new bicycle. But, he's surprised to learn that the family is going to have a new baby. His sister is all excited, and Arthur, in his usual fashion, isn't saying much of anything. All his friends have lots of advice for Arthur for when the baby arrives. When Kate arrives, Arthur comes through in the end.

Activities to Accompany *Arthur's Baby*

1. This is a story to read aloud, and then let the students have an opportunity to talk about new babies at their house. What did they think when they first saw the baby? What is the baby's name? How did this change the family routines? Students can bring in photos of their little baby brother or sister to share.

2. Talk about what students can do to help out when there is a new baby in the house. It makes a lot more work for their parents, so talk about ways the students can help and make a list of at least three. Then have students carry out these helpful ways at home, even if they don't have a new baby brother or sister.

3. Ask students to bring in a baby photograph of themselves. (You may have to write a note home to parents explaining your plan.) Ask parents to label the photos on the back and to put them in an envelope. Then make a bulletin board of baby photos with the caption "Here I Am! Do You Know Me?" Have students try to guess who's who. Don't tell until two days have gone by . . . enjoy the suspense. Then give each student his or her own name card to pin under their photo. You're in for some fun and surprises.

4. "We named her Kate." His parents named Arthur's new baby sister "Kate." Are students named after someone in the family? Let's investigate this. Ask about middle names, too.

5. Taking care of someone other than ourself is a big responsibility. A baby is very dependent and needs attention. Students can think about and discuss how they've grown from being *dependent* to *independent* (two new vocabulary words).

   Sometimes it is a good idea to put children in charge of "living things" that are dependent upon them. Notice that plants are growing in Arthur's classroom. Perhaps plants in your classroom that children must care for will be a helpful experience for them. (A pet in the classroom is even better.)

***Arthur's Eyes* (Boston: Litttle, Brown & Co., 1979)** "Sissy!" "Four-eyes!" Arthur gets a lot of teasing when he has to get new glasses. Is it any wonder that he doesn't want to wear them and keeps forgetting to put them on? He even hides them in his lunchbox and says he forgot them. That makes matters worse, for he keeps bumping into things and even goes into the girl's room by mistake. A kindly teacher, who puts on his own reading glasses, has a talk with Arthur. This gives Arthur the nerve to wear the glasses, and Francine, a classmate, rather likes them. So much so in fact, that she turns up wearing glasses, too—but Arthur discovers they have no glass in them. Francine just thinks they make her look good.

Activities to Accompany *Arthur's Eyes*

1. Read the story, enjoy it—and agonize with Arthur. "When we understand what a story character is feeling, this is called *empathy*. We say that we *empathize* with the character." This is a new vocabulary word and perhaps a new concept for some children.

2. Go back over the story and count the number of mistakes that Arthur makes simply because he isn't wearing his glasses and cannot see. This may be reassuring to someone in class who is having the same problems. Send the message that if they are having problems, they should let the teacher know, let the nurse know, and let their parents know.

3. Determine the "turning point" in the book—when Arthur sees his teacher, a moose, wearing glasses. Now the story is going to have a different focus. Students may wish to incorporate this technique—a turning point, a critical moment—into their own story writing. Be on the lookout for this as stories are read.

4. Everyone can make glasses, just like Francine. Use construction paper or pipe cleaners, and make some fancy creations. Take a cue from the book, and be sure to take a class photo.

5. Talk about "name calling." Arthur was called *sissy* and *four-eyes*. "How does that make people feel? Why is it impolite to do this?" Impress upon children that we don't want to engage in this type of behavior. It's bully behavior.

6. See the world through rose-colored glasses, or blue glasses, or yellow glasses. How do things change? Make a double set (two each) of glasses with colored cellophane for lenses. Or make a big set of "magnifying glasses" with colored cellophane, cardboard frame, and handle.

   Draw and color the same little picture or design three times. Put three different squares of cellophane over them and glue the edges. Frame them. This fosters quite a bit of verbal reaction and exchange on the part of the students as they react to the color changes and differences.

7. Can the children do the math? Arthur's teacher has math problems (3-column addition with carrying) on the chalkboard. If your students are at this level, assign the first row of problems (the first four in the row). Can they do more?

***Arthur's Really Helpful Word Book* (New York: Random House, 1997)** This book is similar to a pictionary, with pictures and words, except that everything is categorized. All subjects are on a two-page spread. Each two-page spread has a border with related items that are not shown within the picture.

This book is a valuable tool for the Reading Center and for the Writing Center. Categories include items in and around the house, zoo, school, supermarket, shopping mall. Then there is a page for counting; a page of opposites; and a page that shows Mom at work, Dad at work, a backyard cook out, and so on. This is a treasury of pictures and words right at your fingertips.

Activities to Accompany *Arthur's Really Helpful Word Book*

1. Even the cover and endpapers have pictures and words. This will prove to be extremely helpful to students. It may be a book that you wish to highlight in your newsletter to parents. It is a good pictionary.

2. *Collections.* One two-page spread is devoted to "collections" because Buster, Arthur's friend, has a collection of dinosaurs that are shown and labeled.

But the question is asked, "Do you have a collection?" Along the borders are many suggestions for collections such as dolls, stamps, buttons, coins, feathers, shells, postcards, caps, and on and on. This may get students interested in a hobby, some of which cost no money.

3. *At the playground.* Have students count the number of games being played. Have they tried some of them? Perhaps this is a suggestion for recess time.

4. *What's inside?* This page will inspire your students to get together a collection of containers, much like the ones on the page. For example, a lunchbox, purse, toolbox, and other containers. Next, the children begin to collect or make (or cut out of magazines) items that would go in each box. Then do as Baby Kate did, and spill them all into a pile! Now we have to categorize them.

5. *When Arthur grows up.* Here is a page of possibilities. The children can tell what the careers are by the uniforms and the tools of the trade. "Can Francine also become engaged in these careers?" *(yes)* "How many more possibilities are there that we don't find on this page? Let's draw some and label them, too."

6. *Things that go.* "This double-page spread is filled with moving vehicles. Let's count them. How many are on land? Sea? How many are big? Little? How many could we ride in? How many other categories can we make?"

   Create a bulletin board. Put up background paper and draw three horizontal lines across, similar to the page in the book. Then cut out an assortment of wheels—big ones, little ones, some spaced far apart, some close together—and paste them on the bulletin board lines. Students can "sign up" for a vehicle and create it on the board. First they use white or yellow chalk to draw it, then either paint or felt-tip pens to color in the vehicles. Gain inspiration from the vehicles on this page.

7. Borders were discussed in the December author/illustrator study. Here is a different use of borders, but just as decorative. Have students begin to think about illustrating journal pages and stories with borders. The bulletin board mentioned in #6 could have a border.

Arthur's Tooth. **(Boston: Litttle, Brown & Co., 1985)** Arthur is the only one in his class who still has not lost any baby teeth—not even one. He does have a loose tooth, but that doesn't count. He can't seem to get this off his mind. And, he's reminded of it every day at school by his friends, who offer to help him by yanking out the loose tooth, knocking it out, and so on. His mother finally decides to take Arthur to the dentist, who proves to be a kind, understanding man who says that *he* didn't lose a baby tooth until he was eight years old. The dentist reassures Arthur that his loose tooth will be out very soon. Back at school, Francine, who has appointed herself the tooth fairy, won't let Arthur play in a game—and that proves to be the best thing she could have done for him!

Activities to Accompany *Arthur's Tooth*

1. This topic is very dear to the hearts of children who range in age from 6–8 years of age. After enjoying the story and empathizing with Arthur, let them tell about their experiences with their teeth.

2. Let's visit the dentist. When Arthur goes to the dentist, you get a good view of the dentist's chair, his assistant, charts on the wall, and some of the tools of the trade. Reread the sign on the toothbrush ("Brush many times a day") and note the "Use These Helpers" chart. "What items are located there?" *(brush, toothpaste, floss)* You also see a poster, in the shape of a tooth, that reads "Eat Healthy Snacks."

3. *Make a tooth booklet.* Explain to students the pages' layout. On page one, create a brush and label it. Write a sentence on the page. On page two, create a container of floss, with yarn circling out of it to represent the floss. Write a sentence. On page three, design a toothpaste tube and label it. Write a sentence. On page four, draw a picture of a dentist. Write a sentence. The cover can show a tooth in the shape of the one on the poster in the dentist's office. Students can make up their own title.

4. *Let's eat healthy snacks.* Bring in two paper bags. Label one "Healthy Snacks" and label the other "Not-So-Healthy Snacks." Use real items (enclosed in paper wrappers, if necessary) so that students can put them in the correct bag. Healthy snacks can include an apple, orange, banana, and photos that students find in magazines of milk, vegetables, and so on. Not-So-Healthy Snacks can include a lollipop, caramel candy in wrapper, fudge brownie in wrapper, soda, and photos that students find in magazines of other sticky, gooey, sugary items that help create cavities.

   Have students check these snack bags regularly because sometimes a not-so-healthy snack can, somehow, end up in the healthy snack bag. Is this Francine at work? At other times, dump the items all together and have students bag them.

5. Make a tooth fairy necklace in the shape of the tooth on the dentist's page. Each student can cut out a gleaming white tooth shape, use a hole punch to create a round circular hole, and insert yarn in the hole. The yarn color can be a code for number of teeth given over to the tooth fairy, or the tooth can just carry a message that reminds students to brush and floss every day. (Reassure students who have not lost any teeth yet that it's a good sign that they have strong healthy baby teeth; when the second teeth do come in, they won't have to work so long.)

   (*Note:* Some of these tooth activities can be used next month during Dental Health Week.)

Arthur's Pet Business. (Boston: Litttle, Brown & Co., 1990) Arthur wants a pet dog. But first, his parents say he has to prove that he's responsible because an animal takes lots of care. Well, that's when Arthur decides to advertise as a pet sitter. His first customer is a growly dog, and then frogs, and then a trained boa constrictor. Finally, his growing pet business is banned to the basement. Will he get his very own pet dog?

Activities to Accompany *Arthur's Pet Business*

1. Let's look at the way Arthur advertises his business. Examine the Want Ads in the newspaper. Then have students design an ad for a Pet Business that

might be helpful to Arthur. What information needs to be included in a short ad?

2. Here's a puzzler. Arthur's ears are on top of his head, and Mrs. Wood, a rabbit, has even bigger ears on top of her head. Yet, they both wear glasses, so the question is, how do they keep them on since glasses usually link over the ears? (Have a pair of underwater goggles available, if possible, to suggest the possibility of a head band.)

3. Solve the problems of glasses for animals with ears in a variety of places. Suppose the animal really wants them hooked over its ears, or around its ears? This is a creative challenge.

4. This story gives students ample opportunity to discuss their pets and their names, and to draw their pets and create stories about them. If students don't have a pet, perhaps they can create a story, like Arthur's, of their Pet Business, or write a story about a pet they would like some day to own.

5. The author solved the problem of Arthur getting a pet in a very clever way. First, Arthur had to prove himself; Arthur had to work for what he got. How else could the story have ended?

6. Students can write about why they would like to have Arthur for a friend. What qualities does he have that make him a potential good friend? Let's single them out after having read an abundance of stories about him.

7. Make an Arthur puppet from a paper bag, or make a stick puppet. "Arthur's common sense might help us to solve problems." Also make stick puppets of Arthur's friends and his sister, D.W. What could the initials D.W. stand for?

Arthur's TV Trouble (Boston: Little, Brown & Co., 1995) Oh, oh! Arthur sees something advertised on TV for pets and absolutely must have it! It will make life easier and solve everything for him because it's a "treat timer." Just push a button, and your pet will get the treat. However, Arthur has no money and has to find a way to earn it. Finally, he assembles the machine that he saw on TV—but it misfires, scares the dog, and makes the lights blink! His sister reminds him there are "no refunds." Arthur learns a lesson from this one, and the children might, too.

Activities to Accompany *Arthur's TV Trouble*

1. How many students have seen something advertised on TV and asked for it? What are these items? Advertising is designed to create a "want." Discuss the difference between "wants" and "needs."

2. Have students ever been disappointed after receiving a toy that they thought they wanted? "Let's tell about it and write about it."

3. Ask students to become a TV person who advertises a product so that children just have to have it! They'll need to write it out and make a poster. They'll have a spot announcement of only 30 seconds (or longer if it's needed). Develop a rubric for this—the advertisers must name the product, tell the cost, tell what it does, tell where buyers can get it, tell why buyers should have it. Plan it, rehearse it, deliver the ad.

4. Students can role-play this story, while other students take turns reading the text in the background.

5. "How many students get an allowance? What work do they have to do to earn it? Arthur is looking for work in this story. To do work for others, you need to be dependable and reliable." Discuss these two traits.

And Many More!

Most children really enjoy reading about Arthur's problems and how they are solved. Students identify with Arthur, who addresses their fears and needs in the comfortable setting of a loving family.

You can use Arthur Adventure books throughout the year and during holiday seasons. Here are just some of them: *Arthur's Nose; Arthur's Valentine; The True Francine; Arthur's Halloween; Arthur's Thanksgiving; Arthur's Christmas; Arthur's April Fool; Arthur Goes to Camp; Arthur's Teacher Trouble;* and many, many more. You can always be sure there will be an Arthur problem and a way to find a satisfying solution to the problem, while learning a lesson along the way.

REPRODUCIBLE ACTIVITY PAGES

Marching Band—Letter Y (Yazoo Yak)

Marching Band—Letter Q (Quinella Quail)

Marching Band—Letter V (Vulcan Vulture)

Marching Band—Letter X (X-Ray Man)

Marching Band—Letter Z (Zachary Zebra)

Reading/Writing Assessment Checklist (A)

Reading Assessment Checklist (B)

Razzle Dazzle Z Chant *(Letter Z)*

Harrison, The Upper Case Snowman *(Writing Practice)*

Kelsey, The Lower Case Snowlady *(Writing Practice)*

Rcky th Rscl Rcn (Ricky the Rascal Raccoon) *(decoding message)*

Children's Literature Activity Page—Arthur's Dream Bubbles *(Marc Brown)*

© DCW99

© 2000 by The Center for Applied Research in Education

© 2000 by The Center for Applied Research in Education

V v

© 2000 by The Center for Applied Research in Education

© 2000 by The Center for Applied Research in Education

© 2000 by The Center for Applied Research in Education

Zz

READING/WRITING ASSESSMENT CHECKLIST (A)

Name _____   **Date** _____   **Comment** _____

1. Can print first name

2. Can print last name

3. Can recognize his/her name

4. Can identify upper case letters

5. Can identify lower case letters

6. Can copy print from a model

7. Can read a line of print

8. Can read a paragraph

9. Is curious about books

10. Likes to listen to stories

11. Exhibits good listening skills

12. Exhibits good speaking skills

13. Can re-tell a story in his/her own words

14. Enjoys listening to stories

15. Shows interest/curiosity in the story

16. Participates willingly during story time

17. Can work independently on written material

© 2000 by The Center for Applied Research in Education

READING ASSESSMENT CHECKLIST (B)

Name _____ **Date** _____ **Comment** _____

1. Can recognize the vowel letters

2. Can "sound out" long vowel sounds

3. Can "sound out" short vowel sounds

4. Can "sound out" letters in a word

5. Is interested in practicing word attack skills

6. Seems to enjoy the reading process

7. Stays with a task. Not easily discouraged.

8. Studies "instant words" (sight vocabulary)

9. Asks appropriate questions for material presented

10. Understands that some words rhyme

11. If given a letter, can produce a word that begins with that sound

12. Enjoys story tapes and picture books

13. Comes to school rested and eager to learn

© 2000 by The Center for Applied Research in Education

Name _____

RAZZLE DAZZLE Z CHANT—LETTER Z

Learn this chant. Color Z with razzle, dazzle colors.

Well, here he is
   our Zither Z,
He's the razzle, dazzle boy
   of our letter family.

He's at the end
   Z closes the door,
And now you know
   what letters are for.

We sound them out
   and get excited
'Cause words come out
   when they're invited.

So take a lesson
   from Razzle, Dazzle Z
And practice every day.

Before you know it
   your effort will show it
You'll be a Reader.
   HURRAY!

You will! U-huh! Yes, sir!
You'll be a reader today!

Z-z-z-z-z-z-z-z-z-z-z-z-z-z-z-z-z-z-z-z-z-z-z.

© 2000 by The Center for Applied Research in Education

Name

HARRISON,
THE UPPER CASE SNOWMAN

Carefully trace the upper case letters and color Harrison.

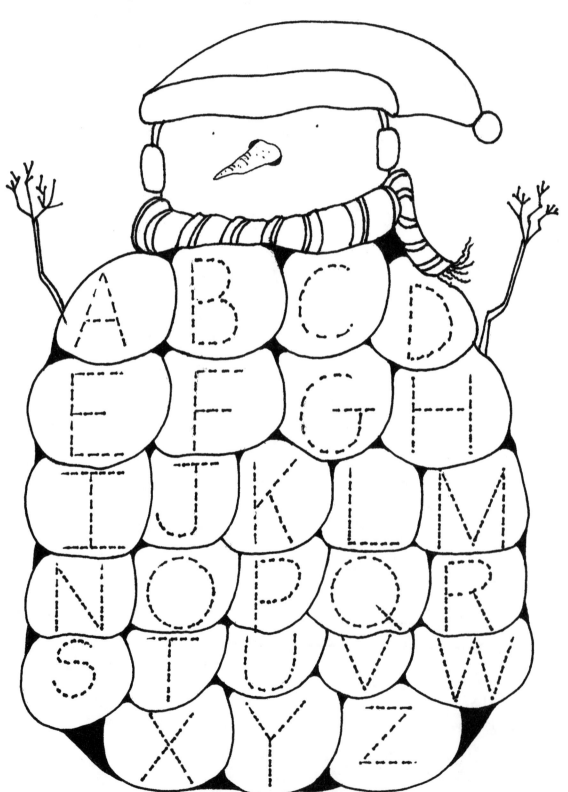

© 2000 by The Center for Applied Research in Education

© 2000 by The Center for Applied Research in Education

Name _____

KELSEY,
THE LOWER CASE SNOWLADY

Carefully trace the lower case letters and color Kelsey.

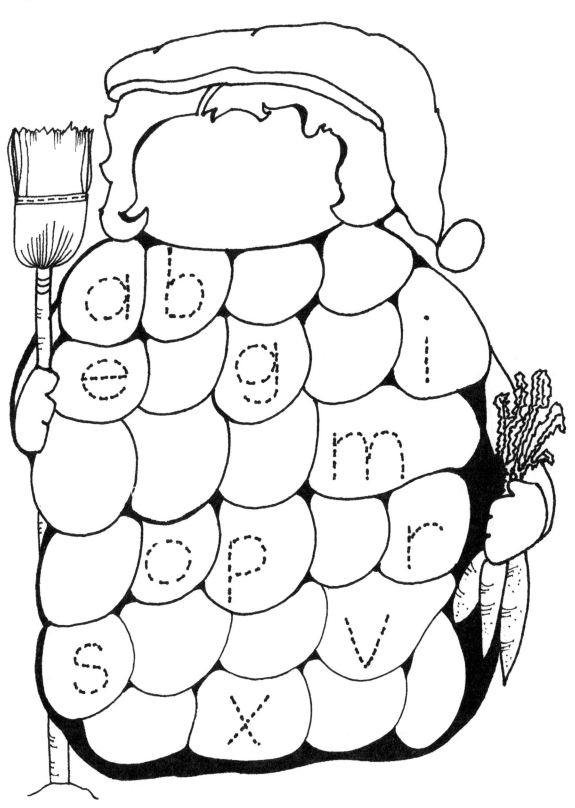

February

CHILDREN'S PICTURE BOOKS

FOR THE MONTH OF

FEBRUARY

Aardema, Verna. *Anansi Finds a Fool, an Ashanti Tale.* **Pictures by Bryna Waldman (New York: Dial, 1992)** In this retold African legend, lazy Anansi wants to fish with a partner who will do all the work. His clever friend, Bonsu, offers to make the fish trap if Anansi will get tired for him, because when work is done someone has to get tired. Is he outsmarted by Bonsu? Read on.

Greenfield, Eloise. *Grandpa's Face.* **Illustrated by Floyd Cooper (New York: Philomel, 1988)** Tamika loves her grandfather's stories and the way he looks. Sometimes his face is not gentle, and one day it looks mean. She doesn't know that Grandfather is practicing for a part in a play. Soon Tamika's unhappiness is apparent and the family must get to the bottom of this—especially Grandfather.

Grimes, Nikki. *C Is for City.* **Pictures by Pat Cummings (New York: Lothrop, Lee & Shepard Books, 1995)** This is a colorful, exciting ABC romp through the city. The pages are filled with colorful images, and the rhyming text helps the reader to locate them. At the end of the book is a Key that lists all of the items on the page. Enjoy "J is for jump shot, for jacks on the sidewalk, for jungle-gym climbing, for jukebox, and jewel." "K is for kosher shops, selling knishes, for kickball, and kite-flying runs after school."

Grover, Max. *The Accidental Zucchini, An Unexpected Alphabet* **(New York: Harcourt Brace & Company, 1993)** This book has simplified, yet bold, bright colored paintings of scenes on each page with a descriptive statement underneath. For example, for the letter "I" there is a large "Ice-cream island" floating along with the boats. The letter "O" shows "Octopus overalls" with eight legs hanging on the line. This book won A Parents' Choice Gold Award.

Lester, Julius. *Sam and the Tigers, A New Telling of "Little Black Sambo."* **Pictures by Jerry Pinkney (New York: Dial, 1996)** In a "new telling" of the classic Helen Bannerman tale, the author gives a new voice to Sam in a land called Sam-sam-sa-mara, where everyone is named Sam. The little boy still outsmarts the tigers and brings home the melted butter for pancakes.

Pilkey, Dav. *Dog Breath: The Horrible Trouble With Hally Tosis* **(New York: Blue Sky/ Scholastic, 1994)** The Tosis family owns a wonderful pet dog, but even skunks avoid her. The family tries everything to help—even taking her on a roller coaster ride to take her breath away—nothing helps! When she overpowers two burglars, the family has to reassess the problem.

Rogers, Jean. *Runaway Mittens.* **Pictures by Rie Munoz (New York: Greenwillow, 1988)** A delightful Eskimo story about Pica, who keeps misplacing his mittens in a snowy land where everything sparkles and crackles. Although the mittens just don't seem to stay in his pocket, they always turn up in the end, even if they are under the dog and her newborn puppies.

Ringgold, Faith. *Tar Beach* **(New York: Crown, 1991)** Inspired by the author/artist's quilts, this story shows a Black American family in a large city who have the tar rooftops as their beach. A little girl, gazing up at the stars, begins to take flight. In this book the backmatter includes a photo of Ringgold's famous story quilt from the Woman on a Bridge series.

Ryan, Pam Munoz. *The Flag We Love.* **Illustrated by Ralph Masiello (Watertown, MA: Charlesbridge, 1998)** A picture book about the flag with beautiful illustrations, this book evokes feelings about the flag of our nation. In her interview with *Booklinks* (1/99), the author said she did not want it to be sentimental, apolitical, or Yankee Doodle Dandy-ish. This book is the grand result.

SanSouci, Robert D. *The Talking Eggs.* **Pictures by Jerry Pinkney (New York: Dial, 1989)** In this adapted tale of two sisters, one is lazy and spoiled and the other is sweet but does all of the hard work. The tale includes a witch with magical powers and wondrous talking eggs. Eventually the story shows what each girl is like on the "inside." A good lesson for all, this is a Caldecott and a Coretta Scott King award-winning book.

FEBRUARY

FEBRUARY GREETINGS! During this month the 100th day of school is usually celebrated. This can be linked with the Second 100 Instant Word List in reading. "How many of those one hundred words do we know? How many can we learn?" You can also link the 100th day of school to counting in the Math section.

Valentine's Day brings joy and color in mid-winter, and there are many opportunities for writing and reading. "Voweltine's Day" on February 13 brings some topsy-turvy activities to the Holiday section and Writing Center. Also, we will be celebrating Black History Month with an emphasis upon folktales and a celebration of several authors and illustrators. Women's History Month also falls in February.

Like the groundhog, it's time to dig in and keep up the good learning attitude toward reading and school.

February's Focus on Reading. The reading skills for February are: (1) The R-Controlled Vowels with Ricky the Rascal Raccoon; (2) Wide Awake and Sleepy Owl Vowel Skillwork; (3) Compound Words and Rebus Reading and Writing; (4) Consonant Blends; (5) Silent E and Silent W; (6) Second 100 Instant Words Served With Pizza; and (7) Spelling.

The R-Controlled Vowels
With Ricky the Rascal Raccoon

Meet Ricky the Tricky Trickster

Ricky Raccoon is playful, pesky, and—as it turns out—a "trickster," just like Anansi the Spider from the African folktales you will read aloud this month. Let's learn how Ricky tricked the vowels. Read aloud this story:

The Story of Ricky and the Mud Giant

One dim night when the moon was just a sliver in the sky, Ricky Raccoon was on his way to visit Owl. They are both "nocturnal," which means they sleep all day but they're up all night. This night, in February, they planned to make valentines and greeting cards.

Along the way to Owl's tree house, Ricky heard some splashing sounds and shouting. He came upon a truck with a logo "The Vowel Company," and it was stuck in the mud. All the vowels were out slipping and sliding and splashing in the mud while they were trying to push the truck. They were so covered with mud that they didn't even see Ricky.

The Story of Ricky and the Mud Giant *(Continued)*

Now Ricky looks like a masked bandit with a black band over his face, so he decided to have some fun. He hid behind a bush and, making his voice deep and low, he called out, "Hark! Who is stuck in my mud?"

"It's 'The Vowel Company,'" called A, E, I, O, and U. "Can you help us?"

"Help you? Anyone who gets stuck in my mud has to pay a fine," growled Ricky. By this time he had scampered up a tree, and dropped a rope around the vowels. They were all tied up in knots.

Then Ricky, looking like a masked bandit in the night, came down from the tree and opened the back of the truck and saw that it was filled with golden coins. He had never before seen such a treasure. He was dizzy with delight! He was rich! He'd never have to work again!

Just then Owl, who had heard the noise, came flying over the truck and called out, "Ricky! Ricky Raccoon, is that you?"

The quick thinking Ricky said, "Yes, yes, it is Owl. I've just chased off a robber and I'm here to help these poor vowels."

Owl and Ricky pulled the knots out of the rope, tied it to the front of the truck, and yanked the vowels free.

"Oh, thank you, Ricky, for being so brave! You chased away a huge mud giant! How can we ever repay you?" the vowels exclaimed.

"Well, since I did save you, maybe I should ride along with you some of the time on your trips. That way, I'll use your sound and mine and I can protect you," said the boastful Ricky.

"Anytime you want to," they agreed. "And you, too, Owl. You can ride along, too."

And so, to this day, both the letter "r" and the letter "w" ride along in words with the vowels. When they do, the vowels let them help do the talking.

The End

The R-Controlled Vowels

Link this exercise to the Ricky Raccoon story. Students need repeated practice with this. "We have the vowel rule that when letters *a, e, i, o,* and *u* are followed by the letter *r,* their sound changes. They are controlled by the letter *r.* Thus, we have the following r-controlled vowel sounds." (See the Reproducible Activity Pages.)

Letter	Sounds Like	Examples
a	ar	far, farm, bark, park, barter, partner
e	er	Bert, fern, perm, concern, clerk, germ
i	ir	dirt, mirth, quirk, smirk
o	or	order, border, corner, corn, forlorn
u	ur	fur, purr, nurse, purse, hurt

Wide-Awake and Sleepy Owl Vowel Skillwork

The Wide-awake Owl Vowel Ride

"Ow! Wow! that hurts," we sometimes say. Those words, and others, remind us that Owl is riding along with the letter *o*. Here are more owl words.

cow   town   brown   clown   frown

Sleepy Owl Words

"Remember that Owl is nocturnal, which means that he sleeps during the day. Sometimes he is snoozing when he appears in a word, so the letter *o* says its *long sound* so as not to wake up Owl. How do we know if Owl is awake or sleeping? We try both sounds, first one and then the other, and use the one that works." Here are some examples of sleepy owl words. (See the Reproducible Activity Pages.)

throw   grow   blow   crow   know

"W" Likes the Owl Vowel Ride

"Sometimes when Owl is sleeping on these day trips, the letter *w* will wake up and sing out, but only rarely, and usually only when the letter *a* or the letter *e* is talking." Here are some samples of the letter *w* changing the sound of the vowels:

aw—caw, hawk, law, lawn
ew—dew, few, mew, new

The Case of the Missing Vowels

"Just suppose that the vowels all caught a bad cold and couldn't talk for a whole morning! What would we do? Could we still read?"

Use junk mail, old magazines, and newspapers, and have students blacken the vowels in five words. Then print them on paper with spaces left open for the vowel letter. Have students work with a study buddy to see if the mystery of the missing vowels can be solved.

A Vowel Work-out

Select a sentence or phrase from the following. Print it on the chalkboard and see if students can figure it out. When they know, have them print it on a piece of paper. Then, at the appointed time, have them choral read the sentence or phrase.

H __ p p y   V __ l __ n t __ n __ 's   D __ y (Happy Valentine's Day)

T __ d __ y   __ s   M __ n d __ y (Today is Monday)

B __   M __ n __ (Be Mine)

Also list the first name of several students and see if these can be figured out by the class. Have students do this for their own first name and last name. Try it with other familiar words, too.

Compound Words and Rebus Reading and Writing

Compound Words

A compound word is usually two or more smaller words put together to make a different big word; for example, *playground, ballpark,* and *firehouse.*

Use the word *under* as a compound word builder. Here are some to get you started: underground, undermine, understand, undertake.

Make a bulletin board display of compound words under a giant construction paper cut-out of an umbrella shape. Entitle it "Under the Compound Umbrella." Words can be put on raindrop shapes and then bunched together to make the compound words.

Compound Word Puzzles

Use a variation of the missing letter technique for compound words. Start off by leaving letters out of only one word. Later, students may be able to build up to missing letters in both words, but go slowly. The object, again, is to get students to see that these are two words joined together.

s c ___ o o ___ / house   (schoolhouse)
p ___ a y / ground   (playground)

Word Sort

Have a wide variety of words printed on small cards. Students can go through these with the idea of building compound words that make sense.

For greater success with this activity, have five compound words in mind. Print the first word on red and the second word on yellow cards or strips of paper. Then have students make their compound words from the ten mixed-up word cards with the aid of the color-coded cues.

Rebus Reading and Writing

A Rebus symbol is a picture that is used in place of a word. The month in which a special holiday such as Valentine's Day falls is a good place to begin (or to reinforce) this because students are interested in valentine cards. (This works well for all major holidays.)

Build up a collection of Rebus symbols and make a focus area of them this month in the Writing Center. Some that will be helpful in general are:

I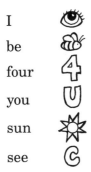
be
four
you
sun
see

Thus, "I see you" can be represented as " ⬤ + Ⓒ + Ⓤ ".

More Rebus symbols can be developed with students. Here are some to get you started. (See the Reproducible Activity Pages also.)

man	(stick figure with hat)
woman	(stick figure with high heels)
boy	(stick figure with small hat)
girl	(stick figure with small high heels)
tree	(stick with round circle resting on top)
moon	(yellow half moon)
animal	(use basic shapes)
bird	(basic shapes with triangle beak)
house	(triangle resting on a square)
school	(triangle resting on a rectangle)

Consonant Blends

Consonant Buddies

"We have pen pals, e-mail buddies, and best friends. Some consonants are best friends or 'consonant blends.' It means that they spend a lot of time together in words and make a nice blend when they are voiced."

Work with blends in families. Make a house shape on the chalkboard or on separate charts, and put the letter blend in a shape that is coming out of the chimney, representing smoke. Do this for each blend.

The Blended Family House of "R"

With a shape of a house and the letters "br" on the shape representing smoke coming out of the chimney (meaning you're cooking), you are off on the "R Family Adventure." Come and meet the blended family: *br, cr, dr, fr, gr, pr, tr, wr.*

Eventually, you will have eight separate houses. Fill them up with words one at a time.

First, have the blend at the beginning of the word. As students use the dictionary or thesaurus (or even magazines and newspapers), they will come upon these blends in the middle of words. Save those for another house shape, but by all means call attention to them (example: a<u>fr</u>aid).

Here are some word groups to get you started:

br	**cr**	**dr**	**fr**
brand	crack	drape	frame
bread	creed	dream	fresh
bring	cringe	drink	fringe
brother	crock	drop	from
brute	crust	drug	fruit

gr	**pr**	**tr**	**wr**
grape	prance	track	wrack
green	pretty	tree	wren
grin	prim	trip	wring
groan	proud	trowel	wrong
grumpy	prune	truck	wrung

Meet the "R" Family Blends

Put two different blend words from the *r* family together that would describe something. For example: *gr*een *tr*ee, *gr*aham *cr*ackers, *cr*acked *br*ick.

Next, use two words from the same blended family to make a statement or phrase. Note that the first two letters of each word in the phrase are identical. Here are some examples:

brown bread	crisp crackers
drip dry	french fries
great grin	practice printing
train tracks	wrong wrap

Meet the "S" Family Blends

This family can be printed on ship shapes. The rectangle can be the base and a big triangle can form the sail. At the base, print the letter "S"; on the triangle top, print the blend. All together you will have seven ships sailing: *sc, sk, sm, sn, sp, st, sw.*

Meet the "L" Family Blends

This family can be printed on lollipop shapes. Put the letter "L" on the stick and the word family blends on the colored circle shapes. The family includes: *bl, cl, fl, gl, pl, sl.* That means you will have six different lollipops to fill in with blend words. Use the dictionary and other available print resources.

Some Three-Letter Blends

Some letters are blended together repeatedly, so that it would be well for students to sound them out. First, they sound out each letter. Then students glide them together to see if they can glide right into a word.

S T R—street, strip, stray, string, strap, stroll, stripe

S P L—splish, splash, splosh, splat, split, splendid

Silent "E" and Silent "W"

Why "E" Is Silent

"There is an old vowel rule: 'The **e** at the end of a one-syllable word makes the vowel say its name.' That rule, while not true 100% of the time, is true often enough that we sit up and pay attention!"

Let's look at some:

bake	cake	fake	Jake	lake
quake	rake	sake	take	wake

Other Silent "E" Endings

Here are some more word families to use when making words with silent *e* endings:

ale	**ane**	**ape**
bale	cane	cape
gale	lane	gape
male	pane	tape
tale	vane	grape
ate	**ave**	**ike**
Kate	Dave	Mike
gate	cave	bike
late	pave	like
rate	wave	pike

For a more complete list of Word Families, or Phonograms, see *The Reading Teacher's Book of Lists,* 3rd ed., by Drs. Edward Fry, Jacqueline Kress, and Donna Fountoukidis (Englewood Cliffs, NJ: Prentice Hall, 1993).

"ITE" Is Mighty Important

The following "ite" words also have silent *e* at the end: *site, kite,* and *bite.* As students are going through magazine ads and newspaper ads, they might notice (or it could be called to their attention) that there is such a thing as "adspeak" or shortened versions of words. The letters "ite" are often used in this regard. For example: lite, nite, rite, tonite.

Other Times "E" Is Silent

Not only in rhyming words, but also in occasional words, the *e* is once again silent at the end, but the vowel is not long. Some of these final *e* silent words include: *one, little,* and *some.* Notice that the rule "Silent *e* at the end makes the vowel say its name" does not apply here. These are words students will have to learn by sight, by heart, or when they meet them in context within a sentence or phrase. Just try sounding them out one way and if it doesn't work, try another way.

Ricky Raccoon and Owl Are at It Again!

"Remember Ricky Raccoon the trickster who controls the vowels when he appears with them?" (See the read-aloud story in the beginning of this month's reading focus section.) "Well, often on these letter journeys when Ricky Raccoon rides along, Owl rides along too. Ricky has agreed to let Owl take his letter 'w' and sit in the front seat, BUT Owl soon gets tired and starts to snooze, so Ricky is the one who speaks up and says the 'rrrrr' sound."

The letter *w* is sleeping, or silent, at the beginning of a word when it appears as the initial consonant in the combination of *wr.* Here are some word samples:

write	wrist	wreath
writing	wring	wren
written	wrap	wrinkle
wrote	wrong	wrestle

Whistle for the Letter "W" Sound

When the letter *w* appears at the beginning of words with the letter *h,* as in *wh,* it makes a windy sound—similar to "hw." Some words for your list include: *whistle, when, wheeze, wheat, what, where.* (Today, in honor of the "wh" sound, whistle a familiar song with the students all together. Some children have learned to whistle and some are still practicing.)

Learning by Heart for Heart Month

"Some words we just have to learn by heart. We call that *memorize.*" A number of these learn-by-heart words appear in the first 100 words list. (See November's reading section.)

Let's start on the second 100 words, if you have not already done so, and do some of the same activities that you did in November. Since the 100th school day of the year is in February, you will do some word counting in the Math section this month.

The Second 100 Instant Word Pizza to Go

To make the second 100 words more appetizing, think of a mini-pizza. You are going to cut it so that it is in four pieces. Each of the four pieces will have 25 new words for students to try to learn by heart. Practice daily. Students can work with a study buddy. Send a copy home.

Make a giant pizza circle in the classroom from red construction paper over tan (crust). Decorate the edges with brown circles (pepperoni) and yellow paper strips (cheese). Then print 25 words on each section. Students can print their own word lists also. (See Reproducible Activity Pages.)

Pizza With Cheese (Round One, 1–25)

over	new	sound	take	only
little	work	know	place	year
live	me	back	give	most
very	after	thing	our	just
name	good	sentence	man	think

Pizza With Cheese & Pepperoni (Round Two, 26–50)

say	great	where	help	through
much	before	line	right	too
mean	old	any	same	tell
boy	follow	came	want	show
also	around	form	three	small

Pizza With Cheese, Pepperoni, & Peppers (Round Three, 51–75)

set	put	end	does	another
well	large	must	big	even
such	because	turn	here	why
ask	went	men	read	need
land	different	home	us	move

Pizza With the Works, to Go (Round Four, 76–100)

try	kind	hand	picture	again
change	off	play	spell	air
away	animal	house	point	page
letter	mother	answer	found	study
still	learn	should	America	world

Include these words with your spelling list of words for the children to learn each week.

Spelling

Spelling Musical Chairs

Make flash cards that contain each spelling word. Have five chairs placed in a circle and tape a flash card to each chair back. Select five students to stand behind a chair. Start the music and have students rotate. When the music is stopped, students scramble for a chair—and each child gets one. Then a designated student in the audience runs the game by circling the chairs, standing behind one, saying the word, and calling upon the student in that chair to spell the word. (If the student cannot spell the word, then he or she may call upon someone else for help, but stays in the game.)

Once the word is correctly spelled, start the music and the rotation. Repeat the procedure. After each word has been spelled, the five students can select a replacement who goes to the circle, and the game is started again. Change the spelling words as needed.

Magnetic Spelling Words

Distribute magnetic letters at random throughout the classroom. Then call out a spelling word and have students bring the letters to the magnetic board, one at a time in order, until the word is completed. Redistribute the letters, call out another spelling word, and repeat the procedure.

How Can We Group the Spelling Words?

"Let's see if we can find any patterns in the words, such as words that begin with the same letter, words that end in the same letter, words that have a rime in them, words that have silent letters when we speak them, and so on. In other words, examine the word list to become familiar with ways we can begin to break them down so that we can gain some spelling clues."

Curve-Ball Word

Each week, when giving the spelling test, throw the students a "curve ball" by giving them one or two words taken from the list of the week before. These can serve as bonus words: students earn extra points if they get them correct.

The curve-ball words can be interspersed with this week's words, or can be given at the end.

READING LINKS TO HOLIDAYS & SPECIAL EVENTS

It's Presidents Month

"We celebrate the birthdays of two of our most famous presidents this month. Their names are George Washington, who was born on February 22, and Abraham Lincoln, who was born on February 12." Check your calendar to see if they are celebrated separately or together as "Presidents Day." Be sure to wear patriotic colors on that day—red, white, and/or blue.

Ask students to name the current president and first family. Check newspapers for photos of them. "How many members are in this family? Do they have pets? What state did they come from before they moved to the White House in Washington, D.C. The White House site and architect was selected by George Washington, but he was the only president not to live there."

President George Washington Visits Betsy Ross

"Remember the last time President Washington visited the home of Betsy Griscom Ross? He wanted her to sew an American flag that he had designed. Well, he's making another visit. This time he wants an American quilt."

He hasn't got it planned, and that's where students come in. He does know that it should be made of red, white, and blue squares. He wants symbols on it, such as the flag, bell, star, Statue of Liberty, and so on.

Students can pool their ideas and design a quilt, working in pairs or in small groups. Each group can contribute squares to the quilt, or each individual can contribute a square. Decide how large the quilt will be and how large each square will be. This calls for some math and art design. It can be done with construction paper, tempera paint, or actual material and fabric crayons.

Picture Books About Presidents

Here are some favorites for students to have in their library area this month: *A Picture Book of George Washington* by David A. Adler, with illustrations by John and Alexandra Wallner. Adler also has a series of information books about famous people designed for the young reader. One is *A Picture Book of Abraham Lincoln.* You might want to also check out *The Buck Stops Here, The Presidents of the United States* by Alice Provenson.

Celebrate Black History Month With Folktales

"This month we celebrate the African American community in our country. One way to learn something about a culture is to study the stories that originate in that culture. In Africa, storytelling is an art. Long ago people did not write down their stories; instead, they passed down stories from generation to generation by word of mouth, or what we call storytelling. Another term is *folktales,* which means the stories of the people."

Be on the lookout for African folktales, as many have been published in recent years, and everyone can learn valuable lessons from them. Some of the retold tales are: *Rabbit Makes a Monkey of Lion* by Verna Aardema, with pictures by Jerry Pinkney; *The Talking Eggs* by Robert SanSouci, with pictures by Jerry Pinkney; *Mufaro's Beautiful Daughters* by John Steptoe; *The Dark-Thirty, Southern Tales of the Supernatural* by Patricia C. McKissack, with illustrations by Brian Pinkney; *The Adventures of Spider* by Joyce Cooper Arkhurst, with illustrations by Jerry Pinkney; *Flossie and the Fox* (a Red Riding Hood variant tale) by Patricia McKissack, with illustrations by Rachel Isadora; and *Zomo the Rabbit: A Trickster Tale from West Africa* by Gerald McDermott.

Anansi the Spider Is in Charge of Storytelling

This famous black spider appears in many African and Caribbean folktales and is a trickster figure. Sometimes the tricks backfire, but not always. Have a "trickster storytelling session" in the classroom this month. In the Uncle Remus stories, Bre'r Rabbit is the outstanding trickster figure. Hare, or Little Hare, is a trickster in the eastern part of Africa. The tortoise is one of the primary trickster figures in the Nigerian tales.

These picture storybooks can be located in the library. Include *Anansi the Spider* by Gerald McDermott and *Anansi Finds a Fool, an Ashanti Tale* by Verna Aardema, with pictures by Bryna Waldman.

The trickster figure is clever, witty, and almost always wins out because of his brilliance. Thus, the trickster is apt to use his wits, or brains, rather than brawn.

Anansi the Spider Gets Devoured

Make the Anansi spider figure for a delicious snack. You will need three large marshmallows and straight pretzel sticks to poke into the middle of the marshmallows to connect the three body parts. Then use straight pretzel pieces (black licorice can also be used) for the eight legs, and poke them into the sides of the marshmallows. Use two red licorice pieces or gumdrops for eyes. Then devour Anansi after the storytelling fest. (There is an African proverb that goes something like this: *"Get rid of your enemy before he is stronger than you."*)

Reading About African Americans in the United States

More books are being printed in this genre, since multiculturalism gained a foothold in the 1990s. The following represent only a few of the fine selections available: *Grandpa's Face* by Eloise Greenfield, with illustrations by Floyd Cooper; *Aunt Flossie's Hats and Crabcakes Later* by Patricia McKissack; *Follow the Drinking Gourd* by Jeanette Winter; *Amazing Grace* by Mary Hoffman; and *Everett Anderson's Goodbye,* a book series by Eloise Greenfield.

Valentine's Day Is February 14

"Long, long ago (13th century) St. Valentine was a priest in Italy, who became the patron saint of lovers. At one time valentines were sent by males only, but today everyone sends valentines."

Set up a post office in the classroom so that each student has a mailbox. Make sure a list of class names (first and last) goes home to parents. Students also enjoy making valentines to give.

If you decide not to have a valentine celebration in your classroom, perhaps students could make valentines for community service people, a local children's hospital, and/or a senior citizen center or nursing home.

Valentine's Day Means Friendship and Love

You can learn to say and to spell love messages in several languages. Here are a few for "I love you":

Swahili—Nini kupenda

Navaho—Ayor anosh ni

German—Ich liebe dich

Russian—Ya tebya liubliu

French—Je t'aime

Spanish—Te quiero

Italian—Ti amo

Ricky the Tricky Raccoon Is Celebrating Voweltine's Day on February 13

Join Ricky and the vowels for a treat on Voweltine's Day. It's the day before Valentine's Day. On this day, things are a bit topsy-turvy, but there's a lot of learning in the air.

There are tricky rules for this celebration—here are some of them. Perhaps students can think up more.

- Tie a yarn ribbon around the wrist of a friend for good luck.
- Paint your thumbnails red for world peace.
- Measure something that is 13 inches long.
- Count the first 13 vowels you meet in a book. (Is Ricky the Rascal Raccoon there?)
- Read a page of print until you find one of Ricky's r-controlled vowel sounds. What is the word? List it on the chalkboard under the following headings: *ar, er, ir, or, ur*. How many can the class find?
- Make up a riddle that has "book" as the answer.
- Make a pink and green heart shape.
- Swallow five times in a row for *a, e, i, o, u.*
- List all of the little words in "voweltine." (*Love* is one of them.)
- Blow up a balloon and say the five vowels before all of the air goes out of it.

Shoo Away Tooth Decay—Dental Health

February is a time for emphasis upon dental health. Make sure this is mentioned in the newsletter for parents. Suggest that a wise new gift for students would be a "Shoo Away Tooth Decay" packet that consists of a toothbrush, toothpaste, and a container of floss. Give a gentle reminder to make sure to get a dental check-up at least yearly, if not twice a year, for tooth cleaning.

In 1999, for the first time, many valuable objects that belonged to President George Washington traveled to museums around the country. One item on display was Washington's false teeth that were made from cow bone and hippopotamus teeth. Today, if teeth need to be replaced, people go to a dentist and have the latest technology available to them for tooth replacements or tooth coverings.

Loss of a Tooth

Younger students are losing baby teeth, which are pushed out by the "second" set. But we only get two sets. If children should have the unfortunate experience of falling and having a second tooth chipped or even knocked out, they should know the procedure to follow which is to immediately immerse the broken tooth in water, or a wet paper towel, and go to the dentist as soon as possible.

One Tooth—Two Teeth

Here is a reading link. Some plurals of words are done internally and do not require an "s" at the end. We say *one tooth,* but *not* two tooths. Instead, we change the letters inside the word from double *o* to double *e;* thus, we say *two or more teeth.*

Here are some words to point out to students. Make it an interesting discovery:

foot—feet

mouse—mice

goose—geese

man—men

woman—women

Others are both singular and plural. Here are some examples:

one fish—two fish

one deer—two deer

one dozen—three dozen

one sheep—six sheep

See the Reproducible Activity Pages for a dental health sheet.

Salute to a Brave Woman—Harriet Tubman

"Harriet Tubman was born a slave in Bucktown, Maryland, in about 1820. She was one of ten children. She grew up on a plantation where she chopped wood and did field labor. She was a strong young woman. When she grew up and married, she wanted to run away to freedom, but her husband wouldn't go north with her. Eventually she ran away and reached the free state of Pennsylvania.

"That's when her work began. Harriet helped other slaves travel the treacherous road to freedom. This route became known as the Underground Railroad, although it was not an actual railroad. It was a system of 'underground' (secret) routes and hiding places used by runaway slaves. Brave people helped them along the route. The slaves followed the North Star and the people who helped them were called *agents*." Find more information at the library about this brave freedom fighter.

Women's History Month

"During February we also celebrate the fact that women have made an important contribution to our country. At one time, girls could only go to elementary school, while boys were able to go on to the higher grades and to college. Girls were taught to sew and paint, and to take care of the home.

"Today, girls in our country can go on to higher grades. Many careers that were formerly thought of as only belonging to men are now available to women. So be thankful for the freedom that this country offers women, and to the women pioneers who made it possible."

A good picture storybook that addresses the voting issue is Emily Arnold McCully's *The Ballot Box Battle.*

Celebrate the Suffragettes

The word "suffragette" was given to women who worked hard to enable women to have the right to vote. Impress upon students that, at one time, women could not vote—only men had this right. The suffragettes deserve a place in history for their bravery for they were ridiculed and scorned in their day. Two famous suffragettes include:

- Mrs. Elizabeth Cady Stanton (1815–1902). She was a feminist and social reformer who helped organize the first Women's Rights Conference, which took place in Seneca Falls, New York, in 1848.
- Miss Susan Brownell Anthony (1820–1906). She worked with Elizabeth Cady Stanton and founded the National American Woman Suffrage Association. She was a feminist leader who battled for women's right to vote. Her home can be visited in Rochester, New York.

What Do We Owe the Suffragettes?

Everyone needs to vote. Students can urge parents to vote in elections by wearing a VOTE badge. In some states, voters use the schools as voting stations. If this occurs in your school, try to arrange to have students line up to look inside the booth—after it has been explained to them. As a good role model, you need to vote and speak positively about this right.

Arrange to vote on an issue in the classroom. Use a secret ballot and count the votes.

READING LINKS TO WRITING

In the Red

Use red felt-tip pens for writing a Valentine story or for printing a message on valentines that are made.

If a person is "in the red," it usually means that person is spending too much money. Are students being thrifty? Students can design "valentine currency" for one day, using white paper and red ink. They can give it to someone they see "doing a good deed." Perhaps students can earn valentine currency today for good deeds in the classroom. The person with the most valentine money gets to be in charge of selecting a game to play or the book that will be read aloud.

In the Pink

Use pink felt-tip pens for writing messages for Valentine greetings. Red, white, and pink are favorite colors for valentines. If a person is "in the pink," it usually means that person is feeling well. Are students feeling well? Students can carefully design "You're Looking Good" tickets using pink paper. Copy a stanza from a poem in a poetry book and deliver it to a friend. Then that person will feel "in the pink."

Whr Hv Ll Th Vwls Gne?

Where have all the vowels gone? This month, have students write puzzle words at the Writing Center. Use the basket of junk mail and newspapers as a resource, and have students copy three words. That is their answer sheet. Then, on another piece of paper, have them print those three words with the vowel letters missing. They can put their initials at the bottom, which indicates that they have the answers.

Have a writing puzzle board or a box, so students can work the word puzzles, and fill in the blanks with letters. Then they can check the correct answers with the person whose initials are at the bottom.

Rebus Messages

Make room at the Writing Center this month for the Rebus symbols. Then students can write messages for others to decipher. Use the Rebus sheet from the Reproducible Activity Pages as one resource.

Students can make up Rebus forms quite easily for people, toys, furniture, animals, plants, clothes, and transportation vehicles. Perhaps they might want to start a Rebus Dictionary for the center.

Write Your Version of an Anansi Tale

Make "Spider Paper" at the Center. Take an oval shape and put two dots at the top for eyes. Staple, or glue, four legs (yarn pieces) along each side. Then, on the body, students can create their own version of a spider trickster tale. (See Reproducible Activity Pages.)

READING LINKS TO MATH

Usually in February school has been in session for 100 days. This calls for a great deal of emphasis upon counting, sets, and even art work with 100 pieces. We're in for a math bonanza this month.

Make a "100 Things" Mural

Send notification to parents in your January newsletter and again a reminder in early February so that they will be thinking about sending 100 items to school on the special "100 Day!" Ask students to bring in 100 items from home in see-through baggies. Some suggestions are:

cotton balls	rubber bands	paper clips
bottle caps	buttons	peanuts in shells
seeds	nuts	old Christmas cards

It is amazing what students and parents can come up with. Make sure the child's name is inside his or her baggie. Hang these baggies on the "100 Things" mural. Enjoy the display. Encourage students to talk about their 100 items and how they decided upon their choice.

A good book to read aloud is *Miss Bindergarten Celebrates the 100th Day of Kindergarten* by Joseph Slate, with illustrations by Ashley Wolff.

More Learning With 100—Grouping

Count out 100 items and have students arrange them in groups of two, then groups of four, five, and ten. Count aloud to 100 by 2's, 5's, and 10's. Students need to memorize this. They can say the numbers while they jump rope, bounce balls, and so on.

Concentric Circles

Count out 100 items, then make five concentric circles. Have 20 items in each circle. Help students notice that the items become further and further apart as the circle gets large.

Create a Sunflower Seed Sun

Use sunflower seeds for this activity. Count out 100 seeds. Make a sun with 20 seeds in the middle. Then, for the rays, make four straight rows of 20 seeds or eight rows of 10 seeds. This can be done on sticky paper and put outdoors for the birds to enjoy.

Each One Plant One

You will need 100 3-oz. (bathroom size) paper drinking cups half-filled with potting soil. Have packets of marigold seeds available, and help each student plant seeds in the 100 cups. Place the filled cups on a sunny window ledge. Water them by squeezing water into the cup with a wet sponge. "How many grow? How can we represent this by a fraction? We can start by putting the numeral 100 on the bottom (total number of cups) and the number that grew on the top." (For example, eighty out of one hundred would be 80/100.)

Make A 100-Paper Mosaic

Time to get out the art scrap box. Have students gently tear 100 pieces of different colored paper for a collage. The paper should be no larger than their thumbnail. Then have each student arrange the 100 pieces into a design on a sheet of 12″ × 18″ paper. Or a picture of one item—such as a person, lamp, computer—can be made from these pieces. After the arrangement has been done, that is the time to paste. Arrange the art work on the bulletin board for display.

Make Toothpick Structures

Each student (or student group) gets 100 toothpicks and creates a structure. You can use regular liquid glue; however, Duco® Cement works very well with these little wooden structures. (**CAUTION:** The cement should only be used by you or another adult.) Have students give a title to the art work. Display it on a colorful paper plate.

Bring on the Geoboards

Get several packages of rubber bands. These come in various colors and sizes. You can use the following to emphasize 100:

   5 geoboards—20 rubber band squares
   10 geoboards—10 rubber band squares
   20 geoboards—5 rubber band squares
   25 geoboards—4 rubber band squares

The Cup Game

Put out a row of ten cups. Have a package of 100 counters. "How many counters will you need to put into each cup so that there is an equal amount in each one? Work it out. Next, try it with just five cups. Now how many do you need? Work it out. Let's talk about it."

Moja Means One

An excellent book to obtain for your use is *Moja Means One, Swahili Counting Book* by Muriel Feelings, with pictures by Tom Feelings. Teach students to count to ten in the Swahili language. Students can sit cross-legged on the floor facing a partner and clap their hands together as they say, "One." Then they clap hands with their partner as they say, "Moja." Clap hands together and say, "Two." Clap hands with a partner and say, "Mbili." Begin with numerals 1–5 and work up to 10.

READING LINKS TO SOCIAL STUDIES

Locate Africa on the Map

"Since February is Black History Month, let's find the homeland of African Americans on the map. Africa is a continent, not a country. There are many small and divergent (new word) countries within this vast continent." Locate Africa on a map or globe and note the vast expanse of land. "There are many countries, with more than 700 languages and many tribes and clans within this continent. Swahili is the name of the language that is most common."

To assist with the emphasis upon folktales this month, cut a large shape of Africa from bright yellow paper and place it on the bulletin board. Students can then pinpoint locations of story settings from the folktales that are read.

Some might include stories about these people in Africa: Ashanti (Ghana), Bedouins (Egypt), Berbers (Morocco), Khosian (Botswana), Dinka (Sudan), Hausa (Nigeria), Kikuyu (Kenya), Masaii (Kenya), Swahili (Eastern coastal countries), and Zulu (South Africa).

Rivers Far and Near

Two important rivers in Africa are the Congo and the Zambeze. Locate these on a map or globe and trace their routes. "There are many animals to be found along the river routes, for they come here to get water."

Students should know the main river near their own city or town. Print the name on the chalkboard and sound it out. Locate the river on a map. "What facts do we already know about our closest river? What would we like to know? What should we know in order to be a knowledgeable citizen?"

Beat the Story Drum

Decorate cylindrical containers with story illustrations from favorite African folktales. A coffee can with a plastic lid makes a good drum. Students can make a variety of sounds and learn to beat the drum as a story accompaniment. A pencil, a dowel rod, or a cleaned and dried turkey *drumstick* can each be used for making different sounds. Thumping with the hand or hands (thumb, fingertips) give another tone quality to the drum.

In Africa, it is said that drummers talk with their drums. The drums can tell everyone how to move. Use the drum and drumstick, referred to above, and have students move to a fast beat, a slow beat, a soft tone, a loud tone, many short beats, several beats with intervals in between. They have to learn to listen, and then move.

Day Names

In West Africa, it was common for children to be named according to the day of the week on which they were born, a custom that also prevailed in Jamaica. The following names representing the days of the week are often common as characters in folktales.

Have students find out on which day of the week they were born. "If we were named after the weekdays, how many students would be called Monday? How many Tuesday?" and so on.

"We can use our West African names of the week. Or write a story about a character who was born on a particular day." Here is the list:

Days of the week	*Male*	*Female*
Sunday	Quashe	Quasheba
Monday	Cudjo	Juba
Tuesday	Cubena	Beneba
Wednesday	Quaco	Cooba
Thursday	Quao	Abba
Friday	Cuffee	Feeba
Saturday	Quamina	Mimba

Make a Travel Poster for a Safari to Africa

There are many unusual animals that can be seen in the wild in Africa. Some include the hippopotamus, giraffe, zebra, lion, leopard, secretary bird, gazelle, gnu, cheetah, hyena, ostrich, water buffalo, elephant, and many, many more. Help the children locate pictures of these animals in magazines to make an ABC Safari Book.

Let's Visit Egypt and Morocco

Many students are surprised to learn that Egypt is located on the continent of Africa. Here is a rich, ancient, once highly developed civilization, with pharaohs, pyramids, and immense statues. From Egypt came papyrus, an original paper made from plant fibers. Read *The Egyptian Cinderella* by Shirley Climo, with illustrations by Ruth Heller.

"While we're in Africa this month, we need to make a stop in Morocco, another developing country. It is said that Morocco is like a tree with its roots in Africa and its branches in Europe." So many country people go to the market riding on donkeys that there are donkey parking lots! A colorful picture book that shows this scene, as well as markets all over the world, is *Market* by Ted Lewin.

Many storks fly free in Morocco and make their huge nests on the tops of chimneys. Some storks spend most of the year in Spain and migrate to Morocco for the warmer climate in winter. To have a stork build its nest nearby is considered good luck. No one would ever harm a stork.

READING LINKS TO SCIENCE & HEALTH

Make Your Dentist Happy

"Special attention is paid to teeth this month, but we must take care of them every day of every month."

- *Brushing.* Explain that brushing is something we do daily for dental hygiene. Demonstrate that we brush with an up-and-down motion from front to back on one side, then the other, and then we do the same thing inside the mouth. Also, at the end we brush our tongue. Then rinse.

- *Flossing.* Some dentists tell us that this is equally as important as brushing. This can be demonstrated for students by using a large comb with teeth that are far apart. Pretend that a piece of string is the floss. Show students how to wrap the floss around the index fingers, holding tight with the thumb. Then gently place the string between each tooth in the comb. Explain to students that we go up one side, make a U-turn and come back down the other side. This is to remove any food lodged between teeth that brushing doesn't reach. It will help eliminate cavities. Leave these materials at the Science/Health Center so that students can practice on the comb.

- *Dentist visit.* Visit the dentist every six months (or at least once a year) for a thorough cleaning by the dentist or the dental hygienist.

Tooth Fairy Tooth Talk

"The tooth fairy knows all about teeth. We have 20 baby teeth that fall out periodically to make room for our permanent teeth. All together, we have 36 permanent teeth. The Tooth Fairy wants you to know that teeth have a purpose." Put the following on the chalkboard:

incisors or front teeth—cut food

cuspids, or front middle—tear food

bicuspids, or back middle—crush food

molars, or back—grind food

"With a piece of toast, we can practice all of these functions. First, bite into the toast with the front teeth to cut it. Then crush and grind it. For the second piece, tear the toast with the cuspids, and then crush and grind it. Eat the piece of toast with an awareness of the teeth doing the work. Of course, we do this with our mouth closed!"

Good Food for Healthy Teeth

Some food is good for your teeth and some is not so good. Students can make a booklet with pictures showing good and not-so-good foods for their teeth. This can be on white paper in the form of a tooth shape:

Good—milk (calcium to help grow strong bones and teeth); fruits and vegetables (vitamins and minerals); hard vegetables help scrape plaque from teeth

Not so good—candy and sweets. The sugar contributes to tooth decay, which causes cavities. Brush after eating sweets if possible, especially gummy candy that sticks to teeth and lollipops that are in the mouth for a long time.

Invite a Dentist for a School Visit

In many areas, dentists will make school visits and talk with children about tooth care. Sometimes, the hygienist will make a short visit. Inquire and invite a dentist, if possible.

Make a Toothpaste Poster

Students can cut out a toothpaste tube shape and design their own brand. "What will it be named? What color is it? Does it have a flavor? What does it claim to do? How often do we use it?" (This activity creates an awareness of all of these important points. Encourage children to go home and check their own brand of toothpaste, color, flavor, and so on.) Be sure to include a note in the newsletter to parents this month about your toothpaste investigation.

Remember: A new toothbrush and tube of toothpaste in a self-closed plastic bag is an excellent prize or reward when you need one.

Children's Books About Teeth

Have a display of books on hand this month to read aloud for your science focus on dental hygiene. These include: *Little Rabbit's Loose Tooth* by Lucy Bate; *Arthur's Tooth* by Marc Brown; *Alligator's Toothache* by Diane DeGroat; and *Albert's Toothache* by Barbara Williams.

LINKS TO AUTHOR-OF-THE-MONTH

Illustrator for February: Jerry Pinkney

This month we are doing something different. We are going to highlight an illustrator! Jerry Pinkney illustrates books for many different authors. He is a "collaborator" in the truest sense of the word, and has won both the Caldecott Medal and the Coretta Scott King Medal—as well as other honors—for his art work. During his career, he has illustrated over 75 books for children.

So this month, we'll learn to recognize the flowing lines and realistic drawings of Jerry Pinkney, while meeting a number of different authors.

It must be exciting to be an illustrator: to receive text (words) only and make the words come to life with the pictures they create in your own mind. The author's words have to create images from which the illustrator can draw. This is difficult and challenging.

Jerry Pinkney's son and daughter-in-law, Brian Pinkney and Andrea Davis Pinkney, are also award-winning picture book illustrators and authors. So, *let's read!*

Hurwitz, Johanna. *New Shoes for Silvia*. Illustrated by Jerry Pinkney (New York: Morrow, 1993) Silvia's aunt Tia Rosita has sent a package home to the family. Included in this package are bright red shoes for Silvia. There's only one thing—they're too big! Silvia can't wait to fit into them. Will the time ever come when she can wear them? Time passes so slowly for her.

Activities to Accompany *New Shoes for Silvia*

1. Read the book aloud and enjoy it. Then look through the book again for the setting. Some scenes take place inside and some are outside of the house. "When outside, are we in a city or country setting? What has the artist included to let us know that we are in a country setting?" (horses, outdoor market, people carrying bowls of items on their head, goats, oxen plowing fields).

2. Find a map or globe that shows the Americas. The author tells us that the setting is "far away in another America," so we know it is Central or South

America. A hint may be in the dedication by the author. But, the story is definitely south of the border of the United States.

3. Tia's red shoes are described in the following way:

    as red as the setting sun (Grandmother)

    as red as the inside of a watermelon (Papa)

    as red as a rose (Mama)

    These words must have inspired the illustrator because he makes sure that the setting sun, the inside of a watermelon, and a red rosebush are drawn into the pictures. Have students search for them.

    Next, have students look at the illustration of the bright red shoes on the last page and add to the descriptions of red. Write them on a chart entitled "Silvia's New Red Shoes Are as Red as . . ."

4. One way the illustrator shows us that time is passing by is through the drawing of the mother. We see that she is pregnant, and eventually she is holding a baby in her arms. Draw this to the students' attention as the way the illustrator chose to show that time has passed by. In what other ways could he have shown time passing? How can students show time passing in their own illustrations?

5. "On the first page, the word 'Correos' appears above a doorway. We do not see that sign again, but it figures prominently into the story. Correo is derived from 'courier' which means post office messenger." Students can learn the word "correos," which would be the equivalent of our post office.

6. "How many different animals are in this village? Let's list them."

7. Discuss receiving clothing gifts that are not our size. Have students had the experience of having to wait until clothing fit them? Have any worn clothing of an older sibling that was too large?

Kipling, Rudyard. *Rikki-Tikki-Tavi*. Adapted and illustrated by Jerry Pinkney (New York: Morrow Junior Books, 1997) This is a classic story of Rikki-Tikki-Tavi, the fearless mongoose. The illustrator tells us at the end of the book that after having illustrated stories by Rudyard Kipling, a favorite of his youth, he decided to expand the story of Rikki the mongoose. In the illustrator's words, "It would take the picture book you hold in your hands to give the frisky and curious Rikki enough room to show himself as the true hero he is." This is an adventure story to be savored and read in sequences to young children. Don't try to read it all at once. Enjoy the adventure.

Activities to Accompany *Rikki-Tikki-Tavi*

1. First, set the stage for the story. Tell students that it takes place in India, a land far away. Locate this on a map or globe. Then tell students that it is a folktale that takes place in the jungle. In that part of the world, the animals are different from the animals where they live; although the animals talk and interact with people, as they do in folktales, the animals will not be ones with which the students are accustomed. Then introduce the *mongoose,* who is furry with a tail like a cat's and a head like a weasel; the *tailorbird,*

with a long, straight upright tail; and the scaly *cobra* snake. Write those names on the chalkboard.

2. Introduce the story characters by name and write them on the chalkboard: Teddy (the boy), his mother and father, Rikki-Tikki-Tavi (mongoose), Darzee (tailorbird), and Nag and Nagaina (two enormous cobras). A minor character is Chuchundra (muskrat) who gives information to Rikki that enables him to learn of the plan of Nag and Nagaina to rid the house of the family.

3. This story has adventure, suspense, and a good character (mongoose) chasing the evil characters (cobras), while Darzee (bird) offers assistance when possible. The humans are helpless against the cobras. But it is the job of the mongoose to rid the area of snakes, so it is an in-born trait—and Rikki-Tikki is a brave warrior.

4. The bird *fluttered,* the mongoose *scuttled,* and the snake *slithered.* At one point, the cobra lifted one-third of himself clear off the ground and "swayed like a dandelion tuft in the wind." "Listen to these descriptive words. Now let's move like the animals. How does the illustrator 'draw' these motions?"

5. Locate the book's drawings of the words, such as the birds that "made a beautiful nest by pulling two big leaves together and stitching up the edges, and had filled the inside with fluff." There is an entire page devoted to this.

6. *Duty before pleasure.* Introduce the expression that is in the book: "a big meal makes a slow mongoose." It served as a caution to Rikki after he killed Karait, a snake. (On a full stomach, the mongoose would not be so swift and so alert, and his job now is to rid the garden of the cobras—*not* to eat a big meal.) Keep in mind that it is important to introduce "expressions" to students; however, if this is not the time, then do it during another reading session. *Aesops Fables* will help with this.

   This calls for a discussion of delaying gratification. "Sometimes we have to do what we need to do, even though we might like to do something else. How does this apply in the life of students?" (doing their schoolwork, then having play time; doing homework and then playing; helping at home before watching TV, and so on)

7. Have students examine the cobra illustrations. Notice the eyes, teeth, and so on. With their pointer finger, trace the artist's rendition of the swooping, swirling snake. Students can make swooping motions in the air, and then on paper with a crayon. Then, fill in the middle with oval shapes, like those in the book, to make a scaly snake.

8. Talk about how the artist's illustrations help to visualize, or give meaning to, the story. "If there could be just one more illustration in the book, what would you like to see?" Talk about planning the text and selecting just what it is that can or needs to be illustrated. The artist shows us all of the characters, the setting both indoors and outdoors, and a lot of action.

Lester, Julius. *Black Cowboy Wild Horses, A True Story.* Illustrations by Jerry Pinkney (New York: Dial, 1998) As lightning blazes in the night sky, Bob Lemmons sees the wild mustangs galloping across the plains. He's been tracking the horses for days, on his horse named Warrior. Can he corral them?

Activities to Accompany *Black Cowboy Wild Horses, A True Story*

1. Enjoy this read-aloud book. It may take more than one time to complete the reading, for it is a long picture book, but worth the time.

2. Go back through the book and track the horses on the pages. They're wild and they're running. "How does the artist show the bend in their legs, the movement of their mane?" Have students trace these lines with their fingers.

3. The author describes the horses in terms such as the quivering of their flesh, the rippling of muscles, the bending of bones in their bodies. Have students close their eyes and try to visualize these horses. Then look again at the horses to see how the artist made the words "come to life." Ask students to put it into their own words.

4. "How does the artist show the reader that Bob cares very much for his horse? How does the author tell us? What words does he use?"

5. "Suppose you were asked to draw a picture that showed: 'the sky was curved as if it were a lap on which the earth lay napping like a curled cat,' and 'high above a hawk was suspended on cold threads of unseen winds,' and 'far away, at what looked to be the edge of the world, land and sky kissed.' What would you do? One thing would be to go outdoors in the wide open spaces and look, and look, and look. An artist must keep looking and seeing. Start thinking in terms of shapes, designs, lines, and textures. Then look at the first page and see how the illustrator depicted the scene for those words."

6. Check the dedications. "To whom did the artist dedicate the book? To whom did the author dedicate the book?" (They each dedicated this book to the other—true collaborative friends.)

7. Check the library for other works by this duo. Together, they've done *Sam and the Tigers; John Henry;* and *The Uncle Remus Tales.*

McKissack, Patricia C. *Mirandy and Brother Wind.* **Illustrated by Jerry Pinkney (New York: Alfred Knopf, 1988)** First, students need to know that this book is the winner of many awards (Caldecott, Coretta Scott King, ALA Notable Book, and a Notable Children's Trade Book in the Field of Social Studies). It is set in the rural south, with southern dialect. It's time for the junior cakewalk and Mirandy is determined to capture first prize. She wants to capture the wind for her partner. The cakewalk was an actual event, where people put on their "Sunday best" and couples arched their backs, held heads up high, and strutted around in a square, making sure to take sharp corners, do dips and turns, and kicks and swirls, in time to a fiddle or a banjo. The cakewalk prize was a decorated cake, which was given for the "best walkin'." The illustrations help to capture that energy and vitality of this African American custom introduced by slaves.

Activities to Accompany *Mirandy and Brother Wind*

1. Before you read the story, tell students that there is a character in the story called "Brother Wind." "If you were the illustrator, how would you portray

(or draw) the wind? How can you capture the wind?" Give them an opportunity to try to draw or to tell about it. Then show how the illustrator portrayed the wind.

2. Next, go through the book and enjoy the story. Explain to students that Black southern dialect is used. (*Note for the teacher:* If you are not polished at reading southern dialect aloud, just read it in your natural voice.)

3. *The cakewalk.* According to the author's note, this is a custom rooted in Afro-American culture. The cakewalk was performed by couples who strutted and pranced around a large square, while keeping time with banjo and fiddle music. The cakewalkers did kicks, swirls, and fancy turns. At the end, a prize was given for the "best walkin'." That prize was a beautifully decorated cake.

   Suggestions are given in the book for creating your own cakewalk. This includes designating a large square space for the walk, either outdoors or indoors; music selections; walking with a partner; making up steps and moves; and finally having the grand contest and sharing the cake. A cake recipe is written at the front of the book.

4. Some vocabulary words are given at the back of the book, along with explanations. These include: *sassy*—quick to give your opinion, but it can also describe someone who is rude; *shackle*—a ring made of metal that is used to secure the ankle or wrist to prevent freedom of movement; *conjure woman*—someone who practices magic, casts spells, and uses charms; *to do someone's bidding*—to perform a service for someone else; and *jubilee*—celebration. These words can be introduced and/or explained as the story is read aloud.

5. Demonstrate for students how to turn a corner in a sharp manner. Walk to the corner, pivot, and walk in the other direction. It takes practice, but it's judged in the cakewalk.

Pinkney, Gloria Jean. *Back Home*. Illustrated by Jerry Pinkney (New York: Dial, 1992) Ernestine, an eight-year-old girl, goes by train to visit her relatives in North Carolina. She lives in the north and this is the first time she has ever visited the south. As soon as her uncle greets her at the station with a bouquet of flowers, however, she feels right at home. Explore the countryside with Ernestine and her Cousin Jack, who teases her about her "citified" ways.

Activities to Accompany *Back Home*

1. Read the story aloud and enjoy it. Talk with students about visiting relatives far away. "How many of you have traveled alone—by bus, train, or plane? We see by the illustrations that Ernestine has a 'tag' pinned to her dress. What do you think might be written on this I.D. tag? If you did travel alone, who helped you?"

2. While in the country, Ernestine's Aunt Beula opens an old trunk and locates a pair of overalls that belonged to Ernestine's mother when *she* was a girl. "Have you ever worn clothing that belonged to your mother or father (or an older relative)? What was the occasion for this?"

3. When Cousin Jack shows Ernestine his new goat, she asks, "May I hold him?" Jack replies, "It's not a him, it's a her!" Then he says he hasn't named her yet, so Ernestine suggests "Princess." Jack is convinced that Ernestine knows nothing about goats and that Princess is a "citified" name. "Ernestine, although willing, can't climb a ladder, and then falls off a goat. Is she, in fact, citified? What might she be able to do that Jack couldn't—something that would make him 'countryfied'?"

4. "How does the illustrator show us that we're in the country? What animals does he show us? How does the artist portray a 'small abandoned farmhouse' in the clearing? What does the porch look like?" (broken flower pots, broken floor boards) "If we were to get inside the house, what would it look like? Perhaps we can draw a room in the house to show what the illustrator chose not to show."

5. "What present does Jack give Ernestine as she packs up to leave? What does it represent? Do presents have to cost a lot of money? What suggestions, from nature, can we name that could be given as a present for someone who is not from our area but who comes to visit us?" (pinecones, chestnuts, buckeyes, acorns, leaves, shells, pretty stone, and so on)

6. "To whom does the author dedicate the book? To whom does the illustrator dedicate this book? What makes this book special?" (based on a true story of the illustrator's wife, who wrote the book) It's her *debut.* That's a new vocabulary word. Have students made a debut in dance, or a piano recital, or in a sports event? This month, they *can* make their debut in the classroom as an author and/or illustrator.

_____. ***The Sunday Outing.* Illustrated by Jerry Pinkney (New York: Dial Books, 1994)** Although this book was written after *Back Home,* the events that are portrayed are those that lead up to Ernestine's trip to North Carolina on the train, and how her family makes her dream come true.

Activities to Accompany *The Sunday Outing*

1. Read the story and enjoy it. It can be read either prior to *Back Home* or after. It would be good for students to know, however, that the two books are part of the same story.

2. Make a comparison between the city and country settings in these two books. "How does the author choose to draw the city? What types of transportation vehicles do we see? Do we see any animals? Do we see anything green? What exactly do we see on the city streets?"

3. Explore Ernestine's bedroom. "Are reading and writing valued in this home? How can we tell? What might be one of her hobbies?"

4. The illustrator shows us a picture of the family scrapbook, so we know that memories are prized. "Do you have family scrapbooks or family photo records in your home?" In your classroom you might be making a photo record of the school year to show that the class's activities are valued. Get

started on this now if you haven't already done so. It can feature the Spring season.

5. The artist uses pencil, colored pencil, and watercolor for the drawings in this book. Have students try making a sketch of something using these three types of media of expression. Begin with something simple and uncluttered, like one flower in a vase.

6. Aunt Odessa is a gentle, reassuring person. She makes Ernestine feel like her dreams might come true. "Do students have a favorite aunt and/or uncle? Why?" What are the characteristics cited by students that make favorite relatives qualify as good people? Stress that it's not necessarily because they give us "things"—we want to know about them as people.

7. "How did Ernestine's dream come true? What sacrifices will her family make for her?" (Her mother postpones getting a new sewing machine and her father decides to work with his old tools for another year so that their daughter can take the train ride and make the connection to relatives back home.) "They want to make her visit possible because they love her." Loving parents make sacrifices for their children—and your students need to be reminded of that.

And Many More!

We are fortunate to be able to get pleasure and enrichment from the books that Jerry Pinkney has so ably illustrated for children.

Be on the alert for the many other books illustrated by this artist. He has collaborated with Robert D. San Souci on the first of three Caldecott awards for *The Talking Eggs,* an exciting folktale set in the south. His collaboration with Robert D. San Souci entitled *The Hired Hand* is a treat, along with *Minty: A Story of Young Harriet Tubman* by Alan Schroeder.

At the time of the publication of *Black Cowboy Wild Horses,* he had already received four Coretta Scott King Awards and two King Honors, as well as three Caldecott honor awards. Hats off to Jerry Pinkney and his wife, Gloria Jean.

Note: Pinkney's son, Brian Pinkney, is also a children's book illustrator, and has chosen the scratch-board design for his medium of expression, although his first book, *The Boy and The Ghost,* resembles the work of his father. Be on the lookout for the Caldecott award-winning *The Faithful Friend,* developed in collaboration with Robert D. San Souci and *Seven Candles for Kwanzaa,* developed in collaboration with his wife, Andrea. Now, he is writing and illustrating his own works. Hats off to this artistic family!

REPRODUCIBLE ACTIVITY PAGES

The Vowel Round-Up *(r-controlled vowel sounds)*

The Wide Awake and Sleepy Owl *(OW)*

Let's Visit the "R Family" Blends

Valentine Rebus Message

Instant Words To Go

The Tooth Fairy Collects Compound Words

Anansi Writes a Special Story

Today's the Day for Blending "S" Words

The Rooster's Crow—Favorite Book Award

Children's Literature Activity Page—The Lady With the Beads *(Jerry Pinkney)*

© DCW99

© 2000 by The Center for Applied Research in Education

Name _____

LET'S VISIT THE "R" FAMILY BLENDS

Have you seen where the "R" families live? Here are their houses. Use your pencil to show who is home today. Learn the names of these family members.

© 2000 by The Center for Applied Research in Education

Name _____

VALENTINE REBUS MESSAGE

Use these Rebus symbols to help Mr. Gage M. Bunny make up a Valentine message. Print the message below.

Message:

© 2000 by The Center for Applied Research in Education

Name _____

INSTANT WORDS TO GO

Here are four instant pizzas to go. How many of these instant words on the pizzas do you know? Keep practicing until you can say them in an instant! Work with a partner. Use your crayons to make the pizzas look delicious!

over
little
live
very
name

new
work
me
after
good

sound
know
thing
back
only

take
place
give
our
man

Name _____

THE TOOTH FAIRY COLLECTS COMPOUND WORDS

During Dental Health Week the Tooth Fairy is extra busy! You can help. Just match up the two little words to make a big word. That big word is called a "compound" word.

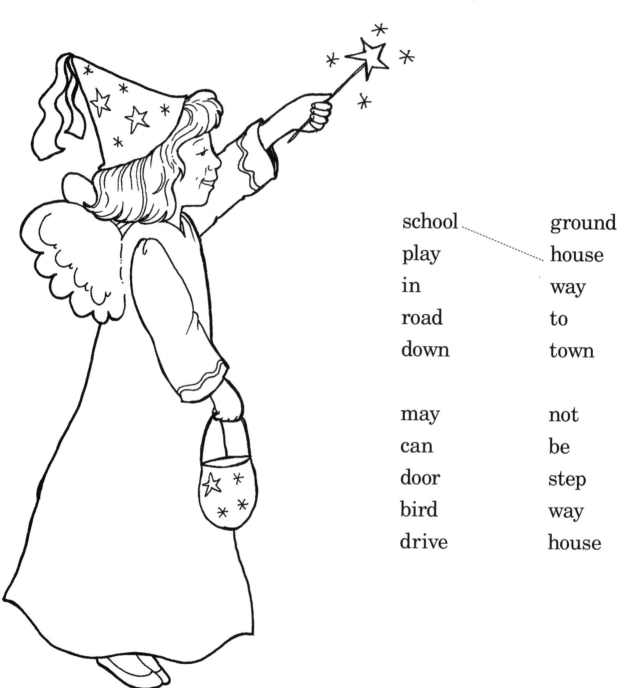

school   ground

play   house

in   way

road   to

down   town

may   not

can   be

door   step

bird   way

drive   house

© 2000 by The Center for Applied Research in Education

Use the back of this page to make up two sentences using the compound words.

© 2000 by The Center for Applied Research in Education

Name _____

ANANSI WRITES A SPECIAL STORY

Anansi is the trickster spider from Africa who enjoys fooling others. Today he was writing a story and BAM! he fell asleep! Let's trick the trickster! Finish writing the story. When he wakes up he won't know who did it!

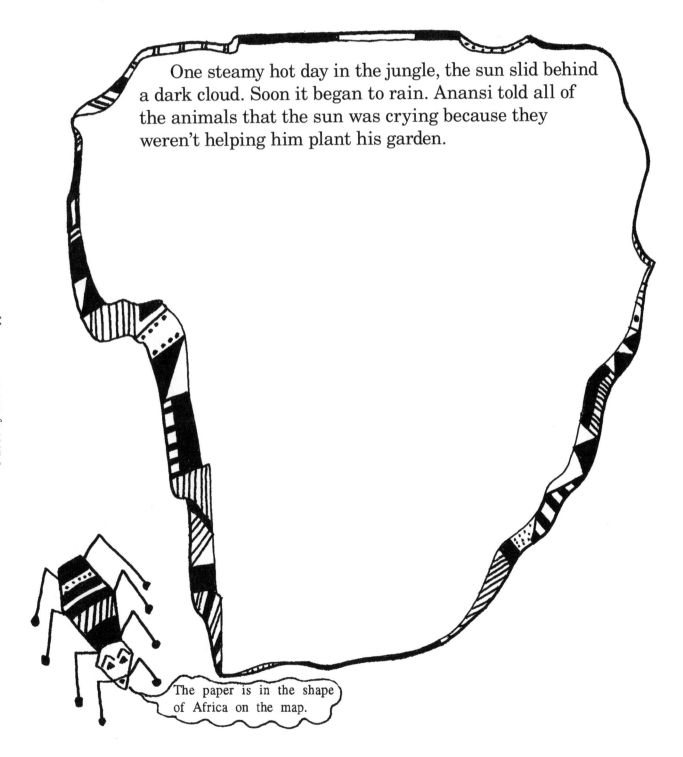

One steamy hot day in the jungle, the sun slid behind a dark cloud. Soon it began to rain. Anansi told all of the animals that the sun was crying because they weren't helping him plant his garden.

The paper is in the shape of Africa on the map.

Name _____

TODAY'S THE DAY
FOR BLENDING "S" WORDS

Shanda is busy blending words today. Please help her pack words that begin with an "s blend" into the correct bags. How many words can you fit into each bag?

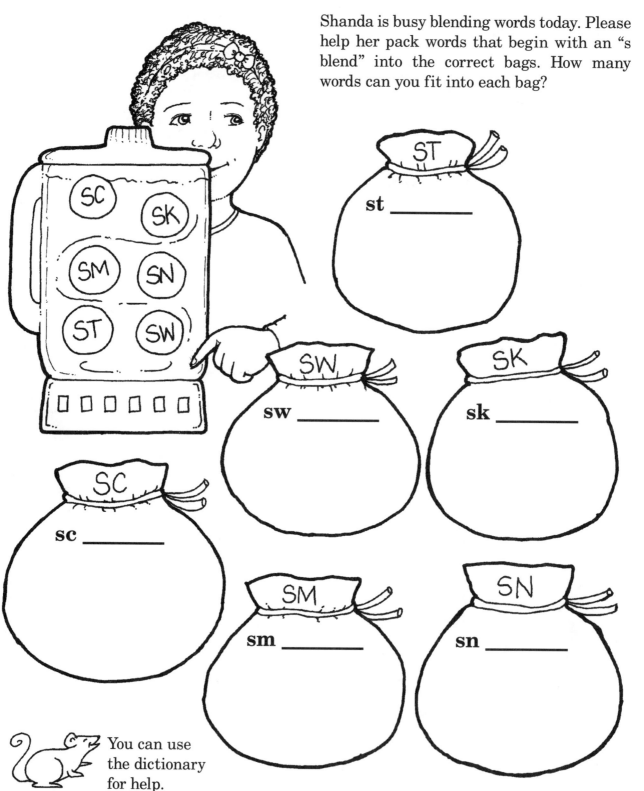

ST

st _____

SC
SK
SM
SN
ST
SW

SW

sw _____

SK

sk _____

SC

sc _____

SM

sm _____

SN

sn _____

You can use the dictionary for help.

© 2000 by The Center for Applied Research in Education

Name _____

The Rooster's Crow Favorite Book Award

When the rooster crows for a book, it means that it is terrific!

What book do YOU think earns this award?

_____
(title)

_____
(author)

_____
(illustrator)

I think this book should receive "The Rooster's Crow Favorite Book Award" because _____

_____

_____

_____

_____

On the back, draw a picture of your favorite part of the story. Share it with classmates.

© 2000 by The Center for Applied Research in Education

Name _____

THE LADY WITH THE BEADS

Let's pretend that this unfinished sketch was found in Jerry Pinkney's art studio.

Complete the beads. Design the head scarf and shawl

Use bright colors.

Work slowly.

© 2000 by The Center for Applied Research in Education

March

CHILDREN'S PICTURE BOOKS

FOR THE MONTH OF
MARCH

Aitken, Amy. *Wanda's Circus* **(New York: Bradbury Press, 1985)** Wanda decides to have a circus and all the kids are willing to sign up, except Wanda says it's only for the "big kids." So, all of the "little kids" decide to leave. But wait, the circus is ready to begin and there's something missing—the audience. Now the "little kids" have the upper hand and have to be wooed back.

Baker, Keith. *Who Is the Beast?* **(New York: The Trumpet Club [Harcourt Brace], 1990)** This is a visual adventure through the jungle. There are stripes and spots and tails and legs scurrying to get away from the prowling beast who resembles a tiger. But is the tiger the beast? Not when he reaches the pond and gazes at his reflection—then he sees the others all around who have similar characteristics.

Bauer, Caroline Feller. *Midnight Snowman.* **Illustrated by Catherine Stock (New York: Atheneum, 1987)** In a town where it rains a lot but hardly ever snows, you have to take advantage of the snow when it happens. Everyone gets into the spirit of the snowfall of the season.

Climo, Shirley. *The Irish Cinderlad.* **Illustrated by Loretta Krupinski (New York: HarperCollins, 1996)** This is an unusual twist on the universal Cinderella tale. Becan the herdboy, like his female counterpart, loses his shoe. It is a giant-size shoe, and is sought after. Like Cinderella he is aided by a magical being—in this case, a bull. (Long ago in Ireland, cattle were thought to have unusual powers, especially one with a white face and red ears.)

Falwell, Cathryn. *Word Wizard* **(New York: Clarion Books, 1998)** By way of a magic spoon, Anna can transform words by looking at the letters and moving them about. For example, the word *canoe* becomes *ocean*. With this new-found skill, Anna helps a little lost boy.

MacDonald, Suse. *Peck, Slither and Slide* **(New York: Harcourt Brace & Company, 1997)** In this concept book, the word "climb," for example, is perched so that it looks like it is climbing over rocks. "Hide" is hiding in a tree behind the branches, and "peck" has holes in it. There is a companion picture for each word, so that the reader can interact with the text and guess which animal might be climbing, or hiding, or pecking. (A rich union of both visual and verbal images.)

Powell, Pamela. *The Turtle Watchers* **(New York: Viking, 1991)** A leatherback turtle lays her eggs on the beach as three island sisters, who have stayed up all night, watch this spectacular event. But, turtle eggs are appealing to hungry sea birds, a boy looking for a snack, and even to an untrustworthy customs officer. The turtle watch begins!

Numeroff, Laura. *Chimps Don't Wear Glasses.* **Illustrated by Joe Mathieu (New York: Simon & Schuster, 1995)** We are treated to a variety of animals reading, cooking, and activities—like hang gliding that are pure fancy. Amusing and entertaining, the book invites the reader to imagine other preposterous things that animals don't do.

Showers, Paul. *The Listening Walk.* **Illustrated by Aliki (New York: HarperCollins, 1961, 1991)** When you go on a walk to listen to sounds in your environment, it means that you must be very quiet. This is a good read-aloud book to prepare a class for a listening walk. At the end of the book, you can close your eyes and count the sounds you hear right where you are.

Westervelt, Linda. *Roger Tory Peterson's ABC of Birds.* **Pictures by Roger Tory Peterson and Seymour Levin (New York: Universe Publishing, 1995)** Go on a bird hunt through the alphabet with colorful birds portrayed realistically from all over the globe. Along with each picture is print information about the bird. A *Guide to Illustrations* at the end of the book tells about the birds, such as where they are located in the world or the type of media used to represent the bird.

 # *MARCH*

MARCH GREETINGS! By this time, many students are reading, but they are in various stages of progress and development. So, while you will want to continue to meet with clusters of students in skill groups, you will also want to give ample time for independent book browsing and reading at the Library Center. With spring on the horizon, it might be a good time to freshen up the Library Center and put a new storybook character in charge. Also, it is time for assessment again—time to take a good look at where students are along the reading continuum. This information needs to be reported to parents, especially if there are concerns, because you do not want to wait until the end of the year to report problems. You'll also want to assess your own performance.

Establish weekly goals with the students and work to meet them. Remember, young students thrive on routine; "if this is Tuesday, it must be _____" is a source of comfort and security for many. With St. Patrick's Day this month—and little green elves here and there—March is an excellent time for a focus on fairy tales, other tales, and a few surprises.

March's Focus on Reading. (1) Phonics Activities; (2) Choral Reading; (3) Wordless Picture Books; (4) Syllables and "The Droll Teller"; (5) Homophones; (6) Assessment; and (7) Spelling.

Phonics Activities

I'm Going to Grandmother's House

Sit in a circle and go around the circle with the ABC's, in order. Students pretend they are going to Grandmother's house and will take something that begins with a letter of the alphabet. All answers are acceptable as long as they begin with the correct letter sound.

Students can repeat all that went before, or just make their own contribution for the letter at hand, depending upon skill level.

- *Example A.*

    STUDENT #1: I'm going to Grandmother's house and will take an apple.

    STUDENT #2: I'm going to Grandmother's house and will take a bird.

- *Example B.*

    STUDENT #1: I'm going to Grandmother's house and will take an apple.

    STUDENT #2: I'm going to Grandmother's house and will take an apple and a bird. *(cumulative)*

Spin-a-Letter

Make a set of spinners using paper plates. When a student spins and lands on a letter, the students must name something that begins with that letter to score one point. This can be played with two or three players. The first player to reach a score of 10 wins. Then begin again.

Sew-a-Letter Cards

Use card stock to create an outline of an object that begins with each letter of the alphabet. Students can, for example, sew around an apple shape for the letter A; sew around the shape of a baby or ball for the letter B; and so on.

Some students can create their own sew-a-letter shape by cutting out a picture of an object from a magazine. Paste it on a sheet of paper. Use a paper punch to punch holes along the edge of the object, and then sew it. This is a kinesthetic approach to the letter–sound relationship.

Peanut Butter Play-dough Letters

You will need peanut butter, nonfat dry milk, a bowl, a mixing spoon, a clean cookie sheet, and an ABC grid.

Mix equal amounts of peanut butter and nonfat dry milk to make the consistency of play-dough. Then roll out the dough to form a letter. Next, roll out more of the dough and make an item that begins with that same letter. Each student can do one letter.

Place the peanut butter play-dough items on a large ABC sheet. When the ABC's are completed, students can name the letter and item, identify the items they made, and then eat them!

Clothesline Letter Socks

You will need 26 lower-case letters and 26 upper-case letters on sock shapes. Students can help make these. You will need ten pairs of real socks, a clothesline, and clothespins. Students can pin the upper-case letter on one sock and the lower-case letter on the other sock in each pair. Then mix them up in a basket. Stretch a clothesline in a secure area, and have students clip the matching socks together as they check to see if the letters match. Then remove the letters and attach ten different sets. Do this until all of the socks have been matched.

Windy Phonics Windsocks

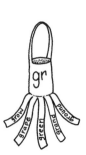

You will need a sheet of construction paper and five long strips of paper. Have students print one of the following letter blends on the windsock—gr, br, tr, fr, and so on. Next, make a cylindrical shape from the paper and staple it together to form the base of the windsock. Then, on the five strips, students will print a word from that blend family. For example, if "gr" is printed on the cylinder, a student can choose five words that begin with that sound (grape, grill) and print one on each strip. When all of the words have been chosen and printed, glue the strip to the bottom of the cylinder. Add several crepe paper streamers, too. Then put a string handle on the top. Hang up in the classroom, if possible, so the letter blend family can wave to the students as the air circulates.

SH! Leprechauns Like It Quiet

"When we put the letters 'sh' together, we get the quiet sound." Often this can be aided by putting the forefinger up to the lips and saying "shhhhhh." Some words are quiet at the beginning and some are quiet at the end. Here are some examples to use:

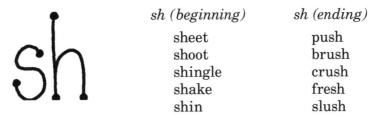

	sh (beginning)	*sh (ending)*
	sheet	push
	shoot	brush
	shingle	crush
	shake	fresh
	shin	slush

Ask students how they would classify the word *shush*. This calls for another category, or a Venn diagram shape for the word lists. Be on the lookout for other words that are quiet at the beginning and ending. "Can we find any words in the newspapers or junk mail that have the quiet sound in the middle?" (pushed, bashed, cashed, eyelashes)

Chippy the Chipper Chipmunk's "CH" Sound

"Chippy is a chipper chipmunk and likes to say 'ch' whenever she can. She likes to make Chipmunk Sentences such as those that follow." Have students repeat these and make up their own:

Chippy chews chocolate chip cookies for lunch.
Chippy chews chocolate chips by the bunch.
Chippy chews chocolate cherries to munch.
Chippy chews chocolate cheese chunks.

"Chippy the Chipmunk's sound can appear at the beginning or ending of the word, just like the 'shhhhhh' sound." Here are some to get you started, and then students can locate more:

	chew	lunch
	chalk	crunch
	chill	touch
	charge	bunch
	chance	much

"The word 'church' gives us an opportunity to show that this sound can appear at the beginning and the end of the same word. How can we categorize this?" Again, the Venn diagram method would be useful.

Root Word Plus "S"

Write these three root words on the chalkboard and have students say them:

> boot   bird   book

Now add the letter 's' at the end of the three words so that they look like this:

> boots   birds   books

Ask students what is different about the words. ("They now have an 's' at the end.") "Does it mean that they are the same words?" ("No, they are plural. The added 's' makes them mean more than one, or plural.") "Can we do this with other words?" ("Yes, some of the time.") Print the root word on the chalkboard, say the word, then have a student add the "s" at the end, and say the word again. Let's try some:

hand	look	run	park
knee	book	turn	bark
cat	lap	pot	flower

Note: The following four activities relate to March's author/illustrator-of-the-month, Tomie dePaola.

Make Strega Nona's Pasta Letters

Use dried pasta to make letter shapes. For example, students can use rigatoni to make the letters "R,r"; linguini to make the letters "L,l"; pieces of elbow macaroni to make the letters "S,s"; and so on.

A Big Kettle of Spaghetti

Obtain a big kettle or pot for the classroom. Put tiny items in the pot, attached to a piece of loopy white yarn (spaghetti). Hang the "spaghetti" over the edge of the pot. Students can gently pull a piece of spaghetti and retrieve an item. Name the item and tell the letter that makes that sound; students repeat the sound. (Use children's miniature toys for the pot.)

Big Anthony's Letter–Sound Relationships

Big Anthony gets a little mixed up and needs some help. Have an assortment of items attached to white loopy yarn, but have the incorrect letter also attached to the item. Ask students to say the item and the letter, such as "Car—B." Does it make sense? No. Have students help Big Anthony to make the corrections. (Create an atmosphere of helpfulness and not ridicule. Many students do get a sense of satisfaction from finding the errors.)

Stuffed Pasta People

Have two students lie down on a double sheet of brown kraft paper. Select a short person and a tall person. Trace around them. The shorter person will represent Strega Nona and the taller person will represent Big Anthony. Use the picture books as an example for helping students paint clothing and facial features on these two figures. When dry, cut out the double figures.

Then staple them three-fourths around the edges, and stuff both figures with tissue and shredded newspapers (spaghetti). Once they are fully stuffed, staple the remainder of the edges. Add details, such as a belt, yarn for hair, a real hat, a real apron, and so on.

Strega Nona and Big Anthony can join the classroom this month and help students with their letter–sound relationships. They can be propped up in the Reading Center, or on chairs at a table. They are both good listeners when it comes to having children read them stories. Students can try to teach them their letters, sounds, and so on. Big Anthony will have some difficulty learning.

Notes to the students can be left from each of these characters (the Author-of-the-Month focus). Big Anthony can do a worksheet (many wrong answers) and students can help correct them. He is a reassuring character for students who are having difficulty with reading. They get another opportunity to teach and learn right along with him. (See Reproducible Activity Pages.) You can fill in several wrong answers on Big Anthony's worksheets, and have them available to use daily. They can be saved in a folder, and brought out during free-choice time, recess, or when you allow time for this activity. It is amazing how many students will select to read and do math work with stuffed characters during free-choice time, especially if the students are cast in the role of helper.

Choral Reading

An Orchestra of Voices

When the whole class reads a line of text together, it is an especially good activity for the student who is having difficulty with reading. It is also a good boost for the student who is just learning the language. The strong voices carry the weaker ones—and your voice is loudest of all to serve as a beacon. Do this often enough and soon the weaker voices begin to strengthen, as children learn to recognize the words. They also feel like they're actually reading, and this serves as a motivation to keep trying.

Encourage Students to Listen Carefully

First, read or say a line of text that students can repeat. Model it by speaking slowly, with good enunciation. Students should be able to hear every syllable in a word. Use this approach when teaching a chant or a poem.

Some students will be preoccupied with the word pronunciation. The student who is fluent in oral language will be able to pronounce the words and focus upon the meaning of the chant or verse.

Cumulative Tales

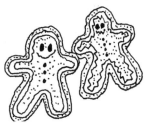

The use of cumulative tales, where the same words are repeated throughout the book and become familiar refrains, serves as an excellent resource for choral reading or choral speaking. *Millions of Cats* by Wanda Gaag is a picture book that offers an opportunity for students to repeat a familiar refrain as they move in time with the rhythm of the words. Other books that offer rich choral speaking opportunities include *There Was an Old Lady Who Swallowed a Fly; The Gingerbread Boy; The Little Red Hen;* and *The House That Jack Built.*

Echo Speaking

Have students stand in two rows, one on either side of the classroom. They can be called the Leprechauns and the Elves, or any other team names you choose. Use flash cards and hold up a letter of the alphabet for all to see. The Leprechauns say the letter in unison; the Elves echo the same letter.

Variation 1. Show the letter card to only the Leprechauns and have them say the letter name in unison. Show three cards to the Elves, and have them select the corresponding letter.

Variation 2. Whisper the letter "E" into the ear of the first person on the Leprechaun team and on the Elf team. In turn, have them whisper it to the next person and the next until the final person receives the letter message. That person on each team says the letter aloud. If it's correct, they gain a point. If it is incorrect, they do not get a point. (This causes children to listen carefully and to speak distinctly, because the letter "E," for example, can easily be passed along as "P" or "B" or "Z" or "T").

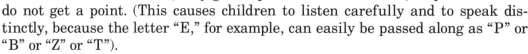

Wordless Picture Books

Going "From Talk to Text"

In wordless picture books, the reader goes *from the visual to the verbal,* and *from the verbal to the text.* Expose students to a variety of wordless picture books this month. Hopefully they may be familiar with some already. If not, go through each book page by page and encourage students to discuss the picture plot.

The concept to try to get across is: "A story is unfolding visually right before our eyes (picture plot). Let's talk about it. Let's get the picture plot 'down on paper' in words. That becomes the story plot, or text. And so we go from pictures, to spoken language, to written language."

By doing this, some students begin to see that:

1. Pictures play an important role in the story.

2. We can figure out a great deal about the story line by the pictures (thus gaining a "sense of story").

3. We can make predictions.

4. We can fill in the gaps, imagining what has happened between pictures.

5. We can use our own words.

6. We can print the words that tell our story (we go *from talk to text*).

7. We can read the story that we just wrote (and that's what reading is—saying words that represent what someone said or thought).

8. We think of words as talk spilling out of a person's mouth and making letters on a page. That's called *print*. (Have students illustrate this as a cartoon.)

Investigate Cartoon Talk

Word bubbles that appear above cartoon characters in comic strips contain words that are spoken or words that the character is thinking.

You can select some examples that show word bubbles and explain to the students that this is "talk written down."

Have students examine cartoon pages (funny pages) of the Sunday paper and the daily paper to get the idea of filling in words in bubble shapes. Also, the lesson to be learned here is that a story is often told with four cartoon pictures—beginning picture, two in the middle, and ending picture. Some are told in six frames or eight frames. Some cartoons have ongoing stories. Students who like to draw can investigate this technique. To help students who are having difficulty with drawing, remember to use basic shapes. Also, only a minimum of visual detail is needed in a cartoon.

Journal Bubbles

Today, while making an entry in their journal, students can tell the event in a bubble shape and draw the accompanying illustration at the bottom of the page. Words in bubble shapes often indicate what a person is thinking silently, but not saying aloud. This is done by tiny circles that go from the character's head to the large bubble shape.

Students can illustrate words that describe what they're thinking but not saying aloud. Have them put themselves in a bakery shop setting or a toy store setting for this exercise.

Bubble Cover-up

Go through a cartoon and cover up the print in the bubble shape. This can be done by cutting and gluing a piece of blank paper to fit inside the bubble. (Now you have a "wordless cartoon.") Make photocopies of this. Have students look at the action taking place and write in words that they think the character is saying. Then make comparisons with other students.

Students can begin to do this on their own, and learn to spell words, print words, and create a short story episode.

Let's Take a Story Walk

Walk through the pages of the wordless picture books, pointing out details. Encourage students to look for details. As the teacher, you will need to keep the thread of information intact as a story begins to unfold.

Before you turn to the next page, occasionally review what has gone on before to keep the story flow in motion.

From this experience, you can do the following:

- Write this wordless story together as a total group.
- Encourage more able readers to work in pairs to write the story.
- Encourage independent readers to write the story.
- Decide how illustrations will be made, because they do not have to be the same as those in the book.

The Familiar Story Cover-up

Many teachers report success by using familiar tales. Cover up the text and go through the book one page at a time. Then students write the text.

Suggested Children's Wordless Picture Storybooks

Some books to help get you started with the transition from the visual to the verbal include: *Tuesday* by David Weisner; *Tabby: A Story in Pictures* by Aliki; *Deep in the Forest* by Brinton Turkle; *The Snowman* by Raymond Briggs; and *Picnic* by Emily McCully.

One word of caution: If you select a book that has objects on a page with no text and no story line (a concept book of shapes, for example), it will not work for the development of a story because there are no connecting visual links.

Create a Four-Page Wordless Storybook

"Take three sheets of photocopy paper and fold them in half. Insert them into a folded piece of construction paper. Then staple them together along the left edge. Now you have a secure book."

The first page is the title page, with title and author information. The next four pages are for the story. The story should unfold visually, with no text. The last page is for the end credits.

These are some ideas for creating a wordless book:

- Create a seasonal book, showing a tree during the four seasons of the year.
- Create a snowy day book with the following format: Page 1—snow falling; Page 2—a snowman; Page 3—the snowman and a big, bright yellow sun above; Page 4—a melted pile of snow.
- Begin with an egg, then the cracked egg, then a broken egg, then the baby chick beside the broken egg.

- Begin with digging a hole in the ground, then seeds being put into the hole, then the seeds beginning to sprout underground and just above the ground with the sun shining up above, and finally a full grown flower.

Students can decorate the construction paper cover. Put these in the Library Center so that all students get an opportunity to read the wordless books. Later, students can add text for their wordless picture book.

Analyzing Children's Books

Work with students so that they will be able to know what is meant by the main idea of the story. "What is the story telling us? What is the theme, or message?" Also, help them identify the major characters and their names. Then they need to understand the setting, or where the story takes place. How many times does the setting shift in a particular story? In *Goldilocks and The Three Bears,* for example, most of the story is set in one place, but in some stories the setting moves from the house to the street to the park and back again. Students can learn to track a story. Also, what new vocabulary words did students learn? Are they able to use the words, or recognize them when they hear them again? Keep working with these ideas in addition to enjoying the books.

Syllables and "The Droll Teller"

"The droll teller of Cornwall was like a peddler who traveled from village to village and from house to house, and traded stories for supper. His story, called a droll, could be sung or told. Some of the characters used by this storyteller have fanciful names—such as the piskies, spriggins, knackers, and small people. Perhaps we can sprinkle a bit of magic dust this month, and use these wee folk to help us with syllables." (They also appear in "Links to Writing.")

Meet the Knackers

"In folktales, the wee elves who lived deep within the mines got the name knackers from the 'tap tap' noises they made as they worked. Although friendly, they did not like to be spied upon.

"We can enlist the aid of the knackers and tap out syllables. What better way to begin than by starting with our names." Have students use their two pointer fingers and tap out syllables (or rhythm beats) to each student's name.

Demonstrate for students that the name *Ann* has one beat, so it gets one tap. *Robert* has two beats, so it gets two taps, and so on. Tell students that another name for these taps is *syllables.*

One, Two, and Three Taps

Put a list of words on the chalkboard and have students say them, tap out the beats (syllables), and then put the appropriate number after them (1, 2, or 3).

Or, use flash cards and a pocket chart with three columns. Use words from the Instant Words Lists or other words from the word wall and place them in the appropriate pocket.

Mary Had a Little Lamb—And How Many Syllables?

Say the familiar four-line rhyme and figure out how many taps (beats, syllables) there are in this rhyme, as students tap it on their forefingers. (*Answer:* 14 one-syllable words—14 taps; 6 two-syllable words—12 taps; total words—20, total syllables 26.)

Mary	had	a	little	lamb
2	1	1	2	1

Little lamb,	little lamb
2 1	2 1

Mary	had	a	little	lamb
2	1	1	2	1

Its	fleece	was	white	as	snow.
1	1	1	1	1	1

This could then be written as follows:

One Syllable (Beat)	*Two Syllables (Beats)*
had	Mary
a	little
lamb	
its	
fleece	
was	
white	
as	
snow	

Work this out with other nursery rhymes for practice with syllables. Students can work together to make puzzles. Chant the chants, sing the songs, and tap the forefingers in time to the beat.

The Words Are Breaking Up

Just like the knackers who are tapping in the mines to break up the coal, words can break up into syllables (or rhythm beats). "The knackers tell us that there are rules we can follow when the words break up, but you can only believe them part of the time because they try to throw us off their path. (Remember, they don't like to be seen)." These are two of the rules:

- CVC. A vowel between two consonants is usually short and gets only one tap for one beat (syllable), so when writing, do not split the word. (hat, cat; run, fun; get, pet)

- VCV. A consonant between two vowels tends to go with the second vowel when the word is split, such as bro' ken, spo' ken, to' ken, and so on. (In this example the consonant letter *k* is between the two vowels *o* and *e*.)

The Spriggins Like to Clap, Snap, Clap

Spriggins are tiny, but mean. It is said that they guard the giant's buried treasures. One thing they like to do to pass the time away is clap, snap, clap to one-syllable (one-beat) words. They clap for a consonant and snap for a vowel.

The word *dog* would be clap, snap, clap. (CVC)

The word *cat* would be clap, snap, clap. (CVC)

The word *ate* would be snap, clap, snap. (VCV)

Hold up flash cards and have students clap and snap to the vowels and consonants. Make a list of words from the rimes, or word families, and have students clap to the consonants and snap fingers to the vowels. This makes a kinesthetic connection to the word.

Can You Find Words With Six Syllables?

It is said that Spriggins have six fingers on each hand. They like to just clap along to *words, a phrase, name* or *title* that has six beats (syllables). These would be long words. "Let's clap some words to see if we can get to six beats."

Note: *Hippopotamus* is a long word but only has 5 syllables. If we say *pink hippopotamus,* we get to 6 syllables. That's acceptable to a Spriggins because it's a special name. Tap out the following for starters:

teddy bear (3) *(not enough exercise for a Spriggins)*

Tyrannosaurus Rex (6) *(just right for a Spriggins)*

spaghetti and meatballs (6) *(just right for a Spriggins)*

peanut butter sandwich (6) *(just right for a Spriggins)*

strawberry lollipop (6) *(just right for a Spriggins)*

double fudge nutty ice cream (7) *(too many for a Spriggins)*

Students can try tapping out their names. Try tapping out items in the classroom, addresses, even library book titles!

Homophones

Well, the leprechauns are at it again this month. They do like to play tricks with words. A homophone is a word that sounds just like another word, but it's spelled in a different way and means something different.

Hear, Here! Concentrate on Listening

"Homophones sounds alike. We can't distinguish one from the other when we listen. So, let's listen to a list of them." Here are some examples:

bear/bare
eight/ate
one/won
two/to/too
hear/here
no/know

See, Sea! Concentrate on Looking

"Homophones, although they sound alike, do not look alike." So this time, print the above list on the chalkboard, one set of words at a time. Point out the differences to students, and have them locate the differences as well.

Write, Right! Concentrate on Meaning

"Homophones can be written in a sentence, but we need to look at the *context* in which they are written so that we can figure out which one to use. In other words, what does the word mean?"

Use the same words listed above for simple sentences on the chalkboard or on a chart. Have students select the correct homophone. These will get you started:

The _____ is in the woods.
    (bear, bare)
Sandy has _____ cookies.
      (ate, eight)
Tom _____ first prize.
    (one, won)
Tim can run _____ .
      (two, too)
Did you _____ the bell?
    (here, hear)
_____ , Ann does not want a cookie.
(Know, no)

Leprechaun Homophone Match

Write homophones on mushroom shapes, because leprechauns like to hide under them. Mix them all together. Then have students match the ones that sound alike. Use them in a sentence.

Leprechaun Homophone ABC Book

Make an ABC Book of homophones. Here are some that the elves and leprechauns found to get you started:

ant/aunt	hair/hare	one/won
be/bee	in/inn	paws/pause
close/clothes	jell/gel	road/rode
dear/deer	know/no	sea/see
ewe/you	lead/led	to/two
flour/flower	mail/male	vein/vane
great/grate	none/nun	whale/wail

(The letters q, u, x, y, and z are leprechaun challenge letters.) For more learning fun with leprechauns this month, see Links to Writing and the Reproducible Activity Pages.

Assessment

Teach Skills Based Upon Assessment

Assess students' strengths and areas that need work. Teach to those areas this month so that students continue to learn and to improve. What is their progress in the following areas:

- identifies letters after hearing them
- isolates the correct letter from a group of letters
- associates letters with sounds
- readily recognizes a number of words
- creates words from word families (rimes)
- taps out syllables with some degree of success
- notices word patterns
- "sounds out" words using clues (blends, letter clusters)
- writes letters and words
- writes a simple sentence, or story, using unconventional spelling
- identifies the ending sound in words
- understands that a letter can represent different sounds (*c, g,* and the combinations of *ph* and *gh* for *f*)
- picks out rhyming words when listening to a word group
- enjoys stories, shows pleasure, participates in discussions
- enjoys looking through books, shows pleasure
- has a "sense of story" (beginning, middle, ending)
- discusses a story after listening to one

What Are the Local, State, National Assessment Goals?

In many states students need to take proficiency tests at the end of certain grade levels. Make sure that you, as teacher, are knowledgeable regarding local, state, and national expectations.

You need to teach children these skills, so that they can meet the standards. These standards are set forth by groups of well-informed professionals who have knowledge of children and what they are capable of learning. School districts across the country are aiming for a solid *knowledge base* at benchmark grade levels.

Check your commercial curriculum materials and teacher's manuals to see where they mesh with state standards. Fill in where they do not. Be flexible, yet have a balanced program.

Assess Yourself as a Teacher

1. Lesson planning is essential for each day. Do you keep detailed plans? Can a substitute teacher come in and take over your classroom with a minimum of confusion?

2. Do you have a weekly plan sheet, or do you use a commercial weekly planner? There are some things that rarely change, so you can set up your own weekly planning sheet, photocopy it, and staple it to your commercial book. The things that remain stable—and therefore need to be in the book each week—are: *Time School Begins; Morning Procedure* (Roll call, Flag Salute, Lunch Count); *Times for Lunch, Recess, Special Classes; and Routine Procedures for End of the Day.* Some teachers print these out once, photocopy them, and cut and paste them for their planner pages.

3. In your planbook, use pencil to write your plans out for at least two days in advance as a beginning teacher, and for the week if you are an experienced teacher. Even then, there will be changes.

4. Mark your subject areas and the plans for each day. Page numbers of texts are not enough, unless you have more detailed information in another spot (which should be noted).

5. Some teachers keep detailed plans in reading books, but note in their planbook where the information can be located—and where the books are kept!

6. In the front of your planbook, keep a list of favorite games, poems, and stories for the classroom. A substitute can make good use of this information.

7. Some school districts require that planbooks be left at school and not taken home. Some other requirements are that plans must be completed for the next day (minimum) before a teacher leaves for the day.
   Find out what your district requires and expects.

8. Do you have a folder entitled "Substitute Teacher"? If not, prepare one. Write a brief letter with information about the day. Spell out procedures; for example, do you take your class to special classes and pick them up? Do you pick up students from outdoor recess? Keep up-to-date information in this folder regarding what book you are currently reading

to the class (if it is a chapter book), what games students enjoy, where your poetry books are kept, where the extra reproducible activity pages are located, and a list of reliable student-assistants.

9. When students are having group time or sharing time, you must be an involved participant. It is *not* the time for preparing a bulletin board or correcting papers; otherwise, students soon get off track and out of control. They need your constant guidance.

Assess Yourself as a Leader

The teacher is the leader in the classroom. Remember, students follow the strongest leader; if it is not the teacher, it is apt to be someone who is acting out and creating problems. So, establish yourself as a firm but fair leader.

- Is your classroom getting out of control? If so, what is your plan of action to remedy the situation? (Spring is often a difficult time for some teachers, but it is not a time to let down your guard.)

- Have you become a buddy or a parent figure, rather than a teacher? If so, what is your plan of action to remedy the situation? Go over the rules again with the students and enforce them.

- Do you have a student who is out of control and influencing the classroom in a negative manner? Plan to have that student out of the classroom while you have a class meeting with the students. Tell them they need to follow *your* cues—*not* those of the student.

- If your class comes in from outdoor recess in a state of agitation, perhaps you can arrange to change your schedule. Talk it over at your grade-level meetings with other teachers. Some teachers find that going out to the playground at a different time with a smaller group of students works wonders for a smoother afternoon. At some schools, the noon outdoor recess is a time for organized games to be played, which includes a focus on games from other countries.

Spelling

Scrabble® Spelling

Work in pairs. Students will need small squares with letters on them. You can use Scrabble® game cubes or make squares with a grid. Print letters on the squares, laminate, and cut. You will need a large assortment, so students can help make these.

Print several of the spelling words on the chalkboard. Put all of the cubes or squares in a bag. Distribute a handful to each student pair. Their challenge is to see how many spelling words they can construct. How many can they almost spell? What letters are missing? Can they spell any in Scrabble® style (vertical and horizontal)?

Collect the squares, give the bag a good shake, and redistribute the squares. How many spelling words can they spell this time?

Butterflies and Caterpillars

Draw a large outline of a butterfly on the chalkboard. Inside of it, draw a caterpillar in the shape of a spelling word (each segment will represent a letter on the first floor, or first floor and upstairs, or first floor and downstairs). This will give the caterpillar a strange configuration.

Have students write the spelling word on a sheet of scrap paper. Then call upon someone to print it in the caterpillar segments on the board. Did it turn into a butterfly? Only if it fits and is the correct word. Then, erase the shape and repeat with another word.

Dictionary Check

Have several dictionaries available for this drill game. Distribute spelling words on a half sheet of paper. The first group (A, B, C, or D) will have to write the definition from one of the dictionaries. Then someone else will have to look up the same word, but in a different dictionary and write the meaning. If the word is not listed in the dictionary (it may be a beginner's book), then the student will need to print or write that on the spelling sheet so there is a record that it has been checked.

This can be an exercise that is carried out during the morning while other reading activities are going on. Then, at the end of the morning or at the beginning of the afternoon session, you can have a "dictionary check report."

Syllable Tap

Tap out all of the spelling words and write them in order by the number of syllables.

READING LINKS TO HOLIDAYS & SPECIAL EVENTS

Reading Across America

The birthday of Dr. Seuss is celebrated on March 2. Many school districts celebrate this day with a host of special reading activities, and you can too. Here are some suggestions.

- Make a black cat and a tall striped hat for a reading badge.
- Invite someone from the community to read a storybook to the class.

- Read some of the Dr. Seuss books this month (and every month), such as, *The Cat in the Hat; Yertle the Turtle; Green Eggs and Ham; How the Grinch Stole Christmas; Oh, the Places You'll Go;* and many more.
- Make white cylinder hats with red stripes and wear for silent reading time.
- Find words that rhyme in the Dr. Seuss books.
- Dr. Seuss is a "pen name." (We talked about pen names in January, since Benjamin Franklin had a pen name.) Can students find the real name of Dr. Seuss in the newspaper or a magazine this week? (Theodore Geisel) Perhaps it's time to take on a new pen name for spring and write some rhymes or silly stories.
- Make scrambled eggs with a touch of green food coloring.
- Make scrambled eggs with a touch of minced green peppers or parsley for green color.
- On a small paper plate, paste a green construction paper shape for eggs and pink construction paper pieces for ham. Put this on a stick. Students can hold this up as they retell the story of *Green Eggs and Ham.*
- Get a used cylinder from an ice cream shop and wash it. Cover it with construction paper to make the hat that the cat wears. Turn it upside down and fill it with Dr. Seuss books for the month. (There are several book clubs that offer these books for a nominal price.)
- Invite guest readers to read aloud to the class today.
- Make "Unscrambled Words and Ham." Scramble the letters in words, unscramble them, and then have a treat of a boiled ham sandwich on rye (wry).
- Visit the Dr. Seuss celebration on the web at *http://www.Dr.Seuss.com* or *www.seussville.com* for more ideas.

It's St. Patrick's Day

"March 17 is a day for 'the wearin' of the green.' Let's all try to wear something green today, whether it's solid, stripes, or polka dots. We can list things that we eat and drink that are green." Here are some to get you started: green beans, green gumdrops, green limeade, green peppers, green cabbage, green lollipops, and, in some foreign countries, children drink green tea. Don't forget the "green eggs" from *Green Eggs and Ham.* Before the day is out, eat something green!

It's a Green Time at the Easel

"Use green background paper and only shades of green for painting. What shall we paint?" Each student can paint his or her version of a leprechaun—and everyone's is different! There is no right or wrong leprechaun because no one has ever really seen one!

"We've heard they have pointed ears, wear a pointed cap, have a long beard, and wear shoes with a turned-up toe. Even if we all paint this into our leprechaun, they will all look different. The little elves want it that way!"

It's Spring!

Celebrate the beginning of spring in March. Take your students for a spring walk and look for little tell-tale signs of spring, such as bulbs beginning to poke green shoots through the ground, trees beginning to bud or blossom, early spring flowers beginning to grow, grass beginning to turn greener, mostly all snow melted, and so on.

Encourage students to look out the window and watch the trees each day. Soon the trees will begin to come out of their dormant state and surprise us with a new green outfit! Don't miss it.

Check the birds at the feeder. "Are they changing? Can we see flocks migrating overhead?"

Making Spring Trees

Having shades of green at the easel also provides an opportunity for creating spectacular trees.

Have students make bare trees on a vertical sheet of paper with construction paper or a felt pen. Just make sure the trees have an abundance of branches.

At the easel, or at a space set up for this purpose, the children use small sponges to dab on the new green growth—but the branches still need to be seen!

Celebrate Birthdays

Each month celebrate the birthday(s) of someone in your classroom with a song. Often there is a treat (depending upon school policy). Create a birthday cake hat from a cylinder for that student to wear all day long.

Special birthdays of famous Americans this month include the physicist Albert Einstein (14th) and four presidents—Andrew Jackson (15th), James Madison (16th), Grover Cleveland (18th), John Tyler (29th).

Mark these on your classroom calendar. What books can your students find on these four presidents who once lived in the White House in Washington, D.C.?

Newspaper in Education Week

"We celebrate newspapers! They bring us news about people, things, places, and events happening in our own community and all over the world."

Create a class "front page" newspaper this month. Spread out a real newspaper and use it for the border. Cover the inside with black construction paper. Then make the columns and spaces by gluing down white strips. Students can write or draw stories about the classroom to fit into those spaces.

A smaller version can be hand-printed by students on white paper, which can be photocopied and sent home. What will the name of the paper be for your classroom?

READING LINKS TO WRITING

"Remember the droll teller of Cornwall from the Reading Section who helped us with syllables? Well, this month the leprechauns have set up shop in the Writing Center. These leprechauns are cheerful and impish and have a long beard, a pointed green hat, green clothes, long stockings as green as new spring grass, and green shoes. Let's have some fun and learn a few things at the same time." Use green paper, yellow paper, and green felt pens so that the Writing Center looks just like spring.

Leprechauns Have Fun With Homophones

"Homophones are words that sound alike, but they are not spelled alike. So we have to use our ears and our eyes."

Print two homophones on a green card. Have students write two different sentences using these words correctly. (Check the dictionary for meaning, if necessary.) It may be easier to work with a partner. (See the Reading section for this month for more work with homophones.)

Some homophones to get the sentences started are:

air	ate	eye	ball	bare
heir	eight	I	bawl	bear
cheap	flour	deer	groan	one
cheep	flower	dear	grown	won

Shamrock Shapes

"On a shamrock shape, write a note to a leprechaun and tell the little elf something that you have learned in school. Include a sentence about your favorite subject. Leprechauns appreciate a border design around the edge of a shamrock, and they like you to take your time. Never rush when you write to the wee folk." Put these shamrocks in a designated spot. Later in the week they can be read aloud and students can try to identify the author.

Long Green Blade of Grass

These wee folk are so tiny that even a blade of grass looks giant to them! Take 12″ × 18″ sheets of light green construction paper, and cut them into strips the long way. Have students use these "blades of grass" to make lists of words that belong in the same category—spring words, reading words, magic words, kitchen words, sports words, and so on. Students can compare word lists with a partner. They can select one of the categories and learn to spell three words from that group of words.

Leprechauns Enjoy Descriptive Words That Tell About Size

"The wee folk like to learn about words that describe the size of objects. Search through picture books, advertisements, and newspapers. Where else can you look? Make a giant green stocking shape. Every time you find a word that describes size, print it on a shamrock shape and tape it to the stocking." Some words to get you started are: big, huge, enormous, giant, tall, tiny, little, slim, microscopic, great.

Leprechauns Enjoy Descriptive Words That Tell About Sound

Since leprechauns never, ever make a sound, encourage students to tiptoe to the Writing Center and—carefully and quietly—print words that describe sounds. "Never shout indoors, because it frightens an elf." These sound words can also be put on a matching giant green stocking shape. Some words to get you started are: bang, buzz, cry, growl, hiss, boom, crack, crash, whisper, purr.

Now Let's Write a Tiny, Noisy Story

"Shhh! Remember, tiny folk don't like noise, they just like to know about noise. So write a story about something very tiny that makes a noise. Use the descriptive words that are hanging on the green stockings to help. You can use as many words to describe something small and as many words to describe sound as you would like." Students may like to work with a partner. Use glossy magazine pictures to help get the story started. Print the story with a green felt-tip pen and make green illustrations.

Writing Skill Pages

If you have a regular writing program for the classroom, students can practice their manuscript printing at this center. Cover a page with acetate and have students trace letters or words with water-base pens. Then erase. They can also practice with chalk and a small chalkboard and eraser. Leprechauns like light green chalk.

Unscramble Familiar Words

The leprechaun imps like to print scrambled words on the chalkboard or on a skill sheet. Make sure they are words with which students have some familiarity. Keep them simple at first with only two or three letters. Once students learn to unscramble and master the technique, try longer words. Make one scramble sheet per week for this center area. (See Reproducible Activity Pages.)

Shifting Vowels

"The leprechauns want to show us how we can take a three-letter word, with a CVC pattern, and *change the vowel only* to get another totally different word."

Have a skill sheet available that has ten or more words on the left in Column A. Then, in Column B, students can print the new word by changing the vowel. Begin, for example, with the shift from the letter *a* to the letter *i*. This will get you started:

Column A (short a)	Column B (short i)
1. f a n	1. f ___ n
2. w a g	2. w ___ g
3. l a p	3. l ___ p
4. s a t	4. s ___ t
5. t a n	5. t ___ n

READING LINKS TO MATH

Let's Use the Newspaper

Since Newspaper in Education Week is celebrated this month, use the newspaper for an abundance of math activities. Here are some general ideas.

1. Count the number of sections in your local newspaper. Record that number. Then count the number of sections in your local Sunday newspaper. Are there more or less in the Sunday paper? How do the figures differ?

2. Get out the ruler and measure the size of a page of newsprint. Is the Sunday comics section the same size? Are the "shoves" (the advertisements) the same size?

3. How are numbers used on the front page in the heading? Are the pages numbered? How are the sections classified? For example, page 2 of the front section is not the same as page 2 of the sports section, so what additional information is needed so a reader knows where to locate information? (Usually sections use letters as well as numerals, such as A–2, C–2, and so on.) Impress upon students that math is a good organizational tool.

Let's Go Shopping

Students can go shopping in the newspaper in the toy section to find something they would like. Record the item, page number, and the cost. Now try to locate a similar item for a lower price. (This can be in the same or in a different newspaper.)

Time for Groceries

Do some comparison shopping. Have one group "shop" at one store and one group "shop" at another store for the same list of items. Add them up. Are they the same at each store? Are there any "two-for-one" specials?

Depending upon the group, coupons can be used for "smart shoppers" to enable them to purchase more.

What Can I Buy for Ten Dollars?

This amount can be changed to five dollars or twenty dollars, depending upon the group and its capabilities. If they had to shop for clothing, what could they buy? Are there any specials?

Coupon Clippers

Cut out all of the coupons in the Sunday paper in the ads. Save them in a little box. Then students might be able to "use them" to help them plan a party. Check the numerals that indicate the expiration date on the coupons.

I'd Like to Shop for a Hamburger

"How much does a hamburger cost at a local fast-food restaurant with the lettuce and tomatoes and pickles and onions and mustard or ketchup? Write that down.

"Now go shopping for a hamburger in the newspaper—you will need to buy ground meat, a head of lettuce, a tomato, a jar of pickles (if they are not sold separately), an onion, and a bottle of mustard and/or ketchup. In a fast-food restaurant, a "quarter pounder" would take ¼ of a pound of meat, so if a butcher is on duty, we can purchase a quarter of a pound of meat. How do we figure that out if we know how much a pound costs?

"Add up the ¼ pound of meat and the other items. How much would it cost to shop for a burger? (How much food would we have left over?) Should we buy more meat and make more burgers? Would the price go down? There are a lot of unanswered questions, so we need to investigate this problem. Keep in mind that we need to spend money wisely, and look for the best value for the money."

Check the Entertainment Section

"Any good events coming to town? How much does a performance cost? How much would that be for a family of four?" (column addition)

We're Job Hunting

"Look through the Help Wanted ads in the Sunday paper. What's available? How much money would you be paid for your effort?"

It's a good idea to compare help wanted ads from papers in various communities to see how the job opportunities vary.

"What is the biggest ad in the paper?" (Measure it.) "What are they looking for?"

Write Want Ad for Missing Dog, Max

After reading the want ads, students can write a want ad for a missing pet. Remember, it has to be short and succinct because often newspapers charge by the word or by the line of print. Give as much information as possible, with as few words as possible.

"Pretend that the newspaper charges a flat rate of $1.00 for the first ten words, and 25 cents for each additional word. How much will your ad cost? Keep editing—avoid words like *and, to,* and other connecting words."

Numbers in Sports

Students can locate numbers on jerseys in sports photos. They can read scores and figure out how many points put the winning team over the top. How many players on a team? Each sport has its own set of numbers that are important for the game. What are they? Students can learn to locate this information in the newspaper. Boys, especially, may become interested in reading the sports page for number information. Girls also can find women's sports given space on the sports pages.

If you live in a suburban area, be sure to bring in the suburban newspaper because students may spot older siblings or people they know in the high school or elementary school sports photos. This makes the math information more real to them.

Newspapers in the Math Center

Newspapers can be used all month long in the Math Center for review, reinforcement, and enrichment. There can be three piles of activity cards from which to select. Keep changing the newspaper supply. Use the *USA Today* Weather Page on the back of section one to your advantage. It can be laminated and used as a worksheet.

Encourage students to mark right on the newspapers—from simple activities such as circling all the "below freezing" numbers (anything 32 and under) on a page, to circling every numeral "5" that they find on this page, or circling all the number words on a page.

Often students do not have an awareness of how much things cost, so the experience of planning an event or planning to buy new clothes are real eye-openers. Working with a partner is helpful for many newspaper activities.

READING LINKS TO SOCIAL STUDIES

People at Work

Make a photo montage (collage) of magazine photographs showing people at work. You will need a blank piece of heavy chart paper. Cut the pictures carefully, large and small, and start in the upper left corner and overlap each picture. Do not leave any blank background showing. This can be an ongoing project in the classroom that may take over a week to finish. The result is worth it.

What Work Do Storybook Characters Do?

"In many picture books we meet with people (or characters) who are busy at work or we see people working in the background. When we look at a picture of a city street, we see buses (bus driver), taxi (cab driver), restaurants (waiters, waitresses, chef), school building (teacher, principal, custodian, secretary, teacher aides), a fire truck (firefighter), an officer directing traffic (police officer), and so on."

When I Grow Up

Have students begin to give thought to what they want to do when they grow up. Then, one by one, have them tell of their choice. Take several sheets of photocopy paper and divide them into fourths. Have each student draw a future picture of him or herself in the chosen career as an adult. They can print their name and perhaps write or dictate a sentence. These pages can be compiled into a book and photocopied so that each student has one to take home.

Write Letters to Community Workers

Have students write letters—or write a class letter—to workers in the city or town. Ask them to tell the students about their work and to send any free promotional material they may have. "How long did they go to school? What do they like about their job?"

The student letter can be sent with a cover letter from you explaining the unit of study. This opportunity offers a good letter-writing experience for students, whereby they learn to address an envelope, put on their return address, fold the letter, seal the envelope, and place a stamp on it.

When the return letters come in, they add authenticity to the letter-writing experience. The letter in itself is enough. Sometimes people send items for the entire class to enjoy, even though requests should not be made. (In one class, for example, a dentist sent toothbrushes for everyone; an airline attendant sent wings for each student; a nurse sent her photo; a surgeon sent a surgical blue paper hat and mask.) Sometimes people graciously volunteer to come in and talk to the group, which is an added bonus.

Community Map

Secure a large piece of canvas or a plastic, fabric-backed tablecloth of one color. Students can plan out their own community using chalk. Plan the center of town or the community where the school is located. When it is sketched, use a felt-tip black pen for the streets. Then use clay, plasticene, box sculpture, and so on to create 3-D models of buildings, statues, trees, stop signs, houses, etc., that can be placed on the map.

Students can bring in toy cars, buses, and so on to travel the streets, or make them from small boxes or blocks. This area can be used for dramatic play as the students learn more about their town.

Who Keeps Our City Running While We're Sleeping?

Talk about the community workers who work through the night so that services are available to people. Make a list of these valuable people: hospital workers, all-night restaurant workers, bakers, truckers, theatre performers, road workers, electrical workers, computer workers, all-night pharmacies, all-night grocery store clerks, airline pilots, airline attendants, railroad workers, and so on.

"THE CITY NEVER SLEEPS" can be a good motto for this part of your unit of study.

All Careers Require Math Skills

It would be just about impossible to name a career in which math is not important. Help students make a list of careers and then learn how math is important to them. Make a web, put the career or job in the center, and write the way in which math is used at the end of the spokes. Students are amazed.

For example, put the career of taxi driver in the middle of the web. Then lead students to uncover the ways in which a taxi driver needs math skills. Complete the web. Here are some ideas: keeping track of distance, figuring gas mileage, reading the meter, calculating money and making change, reading maps, reading traffic signs, having a knowledge of engines and car mechanisms (science), and more.

Try other careers, such as police officer, lifeguard, sports coach, fisherman, waiter/waitress. Note the ways in which they all use math in some way. (Many use science as well.) Thus, math and science are needed in order to function in a complex society.

READING LINKS TO SCIENCE & HEALTH

Careers That Use Science

Today careers in science are open to all. Many more women are going into fields that require science and math than ever before. So girls need to recognize and be reassured that a wide variety of career opportunities are open to them. At one time, this was not the case. Have the children peruse newspapers and magazines, and cut out pictures of both men and women in a variety of careers.

Science Careers

Florist   Vet

"What careers require science?" Some include geologist, plant pathologist, meteorologist, astrophysicist, soil conservationist, medical doctor, medical technician, medical research scientist, and engineer, to name a few.

Other careers that require a working knowledge of science include nursery store operator, landscaper, florist, zookeeper, oceanographer, nurse, veterinarian, pharmacist, museum curator, and so on.

Science Areas

Science is generally divided into three branches: general science, life science, and physical science. Some general science terms that students can learn to pronounce that go with each area are included here:

General Science	*Life Science*	*Physical Science*
balance	bacteria	battery
classify	cell	circuit
degree	digestion	density
environment	flower	sound
planet	infection	vibration
smog	muscle	weight

This is a science "starter vocabulary." Students can get books from the library that deal with the three branches of science. These information picture books, written at the level of a beginner, would be valuable additions to the Science Center throughout March.

Set Up a Science Tool Shop at the Center

First, explain what the science tools are and how they are to be handled. Model this behavior. Introduce only one or two each day and then add materials gradually. Great care has to be taken at this type of center in order to instill a sense of order, cleanliness, and responsibility. This is not a play area, although scientific inventions often do come from "playing around with ideas."

Some tool suggestions include a magnifying glass, microscope, telescope, lever, scale, and slides. Students can learn to use these tools to investigate the properties of items brought in for this area, such as seasonal leaves, rocks, living things (fish, turtle, gerbil), and growing things (plants, seeds, soil, water). (**CAUTION:** Be sure the children carefully handle any living thing. Do this only under adult supervision.)

Set Up a Sink/Float Area

You will need an area set aside for this in the classroom. Use a countertop with newspapers spread over it. Then get a large plastic tub and half fill it with water.

You will need another smaller tub for such items as paper clips, cotton balls, eraser, pencil, chalk, ball of clay, safety scissors, pebble, seashell, paper, cellophane, waterproof toy counting items, magnet, shapes, and so on.

At first, students need to experiment by putting in one item at a time to see if it will sink or float.

Next, have them use a piece of paper divided in half with the word *Sink* in one column and *Float* in the other. They can draw or print the names of the items that do each. Or, the Sink/Float page can be already developed with two columns, one for "yes" (it floats) one for "no" (it sinks). Students need to locate the word or object at the left and check the appropriate square. (See the Reproducible Activity Pages.)

When everyone has had ample opportunity to do this, with two or three at a time, you will want to begin talking about the *properties* of items that sink and those that float. Keep adding and subtracting items.

This is not a play area; it is a learning area. Students need to follow rules and not play, splash, or deliberately spill or throw water. Set up all the rules and consequences beforehand, and post them. If students do not follow the rules, the consequences that you post should also be followed. That way, a student does not have to be punished, but must take the consequences for his or her actions.

Books on Science, Environment, and Health

Some good books by Aliki include *My Feet, My Hands* and *Feelings*. Also find *The Cloud Book* by Tomie dePaola; *The Sky Dog* by Brinton Durkle; *The Boy Who Didn't Believe in Spring* by Lucille Clifton, and illustrated by Brinton Turkle; *Miss Rumphius* by Barbara Cooney; and *Rain* by Peter Spier. Additional books are listed in the Bibliography.

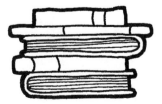

LINKS TO AUTHOR-OF-THE-MONTH

Author/Illustrator for March:
Tomie dePaola

We're in for some good reading enjoyment this month and some fine learning opportunities. First, we'll meet the award-winning *Strega Nona* (Caldecott Honor Book) and the books that ultimately make up some of that wonderful cast of characters, including Strega Nona and Big Anthony, her sidekick, who does not always pay attention to details, and consequently gets into difficulty! We go from magic lessons to art lessons and on to the colorful world of Fin Mc'Coul, the Irish giant.

The artwork of this author is typical of folk art style. Students quickly learn that there are rabbits and hearts on the pages, and they like to find them. They can learn how to draw a number of items in the style of this illustrator, and then branch out on their own.

The text and illustrations are a good match, and the books teach us some important lessons. Tomie dePaola is the author of over 100 books. He is also the illustrator who was asked to create the first cartoon for the Dr. Seuss Book Celebration, for which he drew the famous giant-sized presidents who are carved in stone at Mount Rushmore in South Dakota, each reading a book. We're off on a wonderful reading adventure this month. Hang on to your hats, and *let's read!*

Strega Nona (New York: Scholastic, 1975) In a small town in Calabria, Italy, lives an old lady who everyone calls Strega Nona, which means "grandma witch." Actually, she does have the magic touch and the townspeople seek her advice. She puts up a notice in the center of the town for help, and Big Anthony, who never pays attention, goes to see her. He's hired, with one stipulation—he must not touch the magic pasta pot. Well, the temptation is too great. He hears the chant which sets the pot boiling and making spaghetti, but he doesn't know how to turn off the magic. While Strega Nona is away, he tries it out and the whole town gets flooded with spaghetti! When Strega Nona returns, she knows immediately what has happened. Does the punishment fit the crime? Read and see.

Activities to Accompany *Strega Nona*

1. Read and enjoy the story. Go back through the book and enjoy the folk art animals—the dove, the peacock, the rabbit. These can be found in all of this author's books. Have students draw their own dove, peacock, and rabbit using basic shapes.

2. This would be a good story to act out. Have students dramatize it, using a big pot, an apron for Strega Nona, a hat for Big Anthony, yarn for spaghetti,

and a huge fork. Those not directly involved in the starring roles can be the townspeople and the chorus that chants the magic words.

3. "We don't see the notice that Strega Nona posted in the town square, so let's create one that would resemble the one she made. What will it say? Will it be decorative or plain? Remember, she's advertising for someone to help her with the house and garden."

4. This calls for a good discussion about showing loyalty and doing what is expected. "Big Anthony is disloyal to Strega Nona, for he did exactly what she told him *not* to do. She says 'the punishment must fit the crime.' What do you think this means?" (In this case, he made the spaghetti, so he must eat it.) "We can see from Big Anthony's great big tummy that he doesn't look too comfortable!"

5. "We can learn two Italian words from this story. Big Anthony says 'grazie' (thank you) and 'si' (yes). Let's use these in the classroom after the story."

6. Would students answer the ad in the town square? Would it be exciting to work for Strega Nona? (Think of all the cures that are mentioned in the beginning of the book that Big Anthony might learn how to do.)

7. Have students bring in a variety of dry pastas. Categorize them by shape, size, color. Use them as counters in the Math Center.

Big Anthony and the Magic Ring (New York: Harcourt Brace, 1979) Big Anthony is working for Strega Nona and has a case of Spring Fever. She suggests that it would perk him up to go to the village dance that evening. On second thought, she gets out her magic ring, turns herself into a beautiful maiden, and decides to go too. Big Anthony, of course, watches this transformation and can't wait to see if it will work for him. Soon thereafter, Strega Nona goes away on an overnight visit and he gets his chance to say some magic words over the ring and to become a handsome man. This isn't exactly what he had in mind after all, and Strega Nona has something else in mind for him; she's noticed Bambolona, the baker's daughter, who has her mind on Big Anthony.

Activities to Accompany *Big Anthony and the Magic Ring*

1. Read and enjoy the story. For students, it's like meeting old friends. Stroll through the pages, like one would stroll through a town. "Where are the townspeople? Look for the animals. Do we once again see the rabbit, peacock, birds, cats?" Students can work with basic shapes to make those animals and more.

2. We get a quick glimpse at the inside of Strega Nona's house. Have students draw another room in her house as they imagine it to be. Share drawings with classmates.

3. Notice the roof shapes on the houses. Learn to draw the round-shaped roof tiles as they appear in the story. Then have students put their own stylized lines inside these repeated shapes. They can practice making roof tile shapes with triangles, rectangles, squares, and so on.

4. Locate Italy on the map, since this is where Strega Nona and Big Anthony live.

5. Have students write the next chapter in Big Anthony's life. Do they think Bambolona will win him in the end, or will there be a different ending to this story? The author has left the door wide open for the reader's imagination to take over. Think of the ending as a "story starter."

Strega Nona's Magic Lessons (New York: Harcourt Brace, 1982) We meet Bambolona, the baker's daughter, who is definitely overworked, since she's the only one doing anything in her father's bakery. He is unsympathetic and tells her to get up earlier, even though she's the first one up and the last to go to sleep each day in the village. Angry, she leaves and seeks out Strega Nona, telling her a tale of woe. Sympathetic, Strega Nona takes Bambolona in and promises to teach her magic. Big Anthony overhears this and wants to learn, too, but Strega Nona says "no." Now he's angry and determined to learn magic—and learns another lesson in the process!

Activities to Accompany *Strega Nona's Magic Lessons*

1. Read and enjoy the book. Then create a book of magic lessons, or at least what students think would be in the book. "What are the chants? Remember, we don't fool with magic, according to Strega Nona."

2. This would be a good story for dramatic play. Students can improvise with their props.

3. Introduce the word "alert." "How alert is Big Anthony to the frog at the ending? What is the illustrator telling the audience that Big Anthony does not know?" (Strega Nona can be seen in the background.)

4. Notice the silhouette illustration of Big Anthony stealing into Strega Nona's house to read the magic book. (At least Big Anthony is interested in reading.) The page is done in black, dark blue, white, and a touch of blue/gray for the moon. Students can use these same colors at the easel, or with construction paper, for some dramatic night-time pictures of their own.

5. *Magic measuring box.* Secure a relatively deep box and put some measuring spoons, measuring cups, several bowls, some big wooden spoons, and dry measure (sand, rice, lentils) inside. This can be relatively self-contained; spills will be caught inside the box, so clean-up is minimal.

   Students can gain practice with *dry* measure by reading a recipe, reading the symbols on the measuring spoons or cups, and working with math terms. This can be a magic recipe measuring box; measuring and mixing the same ingredient doesn't matter when it comes to Strega Nona, but the order is important. The following is a sample recipe card:

   Put into small bowl in this order:

   1 teaspoon (sand)

   ¼ teaspoon _____

   ½ teaspoon _____

½ tablespoon _____

¼ tablespoon _____

1 tablespoon _____

Mix and count to 25.

Put into large bowl in this order:

⅓ cup _____

¼ cup _____

½ cup _____

1 cup _____

Mix slowly to the right 6 times, and then to the left 10 times.

Pour the small container of _____ into the large container.

Mix to the right 20 times, counting by one's.

Mix to the left 20 times, counting by two's.

Time for 3 minutes. Pour all ingredients back together.

The recipe card can be altered in any way to meet the needs of the classroom. The spaces have been left blank so that you can insert the word of whatever it is that is being measured. Students can use hour-glass timers, or other times, or just use the clock on the wall to wait out the one, two, or three minutes. Perhaps they want to use one of Strega Nona's chants while mixing. They can also draw a small picture of what this will look like when Strega Nona transforms it into a giant cake or bread or something else.

6. Discussion question: "Why will Bambolona make a good strega, whereas Anthony would not?" (A strega is a female; he also does not pay attention.)

7. Discussion question: "Has Big Anthony finally learned his lesson?" Then, either independently or with a buddy, students write his next adventure.

(retold) *Fin M'Coul, The Giant of Knockmany Hill* **(New York: Holiday House, 1981)** The Fin M'Coul giant stories have been handed down from generation to generation. This Irish giant is best known for the Giant's Causeway, the highway he built between Ireland and Scotland. Another giant, Cucullin, is out to get Fin—and Fin is scared. He runs home to his beautiful wife, Oonagh, who thinks up a way to help him. Children will enjoy this hilarious tale about a giant who is done in by another, right before their very eyes.

Activities to Accompany *Fin M'Coul, The Giant of Knockmany Hill*

1. Read and enjoy the story. Then go back over the book and enjoy the borders. These borders were inspired by early Irish jewelry and metalwork, according to the information in the back of the book.

2. Cucullin, the strongest giant in Ireland, carries a flattened thunderbolt in his pocket. Have students locate the illustration of this. The giant carries

this to show just how strong he is. Can students imagine something else that he might carry to show off his strength?

3. Often in fairy tales and folktales, there is the mention of three's. "Where do we find 'three of something' in this story?" (Oonagh made three braids and wore them in three different places on her body so that nothing she did could fail.) Also have students search for the three wee folk shown in many of the illustrations. Talk about the magic of three that we've met in other stories. (Often it's the third try when someone succeeds; the three little pigs; the three billy goats; and so on.)

4. This story lends itself well to dramatic play. Students enjoy acting out the story. They also enjoy retelling it with flannelboard characters that they draw, or with stick puppets that they create.

5. Locate Ireland on the map or globe. Explain that this is the setting for the giant story. "What ocean would we have to cross to get there?"

***Pancakes for Breakfast* (New York: Harcourt Brace, 1978)** This wordless picture book presents us with an opportunity to create text for the story. Print only appears on two pages—one is the pancake recipe, and the other is a motto hanging on the wall at the end of the story. In this tale, we meet a woman who is determined to make pancakes in spite of the fact that she does not have her ingredients ready and has a dog and a cat only too willing to eat up the supplies that she procures along the way.

Activities to Accompany *Pancakes for Breakfast*

1. "Since this is a wordless picture book, we have to study each page carefully to determine what is going on as the story unfolds." Go through the book repeatedly.

2. This gives the students an opportunity to write text for the book. "How do we do this? We can write about what the character is saying, what the character is thinking, what the character is doing. Write about the setting, describe the setting. Think in terms of beginning, middle events, and ending. We have the option of using 'conversation bubbles' or 'thinking bubbles' and can then include the animals and what's going through their minds." The outcome will depend upon your particular group.

3. Time to make pancakes! Try the recipe in the book, only use an electric frypan rather than a griddle. "Let's take a lesson from the story and have all of our ingredients ready to go before we start mixing!"

4. "In real life in the kitchen, it pays to have everything ready before we begin mixing and stirring. Was this character prepared? In what other ways do we need to think about being prepared before we start doing a task?"

The amusing part of the story is that in the process of making the pancakes, she gets the ingredients as they appear in the recipe. For example, it calls for milk and it is then that she realizes that she needs to milk the cow.

So, discuss with students the idea of being prepared—having materials ready—so that cooking goes smoothly.

5. "If at first you don't succeed, try, try, again." This is the motto hanging on the wall. One new vocabulary word that describes that attitude is *persistent*. It means not giving up, of trying again and again, and then knowing when to give up if it's necessary. This is a good discussion topic for students.

Helga's Dowry, A Troll Love Story (New York: Harcourt Brace, 1977) Helga, a beautiful troll, wants to accept the marriage proposal of Lars, but alas she has no dowry. When Lars goes to a wise man to ask for advice, the man suggests that Lars marry his daughter, Plain Inge, who already has a dowry. Lars agrees and Helga is devastated, but finally decides to go out into the world to seek her fortune so that she can bring it back and marry Lars after all. In the process, she learns a good lesson.

Activities to Accompany *Helga's Dowry, A Troll Love Story*

1. Read and enjoy the story. "Look for the familiar folk art that we find in this author/illustrator's work, along with the stylized heart shape on Helga's house. Draw some of the simple shapes—such as the tree branches with little blossoms sticking out and the face of the cow on the second page. Let's go back to our basic shapes."

2. "Helga burst into tears and caused a thunderstorm. Has anyone been so disappointed that they burst into tears?" This may be a moment to share.

3. "Why should I sit here and pout?" is what Helga said after her disappointment. Then she sprang into action. That might be a good motto for us to adopt in the classroom. Give things another try—it could be spelling or math or reading. Pouting doesn't get the job done, as Helga shows us.

4. "Just prior to the end, a troll pops up next to Helga and says he already loves her. Where did he come from? Let's go back through the book and see if we can locate him." (He is in a bush as she heads down a hill with her laundry cart; he's behind the laundry cart; he's watching her in the beauty shop; he sees her walking down the mountain to the rich man's home; and he shows up in the forest of trees. See if students can spot him—he's been watching all along!)

5. "I wouldn't marry you if you were the last Troll on earth," bellows Helga to Lars. Does he deserve this treatment? Why? Does he get what he deserves in the end? Does Helga?

6. Note the folk art borders around each page. They are the same for each page in the book. Students can renew their interest in borders, especially if they have one design that they can use repeatedly.

7. At the end is a family portrait in a frame. Have students draw an oval shape on paper and cut it out. Then encourage students to draw their family in the oval as if the family were all dressed up and having their photograph taken. Decorate the oval frame, similar to the one in the story.

8. "Compare Helga and Strega Nona. Do they have characteristics in common? How are they alike and/or different? Which one would you prefer to have for a friend?"

And Many More!

There are many more books by Tomie dePaola to read and enjoy. In *Strega Nona Meets Her Match,* a strega with more up-to-date methods tries to take over with her fancy machines and new ways. She hires Big Anthony, who makes the business a disaster and saves the day for Strega Nona.

Read and enjoy *The Art Lesson,* which is taken from a true-life experience of the illustrator who always liked to draw but didn't like to copy. Some illustrators have told us that it is all right to copy art because it trains the eye. This might be an experiment worth trying—some need help, some do not. But, we definitely don't want to copy to the point where every person's results look exactly the same! That's not art. (The sample given in the book is the pilgrim drawing.)

The Popcorn Book gives us much information about popcorn that is factual, along with an amusing story. Other good stories include *Little Grunt and the Big Egg, A Prehistoric Fairy Tale; Tony's Bread; Tomie dePaola's Favorite Nursery Tales; Nana Upstairs & Nana Downstairs* (adjustment to death); *Jamie O'Rourke and the Big Potato*—and others too numerous to mention. Enjoy your time spent with this author, for it adds a lot of humor to the classroom setting.

Note: See the Reading focus for March for additional suggestions for incorporating Strega Nona and Big Anthony into the classroom instructional setting. Your students can make huge stuffed pasta people and read to them; and students can correct Big Anthony's activity pages (remember, he doesn't listen, so he makes mistakes). Maybe the lovable character of Strega Nona will inject a bit of magic into the learning environment—and she always has good advice!

REPRODUCIBLE ACTIVITY PAGES

© DCW99

Name _____

LEPRECHAUN WORD SCRAMBLE

Lucy Leprechaun got into the grocery store and scrambled all the letters on the healthy food signs. Please help unscramble them before the store opens. Thank you!

Key

grapes	apples
carrots	nuts
raisens	bananas

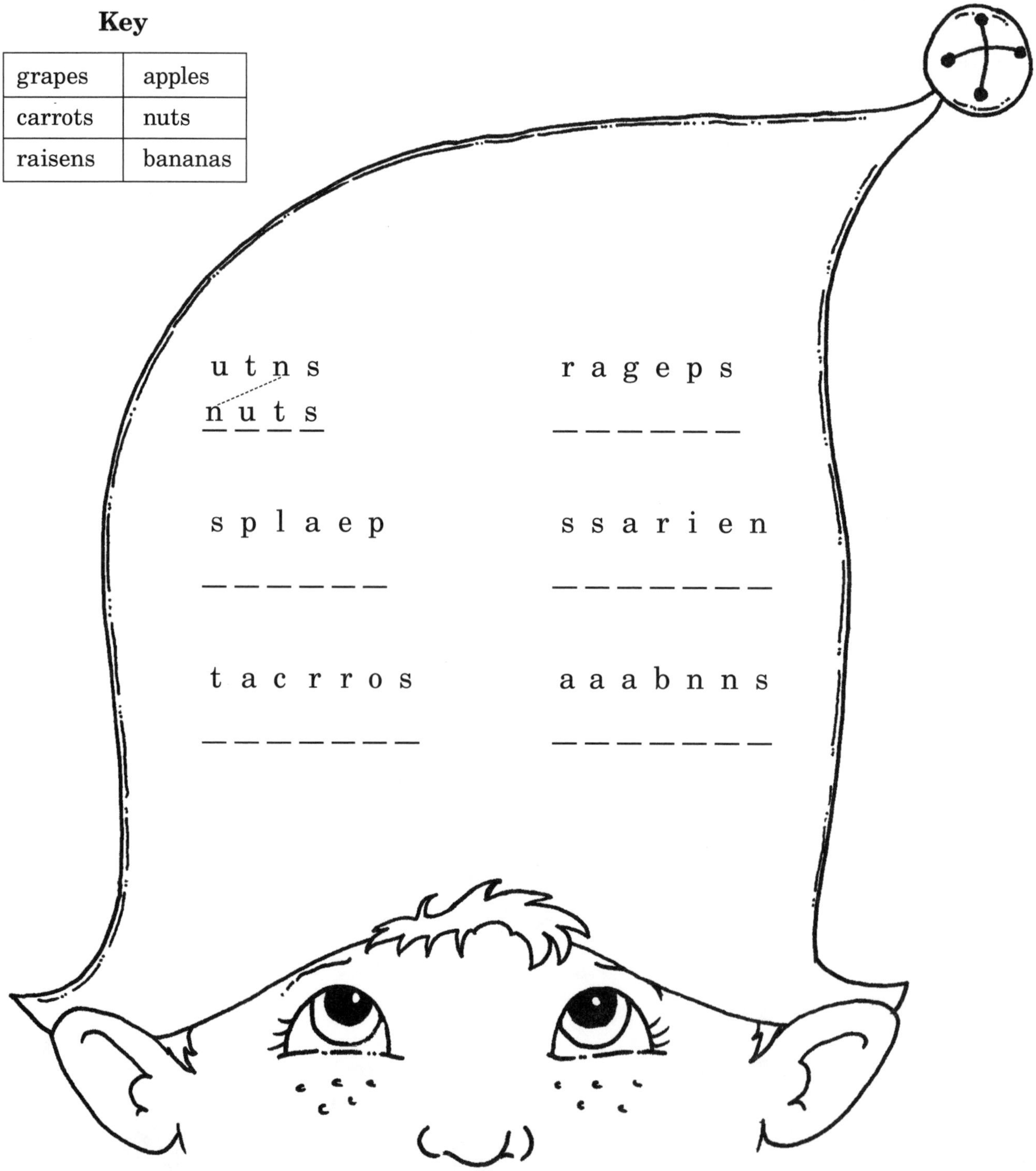

u t n s
n u t s

r a g e p s
_ _ _ _ _ _

s p l a e p
_ _ _ _ _ _

s s a r i e n
_ _ _ _ _ _

t a c r r o s
_ _ _ _ _ _

a a a b n n s
_ _ _ _ _ _

© 2000 by The Center for Applied Research in Education

BIG ANTHONY WRITES A LETTER

Big Anthony went on a trip. He took some of Strega Nona's writing paper with him to write a letter. Here it is. We can see that Big Anthony has not been paying attention to the reading road signs (punctuation marks). Circle the reading road signs that he missed and correct them. Thank you!

Dear Strega Nona ;

Today I went to town. The sun was hot? I saw a cow, and a goat! in the road, I saw a pig . and a duck . and a frog?   The frog can jump "up" high ,   It scared me and then I jumped too ,   I had a good day ?

I am a little bit homesick ?   Do you miss me !   I miss you"   I miss the rabbit too : and I miss your spaghetti.   I will see you tomorrow,   Love "   Big Anthony

© 2000 by The Center for Applied Research in Education

He missed 17.

He needs to practice!

© 2000 by The Center for Applied Research in Education

Name _____

TELEPHONE FOR A HOMOPHONE

These elves have a Homophone Hot Line. They need to link up the homophones listed below. You can help! Color each matching homophone bubble with the same color.

sea

won

road

deer

to

know

two

dear

see

no

rode

one

use two homophones in a sentence.

© 2000 by The Center for Applied Research in Education

Name _____

WANT AD FOR
MISSING STORY DOG

When you write an ad for a missing dog, you must give descriptions. Fill in the information below. When you are finished, do you know what you have? The outline of a character for a story! So, write the ad and then the story.

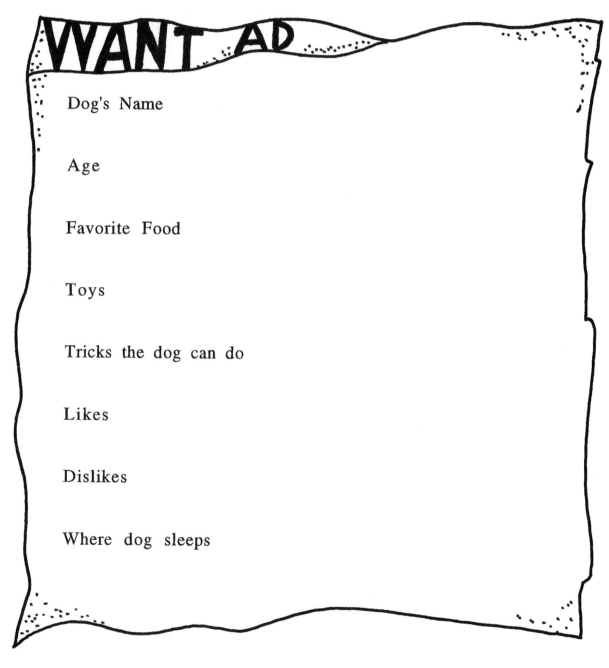

WANT AD

Dog's Name

Age

Favorite Food

Toys

Tricks the dog can do

Likes

Dislikes

Where dog sleeps

Okay, now you have a dog character. Use all of this information for a dog story. Will it be funny or serious? Write on the back of this page. Share it in class.

Name _____

A TULIP BULB BUBBLE STORY

Color the pictures. Then cut carefully on the lines. Paste the four pictures on a long strip and write words or "talk" in the bubbles to make a story.

© 2000 by The Center for Applied Research in Education

Name _____

TIGER IS HUNTING FOR "T" TODAY

Tricky Tara Tiger
     Caught a "t" by the toe.
Draw and color
     four "t" things,
And she will let it go!

© 2000 by The Center for Applied Research in Education

Name _____

WILL IT SINK? WILL IT FLOAT?

use an X.

ITEM	PREDICTION		OUTCOME	
	sink	float	sink	float

What did you learn from this?

© 2000 by The Center for Applied Research in Education

SPRINGTIME PICTURE WRITING

© 2000 by The Center for Applied Research in Education

COOKING UP A STORY POT

Color Strega Nona, Big Anthony AND the pot. Cut the slits in the pot. Insert the story strips into the pot, and it will look like it's full!

I ♡ Pasta

S.N.

How many stories can you re-tell?

© 2000 by The Center for Applied Research in Education

COOKING UP A STORY POT

© 2000 by The Center for Applied Research in Education

1. Print the story titles of books on the spaghetti strips.

2. Cut the strips.

3. Insert the strips into the story pot.

4. Glue strips to back of pot.

HAVE A TOMIE DEPAOLA
STORYTELLING FESTIVAL!

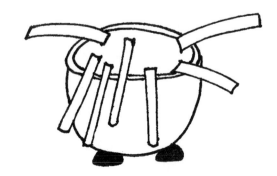

April

Better Bunny Gardens: How to do Fabulous Eggs!

© Deborah C. Wright '99

© DCW '99

CHILDREN'S PICTURE BOOKS

FOR THE MONTH OF
APRIL

Ada, Alma Flor. (retold). *Mediopollito/Half-Chicken.* **Illustrated by Kim Howard (New York: Doubleday, 1995)** This Mexican tale, told in Spanish and English, gives the reader the reason why there is a chicken atop the weather vane.

Bottner, Barbara. *Nana Hannah's Piano.* **Illustrated by Diana Cain Blethenthal (New York: GP Putnam's Sons, 1996)** It's spring and Sonny wants to practice baseball, but his mother wants him to practice the piano. When Sonny complains to Grandmother Hannah, who loves baseball and music, she replies, "Sonny, you'll be great at whatever you do." One day she breaks her ankle and Sonny visits to cheer her up—and she just happens to have a piano.

Kellogg, Steven. (retold and illustrated). *The Three Little Pigs* **(New York: Morrow Jr. Books, 1997)** In this story the pigs run a waffle business, and all is well until the wolf shows up at the door. Then the mayhem begins as the wolf tries to catch the pigs.

Pallotta, Jerry. *The FROG Alphabet Book . . . and Other Awesome Amphibians.* **Illustrated by Ralph Masiello (Watertown, MA: Charlesbridge Publishing, 1990)** From A to Z, this book introduces the reader to frogs, toads, salamanders, newts, and caecilians. Each colorful page depicts a realistic view of the creature and the text is filled with interesting information.

Parish, Peggy. *Play Ball, Amelia Bedelia.* **Illustrated by Wallace Tripp (New York: Harper, 1972)** Amelia Bedelia is taking the all-American game of baseball literally! What does it mean when someone is "stealing a base"? (Children find this book very amusing.)

Rylant, Cynthia. *The Relatives Came.* **Illustrated by Stephen Gammell (New York: Bradbury, 1985)** Well, it's that time of year for the relatives to come and spend the weekend. In this heartwarming book, they come in a jalopy and sleep all over the house and laugh and talk and eat and have a wonderful time—and then they leave. (The book has a nice "family reunion" feel to it.)

Stevens, Janet. (adapted and illustrated). *Tops and Bottoms* **(New York: Harcourt Brace, 1995)** Bear has money and land, but he is so lazy! On the other hand, Hare has no money, no land, and a hungry family. So, Mr. and Mrs. Hare cook up a plan to share the wealth. They'll work the land and Bear gets to choose whether he wants what grows on the top or what grows on the bottom—that's when the fun begins! There are a number of lessons to be learned!

VanLaan, Nancy. *Possum Come a-Knockin!* **Illustrated by George Booth (New York: Alfred Knopf, 1990)** A rhythmic knee-slapping, read-aloud down-home, rhyming tale about a possum come a-knockin' at the old front door of a busy household. (Read it over and over again.)

Walton, Rick. *So Many Bunnies, A Bedtime ABC and Counting Book.* **Illustrations by Paige Miglio (New York: Lothrop, Lee & Shepard, 1998)** A delightful tale in rhyme about Mother Rabbit who lived in a shoe and had so many children, but she knew what to do. The bedtime tale introduces the children by number and name. For example, "1 was named Abel. He slept on the table," and "2 was named Blair. She slept in a chair." The warmth and coziness of the home come through in the soft, pastel art work, especially on the last page when it's time for Mother Rabbit to go to bed, and all the bunnies join her.

Yaccarino, Dan. *Zoom! Zoom! Zoom! I'm Off to the Moon!* **(New York: Scholastic Press, 1997)** A little boy steps out his front door and right into a rocket for a trip into outer space. From the countdown to the splashdown, you land on the moon, float through space, ride in a lunar rover, avoid the asteroids, and return safely home. Sparse rhyming text interspersed with the space enables the reader to experience the adventure and to gain an amazing amount of information.

 # APRIL

APRIL GREETINGS! We're back from Spring vacation, and once again a sense of quiet has descended upon the classroom—but not for too long. The excitement of the new season is in the air, and with it all of the changes that come into the lives of young children. However, one thing needs to be made clear. There is still much ground to cover from now until the end of the school year, and we have a lot of work left to do.

During this season, we can see the physical growth spurt in some children. It is amazing also to find that during this time of year, some students show a growth spurt in learning. Suddenly reading is not such a mystery, suddenly the words begin to look more familiar, and suddenly students are beginning to read or to read more fluently. But, is it suddenly? No, it's what we've been working toward and practicing all this year. That is what is beginning to show—*the effort*. Reading doesn't happen overnight; it takes time, and we're not there yet. Who are students depending upon? You, the classroom teacher, so keep it up!

April's Focus on Reading. (1) April Vowel Review with New Stories; (2) The "KN" Situation; (3) Abbreviations; (4) Contractions; (5) Capital Letters; and (6) Spelling.

April Vowel Review With New Stories

Make New Book Markers

Take the oaktag reading strips out of the books you've been working with for reading and have students replace them with strips that are new and stiff. You may want to give them a set for use at their desks with other books that they are reading or browsing through. A set of strips at the Library Center is also a good idea.

Show students again how to place the strip under the line of print that they are reading from left to right. Then move the "marker" down to the next line, and so on. This helps them to focus upon one line at a time, not upon a whole page of print. For students having difficulty, this is less distracting.

Guess What? "The Long and Short of It" Is That We've Got Twins . . . A, E, I, O, U

The vowels are twins in one sense of the word. When they are on their own and not influenced by other letters, vowels have two sounds—a long sound and a short sound. They are not "identical" twins in terms of sounds, but they do look alike. This can be confusing. So students have to be introduced to the long and short sounds repeatedly, and they need lots of practice in different ways. Fanciful stories and chants will be helpful in introducing, once again, the dual sounds.

The following stories add a bit of April foolishness to this month's learning. Each letter has been given an animal or item name for the long and short sounds, and each comes with a personality. Remember that children do learn from stories, songs, and commercials on television, so let's put that energy to work with the vowels. The following ten characters are in the vowel stories.

	Long	*Short*
A	ape	alligator
E	eagle	elephant
I	icicle	igloo
O	ogre	octopus
U	unicorn	umbrella bird

Meeting the Vowels Through Make-believe Stories

Read the following stories aloud, one per day, and reinforce the letter–sound relationship. Stories can be read repeatedly, or recorded on a cassette tape so that children can listen to the stories over again and learn them by heart. Also, students can learn the chants through repetition. Having a stick puppet of an ape and an alligator, one in each hand, would be helpful once they learn the chant. (See Reproducible Activity Pages for five sets of stick puppets.)

"The Ape and the Alligator" (Long A, Short A)

Once upon a time, Mother Ape gave birth to a little baby ape with curly hair and big brown eyes. The baby was the deep honey color of an acorn, so that's what Mother Ape named her—Acorn.

One day, the mother and baby were down by the river and heard a crackling sound. It was coming from a large egg! Mother Ape and Acorn Ape silently watched as a baby alligator slowly poked his head out of the egg. Then he zigzagged to the edge of the water and walked right in. The alligator swam around for a long time. Finally, he came back on land and settled down. He waited and waited until it was almost dark.

"Well," thought Mother Ape, "if I leave the baby alligator there, a hungry bird will get him." So, she picked the baby up under her arm and took him home. Now she had two babies to care for.

Acorn Ape and the alligator got along well together. Acorn could climb trees and swing from the branches. She would call from above to the alligator as he swam in the river. Although he still couldn't say the long word "alligator," the baby alligator kept practicing and could get as far as "Al–Al–Alli."

"Can I stay with you forever?" asked the happy alligator one evening at dinner.

"Yes, indeed," said the kind Mother Ape. "We can be a family, but now we have to give you a name."

"I already have one," grinned the alligator, snapping his jaws and showing his milky white teeth. "Call me . . . Alli."

Ape and Alligator Chant

Get a rhythm going and make up body motions. Use the stick puppets to aid with rhythm and movement:

Acorn jumps on Alli's back.	*(jump)*
She gives a signal,	
His tail gives a whack!	*(slap hip)*
They float down the river	
But they always come back.	
Yes, that's how the story goes,	*(sway back*
it does.	*and forth)*
Hey!	
That's how the story goes.	
With an "A" and an "Ah"	*(hands on*
and an "A," "Ah, ah!"	*hips; first*
With an "A" and an "Ah"	*kick one*
and an "A," "Ah, ah!"	*foot, then the other)*
A—Ape! Ah—Alligator! RAH!	*(hands overhead)*

Ape and Alligator Sounds

Be sure to point out to the children that the letter *A* has a long sound as in *ape* and a short sound as in *alligator*. The children will readily learn the chant, so when reading text and trying to sound out unfamiliar words, they can try the ape and alligator sounds to help them.

Make a chart with two columns. Print "ape" along the top of one and "alligator" along the top of the second one. Start making a list of words, or have students cut out photographs from magazines and paste them in the appropriate column.

"The Eagle and the Elephant" (Long E, Short E)

One day long ago, a baby eagle fell out of her nest in the middle of the forest. Down, down, down she fell and landed in the curve of a baby elephant's trunk.

Now the eagle was dazed and tried to get back up, but because she had landed in a warm place, she curled up and went to sleep. The baby elephant, not wishing to disturb the bird, stood very still and waited.

When Mrs. Elephant called out "Ellie! Ellie!" to her baby, Ellie didn't come to her. Wondering what was keeping her, Mrs. Elephant went through the bushes and came upon the sight of Ellie rocking a baby eagle back and forth, back and forth in her trunk cradle. The sight was elegant.

Just then, Mrs. Eagle came soaring down from above looking for baby Edith who had fallen from her nest. Ellie told them how the bird fell from out

---

"The Eagle and the Elephant" (Long E, Short E) *(Continued)*

Edith woke up, fluttered her wings, flew about, and landed right back in the curve of the trunk.

"Time to go back to the nest," Mother Eagle said, "but you can come back tomorrow and visit your new friend who saved you from bumping your head on the ground."

To this day, Ellie Elephant and Edith Eagle are best friends. The eagle can fly ahead and tell the elephant where there is water. When they arrive at the water hole, Edith perches on top of Ellie's head and gets a cool spray of bath water.

Eagle and Elephant Chant

Edith Eagle, fell from the sky,	*(fingers make motions like wavy rain)*
landed close to an elephant's eye.	*(point to eye)*
She curled up,	
didn't let out a peep	*(fold arms)*
Ellie rocked her 'til	*(rock folded arms)*
she went to sleep.	
Yes, that's how the story goes,	*(sway to rhythm)*
it does.	
Hey!	
That's how the story goes!	
With an "E" and an "Eh"	*(hands on hips; kick
and an "E," " Eh, eh!"	one foot, then the other)*
With an "E" and an "Eh"	
and an "E," "Eh, eh!"	
E—Eagle! Eh—Elephant! RAH!	*(hands overhead)*

"Iris Icicle and the Igloos" (Long I, Short I)

Now as the story goes, every February when it was still cold and blustery, Iris Icicle packed up her Igloo Repair Bicycle and headed for the far north country to make igloo repairs. The covered bicycle was loaded with icicles, cakes of ice, snowballs, shovels, and snowmen workers.

By the time they got over the icy roads and slippery trails, some of the igloos were already starting to melt.

"What do you need?" called Iris as she approached each igloo. One needed a new icicle leg for a table; one needed a snowball to patch a leaky roof; and one needed a new cake of ice that a snowman carved into a fancy bed. This went on for days.

"Iris Icicle and the Igloos" (Long I, Short I) *(Continued)*

One day, a wood cutter was in the north country selling wood to make houses. "Wood is better than ice," said Ignatz the Wood Cutter. "Wood doesn't melt when the weather turns warm." Some igloos were convinced and turned themselves in for a fancy new wooden house. They shouted, "Go home on your bicycle, Iris Icicle! Ignatz has a power plow! You're out of date! He's our man now!"

And so, Iris Icicle was finished! She felt flushed. She even began to melt a little—and so did the snowmen. But, wait! Why were they melting?

"Look ahead," called a snowman. "Fire! Fire! One of the wooden houses is blazing."

Iris Icicle turned around with her bicycle, went to the scene, and poured ice water on the fire until all the sizzle and snap were gone out of it.

"Oh, Iris! We're sorry!" said the igloo captain. "We need your icy icicles. Please come back next year."

A wise old igloo took Ignatz the Wood Cutter aside and said, "Up here in igloo country, the igloos may melt but we don't catch on fire."

To this day, when you go very, very far north in the winter, you can still catch sight of Iris Icicle on her bicycle.

Iris Icicle and Igloo Chant

Iris Icicle
    took her bicycle
and went to a land
    far away.
	*(arms in front
	hanging on bars;
	circle motions with
	legs)*

She and her team
    patched every seam
on igloos
    night and day.
	(dabbing motions)

They poured icy water
    through a worn-out hose
and Ignatz the Wood Cutter
    nearly froze.
	(pretend to hold hose)

Yes, that's how the story goes, it does. Hey! That's how the story goes!	*(move to rhythm)*

With an"I" and an "Ih"
    and an "I," "Ih, Ih."
With an "I" and an "Ih"
    and an "I," "Ih, Ih!"
	*(hands on hips; kick)
	one foot, then the other)*

I—Iris! Ih—Igloo! YAHOO!	*(hands overhead)*

"The Ogre and the Octopus" (Long O, Short O)

Ogre O'Dell was a big bully. At school, everyone was afraid of her because she wanted to be first. If she knocked the others down, she never noticed. If she stepped on them, it didn't bother her. After all, Ogre O'Dell was a bully.

One day the teacher told the ogres they were going on a field trip to the ocean. There, they would ride in a big boat and go whale watching. They were all excited, except for Ogre O'Dell. You see, Ogre O'Dell was afraid of the water, but she would never admit it.

On the day of the trip, the ogres all climbed aboard and put on their lifejackets. Ogre O'Dell wouldn't put hers on and she shouted, "Lifejackets are for sissies!" She was secretly hoping they wouldn't let her aboard without a lifejacket, so she could stay on dry land. But the captain, who was a giant ogre, yelled in a loud voice that shook the ship, "Put it on!"—and so she did.

Out on the water they watched and waited, but saw no whales. "There's one!" shouted the bully ogre, but it was only a fish. "There's one!" she shouted again, but it was only some seaweed. "There's one!" she shouted, and fell overboard but no one noticed.

Ogre O'Dell was in the water in the arms of a giant octopus named Ollie. "Why are you so mean?" asked the octopus. Ogre O'Dell was too scared to answer. She shook with fright. For the first time she was afraid. So this is how it felt to be scared—how awful! So this is how she made others feel—how terrible!

"Pl–pl–please, let me go," she cried. "I won't be a bully ogre any more."

"You must say 'I promise' three times." So Ogre O'Dell said, "I promise, I promise, I promise."

Just then, the teacher shook Ogre O'Dell by the shoulder. "You fell asleep and missed the whale," she said.

After that day, Ogre O'Dell acted differently. She began to say "please" and she even learned to say "thank you."

Soon the other ogres weren't afraid of her anymore and invited her to play. She learned that it's much more fun to be a friend than a bully. To this day, she's never been a bully again!

Ogre and Octopus Chant

Ogre O'Dell got a
  brand new start.
Thanks to Ollie Octopus,
  she's got a new heart.

*(make heart shape
with hands)*

Oh! she's friendly.
  Oh! she's nice.
Oh! she's sugar
  and a pinch of spice.

(pinch fingers)

Ollie the octopus
    is very glad.
He knows that ogre
    didn't want to be bad.

(smile)

Yes, that's how the story goes,
it does.
Hey!
That's how the story goes!

*(move shoulders back
    and forth)*

With an "O" and an "Aah"
    and an "O," "Aah, aah!"
With an "O" and an "Aah"
    and an "O," "Aah, aah!"

*(hands on hips; kick
    one foot, then the other)*

O—Ogre! Aah—Octopus!
OOOOOOOh—Aaaaaah!

(jump)

"The Unicorn and the Umbrella Bird" (Long U, Short U)

One rainy day, the unicorn was walking along the woods wearing a raincoat and carrying an umbrella. Along came a little umbrella bird, who was carrying his umbrella upside down.

The unicorn greeted the bird and asked what he was doing. The umbrella bird said he was holding his umbrella under the raindrops, trying to catch them. This puzzled the unicorn, who asked what he planned to do with the raindrops. The umbrella bird said, "Why I'll let them go, and then start all over again."

Unicorn laughed and said, "You're getting all wet. You belong *under* the umbrella."

"I do?" asked the puzzled bird.

The unicorn showed him how to get under the umbrella—and this made the umbrella bird feel quite good. They walked along and when they got to Unicorn's home, the umbrella bird was invited in so that he could dry off and get a peanut butter sandwich.

"Help yourself," said the unicorn to the umbrella bird as the jar of peanut butter and the loaf of bread were put on the table.

"Oh, I don't know how to get the bread *under* the peanut butter," fluttered the bird.

"But the peanut butter goes on *top* of the bread. That's what makes the bread look like it's under the peanut butter."

"I see!" exclaimed the umbrella bird, who enjoyed his sandwich.

When it was time to leave, Unicorn asked the umbrella bird where he lived. It was right around the corner. But the umbrella bird sighed and said he lived on the top of a big bush, and he didn't get much sleep when it rained and the wind blew.

> **"The Unicorn and the Umbrella Bird"** (Long U, Short U) *(Continued)*
>
> "Why not make a nest under the bush," suggested the patient Unicorn. "That way you'll be protected." Unicorn gave him a little quilt to borrow so that he would be warm and dry.
>
> When the umbrella bird got to his bush, he made a little nest *under* the thick branches. It was warm and dry and cozy. The tired but happy bird spread out the quilt in the nest. Then he got on top of it, but just before he went to sleep he gave a little shiver and thought maybe he should be *under* the quilt. Oh well, tomorrow he'd ask Unicorn how to get under a quilt. He had found a new friend who would teach him so many new things. Soon the little umbrella bird fell sound asleep.

Unicorn and Umbrella Bird Chant

The umbrella bird   *(Encourage students to create their own movements)*
  is so mixed up.
He doesn't know a saucer
  goes under a cup.

He doesn't know how to
  wear underclothes.
He doesn't know thorns
  grow under a rose.
He doesn't see a worm
  that's under his nose.
He doesn't use a handkerchief
  when he blows!

But Unicorn will change all that,
  for a unicorn's patient and kind.
Before you know it, that umbrella bird
  will have a brilliant mind.

Yes, sir!
He'll have a mighty fine mind.
Uh, huh!
He'll have an A PLUS mind.

U—Unicorn. UH—Umbrella Bird.
U, Uh! U, Uh! U, Uh!

"Underword" Fun

"How would some of these words be explained by the umbrella bird? Remember, he explains things from the bottom up. How would they be explained by Unicorn?" Try:

underground	underdog
underage	undercoat (paint)
underfoot	underhand

Find things in the classroom that would confuse the umbrella bird. "Is the computer on top of the table or is the table under the computer? Is the pair of scissors on top of the teacher's desk or is the teacher's desk under the pair of scissors?" Have students continue this train of thought to make up their own top/under or over/under items list. "We're getting experience with words that are opposite."

Snack With the Letters-of-the-Month

Food serves as a good reinforcement for the letter sounds. Just a taste will do; you don't need huge portions. Here are some possibilities for vowels, but there are many more:

- *Long A*—Acorn Ape loves angel food cake; *Short A*—Alli Alligator asks for apples.
- *Long E*—Edith Eagle eagerly eats eclairs; *Short E*—Elli Elephant enjoys egg salad.
- *Long I*—Iris Icicle idolizes ice cream; *Short I*—Ignatz the Wood Cutter insists on itsy bitsies (small portions).
- *Long O*—Ogre O'Dell says, "Okay to oatmeal"; *Short O*—Ollie Octopus gobbles olives.
- *Long U*—Unicorn likes uniform food pieces and makes a U-turn after eating; *Short U*—The Umbrella Bird eats the "under food" first (likes the cracker *under* the peanut butter, but eats it all; likes the pancake *under* the syrup, but eats it all, etc.).

The "KN" Situation

When the letters *kn* appear side by side in a word, the letter *k* is silent and the *n* does the talking.

Here are some *kn* words:

knee	know	knock
kneecap	knob	knockout
knot	knit	knife

Make Silly "KN" Sentences

Using the groupings above, make silly sentences. For example, the first group includes *knee, kneecap,* and *knot.* A silly sentence might be: "I got a knot in my kneecap in the middle of my knee," or "Mary's knee had a knot in it after she tapped her kneecap." Try some more. Then try the next grouping, and the next.

The object of this activity is to give students experience with seeing and writing the letters "kn" while only saying "n."

How Did the "KN" Situation Happen?

Here's a possible story. One night it was dark and blustery and "n" went to the store for a number of "n" items, like nuts, napkins, and noodles. On the way home, a naughty kangaroo jumped out and kidnapped "n." Kiki Kangaroo ate the nuts, cooked the noodles, and wiped her mouth with the napkins. Then she hid "n" in a knapsack and went to sleep.

The kangaroo's mother came home and knew that something was wrong because her trick knee gave out on her. That always meant trouble.

Kiki admitted that she had been naughty, and promised that she wouldn't do anything bad ever again. Kiki was known for not keeping her promises. So, the judge said that for certain words the letter "k" had to stand guard over the "n" if Kiki Kangaroo was anywhere in sight. The letter "k" can't say a sound; it can only stand guard and let "n" do the talking.

These are some of the guarded words. Remember, when you see "kn" together, it means the "k" is guarding the "n" and the letter "n" does the talking:

knee	knack	knockout	knew
kneecap	knapsack	knock	know
knelt	knit	knothole	known

The "KN" Drama

Have students reenact "The KN Situation" using props and letter cards. This will help them to learn the information in another way.

Abbreviations

Abbreviations for Months

If students didn't get this the first time around, they have another opportunity.

Start with the calendar and work with the abbreviations of the months and the days of the week. For some students, this is still difficult. Begin with April (Apr.) and the day of the week.

Work with the months by the four seasons, so that students are concentrating upon three bits of information at a time. (There are three months that are short and usually not abbreviated.) The seasonal months are:

autumn	September—Sept. October—Oct. November—Nov.
winter	December—Dec. January—Jan. February—Feb.

$$
\text{spring} \left\{ \begin{array}{l} \text{March—Mar.} \\ \text{April—Apr.} \\ \text{May—May} \end{array} \right.
$$

$$
\text{summer} \left\{ \begin{array}{l} \text{June—June} \\ \text{July—July} \\ \text{August—Aug.} \end{array} \right.
$$

Work with the days of the week by school days and weekends. Students are working with chunking information by five's and two's.

Monday—Mon.—M
Tuesday—Tues.—T
Wednesday—Wed.—W
Thursday—Thurs.—Th or R
Friday—Fri.—F

Saturday—Sat.—S
Sunday—Sun.—Su

Shorter Month Names/Longer Days

Work with the months that have the most letters and the least letters, or the longest and the shortest names. Determine which months have the shortest names and no abbreviations—students will discover that these are May, June, and July. These are mainly summer months when the days are longer.

January Complains to June

"We have longer daylight hours and shorter month names in summer." This is the basis for a creative story, especially if January, for example, is complaining that it has shorter daylight hours, but more snow removal work to do, more clothes to put on, and has a longer name to write each day. How will June answer this? Students can be the judge.

Addressing Envelopes—Abbreviations

While there are many abbreviations to learn, for young students the main ones are those that they come into contact with quite often. Encourage them to notice how junk mail coming to their home makes use of abbreviations. Some common ones are found in street titles:

Avenue—Ave.	Lane—Ln.
Boulevard—Blvd.	Road—Rd.
Circle—Cir.	Street—St.
Highway—Hwy.	Trail—Tr.

Ms. Jones
12 Maple Ave.
Anytown, USA 00123

Common title abbreviations include: Miss or Ms., Mr., Dr., and Rev.

Have students learn the abbreviation for their own state. Some students, depending upon their developmental level, are interested in checking out other state abbreviations on the map.

The title "ZIP Code" is an abbreviation for Zone Improvement Plan. Have students learn to say and write their ZIP Code. By now they should be able to say their address, if not print it.

Some abbreviations for subject matter are:

Mathematics—Math
Reading—Rdg
Social Studies—Soc. St. or SS
Science—Sci
Library—Lib
Music—Mu
Physical Education—P.E. or Gym (Gym is part of the word GYMnasium)

Have students make out their own weekly schedule on a calendar grid with an abbreviated name, abbreviations for the days of the week, and abbreviations for subjects written in the grid. If they are unable to do this, then do it as a class exercise on the chalkboard and add to it every day for a week.

Contractions

One way to present contractions (shortening words) is in fanciful story form. This can be done by simply telling students that "Some of the letters work very hard—they work overtime, they even work while we're sleeping (they're busy getting out the morning newspaper). So they need time out for a rest.

"When this happens, we can proceed as usual thanks to the 'apostrophe' which turns the word into a 'contraction.' (Contract means to shorten.) The 'apostrophe' is always looking for overtime work. The apostrophe is dependable, loves to work, and will step in where it is needed. It is sort of a letter 'substitute.'

"The word 'will' and the word 'not' both get overworked and tired. When they need a nap, the apostrophe is called in, some letters drop out, and we can go right on reading and writing. Let's look at some examples." Write these on a chart or on the chalkboard and have students notice that the beginning letters are just the same.

WILL ('ll)	*NOT (n't)*
you will = you'll	cannot = can't
they will = they'll	do not = don't
she will = she'll	was not = wasn't

Next, mix up the word order for the second column, and have students draw a line to match the correct word with its contraction:

you will	they'll	cannot	wasn't
they will	she'll	was not	don't
she will	you'll	do not	can't

Have students look through the newspaper and circle contractions when they find them. Help them to pronounce them. Write them in a "Contraction Book." Also, circle other words that look like contractions and find out what they are.

Flash Card Contraction Match

Make two sets of flash cards. On one set have two words and on the other set have the matching contraction for the words. Students can match the appropriate words and contractions using a pocket chart.

More Contraction Partners

The words "have" and "are" often get in the "substitute apostrophe" and take a rest. Here are some examples:

ARE ('re)	*HAVE ('ve)*
you are = you're	we have = we've
they are = they're	you have = you've
we are = we're	I have = I've

Make a search-and-find sheet for the contractions. (See Reproducible Activity Pages.)

Capital Letters

Let's visit this skill once again, because chances are you have already had opportunities to point out words that are capitalized.

For very young students, be sure they know that each new sentence begins with a capital letter. If you are using Big Books, have the children point to the capital letters. If you have information on the chalkboard in sentence form, have students circle the capital letters.

Making a Tally With Names of People

"We always use a capital letter for people names. Everyone in class has a name that begins with a capital letter." To learn which letters are represented, place an alphabet flash card along the chalkboard ledge, or print it low on the chalkboard. Make a tally mark above each letter every time it is used.

"What about last names—how many more letters are represented?" Use different colored chalk for your tally.

There will still be some gaps, so "Let's try middle names. Can we put marks above/below any more letters?" Again, use different colored chalk.

"How many letters are still not represented? Let's name them." Ask students if they know of any names that begin with those letters so that they can be sounded out and represented in the tally.

Determine which letters are more widely used. Circle the information. Sometimes it is necessary to remind students that this is not a contest; we are simply gathering information.

Check the Newspaper

"Look to see if there is a capital letter at the beginning of each sentence in the newspaper. Circle it. Do the same for a page in a magazine.

"Check to see if the capital letter always appears at the left margin of the page or if it appears in the middle of a sentence." The fact that this happens may be surprising to some beginning students.

Names of Places

Tell students that *specific names* of places are always represented with a capital letter. Say:

I'm going to the park. *(this doesn't tell which one)*
I'm going to Seneca Park. *(this is specific)*

Write this information on the chalkboard using all lower-case letters. Then have students point to the word or words that need to have capitals. Let them erase and make the correction. In the beginning, it's good to use simple sentence repeat patterns. Later, you can branch out.

I'm going to the city.
I'm going to philadelphia. (P)
I'm going to philadelphia with mrs. katz. (P, M, K)

I'm going camping.
I'm going camping in the adirondacks. (A)
I'm going camping in the adirondacks with my cat, suki. (A, S)

I'm going to a wedding in the park.
I'm going to a wedding at rose park. (R, P)
I'm going to a wedding at rose park with nana. (R, P, N)

This is another good opportunity to use your supply of junk mail. If it is addressed, notice where the capital letters are. Notice where the capital letters are in the advertisements.

Sometimes in the ads the whole sentence or certain words in the sentence are capitalized for effect, that is, to get our attention. Writing for advertising is different from newspaper writing and magazine writing (reporting). Be sure to point this out to students. "Environmental print" does not always follow the same rules that we use when we write.

A Tisket, a Tasket, a Letter in a Basket

You will need a basket (with a handle) filled with 26 capital letters. Only one is on top; the rest are under a napkin in the basket. Have the group sit around in a circle, cross legged, and move the basket around as the group sings:

A tisket, a tasket,
A letter in a basket.
I sent a letter on its way.
Can you say its name today?

Whoever is holding the basket when the group stops singing is "It." That person puts down the basket, removes the letter, and says what it is. If they say it correctly, they can keep it in front of them. If they don't know, it's put back undercover in the basket and another one is removed and put on top. Then start the song again. Score one point for every letter a student knows. Then collect them and play it again with upper- or lower-case letters.

Later, lower- and upper-case letters can be mixed together. Some students like to play this during recess time as an option, for two or three rounds. They enjoy the game, and are learning at the same time. Some like to do it in groups of three or five to see how many letters they can collect and points they can score.

Spelling

Ten Guesses

Print the spelling words on the chalkboard and on a set of flash cards. Ask for volunteers to be "It." Then tape a spelling flash card to the back of their shirt. Those who are "It" can ask questions about the word they are wearing that can be answered with a "yes" or a "no." If they guess correctly, that spelling word gets a point (or a tally mark) after it on the chalkboard. When all spelling words are guessed, those who are "It" can choose a replacement. Remember to shuffle the spelling words before making the new attachments. Repeat the procedure.

Make a Vertical/Horizontal Spelling Sentence

Use five of the spelling words. Let's suppose the words are *brush, bring, road, careful,* and *gravel.* A possible sentence could be as follows, but accept silly sentences as well:

Please *bring* the
    brush along as we travel
on the *road* and be
    careful not to get
    gravel in your shoes.

Spelling Buddies

Two students can work together. One acts as the teacher and the other acts as the student; then they reverse roles. The first student has the list of spelling words and says them individually to the partner, who then must spell the word aloud. The spelling buddy gives immediate feedback regarding whether the word is correct or incorrect. Keep going through all of the words and then change roles.

You may want to draw straws for a "spelling buddy for the week." During spare time these two can work together on the words. They can spell them aloud or write them. In this way, students are not always working with the same person.

Can You Catch It?

Deliberately misspell two words in the spelling list on the chalkboard and ask students to find them. They can use their spelling book or spelling list to help them. Call upon students to correct the words.

Then erase the list and write them again, but deliberately misspell different ones. Repeat the detective procedure.

READING LINKS TO HOLIDAYS & SPECIAL EVENTS

April Fool's Day

This is a day for pranks and a little bit of foolishness. In order to have fun and yet keep learning today, declare that all student jokes and riddles need to be done during designated times. You may want to do some organized activities on this mixed-up day. A helpful resource for you is *Tomfoolery, Trickery and Foolery With Words,* collected by Alvin Schwartz, with illustrations by Glen Rounds.

Mixed-up Letters

Tape paper letters to items so that when students come into the classroom from a special class or from recess, these will be noticeable. Make sure that the letter tags are incorrectly placed. You can move right into a phonics lesson by having the letter "M" taped to the sink, the letter "S" taped to the door, the letter "B" taped to the pencil sharpener, and so on. Students can correct the mixed-up letters. Who played this April Fool's joke on them? Perhaps the helpful classroom puppet who is standing by looking quite innocent?

Celebrate Clara Barton

April 12 is a recognition day of Clara Barton, an American nurse who founded the Red Cross. This organization serves the country daily and helps people when misfortune strikes. Some students may have been helped by the Red

Cross if they've been in parts of the country hit by hurricanes, tornadoes, flooding, and so on. The Red Cross often asks for donations of clothing and food.

 Students can make a little construction paper red cross with a heart in the middle and put it on their headings (written work) as a reminder to be a good citizen and to help each other in times of need—and at other times as well.

Easter Time With Children's Books

Don't miss *The Easter Bunny That Overslept* by Priscilla and Otto Friedrich, with illustrations by Adrienne Adams. This classic tale is about that famous bunny who snuggles down for a long winter's nap and then sleeps right through his special holiday! When all of the holidays after Easter roll around, no one is interested in painted eggs. It isn't until he gets to Christmas that Santa thinks of the perfect gift for him, so that he won't be in this predicament for next year. (The gift is an alarm clock.)

R-r-ring! Students can enjoy this story. Then bring an alarm clock into the classroom and set it for certain times during the day, so that as a class the children have ample time to wash their hands and get ready for lunch, and time to get ready to go to a special class, and time to get ready to clean up the room before going home, and so on. Each day, a different student has the opportunity to set the clock and turn off the buzzer. This is a most helpful classroom management tool, and it creates renewed interest in telling time.

Also revisit *Rachenka's Eggs* by Patricia Polacco and work with *Chickens Aren't the Only Ones* by Ruth Heller.

For a celebration of rabbits and other spring animals, introduce students to Beatrix Potter. *Peter Rabbit* is an old favorite. Other animal characters to meet in stories written by this author include Squirrel Nutkin, Pigling Bland, Jemima Puddle Duck, Hunca Munca, Timmy Willie, and Benjamin Bunny.

A good resource book for the classroom is *Things to Make and Do for Easter* by Marion Cole and Olivia H.H. Cole.

Celebrate Pan–American Day

April 14 was declared Pan–American Day by President Herbert Hoover. The Pan–American Union is also known as the Organization of American States (OAS) and includes Mexico, Central America, and South America along with the United States of America.

Locate this vast area of the Americas on a globe. Listen to music with a Latin beat. Invite someone to class who has visited a foreign country to show handicrafts and tell about their experiences of this rich cultural mix of native American Indians, Spanish, Portuguese, and French.

Hollyhocks and Cherry Blossoms

Many Spring festivals are held in honor of flowers. For example, Holland, Michigan has a yearly spring tulip festival, and Rochester, New York has a yearly lilac festival. Is there one in your community?

The Japanese communities celebrate with a Hollyhock Festival and the Cherry Blossom Festival. There are many cherry trees that bloom in our nation's capital, Washington, D.C. These trees were donated to our country by Japan.

Plant Your Own Festival of Flowers

To plant bulbs in the classroom, start about a month in advance. Secure the bulbs from a garden supply store, and place them in a container so that only the bottom of the bulb is in water. Then place them in a dark spot, making sure that the water level is kept up so that the bulb is touching the water. When the sprouts begin to show, you can bring them out in the light of the classroom. As they grow, they can be transplanted into potting soil, or put in a container of pebbles and marbles that are in water. The pebbles help to hold the bulbs securely in place.

Some bulbs that will work well are crocus, daffodil, tulip, grape hyacinth, hyacinth, and any others that are considered spring flowers in your area.

It's Earth Day

April 22 is a special day for calling attention to the care everyone needs to give to Planet Earth. One important way that students can contribute is by becoming aware of recycling cans, bottles, and other materials. Students can make a Recycle Poster. What is the title? the message? What forms, shapes, and colors will the student need to convey the recycle message? This is something to discuss with the class before they are given the assignment, so that results will be appropriate and done well. Display them in the hall.

Make Planet Earth Pudding

This see-through pudding treat represents Planet Earth—the layers of rock and soil underneath our feet. Unlike real dirt, however, this treat is edible.

Ingredients:

1 package Oreo® or sandwich cookies	2 large spoons
1 box chocolate pudding mix	plastic see-through drink
1 box butterscotch pudding mix	glasses
whipped topping	2 mixing bowls
milk	spoons
gummy worms (*optional*)	

Procedure: Place cookies in plastic bags and have students carefully crush them. Set aside. Mix instant puddings according to directions on the boxes. Stir the cookie crumbs into the puddings, but save about one-fourth of them. Spoon the mixtures of the two puddings into the plastic see-through glasses. Put whipped topping on top. These represent three different layers of the Earth's soil. Then sprinkle the top with the remaining cookie crumbs (top soil). Dig in with your shovel (spoon). Some teachers have gummy worms available for the brave and hardy, which can be poked down between the layers with the spoon or with a toothpick.

Go on a Clean-up Walk

You will need garden gloves (or see-through plastic throw-away gloves) and a large trash bag for this hike around the playground and school grounds. Students can take turns wearing the gloves and pick up papers, bottle caps, and dried leaves that are cluttering the edges of the playground fence (inside only). Caution students not to touch any glass. That can be reported by students to the office. This activity will depend upon where your school is located, and whether there are other safety factors to consider.

Arbor Day

April 29 provides a link to the Planet Earth awareness mentioned earlier. Arbor Day is observed in many communities as a day for the community planting of trees. Does your school plan to plant a tree today on the schoolgrounds? Students need to know of the role that trees play in our environment. They are Mother Nature's natural air conditioners. They also provide home and shelter for many birds and animals, as well as beauty.

Students can do bark rubbings of outdoor trees using pale gray construction paper and various colors of crayons. Use the *side* of the crayon rather than the tip. Use the rubbings to cut out a tree trunk and branches. Paste them onto a colored background. Then use green tempera paint and gadgets to print the tree leaves, or use tiny sponges for a filmy effect, or try them both.

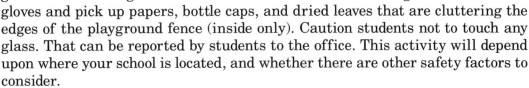

Practice Conservation

The word *conservation* means to take care of trees, in addition to animals, the air, the water, and so on. The Father of Arbor Day is J. Sterling Morton of Nebraska, and his birthday is April 29, the day we make an effort to plant trees. Arbor is a Latin word meaning *tree.* One president who got behind the conservation effort was President Teddy Roosevelt, the same president for whom the teddy bear is named. (Smoky the Bear is in charge of forest conservation.)

Plant seedlings in the classroom and encourage students to take them home to plant. Read *Miss Rumphius,* by Barbara Cooney, to the class. The message here is to leave the world a little better place than you found it.

READING LINKS TO WRITING

Spring Writing Review

Check the manner in which students are holding their pencil for writing. By now, you no doubt have had many whole class sessions with letter formation and the best way to hold a pencil. This spring review might be timely for those who need an extra bit of help.

For right-handed students, the pencil is held between thumb and forefinger, while resting on the second finger. For left-handed students, the same thing is true, except that the student is using the left hand. Some left-handed students have the overhand method, or hook, yet the same fingers are involved in holding the writing implement. Check to make sure students are holding the pencils correctly, for in so doing they are training their hand muscles to use the pencil, and later it becomes difficult to change. **Note:** The thumb does not overlap the forefinger. That creates pinching of the pencil and impedes wrist movement.

Right-handed students slant their paper to the left, and left-handed students slant their paper to the right. Some students seem to be quite comfortable with their paper in a straight position—this is especially true during the printing stage.

Letter Formation Review

Have fresh copies of the alphabet letters for students to practice. A commercially prepared sheet serves as the best model.

Students can practice their name and address.

Students can practice writing from the chalkboard on a daily basis. You may have lines drawn carefully on the chalkboard, with print carefully placed within the lines, for students to copy. It might go something like this:

Name	*(line one)*
April _____, 20___ ___.	*(line two)*
Today is _____.	*(line three)*
	(skip a space)

The robins are visiting our feeder again.   *(message changes daily)*

At the end of each day, students can erase the board and wash it. When students leave, you can redraw lines and reprint the first three lines noted above. The message can be made up by you or by the students. If it is on the chalkboard and ready to go when students first get to school, some like to get started on it rather than getting out a book or a journal. Give students options—one should be handwriting. In your classroom, do not neglect one skill for another.

The above daily writing plan is not in place of a formal writing lesson; it is in addition to it. Students take pride in writing if it is valued by you. They make amazing gains as the year goes on, and are proud of their effort. Again, it's like practicing the piano or the violin or batting a ball. As educators we need to remember that if a student always engages in sloppy writing—and this is left unchecked—then no one can read it and the point of communication is lost. (See rubric information below.)

The Discipline of Writing

When students write a creative story or poem, we accept erasures and cross outs on the draft copy. But a final copy is what we call "camera ready." It has been proofread and corrected in the student's best handwriting, and could be photocopied as is. (**Note:** The computer printout and spellcheck provide the instant gratification of the hard copy, but the discipline is not taught there.)

Allow students the time to slow down and practice. Later in life, handwriting is automatic. In the early years, they are in training.

Check the Newspapers and Magazines

Have students check through the newspaper and magazines for words crossed out, words blackened out, misspelled words, and so on. Occasionally, a word is misspelled. Students can take a cue from this exercise. For final copy, they need a "ready to go to press" attitude. Where do they get that? It's learned in the classroom. It's taught by the teacher. Promote excellence!

Rubrics Are Important

What is a rubric? A rubric is a plan that lists steps along the way for meeting expected outcomes. It can be in the form of a checklist. For example, if a student is going to produce a writing paper that will be judged partially on the form, the rubric checklist might be as follows:

I have done my best writing.

All capital letters are in the correct place.

I have checked all spelling words.

My paragraphs are indented.

My reading road signs are in order (punctuation).

When a student is given a rubric, expectations are spelled out. There is no second guessing.

A rubric for a creative writing story might be something like this:

I have made an attractive cover page.

My title page is complete.

My reading road signs are in order (punctuation).

I have a beginning/middle/ending to the story.

My characters are described with colorful words.

My settings are carefully described.

All story conflicts have been addressed.

My ending is satisfying to the reader.

I have taken care with the illustrations.

Writing on Egg Shapes

Have students write an inventive story on a large egg shape (oval). Have various colors available. They can make a little border around the inside of the egg with spring symbols, such as—tulips, daffodils, rabbits, baseballs, bats, and skates. Place these colorful spring stories on the bulletin board in a giant basket made from construction paper.

Flip-top Bunny Books

Make a large rabbit face from construction paper (pink, violet, purple, yellow) with long ears at the top of its head. Have the ears close together, so that long strips of paper can be stapled to the ears for a flip-top book. The book can be a fanciful story about rabbits or spring, or a real story about rabbits. Look up factual information at the library and include it in the rabbit book.

Also, work on the rabbit face. Be sure to have eyes, pink nose, mouth, and rabbit whiskers. To make the whiskers, cut or tear thin strips of white paper and, one by one, roll them tightly around a pencil. When you slip them off, they are springy. These can be attached to the rabbit face for a 3-D look to the flip-top book.

Variation: Make the face and ears, and then construct a hat for the rabbit. The hat can be the cover for a surprise little flip-top book that students make and glue, or staple, under the hat.

READING LINKS TO MATH

Odd and Even

One way to teach odd and even is to pair things together—that means two of everything. If one is left over, that is referred to as "odd." Students can do this with real items (manipulatives) in the classroom to get the idea of one being left over.

Use the flannelboard and put a row of circles at the top. Then put a square beneath each circle for an "even" number. Count them. Take one away for an "odd" number. Count them.

After students have this concrete concept in mind, you can go to picture matching (semi-concrete) and finally to numerals (abstract).

Counting to 100 by Two's

Use a white grid with ten squares in a row so that students can fill in the squares with numerals from 1–100. After they have done this, have them begin with the numerals 1, 3, 5, etc., and color every other odd or uneven numeral a light color, such as yellow or pink. Students can stop at the end of each row to see if they are correct. At the end, they will have *only* the even numbers highlighted in white.

Students can count to 100 by two's using the grid as an aid. Say only the numerals in the white squares. If students can count to 100 by one's (rote counting), have them whisper *one*, speak out on **two**, whisper *three*, speak out on **four.** Keep going. By counting every other number aloud, they are on their way to counting to 100 by two's.

one   **TWO**   three   **FOUR**   five   **SIX**   seven   **EIGHT**

Echo Counting

Divide the class into two teams. Team One whispers the number "one," then Team Two calls out "two" aloud. Go to 50 or 100. Then change team responsibilities: the team that whispered now calls out the number.

Bouncing Numbers

Have students bounce a ball while whispering on the odd numbers and calling out loud the even numbers. How far can they get? This is a good outdoor recess exercise.

Calculator Count

Introduce students to the calculator if they are not already familiar with one. This can work best in small groups. First, establish with the students that this is not a toy. It is an instrument that we use to check our math, to do our math calculations, and so on. Demonstrate the calculator by explaining what the keys are. Show the "on" and "off" key, and the function keys such as "plus" and "minus." Demonstrate how to press the "on" key; press the "2" key, press the "plus" key, press the "2" key again, press the "equal" key, and check the window at the top of the calculator for the answer. Show students what key to press to clear the operation, and do another as a demonstration. Then distribute the calculators and take them through the process step by step.

For some students who are familiar with a calculator from home, this is a fairly simple review process. Give them a sheet of problems to work on while you rework the calculator with students who are meeting this valuable tool for the first time. For accelerated students, have them create a worksheet and keep track of the answers. They can put their worksheet in a bin to be figured out by another student and then they can use their answer sheet to correct it.

Once the calculator has been demonstrated and students work with it in a serious manner, keep a small supply of them at the Math Center with worksheets.

Or, allow students to spend some time exploring the calculator, first with addition and subtraction, and double-digit numerals, and have them estimate what the answer will be and see how close they are. Often students can begin to sharpen their estimation skills with repeated work on the calculator.

By all means, have them share their findings and discoveries with the class. They can learn from each other.

Work With Number Families on the Calculator

Take the "seven" family, for example. Press "one" and "plus" and "six" and "equals" and the answer should be seven. $(1 + 6 = 7)$. Students can learn that as one numeral gets higher, the other gets lower; this enables them to learn the combinations faster $(2 + 5, 3 + 4,$ and so on). It's like using a market scale with two baskets, one on each side. As one gets lighter, the other gets heavier. Write it down. Talk about it.

Mental Math Challenge

Have a worksheet of problems and have two students do the math "in their head." Record their answer. Use the calculator only as a check.

Computers in the Classroom

One thing to keep in mind is that computers are not to be used in place of manipulating real objects for a basic understanding of numbers. They are used to extend and enrich. For a student with special needs, it can be quite helpful in holding their attention for a longer period of time and for engaging in problem-solving skills.

The physical location of a computer center needs to be carefully thought out. This is especially true because of many wires and cords. Place the computer so that children are not walking and moving among wires. Use a sturdy table and put it against the wall. You would not want to place it next to the play area where students are apt to be physically engaged in dramatic play. Do not locate it next to an art area, because paint and sticky fingers don't mix with computer technology.

- Working together is often facilitated by computer programs, so for that reason place two chairs in front of a computer. This invites students to work together.

- Select software that supports the math program. There may be some that are suggested in the math text you are using.

- Computers, printers, headsets, and software all need care and special handling, so students will have to follow rules that have been set up for computer use. It would be wise to print and attach labels to items, print rules for turning the computer on and off, and for printer use (depending upon the age of the students). It is not uncommon to have several "computer experts" in the classroom; if this is the case, put them in charge of this area.

They will be a tremendous help to students who are less knowledgeable. Chances are they have learned to take this technology seriously, and that attitude is often conveyed to their peers.

Because computers do double-duty in the classroom, they will be effective with reading and writing programs, science, health, social studies, art, music—in fact, all areas of the curriculum.

Computers in Our World—Get With the Program

In our fast-moving world today, computers are at the center. The computer chip is a miniature powerhouse. Computers are being used in banking, on car assembly lines, for traffic control flow, in the health and imaging field, in airports, in travel, in homes—one may even be in your wristwatch.

Take a survey in the classroom. How many students have a computer at home? How many can go to their local public library and access a computer there? How many have computers in the classroom? How many students have been to summer "computer camps"? Computers are very much a part of the lives of young children. Check with the local school district and with your local community, state, or private college in your area to learn about year-round, Saturday, and summer computer opportunities for students.

Computer Robots

Many students will have heard of Seeing-Eye dogs. There is a Japanese robot, called "Meldog," which is about the size of a Seeing-Eye dog but is on two wheels and is operated by a computer chip. This chip has a map of the area built into its memory; when a person tells Meldog to go to a certain location within that area, the robot charts the route. If something gets in its way, it stops and turns in another direction. Meldog communicates with its user by a series of electrical buzzes that are felt on the skin.

Computers are used in physical therapy to send impulses to muscles, thus making them move. This stimulates recovery.

Computer limbs, such as legs, feet, and hands, are being constructed and used by people who have been born with defects or who have suffered debilitating accidents. Some people have learned to play the piano or play sports with these limbs, thanks to computerized signals.

A good resource is National Geographic's *Computers, Those Amazing Machines* by Catherine O'Neill.

Position and Color *(Beside)*

Have students sit in a circle. Print the word "beside" on the chalkboard and explain that it means "next to." You can ask students to raise their hand if they are sitting *beside* someone who is, for example, wearing red.

Go clockwise around the circle and have students say who they are sitting *beside.* For example:

"I'm sitting beside Peggy."

"I'm sitting beside Gage."

"I'm sitting beside Chris."

"I'm sitting beside Miguel."

Then reverse it and go counterclockwise. Students will not have changed position, but will now say a different name with their sentence.

Bat/Ball/Mitt *(Beside)*

Still in the circle, place a bat, ball, and mitt in the center. Direct a student to put the bat in the middle. Ask another to put the ball beside the bat. Ask another to put the mitt beside the ball.

Keep calling out different positions, so students become familiar and comfortable with the concept of *beside*.

Who's Sitting Beside My Teddy?

Have each student bring in a teddy bear (either actual or paper) for the classroom's spring festivities. Then do an activity that involves them. Have students line up the bears in a row. Call upon each student to identify his or her bear, and then describe the bear that is sitting *beside* it. This can be done repeatedly with items that students bring in to share.

More Work With the Concept of "Beside"

These are some questions and activities that can be addressed so that students can gain practice with the concept of *beside* in the classroom and in their world outside of the classroom.

- Who sits beside you on the bus?
- Who lives beside you at home?
- Whose classroom is beside ours in school?
- In the sandbox, let's build a castle beside the wall.
- If you're wearing pink, stand up. Look around for someone wearing blue. Then go and stand beside that person.
- If you're wearing tan, stand up:

    Ann Marie, go and stand beside the door.

    Evelyn and Kaneesha, go and stand beside the sink.

    Ida, go and stand beside the easel.

    John, go and stand beside the computer.

READING LINKS TO SOCIAL STUDIES

Children are consumers in our society. Some have quite a bit of discretionary income and need to learn basic information about money and its value; goods and services; wants vs. needs; and consumers and producers. These topics must first be addressed in a simple way, with activities at their level of understanding. Later, more complex information can be added depending upon their developmental and grade levels.

When We Had No Coins

Students need to know that at one time there were no coins and no paper money as we know it today. People sometimes exchanged goods for services. A farmer, for example, might give you a dozen eggs if you fixed his roof. That was your "pay."

Also, people would *barter* (new vocabulary word) for things. It would be agreed upon that you would shovel out a driveway in exchange for a dozen eggs for the family. The exchange would have to satisfy both parties. Sometimes students barter with baseball cards, magazines, paperback books, and marbles, and may understand the concept if it is personal.

What Did People Use Before Money?

"Before we had minted coins, people used to 'pay' for goods or services by exchanging something that was hand-made—a loaf of bread, a woven blanket, a hand-carved tool."

"People had to 'bargain.' That is, they had to agree, for example, how many potatoes would be exchanged for a loaf of bread." It was not a fixed number. Other foods used for bargaining were grains and corn. People also used feathers and tobacco leaves.

Native Americans used wampum as a medium of exchange. They might wear a wampum belt or necklace. The wampum beads were made from shells and strung together. The darker the bead, the more it was worth. Wampum is from the Algonquin word *wampumpeag*.

Set Up a Grocery Store

To facilitate your experience with money, goods, and services, set up a grocery story in the classroom on a table. Push the table close to a bulletin board, but with enough space to allow the "clerks" to get behind the table. Use the bulletin board for huge letters that call out the name of the store and for student-made information about products, sales, and so on.

In your newsletter to parents, suggest items that could be sent in for the store project; these must all be empty containers so there is no spoilage. You will want cereal boxes, milk containers, frozen food boxes, cans, cartons, plastic bottles, and so on. Have students categorize the items and set up the tantalizing displays. They can make up names for signs and write down the prices.

You will need play money. One way to do this is to cut up different colored pieces of paper to denote different values. Buttons or round chips can be used for coins, or play money can be used. A toy cash register will add authenticity.

Have an "Open" and a "Closed" sign for the store. Initially, work with the store will need to be done as a total group, so that students understand the procedure. Clerks serve behind the counter. A customer comes in with the play money and purchases an item. Change is made. The item is put into a bag. The satisfied customer leaves. (At the end, all play money and goods are returned for another day.)

Eventually, this area can be used during free-choice time before it is finally disassembled. (Not all children go to the grocery store with parents, so for some this is a different experience. Also, many children do not handle money as parents use credit cards, so this is another important learning experience.)

Set Up a Barter Day

There has to be a satisfactory method of exchange on barter day. To begin with, have students make one or two craft items (headband, picture, painting, collage, and so on) and put them on the "barter table." Make sure everyone is included. Then, on the appointed day, students can express an interest in exchanging items. However, set up ground rules so that students know they may say "no" to some offers and "yes" to others. This will vary depending upon the maturity level of the group.

Set Up a Friday Flea Market

This is where you need to write a note home to parents explaining your "consumer" study and asking for a small item worthy of recycling for your flea market. You might decide to use a numbering system. A student can put out his or her item along with a tag that has a number, meaning that's how much this item will "cost." Students can then "work" for tickets in the classroom. For example, everyone gets a ticket worth 5 points if they line up quietly when coming in from the playground. Students can earn tickets worth 1 or 2 points for work well done in the classroom, and so on.

While items are on display throughout the week, some students may notice that they have put too high a number on their item. They should be free to put a new tag on the merchandise, or cross off the old number and put on the new "sale price."

Making Coins

"The first coins in the United States were 'minted' in Philadelphia, Pennsylvania." Locate this city on the map. "Today, coins are also made in Denver,

Colorado." Locate this city on the map. Have students examine real coins for the letter that designates where the coins were minted.

Examine Coins

"Take a good look at our coins. They are all uniform because they are stamped from the same mold. Coins the world over have imprints of people (kings, presidents, rulers) who are important to their history and symbols that represent their society (buildings, torch, eagle, star, etc.)."

Identify the people, buildings, symbols, dates, and writing on coins. This information will help get you started:

	Front	*Back*
Penny	Abraham Lincoln	Lincoln Memorial
Nickel	Thomas Jefferson	Monticello
Dime	Franklin Roosevelt	Liberty torch, olive branch
Quarter	George Washington	Eagle, arrows, olive branch
Half Dollar	John F. Kennedy	Eagle, shield
Dollar	Susan B. Anthony	Eagle, landing on the moon

Students can make coin rubbings for each denomination.

Paper Money

Paper money is printed in Washington, D.C. Locate the nation's capital on the map. Explain to students that it is against the law to write on money. When "bills" get worn, they are taken out of circulation and destroyed, and new ones with new serial numbers are made.

"Let's examine a dollar bill. We'll write down all of the information that we learn by doing this."

How Can Parents Buy Items Without Having the Money in Their Hand?

Today in our complex society, we write checks, use credit cards, use the ATM (Automated Teller Machine), and can make purchases over the phone and the Internet. Instruct students that because it is so easy to spend money, you have to keep careful records of what you owe.

Issue "credit cards" in the classroom made from construction paper, and set a maximum charge limit of $25.00 or $50.00 (this will vary from group to group). Have students go through magazines and newspapers and "purchase" what they'd like to spend for a special holiday or occasion. Keep a record. Do this over a period of a week, so caution students not to spend their money for the first thing they see. Use the calculator to add up the items. Now, if this were a real situation, ask students to determine how they would plan to pay for this. Tell students that if it is not all paid off within a month, they are charged an additional amount (interest) for the loan of the money—and it adds up each month! This is a lesson in problem-solving.

Wants vs. Needs

This is a good discussion topic. Students often cannot distinguish between a *want* and a *need* until it is pointed out to them that there is indeed a difference.

Begin with food and clothing (and shelter, depending upon the developmental level of the group). Make two columns on the chalkboard. List the food that we *need* and the food we might *want*. List the clothing we *need* and the clothing that catches our eye in the store or on a TV ad or in a catalog sent into the home.

Bring up the topic of toys and discuss whether they are wants or needs. "We don't always get what we want, and we don't always need what we get." Have students make a "Wants/Needs" list of their toys, books, and play things.

Resources: Two good resource books for teachers are *Nickels, Dimes & Dollars. How Currency Works* by R.V. Fodor and *The Story of Money* by Betsy Maestro, with illustrations by Giulio Maestro.

READING LINKS TO SCIENCE & HEALTH

Reptiles Aren't the Only Ones. Who's Hatching?

It's the spring season and many forms of life are hatching from eggs. Read aloud the book *Chickens Aren't the Only Ones* by Ruth Heller (our author-of-the-month) and make a list. Here are some to get you started:

Birds

chickens
robins, bluejays, cardinals (all birds)
peacocks
swans

Reptiles

snakes
lizards
crocodiles, alligators
turtles

Fish & Some Sea Life

jellyfish
octopus
snails
tuna
perch
salmon

Insects

caterpillar—pupa—butterfly
ladybugs
grasshoppers
beetles
dragonfly

Use children's magazines such as *My Big Backyard, National Geographic World,* and *Ranger Rick* to locate giant, colorful examples of these creatures.

From Tadpole to Frog or Toad

If possible, bring in a jar of pond water that has tadpoles swimming around inside. This gives students an opportunity to see how they flick quickly through the water. It's the beginning of the life of an *amphibian* (a new vocabulary word). The frog or toad can live on land or in the water. After a classroom visit, empty the contents back into the pond in order for the tadpoles to survive (unless a pond is to be set up in the classroom). Read the storybook *Frog and Toad Are Friends* by Arnold Loebel.

A Turtle Watch

Some turtles are on the endangered species list. In parts of Florida and the Carolinas, there are roped-off areas on beaches where turtles have come ashore to lay their eggs. Often, just before the time for hatching, people go on turtle watches to see the young creatures saw their way out of the hard-shelled egg with their egg tooth, hatch from their egg under the warm sand, make it to the surface, and crawl their way to the ocean. Of all the reptiles, turtles seem to lay the most eggs—but then do not care for them once they have been laid in the sand and covered.

Have students get down on their stomach and move slowly along using their arms and legs and dragging their middle to simulate the turtle entrance into the ocean.

Doing the Tortoise Walk

Tortoises move very slowly. They move on all fours, and often look like they're waddling from side to side. They take a step approximately once every three seconds. Have students get down on all fours and move to a count of three: first the right hand, then the left hand, then the right foot, then the left foot. They won't cover any great distance in a short period of time.

Students can compare this movement with the slithering of a snake, another member of the reptile family.

Reptiles Are Waterproof

"When in the water, reptiles move freely. The water does not come into their body through their eyes, nose, or mouth. It is said that they do absorb salt through their skins, however. Are people waterproof? Not really. Although our skin does help to protect us in the rain, we still have slickers, boots, and umbrellas for rainy days so that we won't get drenched. A storybook alligator, on the other hand, wouldn't mind a bit." Encourage students to write creative stories about a make-believe alligator who goes shopping for a rainy day. A good book that students enjoy is *Dial-a-Croc* by Mike Dumbleton.

Only Alligators and Crocodiles Don't Need Dentists

"Unlike people who get a set of baby teeth and then a second set of teeth, the alligators and crocodiles replace their teeth many, many times over and over again. There's always a tooth waiting to take the place of one that gets caught, or gets yanked out, or cracks and needs to be replaced. So, an alligator or crocodile doesn't need a dentist for that huge mouthful of teeth it carries around."

But students do need to take care of their teeth, and this is time for another reminder to brush and floss daily. "As a treat from the alligators and crocodiles to help clean our teeth, we can enjoy a carrot stick, celery stick, and half an apple today for a special 'Be Good to Your Teeth Snack.'"

The Reptile Rap

The *alligator* has the same beginning sound as *apple*; the *crocodile's* hard sound can be heard in *carrots* and its soft sound in *celery*. Read this aloud all the way through, then go back through and get the rhythm going. Students can join in with rhythmic finger snapping and tapping.

> Alligator, alligator
>   Snap, snap, snap
> Likes to eat apples
>   Tap, tap, tap.
>
> Crocodile, crocodile
>   Bim, bam, boo
> Eats his carrots
>   And celery too!
>
> Big teeth, little teeth,
>   Sharp teeth too,
> Brush 'em, floss 'em
>   You only get two.

A Rake and a Rope

Secure a plastic toy rake and a length of rope. Demonstrate the alligator tooth flossing using these two items. Then have students practice flossing the alligator teeth. This may motivate them to go home and ask for dental floss so that they can take good care of their teeth. Be sure to put this information in your newsletter to parents.

Do Alligators and Crocodiles Communicate?

"How do people communicate?" Be sure that students know that "We need a sender (person talking) and a receiver (person listening). We communicate in the following ways: speaking directly to a person, calling to a person in another room, speaking on the telephone, writing letters, e-mail, writing books, singing, and so on. We also use 'body language' when we wave, frown, smile, droop our shoulders, and so on."

"Alligators and crocodiles communicate with each other by way of sounds, smells, touch, and even 'body language.'" A most common sound is a jawslap. The animal lifts its head out of the water, opens its mouth, and then closes its jaws just at the level of the water. It sounds like a loud slap. Often when one animal starts, another one does this, too.

"An alligator and crocodile can purr, cough, and hiss. If it thrashes its tail about, it means be on the alert! Get out of the way!"

Body Language Exercise

Grin
Frown
Wave with your right hand
Wave with your left hand
Wave to someone far, far away
Smile a "sly like a fox" smile

People language

Open your mouth wide
Quickly close your jaws
Purr
Cough
Hiss through your nose

Alligator language

Resources: Some good teacher resource books to use are *What is a Reptile?* by Robert Snedden, *Alligators and Crocodiles* by Leslie Dow (Facts on File), and an Eyewitness Book entitled *Reptile* by Colin McCarthy.

Ancient Reptiles

Dinosaurs were ancient reptiles that lived millions of years ago. This was long, long before the alligators and crocodiles, turtles and snakes. There were many types of dinosaurs—some were meat eaters and some were plant eaters. *Dinosaur* means *terrible lizard.*

"We have a good opportunity for 'mathasaurus' measuring when we study dinosaurs. Some were as long as three feet—and Tyrannosaurus Rex, the king, was as long as 36 feet!" Go into the hallway or on the playground and take the yardstick or trundle wheel along so that students get an idea of just how long that is.

"Let's do some 'Artasaurus' and make dinosaurs from modeling clay or paint these giants at the easel." It hasn't been established exactly what color some of them were, so students can select their own colors.

"We can engage in some 'Readasaurus' and read many books about dinosaurs that we get from the library." There will be new vocabulary names to learn such as Ankylosaurus, Brontosaurus, Ceratosaurus, Iguanodon, Triceratops, Protoceratops, Tyrannosaurus, and so on.

"Then we can 'Writeasaurus' about what we have learned about these awesome creatures."

How Big Is Tremendous?

Some new vocabulary words for *big* are in order when discussing dinosaurs. Get out the junior thesaurus and find some words that the students can list and add to their vocabulary. Include words such as *gigantic, huge, overpowering, tremendous,* and so on.

Also try to describe a dinosaur by using the "as big as" formula. Have students come up with some descriptive phrases to help picture these giant lizards. Here are some to get you started:

as big as one elephant on top of another
as big as a house
as big as the fire station
as big as a mountain
as big as . . .

LINKS TO AUTHOR-OF-THE-MONTH

Author/Illustrator for April: Ruth Heller

It is fitting that we have chosen Ruth Heller for our April focus because April is National Poetry Month! When Ruth Heller writes, she writes in rhyme. When she illustrates, she does so with beauty.

This author has taken on the task of writing about parts of speech, in rhyme, and has illustrated her verses with colorful pictures that capture the imagination and help with the concepts. The result is that nouns, verbs, adjectives, pronouns, and other parts of speech come to life with bright illustrations and words that enrich our vocabulary development. There are ten books altogether in this picture book language series.

In addition, Ruth Heller has written and illustrated other books that give us a great deal of information. She has at times illustrated books for other authors, such as *The Egyptian Cinderella, The Korean Cinderella,* and *King Solomon and the Bee,* which are listed here. She has a series of coloring books for children, and even postcards of some of the items found in her books. Enjoy the rhymes and the learning this month. *Let's read!*

Chickens Aren't the Only Ones (New York: Grosset & Dunlap, 1982) This book gives a great deal of information to the reader, and is an asset for the study of birds (or eggs at Easter time). Not only are the pictures large and colorful, but by hooking the reader on the rhyme, the reader's attention is captured and held. In some instances, there are few words on the page. For example, in the beginning two-page spread, we see four large chickens and the words "Chickens lay the eggs you buy"; turn the page for a double-page spread of white eggs, some with yolks, and the words "the eggs you boil or fry or . . ."; turn the page for a double-page spread of brightly colored eggs with designs and a baby chick in the corner, and the words "dye! or leave alone so you can see what grew inside naturally."

We go on to wild birds, tame birds, egg sizes, snakes, reptiles, fish and other sea creatures, insects, and egg-laying animals from Australia. By the time we finish, we do see that "chickens aren't the only ones" who lay eggs. The book won Honorable Mention in the Children's Science Book Award.

Activities to Accompany *Chickens Aren't the Only Ones*

1. This is a book that you don't just read and put down, for there is much to be learned here. First, read the book and enjoy the rhyme and the pictures.

2. Go back through the book and talk about all of the creatures that lay eggs. Then categorize them: chickens, wild birds, tame birds, snakes, fish, insects, and so on.

3. "How many of the wild and tame birds can we recognize?" Some—such as the turkey, duck, and swan—are easily recognizable. Try to identify some of the wild birds. Check other resource books, too.

4. Have children find the largest egg (ostrich) and the smallest egg (hummingbird). They enjoy this page, along with the speckled and colorful eggs found there. Most of them are oval, so introduce that shape and term. Have students paint speckled and spotted eggs at the easel this week. Put the background color on first; when it is dry, add another color with paint or with felt-tip pens.

5. What an array of fish! Readers see big spots, little spots, stripes, and patches of color. Some designs run in circles; others seem random. Each student needs a very large fish shape on plain paper: an oval shape with tail and fins. Then have students lightly sketch in their designs using chalk. Next, paint them. Hang these on a bulletin board with a dark blue background, just like the book. Perhaps the rhyme from the page of fish eggs could be copied as an explanation.

6. *Vocabulary development.* The word "oviparous" is a new word to learn. It has four syllables to tap, and the accent is on VIP. For the meaning, look to the words as stated, "Chickens aren't the only ones. There's no more to discuss. Everyone who lays an egg is O.VIP.A.ROUS."

The Reason for a Flower (New York: Grosset & Dunlap, 1987) With colorful illustrations that splash all over the pages, we are observing birds and bees visiting flowers, carrying pollen, and all for one purpose. As the author tells it, "From an anther on a stamen, to a stigma on a style, Pollen grains must travel and stay a little while. And then you'll see the reason for each flower—even weeds. The reason for a flower is to manufacture . . . seeds." We see some other ways that seeds travel and grow in wet areas and in dry areas. We meet the largest flower, and one that smells sweet, and finally meet up with a page filled with products made from flowers. This is an excellent teaching book for a unit on spring growth.

Activities to Accompany *The Reason for a Flower*

1. Go through the book and enjoy the rhythm, the rhyme, and the illustrations.
2. Create a flowers vocabulary list that includes words such as *nectar, pollen, anther, stamen, stigma, style.* Have students draw a picture of the flowers with blossoms, anther, stamen, stigma, style, and pollen, and print these new words in among the drawing, just as the illustrator has done. There is a rhythm to the words and the drawing. This illustration is not stiff. Have students pretend that there is a gentle breeze blowing on this day, so their flower drawings will bend and sway, too.
3. Examine the page that shows that seeds travel far and wide. Locate the seeds that like to hitch a ride. "Where are the seeds on the bike, the shoe, and the burrs that stick to furs? What experiences have you had with seeds hitching a ride on your clothing?"
4. Examine the double page of seeds that grow roots. "How many can we identify? How many can we eat? Let's taste some of them, especially the carrot and radish that can be eaten raw."
5. "Rice, barley, corn, and wheat are cereals we need to eat." These are big illustrations of what these cereals look like as blossoms or flowers. Have students check cereal boxes at home for any of these that they do eat. Check the newspaper ads for these cereals (corn flakes, shredded wheat, and so on). Have a cereal treat one day, instead of sweets.
6. *Language development.* We're introduced to the word "herbivorous" for animals that don't eat meat. Say the word. Tap the syllables, and you'll find there are four. The accent is on BIV. "How many of these herbivorous animals can we name for the wide array shown on the pages?" Also, students are introduced to plants that are meat eaters, and they are called "carnivorous." Say the word. Tap the syllables. There are four, and the accent is on NIV.
7. All flowers are "angiosperm." Say the word. Tap the syllables. Actually, you say this as "an.GEE.o.sperm" with four syllables, but the text blends the letters "gio"—it's an ancient Greek term.

8. *Products made from flowers.* This is an interesting page to examine, for you see a wide variety of materials that you get from plants. The broom represents wood and straw. But students may be able to use the broom at the top of a chart as a Rebus figure, and then list or draw many other items that people use that are made from wood or straw. The origami paper bird can be the Rebus figure for items made from paper that are enjoyed in your daily life. This will be one of the largest of your lists.

Keep going with this page to list cotton products, rubber products, medicines, items made from seeds and beans, and so on.

Bring in real items and have a huge bulletin board of items.

Kites Sail High. A Book About Verbs (New York: Grosset & Dunlap, 1988)
Using simple, lively verse and vivid, realistic paintings, the author/illustrator introduces the reader to the world of words with the focus upon verbs. There are many basic concepts in this book—and with the aid of the verse and the lively and realistic illustrations—the reader is enriched by this book. It's an excellent teaching tool and can be enjoyed on many levels.

Activities to Accompany *Kites Sail High. A Book About Verbs*

1. Read and enjoy the book. Enjoy the illustrations since it is a book of action—"people run, pelicans fly, kites sail high, and rabbits quickly multiply."

2. Verbs are words of *action*. Have students list words that tell how people move (skip, hop, jump, run, dance, and so on). Move in these ways. Then talk about how other things move and simulate the action—such as a cat waking up from a nap, a dog barking, a tree swaying in the breeze, a fish swimming, and a popcorn seed popping.

3. Revisit the vigorous verb pages where fireworks EXPLODE and horses THUNDER down the road. Ask students to examine the art work here. "How has the illustrator made the action come to life?" Point out that the lines flow, they are not straight, and the page with the horses "overlapping" one another is a technique that shows there is movement here. Perhaps students can try some overlapping of their own, using construction paper cutouts for a start.

4. Study the gorgeous crowns on the kings. Then, on paper crown shapes, have students sketch fancy designs. Use gold felt-tip pens to make them vibrant.

5. Find the page that illustrates changing verbs by adding "ed." There are three illustrations to show "I paint," "I painted," "I have painted." Perhaps students can use a three-panel folded sheet of paper to illustrate "I paint" (dipping in the brush and getting ready); "I painted" (showing the item that was painted); and "I have painted" (showing the painted item and cleaning up the brushes to indicate that one is finished).

6. The author tells us to "use every restraint and never, no never, please, never say ain't." Perhaps you can make this one of your standard rules in the classroom. This is written with a quill feather from a peacock. "What can we write with other than a pencil?" (plant stems, stalks, bird quills)

7. The page on verbs that *link* can be used effectively if students copy some of the text, which is, "I AM a cat. My nose IS pink. My fur FEELS soft. I SOUND content. My lifestyle LOOKS most opulent." Use wallpaper designs for pillow backgrounds. Students can draw their own contented cat and be introduced to the word "opulent" (rich).

8. The extent to which you will want to use this book for language development will depend upon the age and language facility of the group. Those listed here are "starters."

A Cache of Jewels and Other Collective Nouns **(New York: Grosset & Dunlap, 1987)** Here we have words to accompany our classifications. Instead of just saying these are whales, we have a "gam" of whales and a "fleet" of ships with purple sails. So everything is grouped for us, but now we're given the correct word that describes— such as bunch, cluster, school, bevy, muster, flock, host, and many, many more. This is an enjoyable teaching book, and children quickly catch on to the new vocabulary.

Activities to Accompany *A Cache of Jewels and Other Collective Nouns*

1. Go through the book, read it, and enjoy the illustrations.

2. Go through the book again, and tell students to notice that there is ALWAYS more than one of an item that is the same. Locate items with which students are familiar.

3. Separate the items by people, animals, and other. Now let's look at the "other" category. How can we classify them? Notice that we have not yet begun to use the words that describe these groups.

4. Once you have the categories set up, begin to introduce the words that describe the groups—a batch of bread, a bunch of bananas, a cluster of grapes, a kindle of kittens, a parcel of penguins, a forest of trees, and so on.

5. Students can create a photo montage of the noun they wish to illustrate. For example, go through magazines and find pictures of puppies. Cut them out, overlap, and paste them on a large page. Then print the word "litter" on a card and attach it to the photo montage. This can be done for as many words as you'd like. Some students may want to do several to make their own books.

6. Say the words and ask students to identify the group. For example, say "army" and have them raise their hand if they have the matching category (ants). More collective nouns illustrated include "drift" (swans), "clump" (reeds), and "pride" (lions).

7. At the end, the author tells us of other group terms that were not illustrated in this book. Students may want to learn some of these, such as a "rafter" of turkeys, a "leap" of leopards, and a "covey" of quails.

8. One collective noun can describe many groups; for example, a HOST of angels, sparrows, daffodils. One group can be described by more than one collective noun, such as a GAM of whales, a MOB of whales, and a POD of whales. Depending upon the developmental level of the students, this gets to be fun because the author/illustrator has devised a clever way to learn the material!

9. Another of Ruth Heller's stunning books about nouns is *Merry-Go-Round, A Book About Nouns*. Use it as a companion book with this book on collective nouns.

Mine, All Mine, A Book About Pronouns (New York: Grosset & Dunlap, 1997) The author tells us that saying one's name over and over and over again gets repetitious and boring, so that's where pronouns come in. Pronouns give us lots of words like *he* and *she,* and *his* and *hers,* and *yours* and *mine,* and a host of other words that make our language rich and flowing.

This book in the language series has playful verse and stunning illustrations. The verse is whimsical and shows readers how much fun we can have with the language.

Activities to Accompany *Mine, All Mine, A Book About Pronouns*

1. Examine the cover of this book and the book jacket. They're covered with gaily wrapped packages, which is what the book is to us—a gift. Explain to students that learning about the language and learning how to use it well is a gift worth having.

2. Examine the endpapers filled with pieces of wrapped candies. "Match those that look alike. Count them. Are they the same on each page? What fancy names could we give these candies? Why did the illustrator use candies on the endpapers? Could it be that the message is that learning is sweet?"

3. Regardless of where the student is in terms of language development and readiness for an abundance of pronouns, everyone is ready for the illustrations. They are a visual feast! Even if you teach very young students and do nothing more with this book, just enjoy the words and the illustrations.

4. As you go through this book, note that Ruth Heller has included illustrations from familiar fairy tales and fantasy stories to help with the descriptive words. Find Goldilocks and the Three Bears. Find Red Riding Hood and the Wolf. Find the double-page drawing of Pinocchio's nose that grew and grew to such a length that it turned into a branch of a tree that houses a bird's nest and birds. Children and adults, who are delighted with this particular page, like to draw Pinocchio's nose as a long stem that branches out and see what they can put in it. It is an extremely imaginative page. (This is a good opportunity to read the Pinocchio story.)

5. Bring on the clowns! They help us learn language, too. Examine the stripes, polka dots, flowers, checks, squares, and other colorful shapes and forms. Then create a colorful language clown from designed wrapping paper, wallpaper samples, glossy magazine designs, and construction paper. "What lesson does this clown want us to learn?"

6. Put yourself last. The author says it best on the last page, "You will never be outclassed if you put 'I' or 'ME' last. Say, 'he and I' or 'him and me,' not 'me and him' or 'I and he.'" This is a good language lesson to learn. Students can easily memorize these lines.

Climo, Shirley. *The Egyptian Cinderella,* **illustrated by Ruth Heller (New York: Thomas Y. Crowell, 1989)** When the blonde, fair-skinned Rhodopis was a small girl, she was stolen by pirates from her home in Greece and taken to Egypt where she was sold as a slave. But she looked different from the others—she had blonde hair and green eyes and skin that burned under the hot sun. When she grew up, the household into which she was sold had dark-skinned beauties who were servants, but since Rhodopis was a slave, they ordered her to do the menial chores. This story continues with the falcon bird as helper and Rhodopis being described as having "eyes as green as the Nile, hair as feathery as papyrus, and skin the pink of a lotus flower." The falcon steals away her slipper which ends up in the hands of the Pharaoh, who must find its owner. The story has an element of truth and fancy, as we can see from the author's note at the end of the book. (**Fact:** A Greek slave girl, Rhodopis, married the Pharaoh Amasis and became his queen during the Dynasty XXVI, 570–526 B.C.)

Climo, Shirley. *The Korean Cinderella,* **illustrated by Ruth Heller (New York: HarperCollins, 1993)** In this story, one of many Cinderella-type stories in Korea, a young girl named Pear Blossom is dearly loved by her mother and father. One day, her mother dies. Her father goes to the matchmaker and gets a new wife who has a daughter, Peony. Alas, Pear Blossom is badly treated, but has helpers in the form of a frog, the birds, and ox. On her way to the festival, she loses her shoe, which is found by the magistrate. The lucky shoe leads him to Pear Blossom, and they marry. Nothing is mentioned at the end of this tale about the mother and stepsister.

Activities to Accompany *The Egyptian Cinderella* and *The Korean Cinderella*

1. Before reading these two tales, make sure students are familiar with the European version of this tale. Select one by Charles Perrault or Susan Jeffers and read it aloud.

2. These two stories are long, so they may have to be read halfway through or until the reader comes to a good stopping point, and then finished at another time. However, they are fascinating and the students will not lose interest.

3. Make sure that, after the stories are read, the illustrations are examined carefully. Note the costumes, the hair styles, and the special hats that the men wear. Have a discussion with students about what they are learning from the illustrations.

4. In both tales, there is the issue of the little shoe. Ask students to compare the shoes, and compare them to Cinderella's slipper. The shoe leads to happiness in all three stories, but they are slightly different. Make the comparisons.

5. In these books, the Cinderella character goes by a different name. Have students learn the name Rhodopis (Ra DOH pes) in the Egyptian version and Pear Blossom in the Korean version.

6. Have students discover who the "helpers" are in these tales—the falcon in the Egyptian version and the frog, birds, and ox in the Korean version. In the European version, Cinderella has a fairy godmother.

7. Learn the words for the magic helpers in different languages. In Korea, a "tokgabi" is the frog and "Ewha" means Pear Blossom. In Egypt, the magic falcon is named Horus. Rhodopis means "rosy-cheeked" in Greek. The ruler in Egypt was a pharaoh, and in Korea the ruler here is a magistrate. In the European versions we meet a prince.

8. Make a CINDERELLA chart using large kraft paper. Draw a grid so students can write in the spaces. Along the left side print TITLE, and then print the titles of each of the three books along the top of the chart. You will need a section for the following: AUTHOR/ILLUSTRATOR, SETTING, CHARACTERS, PROBLEM, HELPERS, ENDING/RATING. Here's a sample:

TITLE	Cinderella	The Egyptian Cinderella	The Korean Cinderella
AUTHOR/ ILLUSTRATOR			
SETTING where/when			
CHARACTERS			
PROBLEM			
HELPERS			
ENDING			
WHAT WE MOST LIKED			

9. **Note:** There are many other Cinderella variants, so you may be interested in continuing with the Cinderella study with *Rough Face Girl* by Rafe Martin (Algonquin Indian), *Mufaro's Beautiful Daughters* by John Steptoe (African), and various other versions such as *The Talking Eggs* by Robert SanSouci. There are over 1,000 versions around the world.

Do *not* make a study of the retold and updated versions of the tales until students are familiar with the traditional versions. The updated versions that take place in cities and towns lose some of the magic of the original tales and become good stories to enjoy and examine afterwards.

Renberg, Dalia Hardof. *King Solomon and the Bee,* **illustrated by Ruth Heller (New York: HarperCollins, 1994)** This is a tale of King Solomon and how, one day while snoozing in his gardens, a bee alighted on his nose. It tickled and, as he went to brush it away, the startled bee stung his nose. The King was furious. Who would dare to sting him! He summoned all of the bees and one little bee came forward with an apology and said that if he was spared, some day he would repay the King. This amused King Solomon, who let the bee go. But one day, the Queen of Sheba and her maidens came to visit the King with puzzles and tests for him to pass. All of the maidens carried a beautiful bouquet of flowers, but only one was real and the king had to guess which one. It was a difficult if not impossible task. But when the King heard the buzzing of the bee, it was no longer impossible.

Activities to Accompany *King Solomon and the Bee*

1. Enjoy the story and the illustrations. Children will find the artist's illustration of the bee sting on the nose to be amusing.
2. Read part of this story and stop after the King lets the bee go. Ask students to imagine what a bee could do for the King some day to repay him. Then continue until the end of the story.
3. Have students make a diorama of a scene from the story.
4. "Why do bees sting?" This calls for a trip to the library to find out about this habit of bees. Students may have been stung and will be eager to tell about their experiences.
5. A bit of honey on crackers might be just the enjoyable treat for an ending to your storytime.

And Many More!

During April Poetry Month, enjoy the poems of many other poets who write and illustrate for children today. (See the Bibliography for suggestions.) In the verse language series by Ruth Heller, there are a total of ten books.

REPRODUCIBLE ACTIVITY PAGES

Name _____

RAINY DAY CONTRACTIONS

Draw a line from the umbrella words to the contraction clouds. Color the umbrellas with bright, spring colors.

© 2000 by The Center for Applied Research in Education

Use each contraction and write six sentences on the reverse side.

© 2000 by The Center for Applied Research in Education

STICK PUPPETS AND CHANT (LONG A, SHORT A)

THE ALLIGATOR AND THE APE

Acorn jumps on Allie's back
She gives a signal
His tail gives a whack!
They float down the river
But they always come back.

Yes, that's how the story goes
It does.
Hey!
That's how the story goes.

With an "A" and an "Ah"
And an "A" "Ah, ah!"
With an "A" and an "Ah"
And an "A" "Ah, ah!"

A—Ape! Ah—Alligator! RAH!

Color and cut the stick puppets. Learn the chant. Put on your own puppet show.

STICK PUPPETS AND CHANT (LONG E, SHORT E)

THE EAGLE AND THE ELEPHANT

Edith Eagle, fell from the sky

Landed close to an elephant's eye

She curled up
Didn't let out a peep

Ellie rocked her 'til
She went to sleep.

Yes, that's how the story goes

It does,

Hey!

That's how the story goes!

With an "E" and an "EH"
And an "E," "Eh, eh!"
With an "E" and an "Eh"
And an "E," "Eh, eh."

E—Eagle! Eh—Elephant! RAH!

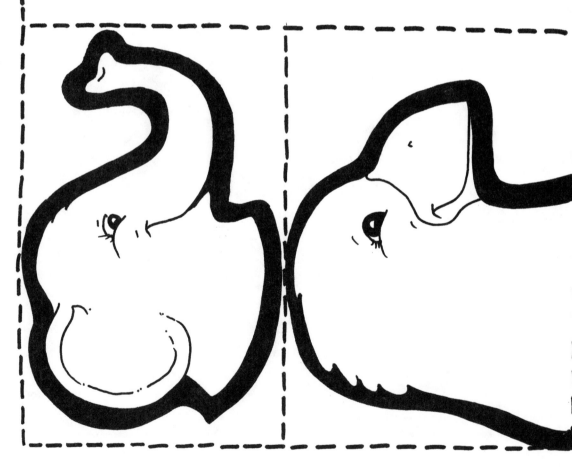

Color and cut the stick puppets. Learn the chant. Put on your own puppet show.

© 2000 by The Center for Applied Research in Education

STICK PUPPETS AND CHANT (LONG I, SHORT I)

© 2000 by The Center for Applied Research in Education

IRIS ICICLE AND THE IGLOOS

Iris Icicle
took her bicycle
And went to a land
far away.

She and her team
patched every seam
on igloos
night and day.

They poured icy water
through a worn out hose
And Ignatz the Wood Cutter
nearly froze.

Yes that's how the story goes
It does,
Hey!
That's how the story goes!

With an "I" and an "Ih"
And an "I" "Ih, Ih."
With an "I" and an "Ih"
And an "I" "Ih, Ih!"

I—Iris! Ih—Igloo! YAHOO!

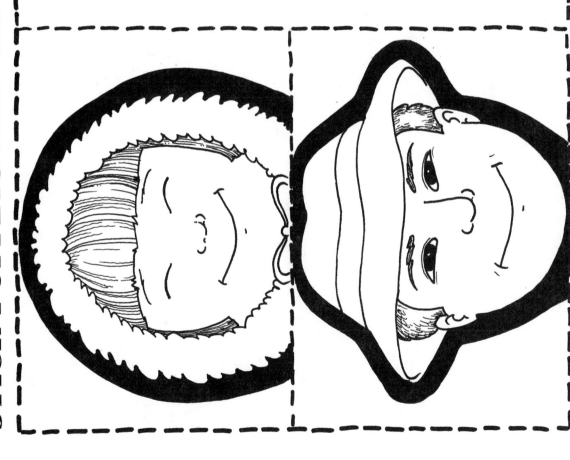

Color and cut the stick puppets. Learn the chant. Put on your own puppet show.

STICK PUPPETS AND CHANT (LONG O, SHORT O)

THE OGRE AND THE OCTOPUS

Ogre O'Dell got a
brand new start
Thanks to Ollie Octopus
she's got a new heart.

Oh! she's friendly
Oh! she's nice
Oh! she's sugar
And a pinch of spice.

Ollie the octopus
Is very glad
He knows that ogre
Didn't want to be bad.

Yes, that's how the story goes
It does,
Hey!
That's how the story goes!

With an "O" and an "Aah"
and an "O" "Aah, aah"
With an "O" and an "Aah"
and an "O" "Aah, aah!"

O—Ogre! Aah—Octopus!
"OOOOOOh-Aaaaaah!"

Color and cut the stick puppets. Learn the chant. Put on your own puppet show.

© 2000 by The Center for Applied Research in Education

STICK PUPPETS AND CHANT (LONG U, SHORT U)

© 2000 by The Center for Applied Research in Education

THE UNICORN AND THE UMBRELLA BIRD

The umbrella bird
is so mixed up
He doesn't know a saucer
goes under a cup.

He doesn't know how to
wear underclothes,
He doesn't know thorns
grow under a rose,
He doesn't see a worm
that's under his nose,
He doesn't use a handkerchief
when he blows!

But Unicorn will change all that
for a Unicorn's patient and kind,
Before you know it, that umbrella bird
will have a brilliant mind.

Yes sir!
He'll have a mighty fine mind.
Uh, huh!
He'll have an A PLUS mind.

U—UNICORN.   UH—UMBRELLA BIRD.
U, Uh!   U, Uh!   U, Uh!

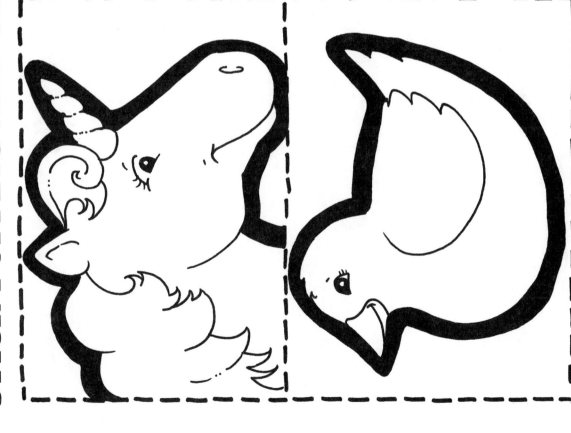

Color and cut the stick puppets. Lean the chant. Put on your own puppet show.

APRIL BOOKMARKS

Please put me to bed with a good book!

Please wake me up with a good book!

My Bookmark _____

My Bookmark _____

© 2000 by The Center for Applied Research in Education

Name _____

KIKI KANGAROO AND THE "KN" WORDS

Kiki has a new job. She matches pictures and words in a sock factory. Today she can use your help. Draw a line from the picture to the word. Then, see how many "kn" words you can use in the same sentence.

knot

knapsack

knife

knee

knit

knob

knight

© 2000 by The Center for Applied Research in Education

ABBREVIATION IN ADDRESSES

Address the two envelopes. Design your own stamps. Use some of these abbreviations:

Mr.   Mrs.   Ms.   St.   Rd.   Ave.   Apt.

© 2000 by The Center for Applied Research in Education

Name _____

JANUARY AND JUNE ARE PEN PALS

Dear June,

   I have more snow to shovel, and more clothes that I have to wear. It takes me longer to write my name. My daylight time is shorter than yours. Do you want to trade places?

   Your friend,
   January

You can answer the letter and cheer up January. Mention all of the GOOD things January can do that June cannot. Design your June stationery, and color January with bright colors.

© 2000 by The Center for Applied Research in Education

Name _____

CHICKEN EGGS ARE BEAUTIFUL

In Ruth Heller's book, *Chicken's Aren't The Only Ones,* there are some beautiful and colorful egg designs.

Here is your chance to design and color three eggs.

© 2000 by The Center for Applied Research in Education

CHILDREN'S PICTURE BOOKS

FOR THE MONTHS OF

MAY AND JUNE

Breslow, Susan, and Blakemore, Sally. *I Really Want a Dog.* **Illustrations by True Kelley (New York: Dutton Children's Books, 1990)** What little boy hasn't said, "If I had a dog . . ." A voice from above, in the shape of a dog cloud, answers the boy's yearning and asks many good questions that lead the boy to think. It shows the responsibility for caring and choosing a pet.

Brown, Ruth. *Alphabet Times Four, An International ABC* **(New York: Dutton, 1991)** Underneath each lovely painting per page is a row of print containing a word in four different languages, representing something from the picture. For example, the "N" page has two little mice huddling by a hole through which a cat is looking. At the bottom, the words *nose, nariz, nez,* and *nase* are printed which represent the word "nose" in English, Spanish, French, and German.

Greenfield, Eloise. *Honey, I Love and Other Poems.* **Pictures by Diane and Leo Dillon (New York: HarperCollins, 1978)** This author is the winner of the 1997 Award for Excellence in Poetry for Children, awarded by the National Council of Teachers of English. Her words are a nourishment to the spirit. Also look for the poetry book *Under the Sunday Tree* by this author, with paintings by Amos Ferguson.

Lewis, J. Patrick. *July Is a Mad Mosquito.* **Illustrated by Melanie W. Hall (New York: Atheneum, 1994)** A month-by-month romp through the sounds, smells, and sights of the year from January through December. At the end the months are woven together in a lyrical poem.

Moss, Lloyd. *Zin! Zin! Zin! A Violin.* **Illustrated by Marjorie Priceman (New York: Scholastic, 1995)** One by one we meet the instruments of the orchestra. The text is rarely in a straight line; it swirls in a rhythmic pattern. When we have met a number of the instruments, in rhyme, they are ready for their entrance to the orchestral performance. (A Caldecott Honor Book.)

Nunes, Susan Miho. *The Last Dragon.* **Illustrated by Chris K. Soentpiet (New York: Clarion, 1995)** A young boy, Peter, is sent to spend the summer in Chinatown with his aunt in an apartment above a noodle factory. How boring! That is, until he spies a dusty, faded, ripped dragon in a store window and wants to bring it back to its old glory. The aunt helps—and soon summer becomes a wonderful adventure!

Sharmat, Marjorie Weinman. *Hurray for Father's Day!* **Illustrated by John Wallner (New York: Holiday House, 1987)** Sterling and Monica Mule vow to make this the best day yet for Dad. One wants to do things for Dad; the other wants to buy presents. At the end of a hectic day of competition for making Dad feel good, Dad calls a halt to it and decides how to best end the day.

Shaw, Nancy. *Sheep in a Shop.* **Illustrated by Margot Apple (Boston: Houghton-Mifflin, 1991)** It's the month of May and the sheep set out on a shopping spree. "Sheep find blocks. Sheep wind clocks. Sheep try trains. Sheep fly planes." The text is in rhyme with whimsical illustrations. Other books in this popular series are *Sheep in a Jeep* and *Sheep on a Ship.*

Talbot, John. *Pins and Needles* **(New York: Dial, 1991)** Did you ever wake up and have a "pins and needles" feeling in your arm or foot? Jean Pierre the Elephant wakes up with pins and needles in his big, long trunk and can't get rid of the feeling all day long. Finally, at bedtime, his friend finds a solution. (Good book for dramatic play—includes plenty of exercise.)

Wynot, Jillian. *The Mother's Day Sandwich.* **Pictures by Maxie Chambliss (New York: Orchard, 1990)** Ivy and Hackett surprise their mother with breakfast in bed on Mother's Day, but what a mess they leave in the kitchen. Make that two messes, for when mother is awakened from a sound sleep, she overturns the tray in the bed and the food flies.

MAY and JUNE

MAY AND JUNE GREETINGS! Unless yours is a year-round school, this is your last opportunity to make the year count. Praise students for what they know, praise them for what they can do, and challenge them to further their skills. For some, this may mean more time with review, repetition, or practicing material that has already been presented. For others, it may mean more time for enrichment and sharpening the skills they have acquired this year. Students should never stop learning and never stop trying.

The temperatures are climbing outdoors—as well as indoors if your school does not have air conditioning! But, champions keep on practicing. Where is the real marching band? Out in the scorching sun, practicing. Where is the real winning sports team? Out in the scorching sun, practicing. The message that students have to learn is that even though it may get to be a bit physically uncomfortable, that does not mean it's time to give up. You must never send that message to students. Why? Because you, as a teacher, are the role model. Students will follow your direction—if you continue to work diligently until the end of the year, so will your students. Expect nothing less, and they will not disappoint you.

So, let's work and enjoy learning right up to the last day of the school year. Leave the message with students, too, that you expect them to continue working on their skills during the long summer vacation. Encourage students and their parents to frequent the library this summer, where they can join library reading programs. They can set up their own play school within their neighborhood and take turns being the teacher. Instill in them this love of learning and achievement.

May/June's Focus on Reading. (1) Phonics; (2) Ricky Raccoon and the Double "OO"; (3) Strategies for Stuck-in-the-Mud Reading; (4) Making ABC Books; (5) Planet Earth to Mars—Be Explicit; (6) Poetry; (7) Folktales; and (8) Spelling.

Phonics

Spring Phonics

It's that time of year for fresh flowers in the classroom. Students often bring in a bouquet of lilacs, tulips, daffodils, hyacinths, irises, and so on. Have students identify the flowers, and tell what letter sound the flower begins with. Students can make a Flower Sound Book. Cut several circles and staple them together at the top. Students can draw or cut out the simple shape of the flower from colored construction paper and paste one on each page. "Label the flower page with the beginning letter sound. Then put a long green strip on the last page and paste some leaves on it. Now we have a flower shape book."

Undercover Sounds

Show students four different objects, identify them, and say the beginning letter and its sound. Next, place these objects deep in a basket under a checkered cloth. Then have students, one at a time, reach under—without looking—and bring out the object that "begins with the _____ sound." Classroom items can be used, such as ruler (r), stapler (s), pencil (p), book (b). Do this several times with the same objects so that different students get a chance. Have students hunt for other objects to put undercover.

ABC Calendars

Distribute a calendar grid to each student. Instead of placing the numerals in the squares, place a letter of the alphabet in each square. Refer to them as the Sunday letters, Monday letters, Tuesday letters and so on, so they are all identified. Then say, for example, "I'm thinking of a Sunday letter and you can bounce it or throw it." Have students raise their hand to give the answer. Do several more in this way. Then have students take turns being "it" to give the challenge to find a letter.

Ball-of-Yarn Letters

Students can use a ruler to help them cut different colors of yarn into 12-inch lengths. Distribute two or three pieces of yarn to each student. First, let them move them around on their own to form letters. Then, call time and have them set the yarn strips off to the side. Next, give a clue about a letter sound. Each student can take one of his or her yarn pieces and make that letter shape on the flat surface in front of him or her. You—as well as the students—get instant feedback.

Variation: Use miniature chalkboards, chalk, and erasers for this same exercise.

Stop-and-Go Phonics

Give each student two construction paper circles—green for "go" and red for "stop." Explain to them that you will make a statement about letters and sounds. If the students agree, they are to hold up the green card so you can continue. If students disagree, they are to hold up the red card, and then it can be discussed.

For example: Say, "Lemon and lime begin with the same letter." *(green card).* "Lemon begins with the letter 'l' and lime begins with the letter 't.' *(red card)*

Phonics Letter Folders

Get 26 file folders, one for each letter of the alphabet. Print the capital and lower-case letter on the outside of the folder. Have students locate pictures in magazines that begin with those sounds. When you have enough, students can arrange these pictures on the *inside* of the folder, both sides, and glue them to the surface. You will soon have a great (spill-proof!) record file of each alphabet letter.

- For vowels, you can have two folders—one for long sounds and one for short sounds—or they can both be in the same folder.
- Students can use these folders on their own, going to them to review the letters and sounds.
- Students can work with a partner, each having his or her own folder. Then they can take turns making up riddles about a sound picture in their folder.
- Students can find more pictures to match the ones glued onto the file folders. Place them in see-through bags and clip them to the folders. Then students can match the pictures. (The pictures won't look exactly alike, but they will be of the same thing. For example, in the letter "T" folder, a toaster picture can be pasted down and a different toaster picture placed in the bag, but they match because they are the same item.)

Alphabet Exercise

Have students exercise regularly, but instead of saying "one, two, one, two" or "one, two, three, four," say the ABC letters. Here are some different routines to get you started:

A—both arms up with elbows bent
B—both arms high overhead
C—both arms back down with elbows bent
D—both arms at sides
} repeat routine three times

E—both arms up with elbows bent
F—both arms out to the sides
G—both arms back in with elbows bent
H—both arms at sides
} repeat routine three times

I—both hands on hips
J—tip body to the right from the waist
K—body upright, hands on hips
L—tip body to the left from waist
M—body upright, hands on hips
N—hands at sides
} repeat routine three times

O—turn neck and look over right shoulder
P—look straight ahead, standing tall
Q—turn neck and look over left shoulder
R—look straight ahead, standing tall
} repeat routine three times

S—stand tall, shoulders back
T—head straight, looking front
U—swivel body to right, and back
V—swivel body to left, and back
} repeat routine three times

W—hands on hips
X—right foot up/down, up/down, up/down
Y—left foot up/down, up/down, up/down
Z—hands at sides, rest

} repeat routine three times

March *in place* to the ABC song rhythm. Lift one foot, then the other, in slow motion, with hands at sides, as the letters are slowly and distinctly called out by the group:

A, B, C, D, E, F, G (pause)
H, I, J, K, L, M, N, O, P (pause)
Q, R, S, T (pause)
U, V, W (pause)
X, Y, Z (pause)
Now I know my ABC's (seven running steps in place)
Tell me what you think of me. (seven running steps in place)

End: Feet together, hands clasped behind back, bow from waist, stand tall at attention (all in unison, just as a gymnast team would do).

Nonverbal, Action-Packed Alphabet Communication

You can play numerous games with the ABC's by using body mannerisms, facial expressions, and dramatizations. Make a standard set of ABC cards that show the letter, the word or words, and the action. (Students can help make these.) Go over all of these together with students in the beginning. Pull a letter card out of the bag, tell students what it says, show them the card, demonstrate the action, have them do the same, and then put it aside. Introduce all letters in this manner.

The student who is "It" takes an action alphabet letter card and acts it out while the group watches. Then students raise their hands to guess what letter it is. The student who guesses the letter correctly is the next "It."

For example, in this action alphabet, the letter "a" stands for *ache*. (See action alphabet below.) If "It" demonstrates this action and calls upon someone who says "rubbing your shoulder," the answer is "no." The person has to say "*a* for *ache*."

Here are some actions to help get you started. For some groups, perhaps in the beginning, it would be best to work with only five cards at a time, and then add more. There is a strong kinesthetic link to the alphabet with these actions—it is helpful for the learner who needs to move about and be physically involved.

A . . . ache . . .   rub shoulder, painful facial expression
B . . . brush . . .   pretend to brush crumbs off lap
C . . . catch . . .   simulate catching a ball
D . . . dog . . .   hands up (paws), panting
E . . . elephant . . .   hands together, bend over, walk heavily,
                               swing arms
F . . . fish . . .   make wavy motions with hand

G . . . gallop . . .	gallop around the room	
H . . . hear . . .	cup hand to ear	
I . . . in . . .	pretend to twist doorknob, open door, walk in	
J . . . jolly . . .	hold stomach and laugh	
K . . . king . . .	stand tall, put on crown, walk magestically	
L . . . lion . . .	open mouth and roar	
M . . . monkey . . .	bend, scamper back and forth using arms and legs (all fours)	
N . . . nose . . .	pick up item and smell it	
O . . . over . . .	make circular motion with hand	
P . . . pick . . .	pick up something	
Q . . . quiet . . .	forefinger to lips for "quiet"	
R . . . run . . .	run in place	
S . . . sing . . .	sing "la, la, la, la"	
T . . . tick-tock . . .	swing arms back and forth	
U . . . under . . .	crouch under desk or table	
V . . . voice . . .	pretend to talk on telephone	
W . . . wink . . .	close one eye	
X . . . X marks the spot . . .	sign name on chalkboard and point to the space before it	
Y . . . yawn . . .	open and close mouth	
Z . . . zipper . . .	pretend to zip jacket	

Even after playing this and enjoying it, some students still do not get the idea that they need to give the precise answer that links to the alphabet letter. For that reason, it may be necessary to either make an action ABC chart for the room or an individual one that can be photocopied for students to have right in front of them.

Ricky Raccoon and the Double "OO"

Raccoon Rhymes With Moon

Remember Ricky Raccoon? He's the trickster we met in February when he pretended to help all of the vowels. (By way of review, it might be a good idea to reread that story.) The letter "r" controls the vowels by changing their sound, as in *ar, er, ir, or,* and *ur.*

Raccoon rhymes with *moon.* Remember, Ricky is a nocturnal animal, which means that he comes out at night—and so does the moon. Point out to students that both words have the double letter "o" in their name and have a cooing sound. List some of the following rhyming words on the chalkboard or on a chart:

raccoon	boom	broom
balloon	goon	loon
moon	noon	pontoon
room	soon	zoom

Raccoon, Moon, Book? (What's Going on Here?)

"Since Ricky sleeps during the day, he isn't always on duty when the sun shines. One day, Double 'oo' saw a robber running away and he dropped something. It was picked up, turned in, and identified as a book. 'Book that rhymes with moon?' asked Double 'oo.' 'No,' said the detective, 'book that rhymes with crook.'"

"Well, since Ricky wasn't there to claim the Double 'oo' sound, we learned that many words with Double 'oo' rhyme with book and crook. How can we tell if Ricky is sleeping or saying his sound? We just have to try both sounds and use the one that makes sense." Here are some double "oo" words that rhyme with *book:*

book	took	crook
look	nook	mistook
hook	cook	cookie

Making Sense of Double "O" Words

Use these simple sentences to help students select the double "oo" sound that makes sense. Does it rhyme with *raccoon* or does it rhyme with *book?*

Oh, *look!* The sun is out! *(rhymes with book)*

She *took* the dog. *(rhymes with book)*

I see the *moon.* *(rhymes with raccoon)*

The *cook* is here. *(rhymes with book)*

The *room* is warm. *(rhymes with raccoon)*

Here's a challenge. There are two different double "oo" sounds in the same sentence. Print it on the chalkboard and see if students can figure it out. Encourage them to work at it until the sentence makes sense. Don't let Ricky the Tricky get the better of them!

The *food* is *good.*

Strategies for Stuck-in-the Mud Reading

Impress upon students that when we say we are "stuck in the mud," it's an expression that means "we're not going anywhere." We can't move on. Sometimes students get stuck on a word or stuck in a sentence, and can't move on. (Even the vowels got stuck in the mud in our trickster tale about Ricky in the February reading focus section.) What can be done about it? Here are some clues that may prove helpful to students.

Stuck-in-the-Mud Decoding Rule #1

Look for little words in big words. Try to find a little word in the word that you don't know. For example, if the word is *trumpet,* perhaps a student can find *pet* and then sound out *tr-uh-m* and glide it into the word *pet.*

Try finding the little words in these words and sound out the rest of the letters in front and behind them.

cabbage (cab age)
another (an other)
carpet (car pet)
character (act)
parsnips (snip)
foolish (fool)
lamp (am)

Stuck-in-the-Mud Decoding Rule #2

Look for the rimes. Look for familiar letters, such as the rimes we've met previously. Some are as follows:

back (ack)
fact (act)
grape (ape)
hand (an)
plate (ate)

There are many, many more rimes, or word families, that can help students.

Stuck-in-the-Mud Decoding Rule #3

Look for blends to help sound out the words. Some blend examples are:

bl	br	cl	cr	dr	fl
fr	gl	gr	kl	mp	pl
pr	st	sl	tr		

Look for three-letter blends. These clusters include:

spl   scr   str   spr

Stuck-in-the-Mud Decoding Rule #4

Look for the root word. In many cases, when students find the root word, they can figure out the endings which are often *s, es, ed,* or *ing.*

swim, swims, swimming
drink, drinks, drinking
color, colors, coloring
dress, dresses, dressed, dressing
press, presses, pressed, pressing
clash, clashes, clashed, clashing

Stuck-in-the-Mud Decoding Rule #5

Is Ricky controlling the vowels? Remember: *ar, er, ir, or, ur.* The vowels are neither long nor short; they are "r-controlled."

arm, were, firm, corn, burn

Is Ricky controlling the double "oo" letters that rhyme with raccoon?

moon, croon, soon, balloon
book, crook, took, look

Is Ricky letting Owl's letter "w" ride in the front seat, but "w" is snoozing?

wrong, wrist, wreck, wrinkle, wrap

Stuck-in-the-Mud Decoding Rule #6

Is letter "k" silently watching over letter "n"?

know, knack, knock, knew, knit
knuckle, knob, knee, knot, unknown

Stuck-in-the-Mud Decoding Rule #7

Go back over the letters once again and sound them all out. Go back over the vowels to determine if they are long or short.

Stuck-in-the-Mud Decoding Rule #8

These are some **other strategies** to use:

- Substitute another word and see if you can make sense of the sentence.
- Check the pictionary.
- Check your word wall.
- Check your Rebus word bank.
- Check your word bank file.
- Check for picture clues.
- Ask a friend; ask the teacher.
- Leave it for now and come back to it later when you have help.

Stuck-in-the-Mud Decoding Rule #9

As a rule of thumb, if a student is asking for help for more than five words on a page of print, then the material is too difficult. Remember, there are three reading levels:

1. *Beginning:* Students need letter–sound relationships, phonics skill building, repetition, reinforcement activities, flash cards, practice, browsing through books, and story time.
2. *Instructional:* Students can read after they get vocabulary words, skill work, and guidance.
3. *Independent:* Students can read on their own.

Making ABC Books

By this time of year, students have looked through and read a wide variety of ABC books in a classroom that is devoted to exposing students to the alphabet in many ways. As the teacher, you have no doubt read aloud many ABC books. Check back through the selections at the beginning of each month to find an ABC book. Also go through the Reading focus for each month where you will find many ABC books listed.

Bring in library ABC books by the bagful. Ask students to share their ABC books with the class. Some that you shared with the group last September or October may be brought in again and take on new meaning as students have matured over the months. (See the Bibliography for more ABC books.)

Make Theme ABC Books

Students can take a theme, such as animals, cities, sports, and make an ABC book on that subject. "Decide whether this will be a book that has one word per page or whether it will have sentences. Decide whether it will show both upper- and lower-case letters, and where they will be placed on the page. Decide whether or not there will be borders. Decide on the media. There are many decisions to make during the planning stage, before beginning the actual book."

Make a Shape ABC Book

"From construction paper, make the shape of a tree, with a brown trunk and flip-top green shape for the tree top. The theme of the ABC book can be animals who live in the tree, sleep under the tree, walk by the tree, and so on. Also, people and inanimate objects can be included in the book as they interact in some way with the tree."

Make an ABC Book of Letters

Cut out alphabet letters. Decorate them and put a Rebus figure on them that is representative of the sound. Then tape the letters together. In the end, 26 letters will be strung (taped) together in a row. Have students work on three at a time instead of all letters at once.

Make a Dot-to-Dot ABC Book

Students can pretend they are book designers who have been asked to make an ABC book for a very young learner. Instead of making the letter on the page, show it as a dot-to-dot shape so that a student can interact with the page and trace the letter.

Make a "Dagwood" Sandwich ABC Book

Dagwood, from the comic strip "Blondie," likes to raid the refrigerator at night and make a big stacked sandwich. Students will need a very long strip of paper with a tan construction paper cut-out of a bun shape at the top and one at the bottom. Then they go through magazines and cut out horizontal strips of food (or other things) that go into the sandwich. Be sure the items are in ABC order. Students can take artistic license for this activity because there is a saying, "he ate everything but the kitchen sink." Let's take an "Amelia Bedelia" approach—the kitchen sink can be included, either for "k" or "s."

Have an ABC Book-making Workshop

Have students collaborate on a big book of ABC letters. They must plan it out; some children are illustrators, some are printers. Then, when the book is assembled and glued, arrange to have students go to other classrooms to share their book. Some planning considerations include:

- Will the book have just upper-case letters, or upper- and lower-case letters on a page?
- Where will the letters be placed on the page?
- Will all the letters be the same color?
- Will there be labels for the illustrations or is this a story?
- Will there be a border?

Be Explicit

Explicit is a new vocabulary word for the students. It means *exact*. Work on the skill of giving explicit (exact) directions and following them explicitly (exactly), so that students can carry out the directions. Students need to learn exactly what is expected, so that it is not open to interpretation. This carries over to the printed page as well.

Say What You See

Use a variety of pictures cut from magazines and determine which ones you can use for this activity. If you have a picture of a bird in a tree, for example, you can work with the position word "in." Paste the picture on a sheet of construction paper and print this sentence at the bottom:

The bird is _____ the tree.
    (under, in, on)

Make a set of ten different pictures and sentences, and place them in a work folder so students can gain practice with simple direction words such as *in, on, under, inside, outside, top, bottom, over,* and so on. Students can also use picture clues to help decipher the words in the sentence.

Say What You Mean

Make a set of sentence strips that students can work with. They will need to figure out the missing word by *seeing* the sentence. The answer can be printed on the back of the strip under a flap. Here are some to get you started.

I like to _____ pizza.
        (eat, ate)

Liddy and Tom _____ to run.
            (look, like)

She likes to _____ flowers.
           (pick, pack)

Please turn _____ the lamp.
          (in, on)

Will you _____ me at school?
        (met, meat, meet)

His socks are _____ .
            (grip, grin, green)

The _____ can bark.
   (log, dog)

We will plant _____ today.
            (seeds, seize)

This exercise can also be done by incorporating listening and seeing. Print the words that are under the blank line on the chalkboard and introduce them. Then tell students that you will say a sentence using first one word and then the other(s). They are to select the one that makes sense, so they must listen carefully. The children can raise their hand to be called upon if they know the answer.

Giving Directions

Give one verbal direction; then two directions; then work up to three directions. This strengthens *listening* skills and requires that students remain focused.

- SIMPLE DIRECTIONS
  One direction: "Pick up the book."
  Two directions: "Pick up the book and put it on the shelf."

Three directions: "Pick up the book and put it on the shelf next to the red book."

- MORE COMPLEX DIRECTIONS

One direction: "Put the scissors on the counter."

Two directions: "Put the scissors on the counter and the rulers in the box."

Three directions: "Put the scissors on the counter and the rulers in the box, and then meet at the rug for a story."

You must be explicit when giving directions. For example, telling students to *put the scissors and rulers away* may be too vague for the student who has difficulty attending. Perhaps that student doesn't decipher "away" and needs more explicit directions, such as "on the counter" or "in the box."

Communicating Verbal Information

Urge students to avoid fuzzy phrases, such as:

"I saw *this thing* on the way to school, and . . . " *(what thing?)*

"We went to *this place* and I got a new baseball." *(where?)*

"Uh . . . *this lady* said to my Mom, . . . uh . . . "Hello" . . . *(who?)*

Have students think things through in their head before they talk out loud. Give some time for thinking, so students can talk "in their head." For some students, this is still a difficult concept, so have them "whisper their talk into cupped hands" for practice.

Learning to memorize a poem or pledge by heart is often easier for some students if they can whisper it out loud into cupped hands, so as not to disturb classmates. Let them know that when they are alone, they can practice by speaking out loud.

Poetry

A Spring Festival of Poetry

Total Group. Have students memorize a poem together as a class. Work on it daily. When ready, say it aloud and record it on a cassette tape recording. Perhaps when the recitation is perfected, you can arrange to have this tape played for the entire school over the public address system during "Special Announcement" time.

Small Group. Have students work in groups of four or five to learn a poem. That means several different poems will be learned by classmates. Set time aside for memorizing the poem. Give each student a copy to take home and learn. When the small group is ready, have them say the poem aloud for the entire group. (Set proper conditions for listening as an audience.) Record it.

Next, send a message to other teachers in the building asking if they would like to have poems said for their group. Give them the choice of two different days and two different times during the day.

Sometimes there are students who do not yet do well with this type of memorization and performance activity. In an effort to have them included, they can go along and announce the poem, or stand silently holding a large colorful prop, or provide sound effects. Their contribution is helping to set the scene, or the mood.

Poetry Display

Have students write their own poetry, either using a formula or something original they want to create. They can illustrate their poetry and make a border. Frame the work with a construction paper frame. To make a splashy display of this poetry, hang it in the hallway along with giant-sized construction paper spring flowers. That means three-foot stems on huge daffodils and tulips! The daffodils can have large cones that stick out from the wall; spray some cologne inside of them for a surprisingly sweet smell of spring in the air.

Poetry Shapes

Make construction paper shapes of trees, rabbits, birds, flowers, and so on. This may inspire students to write a poem about the subject. The poems can be printed directly on the shape or along the outline of the shape.

Another helpful activity is to have students print rhyming words on shapes.

Poetry Favorites

Encourage students to copy their favorite poems from poetry books that are in the classroom. They can make illustrations for them and keep them in their very own Poetry Folder. Perhaps the students can learn some.

Poetry—Work With Expanded Sentences

To enrich children's writing in general, they need to be aware of descriptive words. Put this phrase on the chalkboard:

a   big   dog

"If we think about a 'big dog,' what picture do we see? We need to know more. What color is it? What is the fur like? Is it friendly? Is it snarling? Is it in motion or standing still or crouching?" Little by little, have students contribute descriptive words that you print on the chalkboard. Before everyone's eyes, the phrase builds to tell more about this dog:

a		big brown	dog
a		big brown, shaggy	dog
a	pretty	big brown, shaggy	dog
a	pretty, calm	big brown, shaggy	dog

Now everyone can get more of a picture of this dog, making the picture turn out entirely different by the words used. Try this next with "a small cat." Students can do this again and again—and just by the words they select—can turn the cat, dog, horse, rabbit, etc., into a sweet or sympathetic or monstrous animal. It's a good exercise for the use of descriptive words. Perhaps in the end, it can become a poetic phrase that a student wishes to illustrate, or turn into a poetry character, or even be honored as a poem.

a		small		cat
a		small	scrawny	cat
a	frightened,	small,	scrawny	cat
a	frightened, snarling,	small,	scrawny	cat
a	frightened, snarling,	small,	scrawny, tiger	cat

A Formula for Poetry

Next, students need to find out more about this animal, so use the following formula. Save the title for last.

TITLE: _____

A frightened, snarling, small, scrawny, tiger cat

_____ (a word that tells how it moved)

_____ (a phrase that tells where it went)

_____ (a phrase that tells what it was after)

_____ (a phrase that tells what you hope for the cat)

_____ (a word that sums up the cat or the situation)

Here are two examples that could be read aloud, then taken apart for students so that they understand the formula. Then they can make suggestions and come up with their own cat poem.

A Hungry Cat

A frightened, snarling, small, scrawny, tiger cat
leaped
around the corner
after a sparrow eating worms.
I hope it is healthy.
Hisssss!

TITLE: _____

A frightened, snarling, small, scrawny, tiger cat
slinked
under a bush
to get shelter.
It needs a good family.
Homeless.

Poetry Books for the Classroom

There are many fine poetry books for children available in bookstores, at the public library, and through the school library. Here are several authors and titles for your celebration of spring through poetry: *The New Oxford Treasury of Children's Poems,* edited by Michael Harrison and Christopher Stuart–Clark; *Tasty Poems* and *Noisy Poems,* compiled by Jill Bennett, with illustrations by Nick Sharratt; and *Dinosaur Poems* and *Dragon Poems,* compiled by John Foster, with illustrations by Korky Paul.

Some favorite poets to check for at the library include: X.J. Kennedy, J. Patrick Lewis, David McCord, Eve Merriman, Mary O'Neill, Jack Prelutsky, and Shel Silverstein. (See the Bibliography at the end of the book.)

Folktales

Folktale Festival

Folktales have been passed down to us by word of mouth, so they are excellent choices for storytelling. Have students select a favorite folktale to memorize and tell the story. Some students like to dress up as a character when telling the story. Some like to make stick puppets or sock puppets. You might want to have a spring folktale festival and capture the event on videotape. (Sometimes parents like to have a copy of this tape, so if they provide the tape, perhaps the school district can arrange to make copies. Or a parent might be helpful here.)

What Do Folktales Teach?

Values. Folktales teach values by rewarding honesty, goodness, kindness, helpfulness, and so on. The characters who are evil, unkind, foolish, selfish, or harmful are not rewarded, so bad deeds do not go unpunished. The good win out in the end. That means good on the inside—looks do not always count in the folktales. Often the weak win over the strong, and the plain win out over the beautiful.

Folktales are born of the oral tradition, meaning they were passed down for generations by word of mouth. The purpose was to teach a lesson or to instruct the listener. Much later, the tales were written down and, thanks to the Grimm Brothers—who recorded but did not write original tales—many of the tales have been saved for us to enjoy today.

Appreciation of Language. The tales have colorful language. Rich descriptions paint pictures in our head, and many rhymes and chants—when learned as a young child—stay with us forever. Many of the sayings in stories and fables are used as adults in everyday speech, including: "Don't count your chickens before they're hatched"; "Don't talk to strangers"; "Don't cry over spilled milk"; and "A leopard doesn't change its spots."

Teach Reading With Folktales

First, you need to enjoy folktales for the good stories that they are, and for the rhythm, rhyming, and repetition. Then, you need to talk about the descriptive words, the visual images, and the lesson to be learned. Read several versions of the same tale to the children and make comparison charts, which is helpful in reading. Set up the chart on a grid, with two or three stories per chart. Include the following categories: (1) title; (2) characters; (3) setting; (4) problem; and (5) solution, or how the problem was solved. The author and illustrator may also be included. (See the Reproducible Activity Pages.)

Chants.   Many of the folktales have chants with rhyming words. This may be helpful to students in the reading process because of the repetition. *Once they learn to say it, it becomes easier to read it.*

Making Circle Story Maps.   Decide what are the important parts of the story and list them. "What symbol or figure can you draw to represent each one?" After working that out, help the students to use a circular shape for the story map. Draw something that represents the beginning of the story at the top of the circle, and move clockwise as the rest of the story is represented pictorially. End up at the top. Then go around the circle and tell the story. The pictures serve as visual prompts.

Colorful Words.   Many of the descriptions of characters or settings are quite colorful, and are new to students. Go back through an already-read folktale for words that describe the castle, words that describe the ogre's appearance and habits, and so on. This may help students in their own writing.

Reading Level.   Remember that most picture books are written at a third-grade level. Picture books also do not have a controlled vocabulary, so children do not meet the same words in a repetitive pattern that helps with the reading process. Folktales are not "starter books" for teaching reading, even though young children enjoy listening to the stories, retelling them, and looking through the books over and over again.

A Multicultural Folktale Approach to Storytelling

As we have had a bonanza of multicultural books published in the 1990s, we are fortunate to be able to take students on journeys around the world with folktales. We get information from the lovely illustrations about the people and the way they dress, houses, food, animals, and surroundings. We can go to a village in Africa, to the countryside in Mexico, to Alaska, to New Zealand, to Europe, and hop all over the globe, depending upon which book we pick up and look through and read aloud. It's a wonderful opportunity for discovery and learning.

Have a globe available. Each time a story is read from that part of the world, attach a little piece of plasticene to that spot with a colored counting stick and label for a marker. (See the Bibliography for folktales.)

Multicultural Tricksters

The trickster figure in folktales is one that children enjoy. The trickster is usually clever and cunning, and uses its wits to get what it wants. Sometimes it gets its comeuppance, but more likely than not it gets others to do its bidding—and gives us a good story treat along the way. Introduce stories that feature the trickster figures. One favorite is Anansi the Spider (Africa). Others include Reynard the Fox (France), the Jackal (India), Brer Rabbit (American, Southern Black tales, originally from Africa), the Mousedeer (Indonesia), and the Raven (Northwest Native American). Other animals that serve in this role in different cultures include the monkey, hare, wolf, and crocodile.

After reading a trickster tale, discuss the character and the qualities it has. "What does this character do to make people believe things or act in certain ways?" Make a list of traits (can act very polite; uses flattery; gets others to do its bidding; stretches the truth).

Folktales and Quilts

These two seem to go together naturally. Students can make a story quilt on cloth squares using fabric crayons.

- Select a favorite folktale character, draw and color its picture, and use iron-on tape to affix it to a cloth background. Then, use iron-on tape strips to make the divisions between the squares. (**CAUTION:** The hot iron is used only by an adult.)

- Make a construction paper quilt. Select a color scheme for every other square (purples or greens?). Each student gets a square to make a symbol for the quilt, such as a wand, tree, slipper, coach, gingerbread man, castle, house of candy, house of straw/sticks/bricks, and so on. Use torn paper collage to make the pictures, and then glue these to a kraft paper background.

- Make a quilt of a scene from a story. Cut large figures from calico and gingham prints, and glue these onto the background. Use yarn for hair, buttons for eyes, real lace for aprons, and so on.

- Make a crazy (paper or cloth) quilt of trickster figures. Each student can do a favorite trickster, and even put the trickster in "disguise." (Several students can do the same trickster when it's wearing a disguise.) Place these characters in helter-skelter fashion all over the quilt background. Make a colorful border for the quilt.

For more ideas, see the wide selection of books on quilts in the Bibliography at the end of this book.

Additional Suggestions for Using Children's Literature in the Classroom

Here are some suggestions for integrating picture books into the activities of the classroom. Many of these can also be found in the Author-of-the-Month sections at the end of each month. Here are some effective activities that you may wish to try:

- Make a poster to advertise the book.
- Give a one-minute radio speech telling the audience why this is definitely a good book to read.
- Make a shoebox diorama to show the setting of the story.
- Make the story into a play.
- Have students keep a list of books they've read and enjoyed.
- Read the book to students in lower grades.
- Read the book into a tape recorder so others may enjoy it.
- Create a new book cover for this book.
- Make a bookmark that goes along with the book.
- Make an endpaper design if the book does not have one.
- Make your favorite character using clay, papier-mâché, pipe cleaners, etc.

Do a "Book-in-a-Box" Project

For this project you will need a sturdy box (any size), a favorite book, four compartments inside the box, and materials for the projects you are going to suggest.

First, convert the outside of the box into a colorful, exciting "can't wait to open the lid" box. Inside, the book goes into one compartment; that leaves three more compartments. Think of a related writing activity for one section, an art activity for another section, and—for the last section—select an activity that is related to math, science, or social studies. This becomes a portable learning center in the classroom.

The box can be made as a total group, or in small groups, or individually. If made in the classroom, use a very large one. Some students like to make these at home and bring them in for others to enjoy.

Make a Giant-Size Puppet Theatre

Secure a stove or refrigerator box from an appliance store and transform it into a theatre. Turn it on its side so that the back can be opened and students can step inside. Cut a square in the opposite side for the performances. A piece of material doubled over and put on a strong string or dowel rod can be used as the curtain.

Cover the outside of the box with tempera paint, construction paper, or prepasted paper so that it looks attractive. Perhaps a title could be put on one side or on the front to name the theatre. Students can reenact stories for audiences using a variety of puppets. They can also be a TV reporter and tell a story from inside as the "talking head."

Arrange for an Author Visit

This is a memorable event. It is often costly, so it's a good idea to link up with another school district, if possible. First, form a committee to gather background information. Write to the publisher to find out if the author does make visits. How far in advance does the person need to be booked? Determine the cost, which includes travel, meals, overnight stays, and the fee. Where will the funds come from to pay for this? Work out all of the organizational plans at the teacher-planning level. Talk to someone who has already planned an author visit. Get information from the children's librarian at a public library or in the school library. You will want to do a study of the author's works before the big day arrives.

Students can be involved in the planning *after* arrangements for an author/illustrator visit are set. Once plans are underway, secure a number of books by the author or illustrator. Read them to the children and discuss the stories. Have students do projects that stem from the books. Getting the art teacher involved in the process is extremely helpful. Also, use ideas from the Author-of-the-Month sections of this book.

Some schools invite an author to visit the primary classrooms, for example, and each grade level concentrates on projects from a different book. Display the work in the hallways. Make the foyer a print-rich environment to welcome your guest. This is an exciting reading event! Also, have students prepare questions they would like to ask the author/illustrator about a particular story, a character, or about illustrating and writing books. There won't be time to answer all of them, but it's best to be prepared.

Spelling

Spelling Construction

Use Cuisenaire® rods to construct spelling words. The words can lay flat or be built up.

Coded Messages

Devise a number and letter code. The easiest is to use the following: 1 = A, 2 = B, 3 = C, 4 = D, and so on. Have a grid available with the code so that all students have access to this information. Then print out the spelling words in code and have students decipher them. For example:

$$19\ 16\ 5\ 3\ 9\ 1\ 12 = \text{SPECIAL}$$

This will generate a lot of interest in coded messages. Students can make up their own codes for the spelling words or their own sentences in code.

How Much Does This Word Cost?

Use the same code as the one above, only this time the number can stand for cents. Add up the spelling words to see how much they would cost. (The word SPECIAL, for example, would cost $19 + 16 + 5 + 3 + 9 + 1 + 12 = 65$ cents.)

Spelling Sense

Write a spelling word in a sentence. Then rewrite the sentence using a similar word so that the meaning is not changed. Do this for all of the words. For example, suppose that *pretty* is a spelling word. The student can write:

That is a *pretty* cat.
That is a *beautiful* cat.

Then ask students to read their "similar" sentence aloud, and see if other students can guess the spelling word.

Sign the Words

Use sign language to spell out the individual letters of the words. Work with a study buddy for this activity.

Snake Coils

Use clay or plasticene to roll out long coils. Then use the coils to print or write the spelling words.

READING LINKS TO HOLIDAYS & SPECIAL EVENTS

Happy May Day

The first day of May is a celebration of spring that began many, many years ago in Europe. The maypole often is placed in the center of town and people dance clockwise around the pole in fancy costumes. There is food, drink, and the joy of being out in the sunshine!

In some European villages, to this day, there is a contest for the most gaily-decorated pole. People decorate the pole at night and hide the pole in a secure place so that no one sees it until May 1. Then prizes are awarded for various categories, such as originality, beauty, and so on.

Use an outdoor umbrella stand, or a pole from the gymnasium, for your class's maypole. Make flowers from tissue paper and decorate the pole. Hang streamers from the top. Students can take hold of the end of a streamer, and go 'round and 'round the pole. To weave the streamers around the pole, half the students go clockwise while the other half go counterclockwise, going over and under with the streamers. Then reverse the process to untangle the streamers. Enjoy cookies and lemonade at the end, play music, and read some spring poetry.

Happy Mother's Day

Mother's Day ranks as the third most popular holiday in the world, after Christmas and Easter. Long ago people in England honored their mothers on a day called "Mothering Sunday." The special flower for the day is a carnation.

Anna M. Jarvis (1864–1948) was the founder of Mother's Day in the United States. It was her own mother's idea, and Anna carried it out. President Wilson proclaimed Mother's Day on the second Sunday in May. We take this day to honor good mothers everywhere, and to bring families together.

Have students make out an I.O.U. certificate for their mother for this special day. It is a coupon that Mother can cash in for: helping with the dishes, taking out the trash, helping to put groceries away, and so on. Read the storybook *The Mother's Day Mice* by Eve Bunting, with illustrations by Jan Brett.

Memorial Day

Memorial Day, observed on the last Monday in May, is a day set aside to honor the soldiers who died in any war in which the United States was a part. It is a day marked with parades, patriotic speeches, and flags flying in the breeze. Often, Veterans of Foreign Wars and American Legion organizations place flags on cemetery graves of those who fought for the United States, even if they did not lose their life in the war.

Students should know that men and women join the armed forces to protect our country. They enlist in the Army, Navy, Air Force, and Marine Corps. Some men and women also protect us by joining the National Guard and the Coast Guard.

"Today at school, we can make our own flags from construction paper and our own folded hats from newspaper. March on the playground, and up and down the hall. Back in the classroom we can march to patriotic music, such as 'Stars and Stripes Forever' by John Phillip Sousa." Sending greeting cards to a nearby veteran's hospital would be greatly appreciated.

Flag Day

The flag is one symbol for the United States and on Flag Day, June 14, it is flown high in the breeze all over the country. If students did not make individual flags for Memorial Day, now would be the time to do so. Instead of using cut paper, have students fill in the red spaces and white spaces with torn paper to make a collage flag. Or, use fabric paint to make a real cloth flag. This can be glued to a stick or dowel rod and used in a class parade.

Good resource books are *Patriotic Holidays and Celebrations* by Valorie Grigoli; *Fireworks, Picnics, and Flags* by James Cross Giblin, with illustrations by Ursula Arndt; and *Fiesta U.S.A.* by George Ancona.

What Is Your Flag I.Q.?

Students can do a flag study if they have not already done so. For some it would serve as review and a memory jogger.

- How many red stripes? (seven)
- How many white stripes? (six)
- How many stars? (50)
- How many colors on the flag? (three—red/white/blue)
- Will the flag always have thirteen stripes? (Yes. They stand for the original thirteen colonies. Any new state would be added to the star section, by act of Congress.)
- What is the flag made of that was placed on the moon in 1969? (metal, to withstand dust and particles from space that bombard it)

Happy Father's Day

"We're happy to honor good fathers on this special Sunday in June. Our hard-working fathers put in long hours at work so that they can provide a home and special activities for us all through the year." Sometimes this is taken for granted, so students need to think about what their fathers do for them, what they like to do with their dad, and what they'd like to be able to do with their dad.

What do students call their father? Some common names are Dad, Daddy, Papa, Papa Joe, and Pa. Have a discussion of this; be sure to accept all answers as some students are from extended families, so sometimes a grandad or uncle fills in as Dad.

Students can write a letter to Dad telling what they like about him. They can draw a picture of a favorite day they had with Dad and be prepared to give or mail it to him. A hand-made greeting card is also always a special remembrance. This can be on paper shaped like a baseball or an elongated baseball bat, with "You're a Hit With Me, Dad!" printed on the front, and the child's message inside.

Read *A Perfect Father's Day* by Eve Bunting, with illustrations by Susan Meddauth.

First Day of Summer

Link this special day to outdoor activities and sports. Have students list all of the ways they use balls in sports (kick, throw, bat, hit with racket, etc.). "How many ways do we use water for sports?" (boating, swimming, skiing) "In what sports do we run?" (baseball, football, soccer, etc.) "In what sporting activities do we use air?" (ballooning, hang gliding, kite flying, etc.)

Celebrate with some old-fashioned games on the playground, such as the three-legged race. Two students work as a team and stand side by side. Use a rope to tie their adjoining legs together, to serve as one leg. Ready, set, go! Run to a designated spot. Time it. Who's the winning pair?

READING LINKS TO WRITING

Printing a Letter

Have students number their paper from 1–5. Say five letters of the alphabet one at a time, and have students write them down. Do they know them? If not, they need to focus upon these five and learn them by heart. Then add two more at a time.

Double Consonants

When students are learning to write a line of print, a good rule is to begin by teaching them to *not* start a new word if they can't fit it on the line.

Students are apt to encounter hyphenated words in picture books, magazines, and newspapers long before they will use this tool themselves. However, some students will begin to show an interest in this and may be ready to learn about it. To show students how to divide words with a hyphen, begin with words that have a double letter in the middle. Students can practice on these words:

apple	bubble	cattle	dollar
effort	follow	giggle	hidden

Another place where words are "separated" or hyphenated is just before the "ing" ending. Also tap out the beats (syllables) of the word, and divide the word between each syllable. **Hint:** At least one vowel is usually in each syllable.

Make a Flag Etiquette Book

There are many rules and procedures for handling the U.S. flag. Make a colorful cover that shows the flag or "symbols" made from the colors of red, white, and blue. Symbols can be stars, the Liberty Bell, the Statue of Liberty, Uncle Sam, and so on. Students can illustrate the following actions and print directions under their pictures:

- Flags should be raised quickly, but lowered slowly.
- Flags should not be allowed to touch the ground.
- Flags should be flown from sunrise to sunset.
- Flags should not be flown in the rain.
- The flag is flown at half-mast (halfway up the pole) when the nation is in mourning over the death of an important person.
- "Old Glory" and "Stars and Stripes" are nicknames for our nation's flag.
- Here I am saying the Pledge of Allegiance:

> I pledge allegiance to the flag
> of the United States of America
> and to the Republic for which it stands,
> one nation under God, indivisible, with
> liberty and justice for all.

A good resource book is *I Pledge Allegiance* by June Swanson, with pictures by Rick Hanson.

Invented Spelling

As students are writing poetry, folktales, and stories this time of year at the Writing Center and in their journals, they will still be using invented spelling (depending upon their age and developmental stage). Younger children, especially, will invent spelling, which is acceptable at this stage. Students are using phonetic principles when they put together letters to make words. They actually tell us what they already know.

For example, a student is writing about a big elephant and spells "Th luhfnt is beg"—let's see what the child knows. You can see that the child knows the following:

- The word at the beginning of the sentence, in this case *The,* begins with a capital letter and the "th" sound.   luhfnt
- The student is sounding out "el" (l) and the "uh" and the "f" (for "ph") and "nt." Thus, you can see that the letter–sound relationship is at work in this long word—*elephant.*
- The word *big* begins with the letter "b" and ends with the letter "g."

This child is on target. So the process is working and the sounds are written, even though *elephant* appears as "l uh f nt." You are looking at what the child knows, rather than what the child does not know. Many times the consonants appear and the vowels are left out. It is later, during the editing sessions, that you can begin to develop the correct spelling of words. Writing is complex: it is slower to develop than reading, which is slower to develop than speaking. But these skills are, at the same time, intertwined.

READING LINKS TO MATH

Fairy Tale Number Bags

Decorate two or three paper bags. Label them: "Big Bad Wolf's Bag," "Three Billy Goats Gruff Bag," and "Rapunzel's Math Bag." In each bag can be math strips that these characters are supposedly working on. "Let's see if we know them, or need to work on them, too."

Select a strip from one bag and print the information on the chalkboard. For example: 2 _____ 4. Students have to print the number that comes in the middle, or between these two numbers.

Select a strip from another bag and print the information on the chalkboard. For example: _____ 7 _____. Students have to print the numbers that come before and after.

For the third bag, do a variation of the above and use larger numbers.

Double, Double

To teach the concept of "doubles" (or pairs), have a stack of items (four of each) and sort them by two's. Use grocery items, socks, pencils, erasers, and so on. Be sure to have one set with three items (not doubles), and only one of another item (not doubles).

"Go through the items and put all of the doubles (two of something) together. When we come to items that do not match up, they are known as 'not doubles.'" Students can write their items as 3 + 3, 2 + 2, and so on.

Often students have less difficulty memorizing doubles, such as:

$$1 + 1 = 2 \qquad 2 + 2 = 4 \qquad 3 + 3 = 6$$

so if we can get them to think in terms of "doubles plus one," it may be easier for some students to grasp addition facts.

Doubles in Our Language

The word *double* is used in many of our language phrases. Here are some that students may be aware of; if not, then explain what the phrase means:

- Double house (side by side)
- Doubles (tennis)
- Double trouble (twice the amount of trouble)
- Double up (line up by two's)
- Double the fun (twice as much fun)
- Double dip (two dips of ice cream)

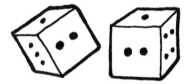

Ask students if they know of any other phrases that use the word *double*. Challenge them to be on the alert for this word and report it to the class when they hear it used.

Doubles Plus One

Review doubles so that students can see three books in one pile and three books in another pile and call out "3 + 3." Next, add one more item. Now it can become "3 + 4" or "4 + 3" depending upon where you place the book. Encourage students to look for a "double pattern" and add on whenever they can.

Distribute an even number of Unifix® cubes to each student or to students working with a partner. For example, give them eight and have them write out the number sentence using doubles $(4 + 4 = 8)$. Next, distribute one more cube and have students add it to the first group and write it as $5 + 4 = 9$. Remove it from the first set, add it to the second, and write it as $4 + 5 = 9$.

Look for doubles in the room. Check windows, window panes, door panels, overhead lights, radiator grates, etc. Next, look for "doubles plus one" in the classroom (3 of something, 5 of something). Impress upon students that they can always be thinking in terms of doubles when working pencil-and-paper problems. (For example, if they see $3 + 4$, and they know that $3 + 3 = 6$, they just need to add one more to the double set.

Math Double Balloons

Make construction paper balloon shapes with a string tail with various numerals printed on the balloon, and hold them up one at a time. For each double inside the balloon, ask students to put a bow on the tail. How many doubles (twos) are inside? For example:

- math balloon with "5" (two bows)
- math balloon with "7" (three bows)
- math balloon with "3" (one bow)

The strings can get longer as the numbers get higher. Also, bows can be color coded so that red is equal to double and blue is equal to a "not double."

Exploring Probability

You will need a paper bag, 7 black squares of construction paper, and 3 white squares of construction paper.

Then follow this procedure:

1. Show students the white squares and count them (1, 2, 3). Then show the black squares and count them (1, 2, 3, 4, 5, 6, 7). Place them all into the bag.
2. Explain that you will shake the bag to mix up the colors. Then reach in and pick out one square. *Print the color name on the chalkboard.*
3. Reach in again and again, each time writing the color name on the chalkboard.
4. Hmmmm. There are more black than white squares listed on the chalkboard. Have students "guess" what the next one will be.
5. Point out to students that since there are more black than white squares in the bag, the black ones are being selected more often.
6. Repeat the above procedure, but change to 4 red and 10 blue squares; then 3 green and 9 purple squares. Have students come up and select the next square. Each time, have them ESTIMATE what color will appear next. (They get quite excited and motivated by this activity.)

What Are the Chances (Probability) of Yellow Being Selected?

Tell students that you have 2 yellow and 10 purple squares. Ask which color is most apt to be selected. If students don't immediately say "purple," then they need to go through the modeling process again.

Students need to learn that the color that has the *most* squares is likely to be chosen the *most*. Repeat with the following, so that the children are not just guessing, but have caught onto the concept:

6 green, 1 blue
14 red, 17 yellow
6 purple, 7 white
8 black, 7 orange

For Students Who Need Extra Help

Reteach this concept in small groups using real objects. Show students what you are putting in the bag (for example, 6 blue felt pens and 3 yellow felt pens).

Reach in until all are taken out—even the three yellow so students *see* that the probability of getting a blue is greater because there are more.

Weather Probability

Keep a weather chart. "Sunshine today or no sunshine today? How many sunny days have we had this week? Let's check the weather news for the predictions. Now, we can predict. How many think the sun will shine tomorrow?" (Record the number.) "How many think the sun will not shine tomorrow?" (Record the number.) Check the next day.

You can also make a chart with students' names and predictions. How many times do they predict well?

Math Matching Treat

Have a jar filled with real jelly beans. Students can reach into a bag with construction paper jelly beans, pick out a color, match that color to the real color, and reach in and take their jelly bean treat.

READING LINKS TO SOCIAL STUDIES

Introducing Transportation

Students are no strangers to transportation since they've no doubt used many types to get from one place to another. However, they may not realize that they already do know information about transportation, and that there is still more to learn about the topic.

Start off with what students know. Have them discuss the types of transportation they've used. Then classify them by *land, sea,* and *air*. The list you make on a chart may eventually look something like this:

Land	Sea	Air
foot	motorboat	jet plane
bicycle/tricycle	sailboat	helicopter
wagon	cruise ship	twin-engine prop
car	paddle-wheeler	hot-air balloon
train	pontoon	private plane
motorcycle	canoe	
horse-drawn buggy	schooner	
truck	QE II	
Jeep	raft	
van	ferryboat	
trolley	submarine	
subway		
monorail		
moving sidewalk		

Let's Look at History

"Long ago in our country, we had no roads. Native Americans traveled on foot by way of trails. Then people traveled by stagecoach, and the trails got muddy and filled with ruts. Logs were rolled over the roads, but these made the trails very bumpy. Sometimes they were referred to as 'corduroy roads.' Why would they be called corduroy roads?" Have a sample of corduroy cloth so that students can see it is a bumpy—rather than smooth—surface.

Stagecoach Was the Way to Go!

"For over 100 years, people traveled by stagecoach and were lucky to go ten miles per day! How far is it to get from one end of our town to the next, or from one town to the next? Let's figure out how long it would take to get there by stagecoach. Sometimes people traveled only during the day, under threat of attack by robbers or Indians, and stayed at wayside inns during the night. Sometimes they rode all night, sitting on hard benches."

Point out to students the progress that has been made in transportation. Stagecoaches had wooden wheels and the ride was extremely bumpy. Today's vehicles have tires and springs, which make for a smooth ride.

The very first paved road in our country was the Pennsylvania Turnpike. Let's find Pennsylvania on the map.

Rivers, Lakes, Seas, Oceans

This study leads you to rivers, canals, and lakes. For young children, limit this to a study of the bodies of water in your immediate area. Print the names of the rivers, lakes, ponds, and so on, on the chalkboard and have the children learn them. For older children, branch out into the greater community, then the state, and finally the country.

You can do this by following a river on a map and see where it takes you. What state(s) do you pass through?

Steamships and Then Railroads

Make a timeline in the classroom of the different types of transportation as you read about them.

Get a Hobby Horse!

"The first bicycles had no pedals. They looked like a regular bike, with handlebars, a seat, and two wheels—except that the front wheel was quite a bit larger than the rear wheel. The rider, generally a male, mounted the bike and moved the bike by walking. The rider's feet touched the ground and the seat was used as something to lean against or perhaps sit on if the rider had long legs. This type of bike was referred to as a 'hobby horse.'"

"Children long ago had a toy version of the hobby horse, which was a toy horse head on a very long stick. The stick was placed between the feet and lower legs, and the child 'galloped' away on the horse. A rocking horse, another child's toy, was for younger children who could pretend to ride, but the horse only moved back and forth on the curved runners."

Make hobby horses by using long dowel rods. Attach a horse head made from a paper bag, and have a good ride around the playground! Children in Colonial days used to "ride the kitchen broom" for play.

Who Has a Bicycle?

Check with students to see how many have bicycles. Do they wear their safety helmets? Today's bikes are ten-speeds (and more), with brakes on the handlebars, computerized controls, and so on. Children have a much easier time riding bicycles than their ancestors of years ago. "What will bicycles of the future look like? Let's speculate."

Simulate a Train Trip or Plane Trip

In the classroom, prepare for a trip. Arrange the chairs in rows with an aisle down the middle. If it's a plane trip, for example, a pilot and co-pilot are seated in front, and attendants greet students as they "board" with their tickets to designated seats. When everyone is seated, simulate the strapping on of the seatbelts. Prepare for takeoff. Once airborne, the attendants can serve a snack. An informational video of transportation, or of something that has to do with a social studies or health unit, can be shown. Then prepare for landing. Collect trash in bags. Sit and wait for the plane to land. Unbuckle seatbelts. File off at the designated "doorway" in an orderly manner. The children must not barge ahead of others, but need to wait for their turn.

This is as much a lesson in good travel manners as it is in transportation and the information learned from the videotape.

Resources

Books and videotapes are an excellent source of information about the past. This is one unit that students really enjoy. Some helpful information picture books include: *The Wonderful World of Transportation* by Laurie Lee and David Lambert; *Early Travel* by Bobbie Kalman (Early Settler Life Series); and *Story of Transportation* by Wilma Wilson Cain.

Also, have students be on the alert for modes of transportation in picture books. Remember, Cinderella used a pumpkin coach. Some characters use rockets or space ships.

Transportation Songs and Poems

There are many songs that deal with transportation and are enjoyable for youngsters to sing. (Check with the school librarian for audio or video cassettes, check with the music teacher, and check the community library.) There are many songs about the railroad to enjoy learning, including "She'll Be Coming 'Round the Mountain When She Comes." There are many verses and phrases such as "Toot, toot!" and "Whoa, back!" The song is from a bygone era, but still fun to learn and sing. Look for songs that have transportation in the titles. Find poems about travel today and in the future, and enjoy them also.

Writing About Retreads

"Write a poem or story about tire retreads from an 18-wheeler that end up being recycled, and now they're on the bottom of athletic shoes. How is the tire's life different?"

You could also have two students write to one another on shoe shapes. One can write from the point of view of missing life on the big highway in the fast lane, and the other student can write from the point of view of enjoying walking on streets, being able to play sports games, kicking a ball, and so on.

READING LINKS TO SCIENCE

Introducing Birds

Introduce the topic of birds by having the entire class brainstorm all that they know about birds. Synthesize and list that information. Then talk about what they'd like to know about birds—feet, beaks, habitats, wings, etc. List that information. Now the students need to find out where the information can be located. Go to the school library for books and magazines. See if any videos are available, as well as sound recordings of bird calls. Set up the Science Center as a bird study area.

Our Fine-feathered Friends

"Birds are the only living things that have feathers. They spend time preening themselves, or cleaning dirt and dust from their feathers by using their beak. The feathers help keep them warm because they are windproof. Sometimes we find a bird feather on the ground—often in the autumn. Most birds lose one feather at a time, and then it grows back."

Make an outline of a bird on the bulletin board and have students label the parts, such as beak, wing, breast, legs, feet, and tail feathers. Then decide what color or colors to paint the bird, depending on what kind it is. Find out what the bird is for your state; perhaps that's the one that could be used.

Bird Bones

A bird has a bony skeleton. Although the bones are strong, they are not solid. They're hollow. Therefore, the bones add very little weight to the bird, so assist with the process of flying.

In many Central American countries, the bones of birds are collected and used as a type of flute. Holes are finely chiseled into the side, and air is blown through the hollow bone. It makes a lovely sound. The bones of vultures are used in this way, and that makes a nice story because vultures have no voice—yet, their bones are used to make melodies long after the vultures are gone.

Birds Come in Many Families

Birds are listed in categories, including Ground Birds, Sea Birds, Waterbirds, Birds of Prey, and Songbirds. List these categories on a big chart. Have students list birds underneath the categories that they come across in the resources at hand. For starters, the list may look something like this:

Birds of Prey	**Songbirds**
Bald Eagle	Robin
Vulture	Cardinal
Barn owl	Blue jay
Osprey	Oriole
Falcon	Nightingale

Birds Come in Many Sizes

"The ostrich is the largest bird, measuring over six feet tall. This bird is too heavy to fly, but it can run fast. The hummingbird is perhaps the smallest." For a good look at the ostrich's and hummingbird's egg sizes, in comparison to other birds, check out the book *Chickens Aren't the Only Ones* by Ruth Heller, the April Author-of-the-Month.

Do Birds Hibernate?

"The poor-will bird is eight inches long and sounds like it's singing 'poor will,' which is how it got its name. So far, it's the only bird we know of that hibernates in the crevice of a rock. It's a night bird that hunts beetles and moths."

Make a Bird Treat

You will need pinecones, peanut butter, and bird seed. Help the children use the pinecone as the feeder, with dollops of peanut butter on the ends. Sprinkle seeds on top of the peanut butter. Tie a string around the pinecone and hang it from a tree outside the window. Wait patiently, for eventually a bird will see it and investigate!

Hatch Chicks

If possible, bring an incubator into the classroom and place some fertile chicken eggs inside. (**CAUTION:** Be sure to carefully follow the manufacturer's instructions.) Some teachers have also used duck, goose, or wild pheasant eggs. There is a lot of care that goes into regulating the temperature of the incubator and it needs to be checked on weekends. Once chicks are hatched, they too need to be tended to on weekends until a permanent home is found for them. This is a fantastic experience for students, and one that needs guidance from the teacher.

Set up an easel outside the door to the classroom and give an hourly up-date on the progress of the hatchlings. The whole school will be interested, and you will have many classes that will want to visit.

This is a rich opportunity for photographs, stories, journal writing, and observation.

What Can We Learn from Birds?

Make a list of what the children learn about the habits of birds in their own backyard or neighborhood throughout this study. It may look something like this:

- They are nature's "weavers" when nest building.
- Some build a nest of sticks and twigs (eagle).
- Some use mud to form a nest (robin).
- They use their beak for building, gathering food, feeding young.
- They can build a nest that rocks in the breeze (oriole).
- They are good parents. They stay with their young and feed them until the young can fly.
- They will swoop down on animals and people who get too near their nest.

Let's Make Birds

Use clay to mold birds, or put bright paint at the easel for students to use for colorful parrots. Students can also use construction paper to create colorful birds with round shapes, or rectangular shapes, or square shapes. These can be stuffed and hung from the overhead lights by a long string, appearing to fly in the breeze.

The Birds Are Back

By this time of year many familiar birds are back home until it's time to migrate again. This is a time for nest building, egg laying, and raising families, so caution students to not collect nests in the spring. If you didn't have the opportunity earlier in the year to set up a birdwatching station at a window, now is the time to do so. Have a pair of binoculars handy. Also put a small bird feeder, the kind that can be attached with a suction cup, on the window pane. It won't take long for the birds to find it, especially when it's very quiet. They are easily startled by noise and quick movements, so this must be a quiet area in the classroom. Keep track of the birds that visit the feeder.

Two good resource books are *Outside and Inside Birds* by Sandra Markle and *Simon & Schuster's Children's Guide to Birds* by Jinny Johnson, with Dr. Malcolm Ogilvie.

LINKS TO AUTHOR-OF-THE-MONTH

Author/Illustrator for May and June: Aliki

Aliki, whose complete name is Aliki Brandenberg, has written and illustrated more than 40 picture books for young children. Some are storybooks and some are information books. But they all teach lessons and they help us to learn. Many are done with small drawings and cartoon-like bubbles overhead that contain the print. This is often helpful when there is a lot of information to impart.

The following sampling of books will show the wide range of this author/illustrator. Aliki lives in England, but she visits Europe and also the United States. *Let's read!*

Painted Words, Spoken Memories **(New York: Greenwillow Books, 1998)** In this tender book, a little girl named Marianthe is new to this country and a new girl at school. She can't speak the language and the words mean nothing to her, but her mother is a strong woman and an exceedingly fine influence in her life. For every doubt Marianthe has, the mother has a loving answer. At school, the children soon discover that "Mari" can draw, so that is how she communicates.

Halfway through the book, the story of *Painted Words* ends. But turn the book upside-down and around to take up where the first story left off. With *Spoken Memories* Mari can now put language to her drawings and tell her story. (A touching tale and right on the mark for the immigrant newcomer.)

Activities to Accompany *Painted Words, Spoken Memories*

1. Read and enjoy both stories. If you have any newcomers in your classroom, or students who have not been in this country for long, they will be able to tell their stories about how it felt to be the new person who couldn't speak the language and couldn't understand. Let's hear from them, and learn from them.

2. When Marianthe is fearful that no one will understand her, her wise Mama says, "a body can talk." (Discuss nonverbal communication, and how we can tell what people are trying to express or what they are feeling.)

3. When Marianthe says that everything is different in this new place, her wise Mama says, "only on the outside. Inside people are the same." Again, this calls for a discussion of the way in which people are more alike than different in their hopes, dreams, loves, fears—through the whole range of emotions.

4. Ask students to try to remember their very first day at school and how it felt to be there. Marianthe says, "I am a little afraid, but not enough to cry." Again, try to discuss fears and how we can deal with them.

5. "I am drawing what I can't talk," says Marianthe. Have students draw their feelings or expressions of an experience, and "let's just enjoy the painting. Later we can talk about it, but for now just enjoy it." This would make a good week at the easel—students draw or paint what they can't talk about.

6. When Marianthe is able to tell her story, we see that her life in another land is indeed very different from life here. Go through the book and see how the people dress and the work they do, so that the children gain some idea of where this girl came from.

7. Marianthe and later the twins were welcomed into her home. Ask students to interview their parents to find out "who was waiting for them, and who decided on their name, and who couldn't wait to hold them."

The Two of Them (New York: Greenwillow Books, 1979) This book captures the essence of the love that a grandfather feels for his grandchild. Before the child is born, Grandfather makes her a wooden bed. He also makes a ring of silver and a polished stone, because someday he knows it will fit her finger. The book is a loving story of these two as the little girl grows up and as the grandfather grows old. Then there is the aloneness after Grandfather has gone, but a treasure house of memories.

Activities to Accompany *The Two of Them*

1. Read and enjoy the story. This story is a celebration of the love between Grandpa and his granddaughter. Have children think about special times they have had with their grandfathers, and then share them with the class. (**CAUTION:** Be sensitive to those students who may never have known their grandfathers and those whose grandfathers may be in very poor health.)

2. The book addresses the subject of death. You have the words "She knew that one day he would die. But when he did, she was not ready, and she hurt inside and out." This may be an opportunity for some students to express their experience of loss of a loved member of their family, or a neighbor.

3. "Let's talk about the good times we have had on vacation—either with a grandfather or another special member of the family." Have students tell about their favorite day—one they would do all over again. It may be a trip to the zoo, or the day the family went to get ice cream, or the day they all flew to a theme park. Accept all responses.

4. Grandfather plays the guitar and the girl plays the flute, and they make music together. "Do we have students who come from families who have music as part of their special times together? Does a family member create the music? Can we possibly invite that person to class to play for us?"

5. "We see the inside of Grandfather's store. Can you spot the name of the store?" (Jimmy's M ... [market] on the awning in the black-and-white sketch next to the page that shows the store.) "What is the address? How can we tell from the printing on the window what holiday season this is?"

6. Have students print their name on tracing paper. Then hold it up to the window for them to see what their name looks like from the inside out. Do this with other words, and have students figure them out.

***Hello! Good-bye!* (New York: Greenwillow Books, 1996)** The author tells us that every day we use the words "hello" and "good-bye" again and again. They are a beginning and an end. She takes these two words and shows a variety of contexts in which they are used. After we read this book, these two words have expanded to have a wealth of meaning for us.

Activities to Accompany *Hello! Good-bye!*

1. Each page has a lesson. But first, just enjoy the book.

2. "How many ways can we say hello?" The book is rich in language development. Print the words on the chalkboard so students can read some of the messages in the speech bubbles, such as "Greetings!" and "Howdy!" and "Good Morning!"

3. "How can we say 'hello' with no words? There are nine different illustrations on this page and nine separate words for us to print and learn. We can 'shake' hands, 'hug,' 'bow,' 'wave.'" Print these words on flash cards. Hold them up and have students carry out the action.

4. "We can learn the words for 'hello' in four different languages. Let's print them and say them: Shalom (Hebrew), Yiasou (Greek), Aloha (Hawaiian), Nameste (Hindi). And there are words for 'good-bye' in six different languages. Let's print them and learn to say them, too."

5. "We even have good-bye words for travelers, such as 'Bon Voyage,' 'Pleasant Climbing!' and 'All Aboard,' and more on this page." Have students act out the greetings for both "hello" and "good-bye."

6. "Each page has a separate lesson for us to learn about greetings. Let's take them one at a time. Remember what the author tells us. It is rude to *not* say goodbye."

***Communication* (New York: Greenwillow Books, 1993)** The message of this book is that it takes two to communicate, and that there are lots of ways that people do communicate. Even the endpapers have the upper- and lower-case alphabet printed on them, along with the Braille Alphabet and the Sign Language Alphabet. For a unit on the topic of communication, this book is a must. It's enjoyable reading too.

Activities to Accompany *Communication*

1. Print the word "communication" on the chalkboard. After you have read the book, go back over it page by page. Take your time. Don't do this all in one day. By the end of the book, the children will have learned a lot about communication.

2. Students can make their own four-page book of communication, and can use the words from the book to print under the pictures they draw. The messages are: "We speak words"; "We listen to words"; "We write words"; and "We read words."

3. Find the page that shows all of the different means of communication that people use. It's entitled "There Are Other Ways" and shows signs and symbols, Rebus symbols, the arts, and other means of communication via speech and print. This, too, would make a good wordless picture book on the topic.

4. Students can also use this page as the basis for a guessing game. The game is "I'm thinking of something that _____ and you can _____." Remember to call upon students who have their hand raised. (Later in the book the author addresses the habit of shouting out the answers instead of raising a hand. We learn that it really irritates some people who *do* know the answers.)

5. "*Feedback* is a word we hear often. What does the author have to say on this topic? What can we learn from her? Let's talk about it . . . and let's listen."

6. Ask students if they are good listeners. "What makes a good listener? This book addresses the topic of people who may talk too much and not give others a chance to talk. It gives us plenty to think about as we go about the business of trying to learn to communicate. It's fun, but there are certain rules that make for polite communication."

How a Book Is Made (New York: Trumpet Club Special Edition, 1986) This is a good opportunity to talk about how the publishing companies put together the picture books students have been reading throughout the year. If they've been publishing their own books, now they may have some new vocabulary words that are used to label certain parts of the book. They will certainly get an idea of the immense amount of work that goes into making a book and the number of people we have to thank in the process.

Activities to Accompany *How a Book Is Made*

1. The characters in the book look like cats. The style of the book is such that the characters are making comments by way of overhead talk bubbles, with text underneath the pictures. Done in "comic book" fashion, the book holds the attention of the reader because of the vast information in the book.

2. Students will learn the parts of a book if they haven't already done so: front flap, dust jacket, endpapers, spine, gutter, title page, title, copyright page, author/illustrator, publisher, back flap. The sketch with labels and arrows is very helpful. Perhaps a chart can be made of this for the classroom, if students are interested in publishing their own books. Some classrooms have an emphasis on book-making throughout the year.

3. Who made this book? The people responsible are the author/illustrator, editor, publisher, designer, copyeditor, proofreader, production director, color separator, printer, publicity and promotion director, and the salesperson. Their various duties are spelled out for us throughout the book. Ask students which jobs appeal to them.

4. Do students know that a full-color book is printed using only four colors— yellow, blue, red, and black? The colors are combined to make more colors, and lighter shades of each color are combined to make up still more colors. "Perhaps we can each have an opportunity to do some paint mixing, and create a scene from one of our own books." (For starters: yellow + blue = green; blue + red = purple; red + yellow + blue = brown; red + yellow = orange. Go easy on the black; otherwise, the paint can look muddy.)

5. Printed colors are made up of tiny dots. The darker the color, the bigger the dots. Have a strong magnifying glass available so that students are able to see the dots. (Bring in some newspaper photos and notice that they are also made up of dots.) This may start some students on an investigation of color printing, or of making pictures with dots.

6. Point out to the students that making a book is a "process." It is not done hurriedly. There is much checking, rechecking, proofreading, and doing things over again. This information may be helpful to the hurried child who wants to get the job "over with." The idea is to enjoy the work and to be proud of the end results.

7. The author gives us a good message, especially in this age of television and computers: "I like books. I like the way a book feels. I like the way a book smells. I like to turn each page, read each word, look at the pictures." Have students feel the glossy pages of a book or cover, or the rough pages of a book. "Take pleasure in slowly turning over each page one by one. The author is telling us to enjoy the 'feel' of a book in our hands, and the smell of the pages. A book, then, appeals to our senses."

8. Although it may seem unlikely, a companion book to this one for the older readers is *The Stinky Cheese Man and Other Fairly Stupid Tales* by Jon Szieska, with illustrations by Lane Smith. You can teach and reteach the parts of the book and in which order they belong because in this book, they're out of order. Students who can already read, and who won't get too sidetracked by these zany retold tales, find pleasure in noting that the Table of Contents is in the wrong place, and they, along with the Little Red Hen, note that the book begins before the introduction. For others, it is a good instruction opportunity. Also, readers get to answer the question at the end: "Who is this ISBN guy, anyway?" That sets students off on an ISBN adventure, when previously, most students had not noticed this number that is different for each book, yet appears on all publications.

***Keep Your Mouth Closed, Dear* (New York: Dial Books, 1966)** This is a good book that is just for fun. Charles, a young crocodile, eats everything in sight. He's not hungry—he just eats practically everything he sees. One day he swallows Father's alarm clock. It keeps ticking inside him—and the alarm even wakes him up out of a sound sleep! Mother tries zipping up his mouth, but that doesn't feel too good. She tries putting a paper bag over his mouth, and even a sock. Charles is getting heavier and heavier. Who would ever guess that spring cleaning offers the answer, when Charles tries to swallow the vacuum cleaner suction hose. Children will take delight in this story that is designed to entertain.

Activities to Accompany *Keep Your Mouth Closed, Dear*

1. Go through the book and enjoy the story. Then go through it again and make a circle web of the story. Start at the beginning of the circle and, in a clockwise position, draw a picture around the edge for everything Charles swallows and everything Mother uses to cover his mouth. End back at the top. Use this circle web to retell the story of Charles.

2. Make alligator puppets from paper bags. Use the puppets to retell the story of Charles.

3. "Suppose the story went on for four more pages, with four more things to swallow. What do you think Charles might swallow? Would it make sounds?" This calls for some illustrations.

4. Go through the book and check the reactions of the people as they see Charles. What might some of the people be thinking or saying as Charles walks down the street with a paper bag, or a sock, or band-aids over his mouth? What other ways can children think of that his mother might be able to use to keep his mouth closed?

5. Have a discussion about putting things in our mouths. "Only food and drink should go into our mouths—not fingers and not anything else that we could swallow that could cause choking or something else just as serious." For students who have baby brothers or sisters, caution them to remove items from around the baby that could be put in the mouth and get clogged. Remember, in case of an emergency, instruct students in the use of the 911 emergency number.

We Are Best Friends (New York: Greenwillow Books, 1982) Robert and Peter are best friends, but one day Peter tells Robert that his family is moving. Robert is most unhappy. "Who will you play with? Who will you fight with? Nobody fights like best friends! You'll miss me." But Peter moves and Robert is in the doldrums for he has no one to play with, no one to fight with. One day a new boy named Will comes to school. At first, Robert doesn't like him. Slowly, however, their friendship grows. Peter and Robert exchange letters, and they are fun to read. (This is a reassuring story for anyone who has ever had to move and leave best friends, and then make new friends.)

Activities to Accompany *We Are Best Friends*

1. "Enjoy the story and the lesson learned here. It's difficult to lose good friends, but we can stay in touch by writing. We can make new friends, too, although it takes time."

2. The children in this story are young, but the message is valuable for all children. Check the beginning text. "Is Robert thinking more of himself or of Peter?"

3. "Look closely at the page of the classroom. What are some of the activities that this classroom is busy engaging in?" (reading, art, studying dinosaurs, planting a variety of seeds)

4. Have students read the letters that the boys exchange. They are both printed in upper-case letters. Notice the variety of colored pencils used for the text. Arrange to set up a letter-writing experience for your classroom, either with students within the building or from a different class in the school district. You can even arrange to write to a class in another part of the country, and have a grand experience with writing and meeting new friends.

5. "If you were to invite a new friend to your house, what would you enjoy sharing with that new friend? In this case, Charles had a frog in the garden that Will enjoyed."

Showers, Paul. *The Listening Walk,* **illustrated by Aliki (New York: Harper-Collins, 1961, 1991)** This is a joyful book of sound. A girl, her father, and the dog, Major, take a walk one nice day. On a Listening Walk, there is no talking, just listening to the sounds in the neighborhood, on a busy street, past children playing and workmen with jackhammers. Finally they arrive at the park, and we leave the city sounds and enter into the world of country sounds. This book can enrich a unit of study on sound, or help us to concentrate on sounds in our environment as we take our own Listening Walk.

Activities to Accompany *The Listening Walk*

1. First, explain to students that you are going on a Listening Walk via the book. Set the stage for good listening. Then go through the book and enjoy the sounds.

2. It's fun to "sound out" the sounds that are in the book. One way to do this is to write the sounds on the chalkboard or make a list of them on a chart. A beginning list would include:

Sound It Out	*This Is It*
twick, twick	Major's toenails
dop, dup, dop, dup	father's shoes
z-z-zzzzoooooommmmm	power mower
thhhhhh	sprinklers
hmmmmmmmm	new cars
brack-a, brack-a	old cars
eeeeeeeeee	brakes
trring, trring	bicycle bell
waaa, awaaa	baby crying
bik bok bik bok	lady with high-heeled shoes
pfssssssss	bus door opening
dak-dak-dak-dak	jackhammer
prrrooo, prrrooo	pigeons cooing
gank, gank	ducks
rat-tat-tat	woodpecker
creet, creet, creet	crickets
bzzzzzzzzzz	bees buzzing

Here is a wonderful opportunity for a phonics lesson!

3. "In the book, we are encouraged to sit very still and listen. We can do that in the classroom for one whole minute. That's a long time to be very quiet. But we're listening for sounds, and then we will talk about what sounds we heard—what they were and the sound they made."

4. In the book, the girl sits in her own home, closes her eyes, and listens. Encourage children to do that and then tell what they heard. They can take a Listening Walk around the playground. "Are there birds chirping? Airplanes flying overhead? Dogs barking? Children playing? What sounds do our shoes make on the pavement, on the gravel? What sounds does the swing set make in the breeze or when we're on it?" There are many possibilities for listening on the playground.

5. Again, on the playground, have a group of students play a game while another group listens to the sounds. It can be the thwack thwack of a jump rope, or the creaking of a slide, or just the sound of voices.

6. *The Listening Bag.* Put five items in a bag and have students close their eyes. Make sounds with the items. Have students guess the items. You can use items from the classroom (stapler, scissors, three-hole punch, bell, and so on).

    Then, after the items have been identified, listen to the sounds again. This time, however, ask what could be making that sound in the city and/or in the country.

    Also, use items to accompany your read-aloud stories, so that they become sound stories. Students can make up a "sound story" with the items from the Listening Bag.

And Many More!

Look for additional books by this author/illustrator. She has some books that will enrich your unit of study and others that are just plain good stories. Several informative books include *Digging Up Dinosaurs; Dinosaurs Are Different; Dinosaur Bones; My Visit to the Dinosaurs; Wild and Woolly Mammoths;* and *Corn Is Maize, The Gift of the Indians.*

Good read-aloud stories include *Best Friends Together Again; At Mary Bloom's; Overnight at Mary Bloom's;* and a fine book on *Manners* and one on *Feelings.*

REPRODUCIBLE ACTIVITY PAGES

The ABC Baseball Champ

How Does Your Garden Grow? *(oo)*

The Teddy Bear Drum Major Syllable Tap

There Was an Old Lady Who Swallowed a Fly *(Song)*

There Was an Old Lady Who Swallowed a Fly *("Old Lady" Puppet Pattern)*

There Was an Old Lady Who Swallowed a Fly *(Animal Props)*

There Was an Old Lady Who Swallowed a Fly *(Animal Props)*

I'm Proud To Be a Poetry Animal!

Make a Double Storytelling Puppet

Two-Story Comparison Chart

Children's Literature Activity Page—A New Book Cover (Aliki)

© DCW99

THE ABC BASEBALL CHAMP

This baseball player likes to make ABC books. He has some suggestions for helping you with ideas for *your* ABC Book.

ABC's of *SOUNDS*

A—Ah-choo!
B—Boom!
C—Cock-a-doodle-doo!
D—
E—
F—
G—
Z—Keep going all the way to z-z-z!

ABCs of *THINGS WE EAT*

A—Apples
B—Banana
C—Carrots
D—Dates
E—Eggs
F—
G—

Keep going. Draw illustrations.

ABCs of _____

Think up three more ideas for ABC books. Perhaps you could use something that you are studying in science or social studies.

    1. ABCs of _____

    2. ABCs of _____

Always put a fancy, colorful cover on your ABC books!

© 2000 by The Center for Applied Research in Education

Name _____

HOW DOES YOUR GARDEN GROW? (OO)

Ricky Raccoon is watching his Double O Flower Garden. Print the word on the line. If the "oo" words rhyme with *raccoon,* color the flower red. If the "oo" words rhyme with *book,* color them a different color. Then color Ricky.

raccoon   _____ oo _____   _____ oo _____   _____ oo _____

_____ oo _____   _____ oo _____   _____ oo _____   _____ oo _____

© 2000 by The Center for Applied Research in Education

© 2000 by The Center for Applied Research in Education

Name _____

THE TEDDY BEAR DRUM MAJOR SYLLABLE TAP

This drum major won first prize in the Syllable Tap Contest. This is what he does: (1) Listens to a word; (2) Repeats the word; (3) Taps out the beats (syllables). You can do it too.

Color Teddy

Listen, Repeat, TAP! Write the number of taps (beats) on the line.

1. old _____ 1

2. another _____ 3

3. show _____

4. only _____

5. over _____

6. under _____

7. big _____

8. little _____

9. tulip _____

10. daffodil _____

11. rose _____

12. pansy _____

13. monkey _____

14. bear _____

15. elephant _____

16. alligator _____

THERE WAS AN OLD LADY WHO SWALLOWED A FLY (SONG)

There was an old lady who swallowed a fly.
I don't know why she swallowed a fly.
Perhaps she'll die.

There was an old lady who swallowed a spider,
    that wriggled and wriggled and jiggled inside her.
She swallowed the spider to catch the fly.
I don't know why she swallowed a fly.
Perhaps she'll die.

There was an old lady who swallowed a bird.
How absurd, to swallow a bird!
She swallowed the bird to catch the spider, etc.

There was an old lady who swallowed a cat.
Well, fancy that, she swallowed a cat!
She swallowed the cat to catch the bird, etc.

There was an old lady who swallowed a dog.
What a hog, to swallow a dog!
She swallowed the dog to catch the cat, etc.

There was an old lady who swallowed a cow.
I don't know how she swallowed a cow!
She swallowed the cow to catch the dog.
She swallowed the dog to catch the cat.
She swallowed the cat to catch the bird.
She swallowed the bird to catch the spider,
    that wriggled and wriggled and jiggled inside her.
She swallowed the spider to catch the fly.
I don't know why she swallowed a fly.
Perhaps she'll die.

There was an old lady who swallowed a horse.
She's dead, of course.

DIRECTIONS FOR MAKING SONG PUPPET AND PROPS

1. Color and cut the shapes. Use a see-through plastic sandwich
   bag for the stomach. Staple the shapes to the bag to create the
   old woman.

2. Color the animals. Cut around the dark outline.

3. Sing the song and place the animals, in turn, into the see-
   through bag (stomach).

© 2000 by The Center for Applied Research in Education

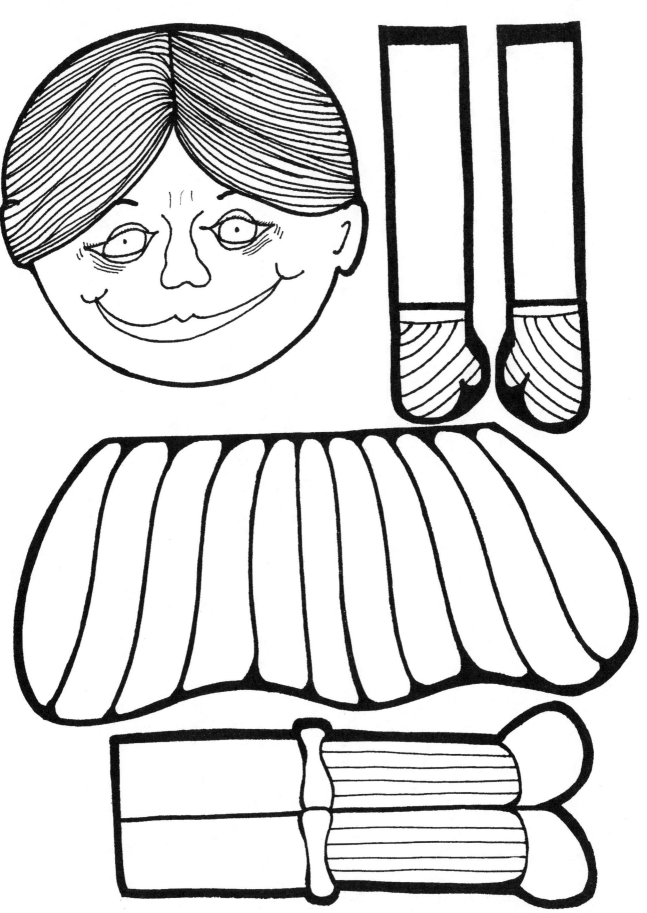

© 2000 by The Center for Applied Research in Education

© 2000 by The Center for Applied Research in Education

© 2000 by The Center for Applied Research in Education

Name _____

I'M PROUD TO BE A POETRY ANIMAL!

May is Poetry Month! This animal likes the rhythm and rhyme of poetry. Find a short poem for each category below. Copy it in the space provided. Say it. Memorize it. Jump to the rhythm.

Weather

sports

food

© 2000 by The Center for Applied Research in Education

MAKE A
DOUBLE STORYTELLING PUPPET

Color the hand puppet. Carefully cut it out around the edges. Next, trace around it on a sheet of construction paper. Make a different animal face on that shape. Put the two pieces together back-to-back. Your teacher can help you staple it together.

Use the back-to-back puppets for storytelling.

© 2000 by The Center for Applied Research in Education

Name _____

TWO-STORY
COMPARISON CHART

TITLE		
CHARACTERS		
SETTING (where)		
SETTING (when)		
PROBLEM		
SOLUTION		
ENDING		
NEW WORDS		
MY THOUGHTS		

© 2000 by The Center for Applied Research in Education

Name _____

A NEW BOOK COVER

Mrs. Polly Puffin won first prize in a contest to make a new cover for a book by Aliki. She wants you to select the book and help her in the space below. Remember to use the title and author's name. Work slowly.

© 2000 by The Center for Applied Research in Education

BIBLIOGRAPHY

Picture Books—ABC

Ada, Alma Flor. *Gathering the Sun, An Alphabet in Spanish and English.* Illustrated by Simon Silva. (English translation by Rosa Zubizarreta.) (New York: Lothrop, Lee & Shepard, 1997)

Base, Graeme. *Animalia* (New York: Harry N. Abrams, Inc., 1987)

Brown, Ruth. *Alphabet Times Four, An International ABC* (New York: Dutton Children's Books, 1991)

Bruchae, Joseph. *Many Nations, An Alphabet of Native America* Illustrated by Robert F. Goetzl (Mahwah, NJ: Troll, 1997)

Demerest, Chris. *The Cowboy ABC* (New York: DK Publishing, 1997)

Dodson, Peter. *An Alphabet of Dinosaurs* Paintings by Wayne Barlow (New York: Scholastic Hardcover, 1995)

Downie, Jill. *Alphabet Puzzle* (New York: Lothrop, Lee & Shepard, 1988)

Drucker, Malka. *A Jewish Holiday ABC.* Illustrated by Rita Pocock (New York: Harcourt, 1992)

Emberly, Ed. *Ed Emberly's ABC* (Boston: Little, Brown 1978)

Fain, Kathleen. *Handsigns, A Sign Language Alphabet* (New York: Chronicle, 1993)

Gustafson, Scott. *Alphabet Soup: A Feast of Letters* (New York: Greenwich Workshop Press, 1994)

Heller, Nicholas. *Goblins in Green.* Illustrated by Joseph A. Smith (New York: Greenwillow, 1995)

Holtz, Lara Tankel. *DK Alphabet Book.* Illustrated by Dave King (New York: DK Publishing, 1997)

Kitchen, Bert. *Animal Alphabet* (New York: Puffin, 1988)

Marshall, Janet. *Look Once, Look Twice* (New York: Ticknow & Fields, 1995)

Mayer, Marianna. *The Unicorn Alphabet.* Pictures by Michael Hague (New York: Dial, 1989)

Nathan, Cheryl. *Bugs and Beasties ABC* (New York: Cool Kids Press, 1995)

Palotta, Jerry. *The Icky Bug Alphabet Book.* Illustrations by Ralph Masiello (New York: Trumpet Club, 1986) (There are fifteen alphabet books in this author's series.)

Radunsky, Vladimir. *An Edward Lear Alphabet* New York: HarperCollins, 1999)

Rankin, Laura. *The Handmade Alphabet* (New York: Puffin, 1996) (Sign language)

Sandved, Kjell B. *The Butterfly Alphabet* (New York: Scholastic, 1996)

Shannon, George. *Tomorrow's Alphabet.* Illustrated by Donald Crews (New York: Greenwillow, 1996)

Wilbur, Richard. *The Disappearing Alphabet.* Illustrated by David Diaz (New York: Harcourt Brace. 1997)

World Wildlife Fund. *Animal ABC's* (San Rafael, CA: Cedco Publishing, 1997)

Picture Books—General

Aylesworth, Jim. Old Black Fly. Illustrated by Stephen Gammell. _____ . Teddy Bear Tears. Illustrated by Jo Ellen McAllister-Stammen. (New York: Atheneum, 1997)

Bunting, Eve. *Going Home.* Illustrated by David Diaz (New York: HarperCollins, 1996)

Cooney, Barbara. *Miss Rumphius* (New York: Viking, 1982)

Ernst, Lisa Campbell. *Zinnia and Dot* (New York: Viking, 1992)

Gammell, Stephen. *Is That You, Winter?* (New York: Harcourt Brace, 1997)

Hoban, Tana. *I Walk and Read* (New York: Greenwillow, 1984)

Hoffman, Mary. *Amazing Grace.* Illustrated by Caroline Binch (New York: Dial, 1991)

Kasza, Keiko. *A Mother for Choco* (New York: Putnam, 1992)

Kuskin, Karla. *The Philharmonic Gets Dressed.* Illustrations by Marc Simont (New York: Harper & Row, 1982)

Leedy, Loreen. *Messages in the Mailbox: How to Write a Letter* (New York: Holiday, 1991)

Mahy, Margaret. *The Boy Who Was Followed Home.* Illustrated by Steven Kellogg (New York: Puffin, 1986)

McKissack, Patricia C. *Ma Dear's Aprons.* Illustrated by Floyd Cooper (New York: Simon & Schuster, 1997)

Martin, Bill, Jr. *The Maestro Plays.* Illustrated by Vladimir Radunsky (New York: Voyager, 1996)

Martin, Jacqueline Briggs. *Snowflake Bentley.* Illustrated by Mary Azarian (New York: Houghton Mifflin, 1998) (Caldecott Award)

Polacco, Patricia. *Aunt Chip and the Great Triple Creek Affair* (New York: Philomel, 1996)

Shannon, David. *No, David!* (New York: Blue Sky Press, 1998)

Stevens, Janet (adapted). *Tops and Bottoms* (New York: Harcourt, Brace, 1995) (Caldecott Honor Book)

Wildsmith, Brian. *The Little Wood Duck* (New York: Franklin Watts, 1973)

Yolen, Jane. *Owl Moon.* Illustrated by John Schoenherr (New York: Philomel, 1987)

Yorinks, Arthur. *Hey, Al.* Illustrated by Richard Egielski (New York: Sunburst, 1986)

Picture Books—Holiday

Child, Lydia Maria. *Over the River and Through the Wood.* Pictures by Brinton Turkle (New York: Scholastic, 1974. (Thanksgiving)

Diane Goode's American Christmas (New York: Puffin, 1998)

Diane Goode's Book of Scary Stories and Songs (New York: Puffin, 1998)

Flournoy, Vanessa and Valerie. *Celie and the Harvest Fiddler.* Illustrated by James Ransome (New York: Morrow, 1995)

Grifalconi, Ann. *The Bravest Flute* (Boston: Little, Brown, 1994) (New Year)

Hague, Michael. *The Perfect Present* (New York: Morrow, 1996) (Christmas)

Hirsh, Marilyn. *I Love Hanukkah* (New York: Holiday House, 1984)

Lewis, J. Patrick. *The Christmas of the Reddle Moon.* Illustrated by Gary Kelley (New York: Dial, 1994)

Pinkney, Andrea Davis. *Seven Candles for Kwanzaa.* Illustrated by Brian Pinkney (New York: Puffin, 1998)

Polacco, Patricia. *The Trees of the Dancing Goats* (New York: Simon & Schuster, 1996) (Hannukah, Christmas)

Spinelli, Eileen. *Thanksgiving at the Tappletons'.* Illustrated by Maryann Cocc-Leffler (Philadelphia: J.B. Lippincott, 1982)

Picture Books On Quilts

Bolton, Janet. *Mrs. Noah's Patchwork Quilt* (Kansas City: Andrews and McMeel, 1995)

Ernst, Lisa Campbell. *Sam Johnson and the Blue Ribbon Quilt* (New York: Mulberry Paperback, 1983)

Hopkinson, Deborah. *Sweet Clara and the Freedom Quilt.* Paintings by James Ransome (New York: Alfred A. Knopf, 1993)

Jonas, Ann. *The Quilt* (New York: Puffin Books, 1984)

Lyons, Mary E. *Stitching Stars, The Story Quilts of Harriet Powers* (New York: Aladdin Paperbacks, 1993)

Paul, Ann Whitford. *The Seasons Sewn, A Year in Patchwork.* Illustrated by Michael McCurdy (New York: Harcourt Brace, 1996)

_____. *Eight Hands Round, A Patchwork Alphabet.* Illustrated by Jeanette Winter (New York: HarperCollins, 1991)

Picture Books—Folktales/Fairytales

Aardema, Verna. *Anansi Does the Impossible.* Illustrated by Lisa Desimini (New York: Simon & Schuster, 1997)

Andersen, Hans Christian. *The Emperor's New Clothes.* Illustrated by A. Barrett (Cambridge, MA: Candlewick, 1997)

_____. *Little Ida's Flowers.* Illustrated by L. Allen (New York: Philomel, 1989)

Dupre, Judith. *The Mouse Bride: A Mayan Folktale.* Illustrated by Fabricio Vanden Broeck (New York: Knopf, 1993)

Faulkner, William J. *Brer Tiger and the Big Wind.* Illustrated by Roberta Wilson (New York: Morrow, 1995)

Gill, Shelley. *The Alaska Mother Goose.* Illustrations by Shannon Cartwright (Homer, AK: Paws IV Publishing Co., 1987)

(Grimm Brothers). Jarrell, Randall. *The Fisherman and His Wife.* Pictures by Margot Zemach (New York: Farrar, Straus, Giroux, 1980)

(_____). Rockwell, Ann. *The Three Sillies and 10 Other Read Aloud Stories* (New York: Thomas Y. Crowell, 1979)

(_____). Shub, Elizabeth. *The Bremen Town Musicians.* Pictures by Janina Domanska (New York: Greenwillow, 1980)

(_____). Spirin, Gennady. *Snow White and Rose Red* (New York: Philomel, 1992)

Kimmel, Eric A. (retold) *Baba Yaga, A Russian Folktale.* Illustrated by Megan Lloyd (New York: Holiday House, 1991)

_____ (retold) *Onions and Garlic*. Pictures by Katya Arnold (New York: Holiday House, 1996) (European)

Knutson, Barbara. *How the Guinea Fowl Got Her Spots: A Swahili Tale of Friendship* (Minneapolis: Carolrhoda, 1990)

McDermott, Gerald (retold) *Musicians of the Sun* (New York: Simon & Schuster, 1997) (Aztec)

_____. *Zomo, the Rabbit, A Trickster Tale from West Africa* (New York: Harcourt Brace, 1992)

_____. *Coyote, A Trickster Tale from the American Southwest* (New York: Harcourt Brace, 1994)

Paye, Won-Ldy and Margaret H. Lippert. *Why a Leopard Has Spots, Dan Stories from Liberia* (Golden, CO: Fulcrum Publishing, 1998)

Perrault, Charles. Retold by Amy Ehrlich. *Cinderella*. Pictures by Susan Jeffers (New York: Dial, 1985)

Scieszka, John. *The True Story of the Three Little Pigs*. Pictures by Lane Smith (New York: Puffin, 1996)

Scieszka, John and Lane Smith. *Squids Will Be Squids*. Designed by Molly Leach (New York: Viking, 1998)

Tejima. *Ho-Limlim, A Rabbit Tale from Japan* (New York: Philomel, 1990)

Temple, Francis. *Tiger Soup*. (New York: Orchard, 1994)

Wilson, Barbara Ker. (retold) *Wishbones, A Folktale from China*. Illustrated by Meilo So (New York: Bradbury, 1993) (variant of YehShen)

Picture Books—Math

Anno, Mitsumasa. *All in a Day* (New York: Philomel, 1986)

Chandra, Deborah. *Miss Mabel's Table*. Illustrations by Max Grover (New York: Browndeer Press, 1994)

Grossman, Bill. *My Little Sister Ate One Hare*. Illustrated by Kevin Hawkes (New York: Crown, 1996)

Hague, Kathleen. *Numbears* (New York: Henry Holt, 1986)

Haskins, Jim. *Count Your Way Through India*. Illustrated by Liz Brenner Dodson. (Minneapolis: Carolrhoda, 1989)

Hoban, Tana. *More, Fewer, Less* (New York: Greenwillow, 1998) (Look for many math concept books by this author.)

_____. *26 Letters and 99 Cents* (New York: Greenwillow, 1987)

McCourt, Lisa. *The Rain Forest Counts*. Illustrated by Cheryl Nathan (New York: BridgeWater, 1997)

Merriam, Eve. *Ten Rosy Roses*. Illustrated by Julia Gorton (New York: HarperCollins, 1999)

Parker, Vic. *Bearobics, A Hip-Hop Counting Story*. Illustrated by Emily Bolam (New York: Puffin, 1999)

Rankin, Laura. *The Handmade Counting Book* (New York: Dial, 1998) (Sign language)

Toft, Kim Michelle and Allan Sheather. *One Less Fish* (Watertown, MA: Charlesbridge, 1998)

Wells, Rosemary. *Bunny Money* (New York: Dial, 1997)

Picture Books—Multicultural

Baer, Edith. *This is the Way We Go to School* (New York: Scholastic, 1990)

Baker, Jeannie. *Where the Forest Meets the Sea* (New York: Greenwillow, 1987) (Australia)

Cohn, A.L. (compiler). *From Sea to Shining Sea: A Treasury of American Folklore and Folksongs* (New York: Scholastic, 1992)

Goble, Paul. *Iktomi and the Coyote, A Plains Indian Story* (New York: Orchard, 1998)

Green, Mona. Retold by Pamela Lofts. *The Echidna and the Shade Tree* (San Diego: Slawson Communications, Inc., Mad Hatter Books, 1977)

Nunes, Susan Miho. *The Last Dragon.* Illustrated by Chris K. Soentpiet (New York: Clarion Books, 1995)

Polacco, Patricia. *Chicken Sunday* (New York: Philomel, 1992)

Pomerantz, Charlotte. *If I Had a Paka: Poems in Eleven Languages.* Illustrated by Nancy Tafuri (New York: Greenwillow, 1982)

SanSousi, Robert D. *Cendrillon, A Caribbean Cinderella.* Illustrated by Brian Pinkney (New York: Simon & Schuster, 1998)

Say, Allen. *The Bicycle Man* (New York: Parnassus, 1982)

Schroeder, Alan. *Minty: A Story of Young Harriet Tubman.* Illustrated by Jerry Pinkney (New York: Dial, 1996)

Steptoe, John. *Mufaro's Beautiful Daughters: An African Tale* (New York: Lothrop, Lee & Shepard, 1987)

Taback, Simms. *There Was an Old Lady Who Swallowed a Fly* (New York: Scholastic, 1997) (Caldecott Honor Book)

Picture Books—Science

Barner, Bob. *Dem Bones* (New York: Chronicle, 1996)

Barton, B. *Machines at Work* (New York: Thomas Y. Crowell, 1987)

Campbell, Jackson. *How a House Is Built* (New York: Scholastic, 1994)

Cannon, Janell. *Verdi* (New York: Harcourt, 1997)

Cole, Joanna. *The Magic School Bus Lost in the Solar System.* Illustrated by Bruce Degan (New York: Scholastic, 1990) (Many books in this series.)

Edwards, Pamela Duncan. *Some Smug Slug* (New York: HarperCollins, 1996)

Gibbons, Gail. *The Moon Book* (New York: Holiday, 1997)

Hirschi, Ron. *Headgear.* Photographs by Galen Burrell (New York: Dodd, Mead, 1986)

Horvatic, Anne. *Simple Machines.* Photos by Stephen Bruner (New York: E. P. Dutton, 1989)

Leedy, Loreen. *Postcards from Pluto: A Tour of the Solar System* (New York: Holiday, 1993)

Norden, Beth B. and Lynette Rushchak. *Magnification* (New York: Lodestar, 1993)

Paulsen, Gary. *Full of Hot Air* (New York: North–South Books, 1993)

Simon, Seymour. *Shadow Magic* (New York: Lothrop, Lee & Shepard, 1985)

Picture Books—Poetry

Bruchac, Joseph and Thomas Locker. *Between Earth and Sky* (New York: Harcourt Brace, 1996)

deRegniers, Beatrice Schenk. *Sing a Song of Popcorn: Every Child's Book of Poems* (New York: Scholastic, 1988)

Dragonwagon, Crescent. *Half a Moon and a Whole Star.* Illustrated by Jerry Pinkney (New York: Aladdin, 1986)

Hoberman, Mary Ann. *The Llama Who Had No Pajama.* Illustrated by Betty Fraser (New York: Harcourt Brace, 1998)

Kennedy, X.J. and D.M. Kennedy. *Knock at a Star: A Child's Introduction to Poetry* (Boston: Little, Brown, 1982)

Lewis, J. Patrick. *A Hippopotamusn't.* Illustrated by Victoria Chess (New York: Dial, 1990)

_____. *Doodle Dandies.* Illustrated by Lisa Desimini (New York: Atheneum, 1998)

Merriam, Eve. *Fresh Paint* (New York: Macmillan, 1986)

O'Neill, Mary. *Hailstones and Halibut Bones* (Garden City, NY: Doubleday, 1961)

Prelutsky, Jack and Arnold Lobel. (anthology). *The Random House Book of Poetry for Children* (New York: Random House, 1983)

_____. *A Pizza the Size of the Sun.* Drawings by James Stevenson (New York: Greenwillow, 1994)

Shively, Julie. *Barefoot Days, Poems of Childhood.* Illustrated by Russ Flint (Nashville, TN: CandyCane Press, 1998)

Steptoe, Javaka. *In Daddy's Arms I Am Tall* (New York: Lee and Low, 1997)

Silverstein, Shel. *Where the Sidewalk Ends* (New York: HarperCollins, 1987)

Thomas, Joyce Carol. *Gingerbread Days.* Illustrated by Floyd Cooper (New York: HarperCollins, 1995)

Yolen, Jane. (selected). *Sky Scrape/City Scape, Poems of City Life.* Illustrated by Ken Condon (Honesdale, PA: Boyds Mills, 1996)

_____. (selected). *Snow, Snow: Poems About Winter* (Honesdale, PA: Boyds Mills, 1998)

Videotape/Computer

Broderbund, P.O. Box 6125, Novato, CA 94948

Educational Resources, P.O. Box 1900, Elgin, IL 60121

Reading Rainbow Video, University of Nebraska, P.O. Box 80669, Lincoln, NE 68501

Sunburst, 101 Castleton Street, Pleasantville, NY 10570

Weston Woods, Weston, CT 06883

Magazines for Children

Booklinks (older children)

Chickadee

Cobblestone

Cricket
Highlights for Children
Hopscotch
Jack and Jill
National Geographic World
Spider
Your Big Backyard

Teacher Resource Books

Bernstein, Rosella. *Phonics Activities for Reading Success* (West Nyack, NY: The Center for Applied Research in Education, 1997)

Carle, Eric. *You Can Make a Collage* (Palo Alto, CA: Klutz, 1998)

Edmonds, I.G. *Trickster Tales.* Illustrated by Sean Morrison (Philadelphia: Lippincott, 1966)

Fry, Edward Bernard, Jacqueline E. Kress, and Dona Lee Fountoukidis. *The Reading Teacher's Book of Lists,* 3rd edition (Englewood Cliffs, NJ: Prentice Hall, 1993)

Gardner, Howard. *Frames of Mind: The Theory of Multiple Intelligences* (New York: Basic, 1983)

Getting to Know the World's Greatest Artists Series (New York: Orchard, 1996)

Johnson, Jinny. *Children's Guide to Birds* (New York: Simon & Schuster, 1996)

Lowenfeld, Viktor and W. Lambert Brittain. *Creative and Mental Growth,* 6th edition (New York: Macmillan, 1975)

O'Neill, Catherine. *Computers, Those Amazing Machines* (Washington, D.C.: National Geographic Society, 1985)

Piazza, Carolyn L. *Multiple Forms of Literacy, Teaching Literacy and the Arts* (Upper Saddle River, NJ: Prentice-Hall, 1999)

Poppe, Carol A. and Nancy A. VanMatre. *K–3 Science Activities Kit* (West Nyack, New York: The Center for Applied Research in Education, 1988)

Rief, Sandra F. *How to Reach and Teach ADD/ADHD Children* (West Nyack, NY: The Center for Applied Research in Education, 1993)

Ringgold, Faith, Linda Freeman, and Nancy Roucher. *Talking to Faith Ringgold* (New York: Crown, 1996)

Stull, Elizabeth Crosby. "Drawing a Story and Listening to a Picture, A Visual–Verbal Relationship." *Arts and Activities,* January 1982.

Taylor, Barbara J. *Science Everywhere, Opportunities for Very Young Children* (New York: Harcourt Brace, 1993)

Warner, L. and K. Craycraft. *Fun With Familiar Tunes* (Carthage, IL: Good Apple, 1987)

Wilcox, Jane. *Why Do We Celebrate That?* (New York: Franklin Watts, 1996)